I0824960

OLD GLORY

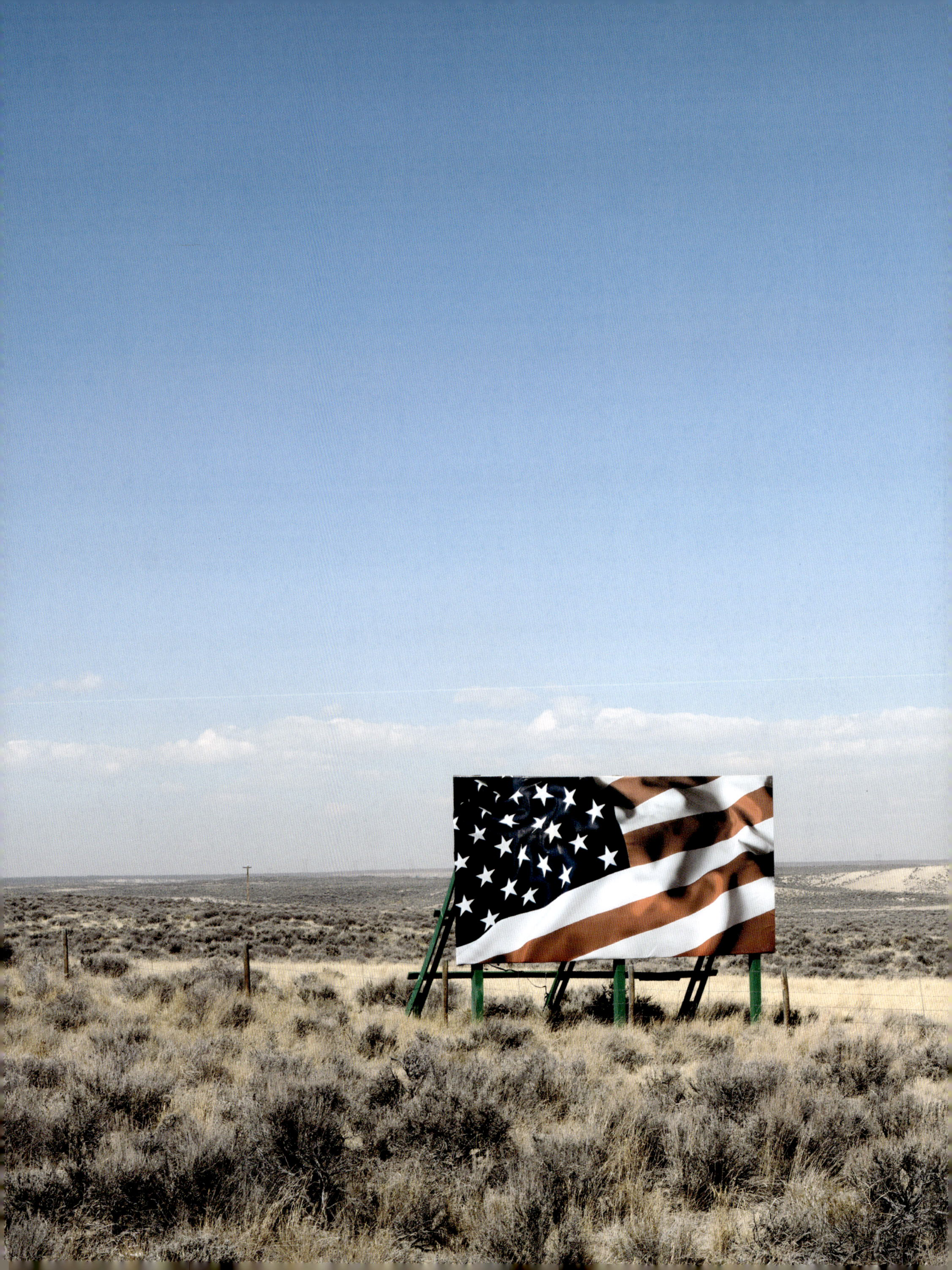

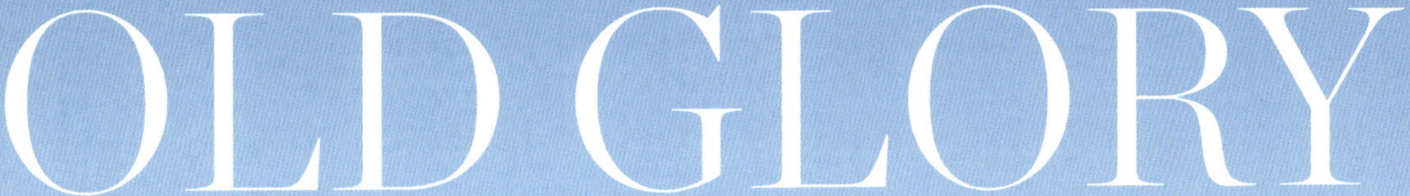

OLD GLORY

Iconic Flags and the Stories They Tell of America's 250-Year History

ROLAND MILLER

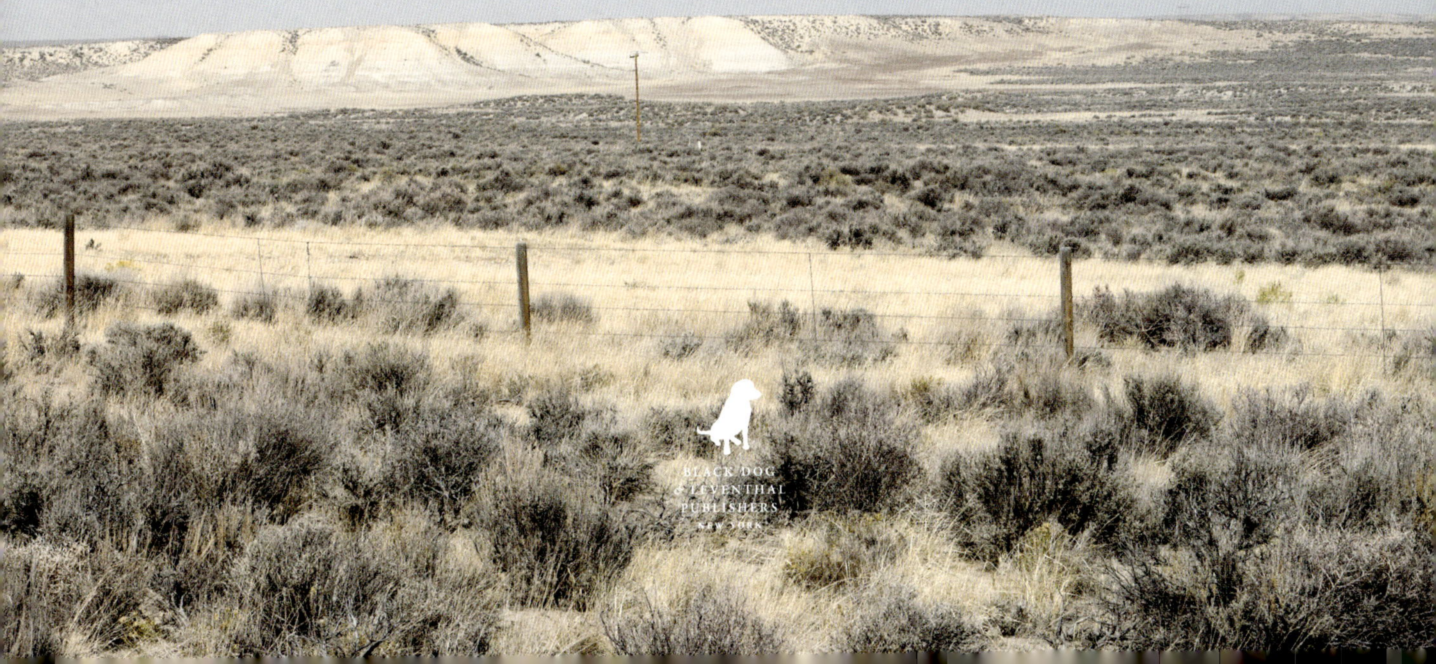

BLACK DOG & LEVENTHAL PUBLISHERS
NEW YORK

Previous: *Little America, Wyoming, 2023*

Opposite: *Superior, Arizona, 2024*

Black Dog & Leventhal Publishers
Hachette Book Group
1290 Avenue of the Americas, New York, NY 10104
www.blackdogandleventhal.com

BlackDogandLeventhal @BDLev

First Edition: June 2026

Published by Black Dog & Leventhal Publishers, an imprint of Hachette Book Group, Inc. The Black Dog & Leventhal Publishers name and logo are trademarks of Hachette Book Group, Inc.

Black Dog & Leventhal books may be purchased in bulk for business, educational, or promotional use. For more information, please contact your local bookseller or the Hachette Book Group Special Markets Department at Special.Markets@hbgusa.com.

The publisher is not responsible for websites (or their content) that are not owned by the publisher.

Additional photo credits appear on page 220

Print book cover and interior design by Nina Simoneaux

Library of Congress Cataloging-in-Publication Data has been applied for.

ISBNs: 978-1-6482-9214-9 (hardcover); 979-8-8941-4366-8 (ebook)

Printed in China

TLF

10 9 8 7 6 5 4 3 2 1

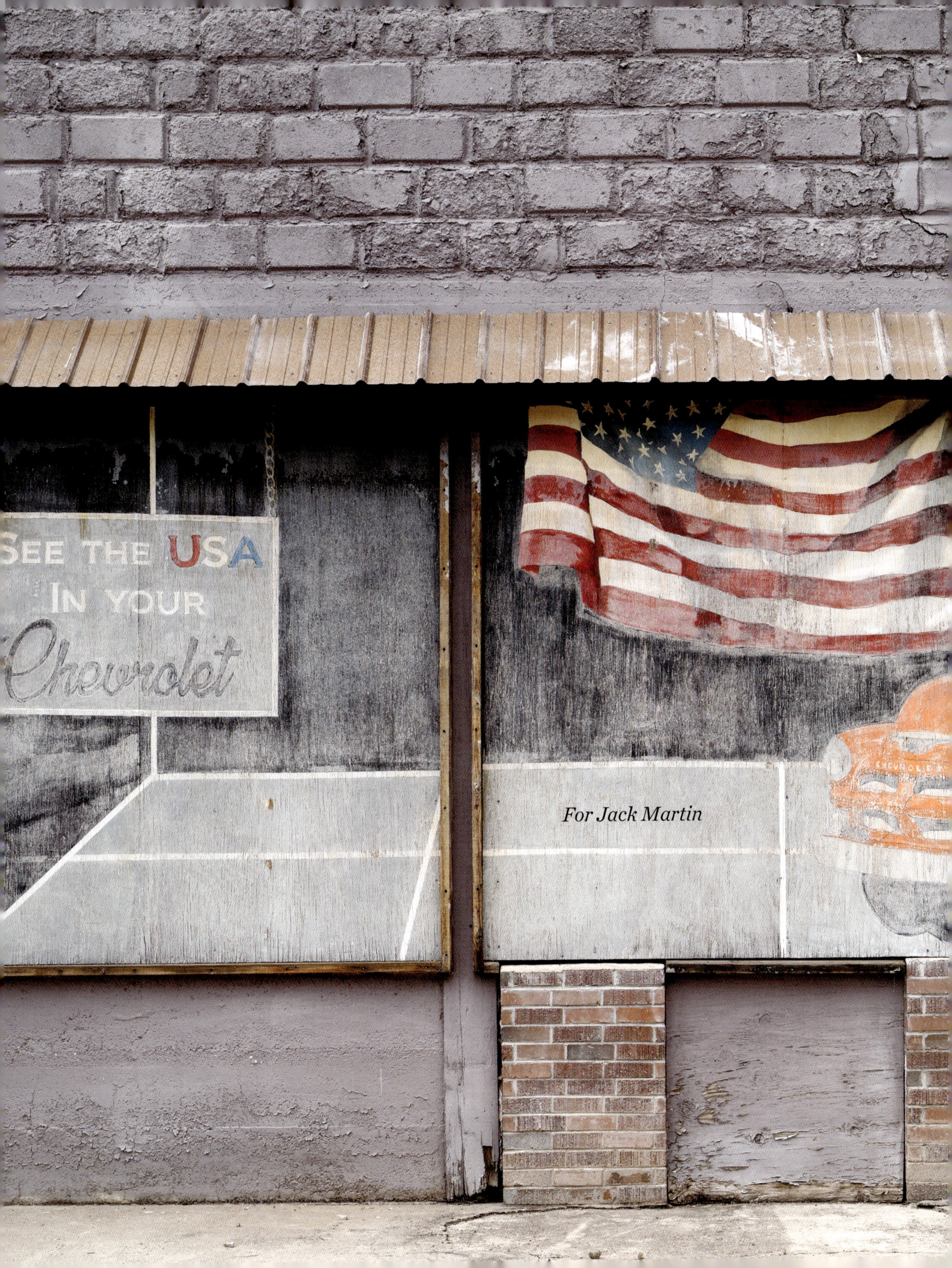

For Jack Martin

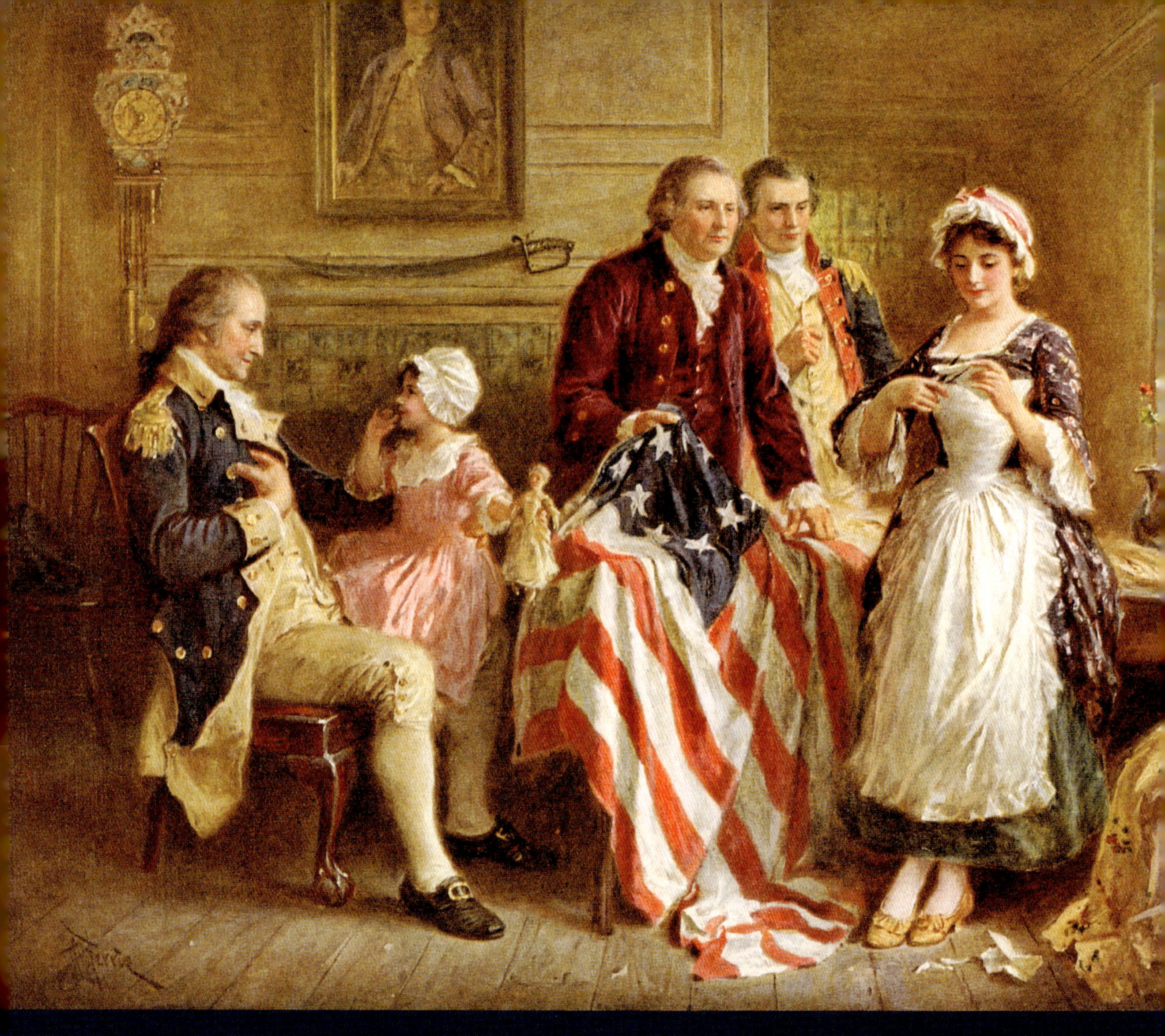

Betsy Ross demonstrating how she cut five-pointed stars for the flag in Jean Leon Gerome Ferris's painting Betsy Ross 1777, circa 1920

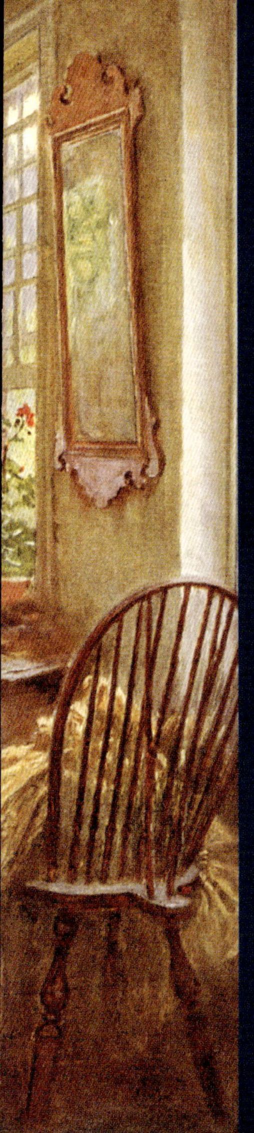

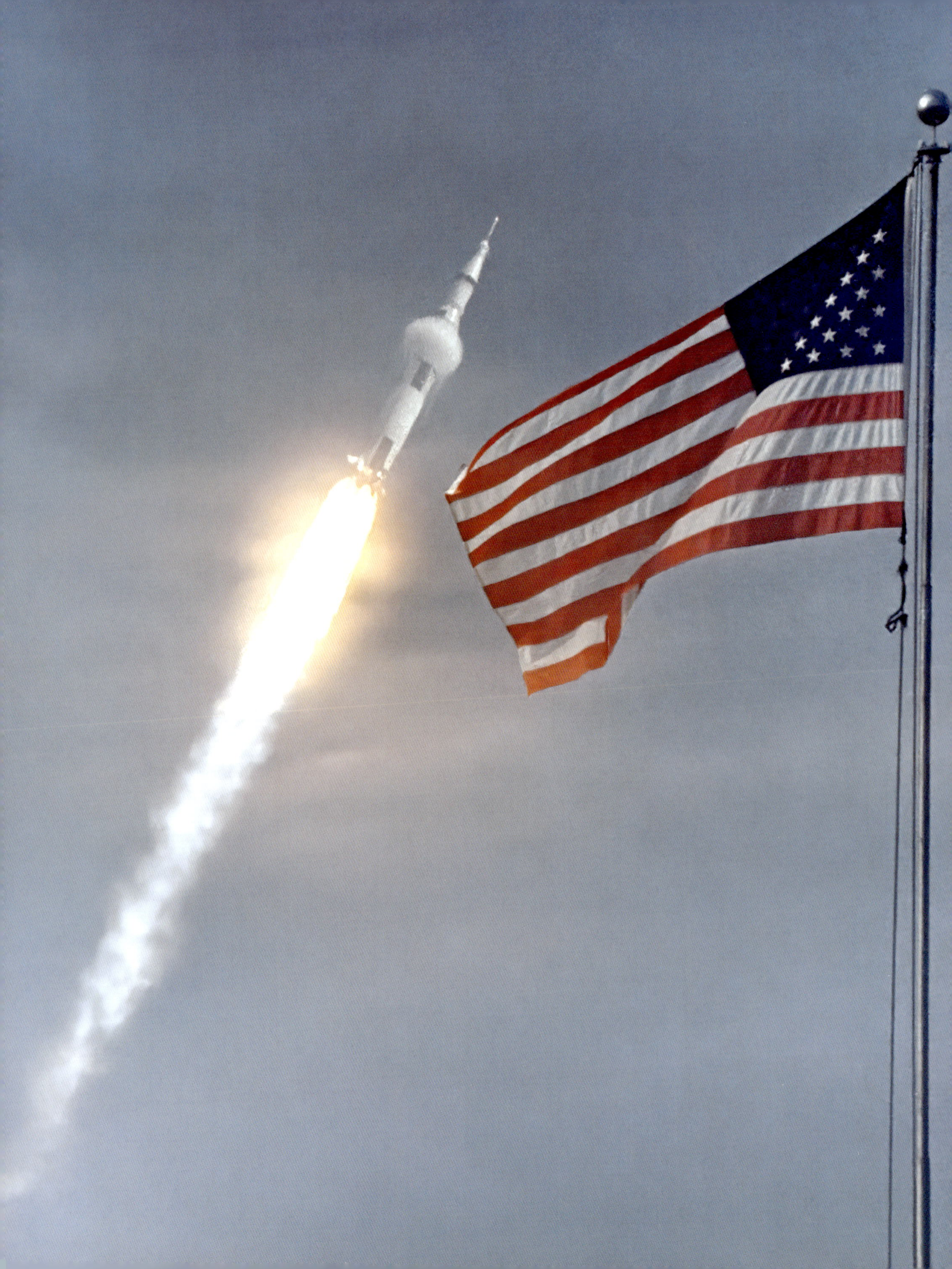

INTRODUCTION

FEW SYMBOLS HOLD THE POWER and inspiration of the American flag. It has encouraged heroics in trying times, soothed the nation after tremendous trauma, brightened the eyes of citizens, and shrouded the coffins of our best and bravest. It inspires and excites. It offers comfort and hope. The American flag tells the story of the country's heritage. It is a symbol of democracy and freedom.

On July 4, 2026, we celebrate the 250th anniversary of the United States' independence from Britain—America's semiquincentennial (also known as the sestercentennial and the bisesquicentennial). By looking at the nation's flags, both formal and informal, and how they changed over its history—and how history changed them—we can trace a story of goodwill, stalwart support of our allies, and belief in the Declaration of Independence's notion "that all men are created equal, that they are endowed by their Creator with certain unalienable Rights, that among these are Life, Liberty and the pursuit of Happiness."

Opposite: *Apollo 11 launches with the American flag in the foreground, July 16, 1969.*

Flags were initially flown almost exclusively by armed services from ships, at military installations, and on battlefields. They were used to communicate where troops and leaders were located during battle. Beginning with the Civil War, private citizens began showing their support for America by displaying the Union's flag at their residences. Today, it is difficult to pass along the streets of any American city and not find an American flag flying in the breeze. It's displayed at homes, businesses, schools, government offices, military facilities, polling places, sporting contests, and almost any event where a large group of Americans is gathered. American flags abound during national holidays, especially Memorial Day, the Fourth of July, Veterans Day, and

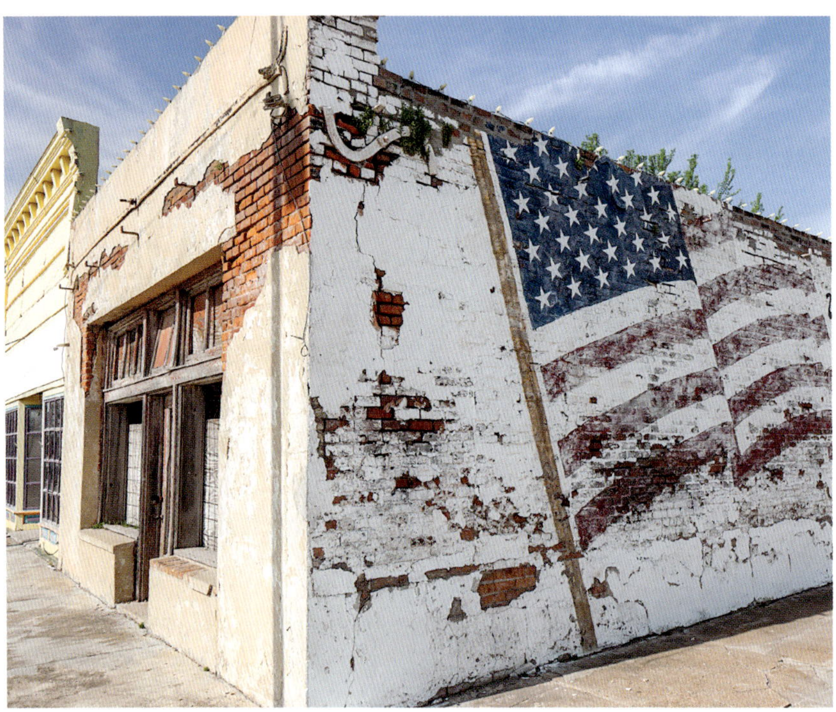

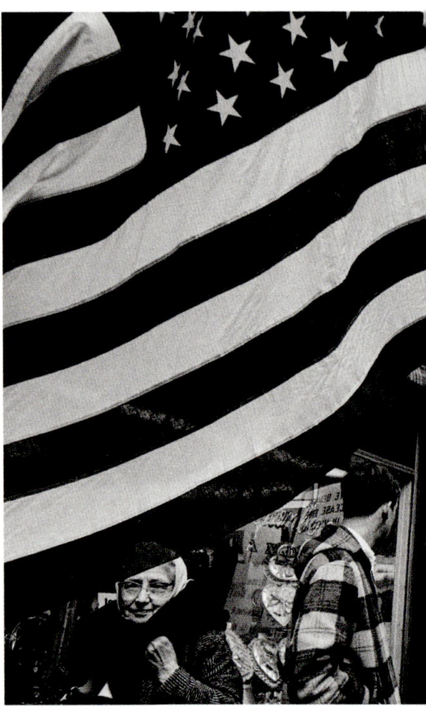

of course Flag Day, which is celebrated on June 14 every year to commemorate the designation of the first official American flag by Congress on that date in 1777. Honor and color guards present the flag with dignity and solemnity at ceremonies. Murals across America at schools, civic buildings, and VFW halls feature the flag to inspire students and visitors at these institutions.

Too often people confuse the symbolism of the flag with the article itself. It is not the bits of colored cloth we should revere, but the ideals, values, and morals the banner represents that should be honored. At times, the flag is used as a symbol of protest. Burning an American flag has become a powerful and alarming remonstration of the government (page 153) or as a response to a specific incident, like the murder of George Floyd (page 192). In contrast, when American flags are burned on foreign soil, it's generally an expression of hatred for America and its policies.

Despite the flag's use in a range of protests over the past two centuries, it's only relatively recently that the flag has become a direct political symbol. Beginning around the 1970s, politicians began to face a litmus test of sorts, in which their patriotism for the country was inferred by whether they wore one. Barack Obama, running for president in 2007, was one of the first politicians to stop wearing an American flag lapel pin; he felt that measuring a person's devotion to the United States based on the flair they wore on their jackets was misguided:

> *My attitude is that I'm less concerned about what you're wearing on your lapel than what's in your heart. You show your patriotism by how you treat your fellow Americans, especially those who serve. You show your patriotism by being true to our values and ideals. And that's what we have to lead with, our values and ideals.*

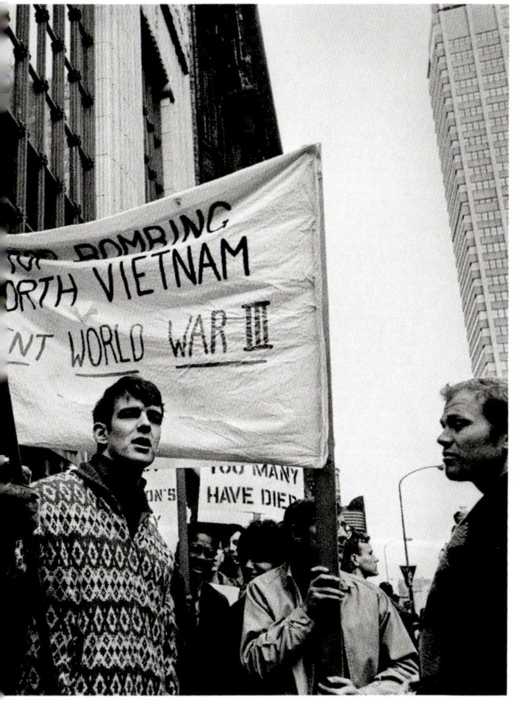

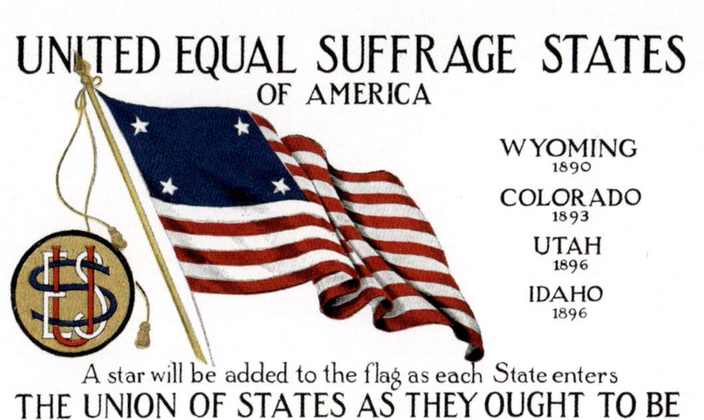

Above: *Suffrage postcard, 1910*

Opposite, left: We the People *mural, Calvert, Texas, 2016*

Opposite, right: *Students protesting the first bombing of North Vietnam, 1965*

Over the past few decades some political groups have started to utilize the American flag as if it were their private icon, representing their specific beliefs—including some disturbing distortions of the very ideals America was founded on—and belying the notion that America has a duty to treat and protect every citizen equally. This approach minimizes the value that divergent ideas, experiences, and backgrounds in society bring to the nation's culture, creativity, and innovation. It's the very contributions from diverse groups that are so much a part of the nation's success.

The same upsurge in patriotism that occurred during the Civil War also took hold at the beginning of World Wars I and II and after the attacks on September 11, 2001. It often takes a national tragedy or crisis to remind the country of its patriotic history. There are many examples of when the United States, facing difficult times, took the high road and stood by the tenets embodied in the Constitution: responding to the Great Depression with government programs to provide relief to struggling citizens and joining World War II to defeat fascism, to mention a few.

For the past 250 years, the United States has been the leader of the free world for a good portion of that time span, yet there are chapters in American history where the country's stance has been misguided: the building of wealth upon the backs of enslaved people, the relegation of women to second-class citizens, and the internment of Japanese Americans during World War II, for example.

Even with these darker passages in history, the American flag has been a persistent reminder of the noble ideals of this country. Most citizens have a certain reverence for the flag, which is codified in the United States Flag Code. The Flag Code is a recommended but nonbinding set of guidelines for presenting and handling the American flag that was first enacted into law on June 22, 1942 (Honoring the Flag, page 206). The code clearly defines what the flag should look like, appropriate uses of it, how it should be displayed, and how it should be treated. There is no legal jeopardy in not following the Flag Code, but anyone not doing so is disrespecting the flag. For example, using the flag in advertising, on clothing, or for other commercial purposes is considered insolent. Even the famed illustration of Uncle Sam declaring "I Want *You* for U.S. Army," which was used as a recruitment poster during World War I and depicts him in a top hat that has a blue band and white stars, could be seen as a transgression of the Flag Code.

Some of the fifty flags discussed in *Old Glory* would violate the Flag Code. Yet, all of them stand as symbols of American ideals. Some of these flags predate America's independence and served as models for the current Stars and Stripes, like the Liberty Tree flag (page 3) and the flag used at George Washington's headquarters (page 5). Some were used in protest (pages 130 and 160), highlighting the value of our First Amendment rights. Some commemorate tragic events (page 187); some celebrate our country's brightest moments (page 201). Some, like the Star-Spangled Banner (page 25) and the *Landing Craft Control 60* flag (page 107), stood witness to dramatic historical events. Others manifested in popular culture, such as Wonder Woman's costume (page 89) and the flag motif in the film *Easy Rider* (page 135), and more.

The book covers two and a half centuries of the flag's history—from 1765 to 2026—through political evolutions, dramatic events, and social upheavals. By studying the evolution of the flag and its intersection with the nation's story over the past 250 years, one can gain a clearer understanding of the United States and its history. Through all that history, the American flag has stood as a singular constant symbol that reminds us of everything that makes this country exceptional.

ANATOMY OF A FLAG

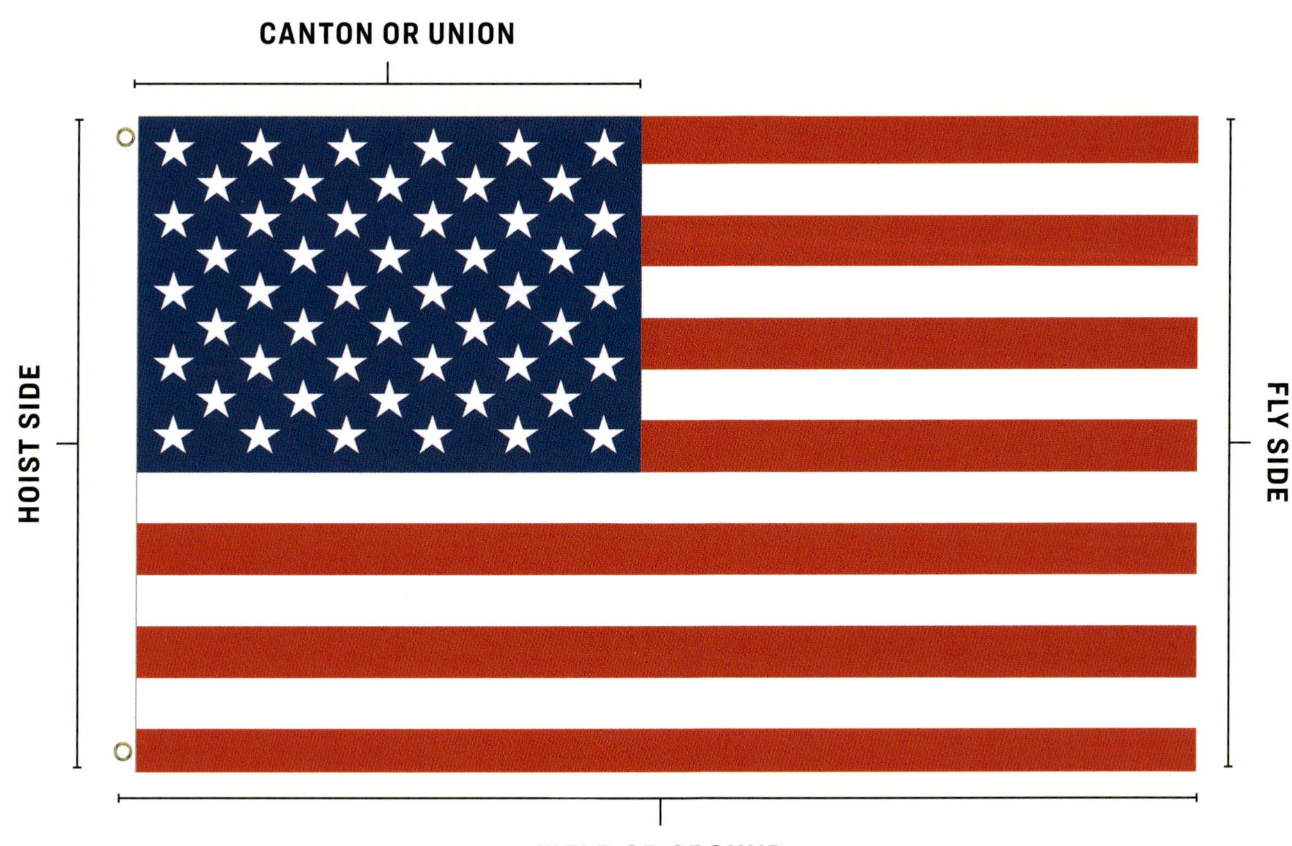

250 YEARS OF FLAGS AT A GLANCE

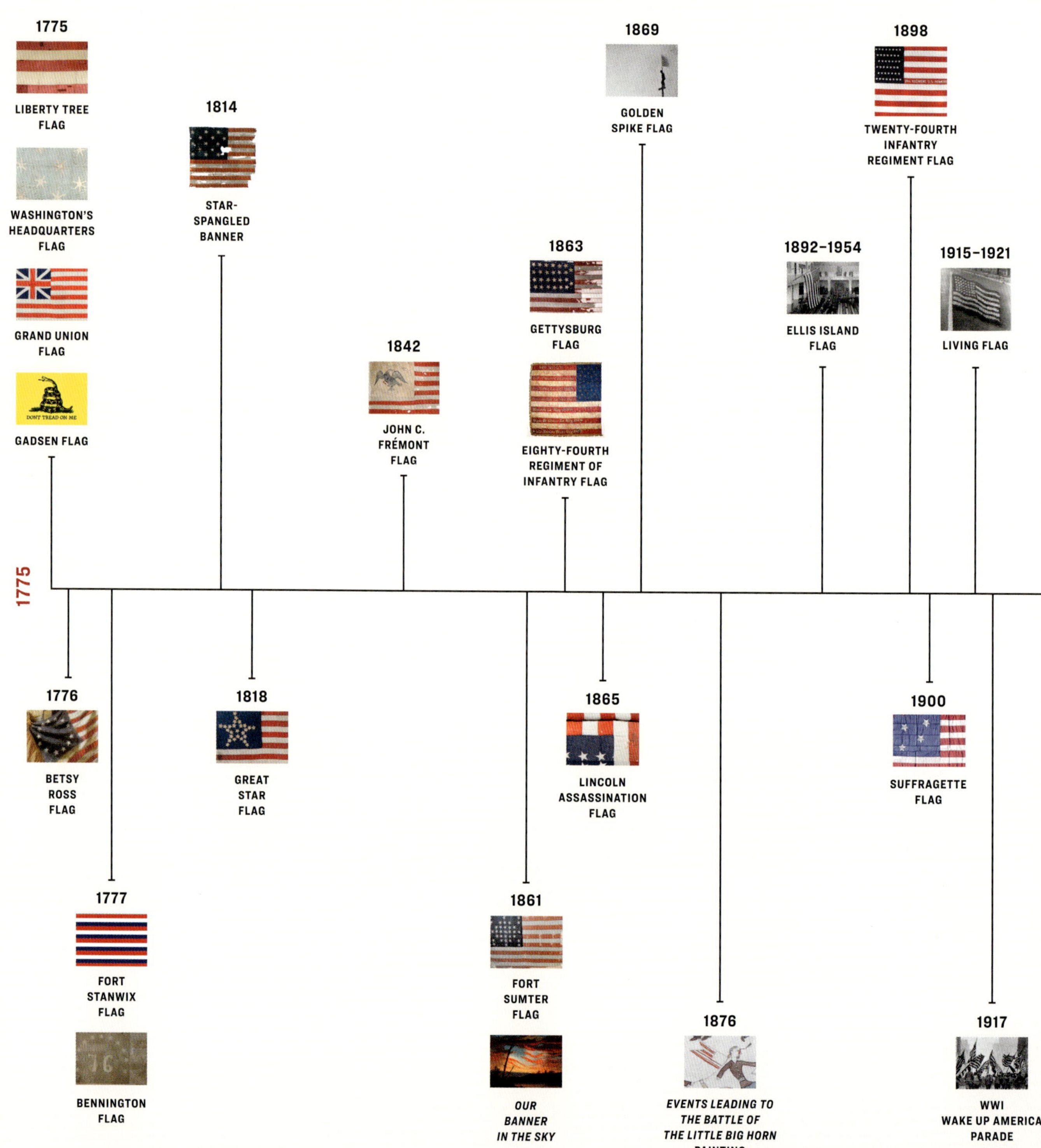

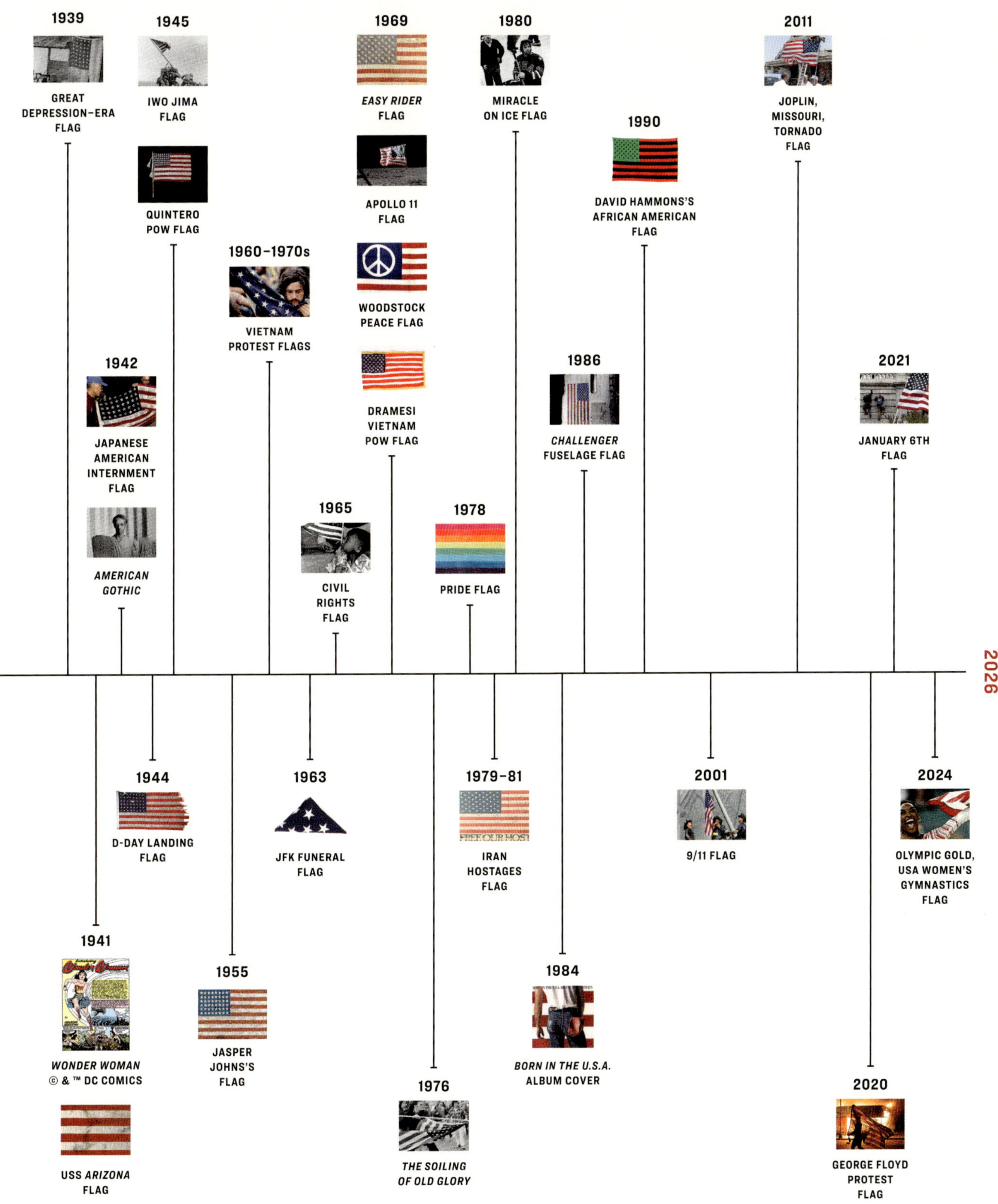
1939
GREAT DEPRESSION-ERA FLAG
1941
WONDER WOMAN © & ™ DC COMICS
USS ARIZONA FLAG
1942
JAPANESE AMERICAN INTERNMENT FLAG
AMERICAN GOTHIC
1944
D-DAY LANDING FLAG
1945
IWO JIMA FLAG
QUINTERO POW FLAG
1955
JASPER JOHNS'S FLAG
1960–1970s
VIETNAM PROTEST FLAGS
1963
JFK FUNERAL FLAG
1965
CIVIL RIGHTS FLAG
1969
EASY RIDER FLAG
APOLLO 11 FLAG
WOODSTOCK PEACE FLAG
DRAMESI VIETNAM POW FLAG
1976
THE SOILING OF OLD GLORY
1978
PRIDE FLAG
1979–81
FREE OUR HOST
IRAN HOSTAGES FLAG
1980
MIRACLE ON ICE FLAG
1984
BORN IN THE U.S.A. ALBUM COVER
1986
CHALLENGER FUSELAGE FLAG
1990
DAVID HAMMONS'S AFRICAN AMERICAN FLAG
2001
9/11 FLAG
2011
JOPLIN, MISSOURI, TORNADO FLAG
2020
GEORGE FLOYD PROTEST FLAG
2021
JANUARY 6TH FLAG
2024
OLYMPIC GOLD, USA WOMEN'S GYMNASTICS FLAG
2026

Bridger, Montana, 2023

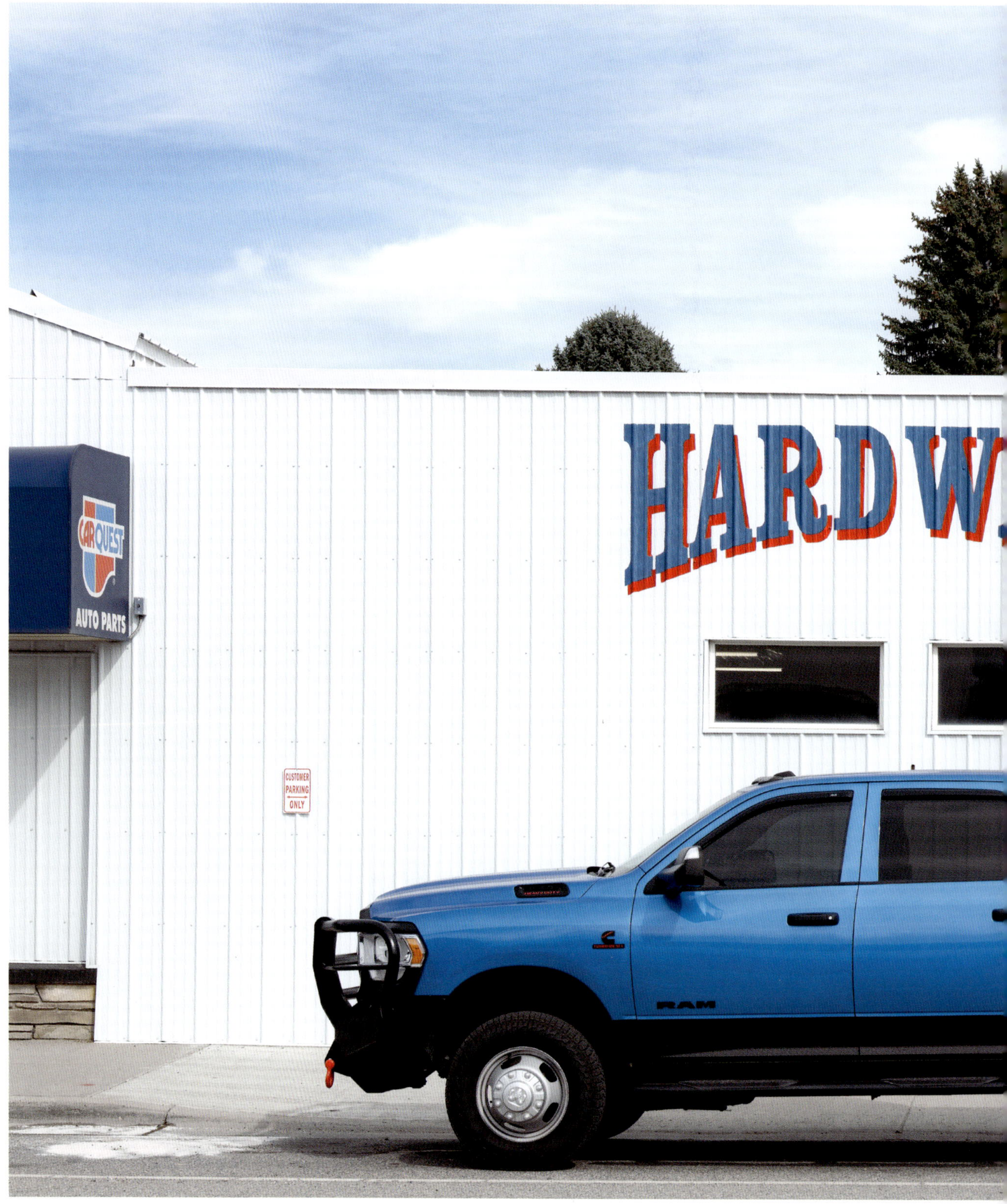

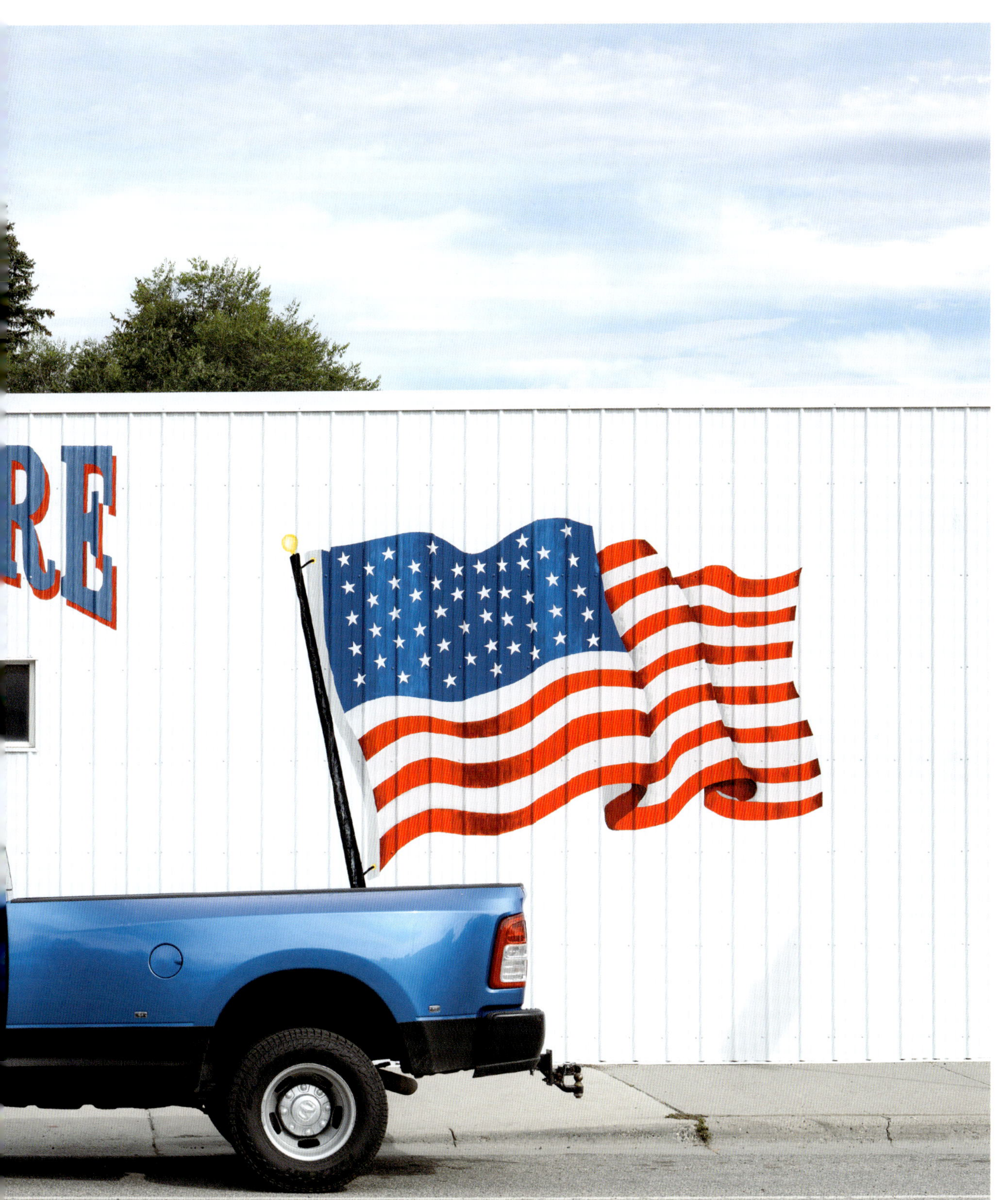

1765

to

1775

The Birth of the United States of America

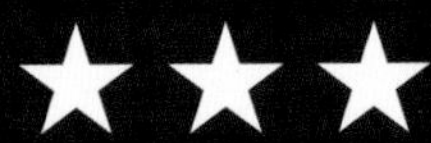

AMERICA'S FIRST FLAGS WERE BANNERS CARRIED by early patriots. These unofficial standards aimed to symbolize the colonies' break from the British Empire. Before the Revolutionary War, military units across the colonies and regions used their own flags to identify themselves and show their support for liberty.

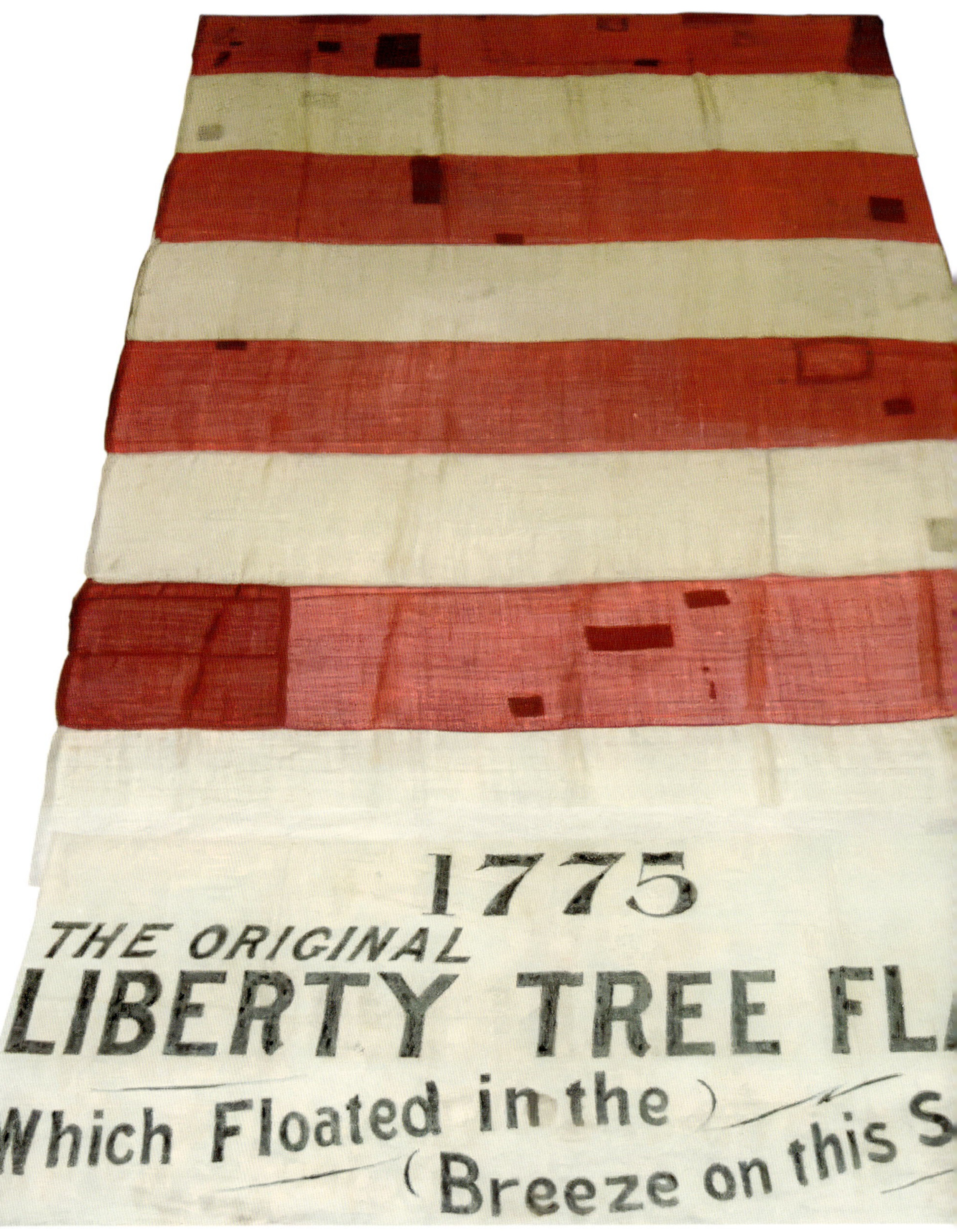
1775
THE ORIGINAL
LIBERTY TREE FL
Which Floated in the
Breeze on this S

LIBERTY TREE FLAG

Tea, Taxes, and Tyranny

DATE: 1760s–1770s

EVENT LOCATION: Boston, Massachusetts

CURRENT FLAG LOCATION: Revolutionary Spaces, Boston, Massachusetts

On August 14, 1765, colonists gathered at a large elm tree near Boston Neck (the narrow isthmus that connected Boston to Roxbury) to protest the Stamp Act—which had nothing to do with postage. The Stamp Act was a British law passed in 1765 requiring colonists to pay a tax on various forms of paper documents—mainly official documents, but also including pamphlets, newspapers, and even playing cards—that were produced in the colonies. The "stamp" was an embossment signifying that the tax had been paid. The protest was successful, and the Stamp Act was repealed. Following this, colonists began calling the elm the Liberty Tree.

The Liberty Tree became the focus of other demonstrations in which American colonists continued to express their frustration with the rules and taxes imposed by the British. At some point, as a symbol of their protest, they hung a banner from the tree: the Liberty Tree flag. It was made of nine vertical stripes—five red and four white. Lore states that when the flag was eventually banned by Britain, the colonists rotated the stripes

Previous: Liberty Tree Flag, circa 1770s

to a horizontal position to get around the ban on the vertically striped flag. Around 1775, the flag was expanded to include thirteen horizontal stripes, seven red and six white, to represent the thirteen colonies.

The Liberty Tree flag may be the originating source of the red-and-white stripes the flag features today. It likely served as a model for the Grand Union flag (page 7), which consisted of seven red and six white horizontal stripes and had the British Union Jack as its canton. (A canton, also known as a union, is the rectangular or square design located in the upper left-hand corner of a flag.) Every official United States flag from the Grand Union flag forward incorporated red-and-white stripes.

BOSTON TEA PARTY

★★★

On the night of December 16, 1773, a group of about a hundred colonists dumped 340 crates of loose tea, over 90,000 pounds in total, into Boston Harbor in what would become known as the Boston Tea Party.

Tea was an important commodity for the colonists, who, like most émigrés from or descendants of Britain, had a love affair with the brew. The British government applied a 25 percent tax on tea in the American colonies, and eventually the colonists, in protest, declared a boycott, driving down demand. Britain responded with the Tea Act of 1773. This was designed to keep the main British tea importer, the East India Company (EIC)—which was in dire financial trouble—afloat by granting the company a monopoly on tea sales in the colonies.

In the late fall of 1773, three ships—the *Beaver*, the *Dartmouth*, and the *Eleanor*—had arrived in Boston Harbor with stocks of tea. Boston residents protested and intimidated the colonist merchants who were receiving the tea on behalf of the EIC. They kept the tea from being off-loaded from the vessels. When the citizens of Boston learned that the governor, Thomas Hutchinson, was refusing to let the ships return to England with their cargo still on board, the Boston Tea Party ensued.

The Boston Harbor uprising was most likely led by the Sons of Liberty, a loosely organized radical group of colonists who opposed the taxes and laws being imposed on the American colonies by the British government. Their flag was the Liberty Tree flag. The Sons of Liberty were wary of being connected to the Boston Tea Party, so no identifying flag was flown during the event.

The Liberty Tree flag and the Boston Tea Party are both connected to the birth of the United States. These protests set in motion other events that would steer the colonies into the Revolutionary War. They showed the colonists that they could stand up to the British and gave rise to the first modern democracy.

WASHINGTON'S HEADQUARTERS FLAG

The General's Standard

DATE: Revolutionary War, ca. 1775–1783

EVENT LOCATION: Various

CURRENT FLAG LOCATION: Museum of the American Revolution, Philadelphia, Pennsylvania

George Washington's Headquarters flag (also known as Washington's Commander-in-Chief standard) was reportedly the first flag to feature thirteen stars, representing the thirteen colonies. It is believed to have been created prior to 1776, meaning that, like the Liberty Tree flag (page 3), it predated the formation of the United States. The flag was known as a "standard," which meant it was used to designate a military leader's location in the field so that officers knew where to contact the command structure. (In the navy, a standard would mark the admiral's ship as the flagship.) Washington's Headquarters flag would have been flown wherever George Washington was stationed, on or near the battlefield.

The provenance of Washington's Headquarters flag is based almost entirely on family stories. Ellen Lovell Crosby and Fannie Lovell, descendants of George Washington's sister, Betty Washington Lewis, gifted the

Below: *Washington's Headquarters flag, mid-1770s*

flag to the Museum of American History at Valley Forge, Pennsylvania, in the early 1900s. They claim that the standard had traveled with Washington during the Revolutionary War, and that it had a blue field with thirteen six-pointed stars laid out in five rows. There are conflicting historical accounts of what Washington's Headquarters flag looked like—for example, Charles Willson Peale's 1779 painting, *Washington at Princeton,* depicts the flag with its stars arranged in a circle. However, there is also no definitive proof that this isn't the actual flag that Washington used during the Revolutionary War.

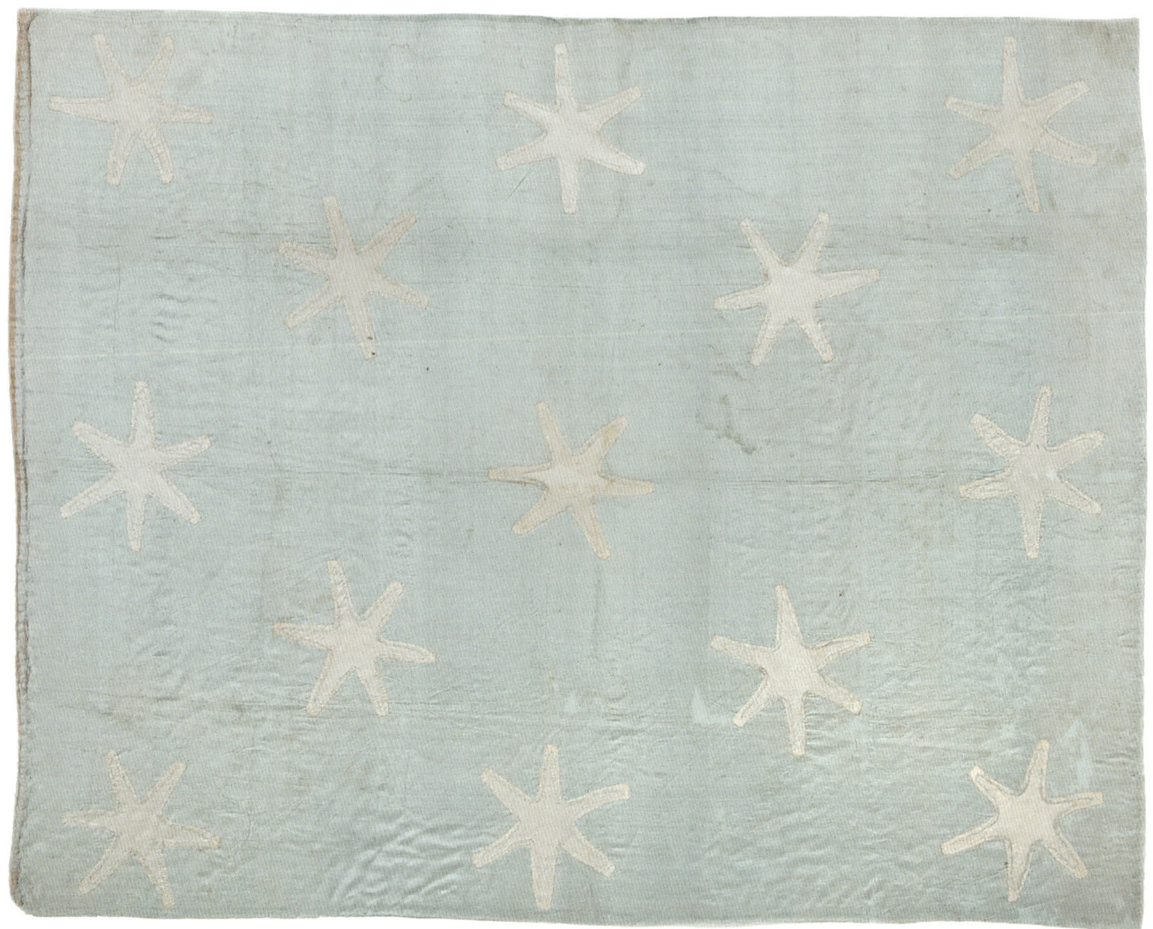

GRAND UNION FLAG (OR THE CONTINENTAL COLORS)

The Flag of Appeasement

DATE: December 3, 1775

EVENT LOCATION: Aboard the colonial warship *Alfred* in Philadelphia Harbor

CURRENT FLAG LOCATION: Unknown

Following: *The Grand Union flag, 1775*

Before the Revolutionary War, America's thirteen colonies were separate entities. Each colony had its own flag, and in some cases so did the various districts and regions. The colonies came together as a nation mainly due to the colonists' frustration with Britain's tax acts of the 1760s and 1770s. The Grand Union flag became their unofficial flag, a symbol of their unity as a new nation.

The designer of the Grand Union flag has been lost to time (as is the original flag), but it's surmised that the inspiration was the British navy's Red Ensign, which features the Union Jack on the canton in a field of red. The same Union Jack appears on the canton of the Grand Union flag, along with thirteen alternating red-and-white stripes, the identical arrangement that would be used on almost every future American flag.

Though designing a national flag for the American colonies was a revolutionary gesture, the British Union Jack on the canton may have signified a desire to maintain ties to the British motherland. Many colonists

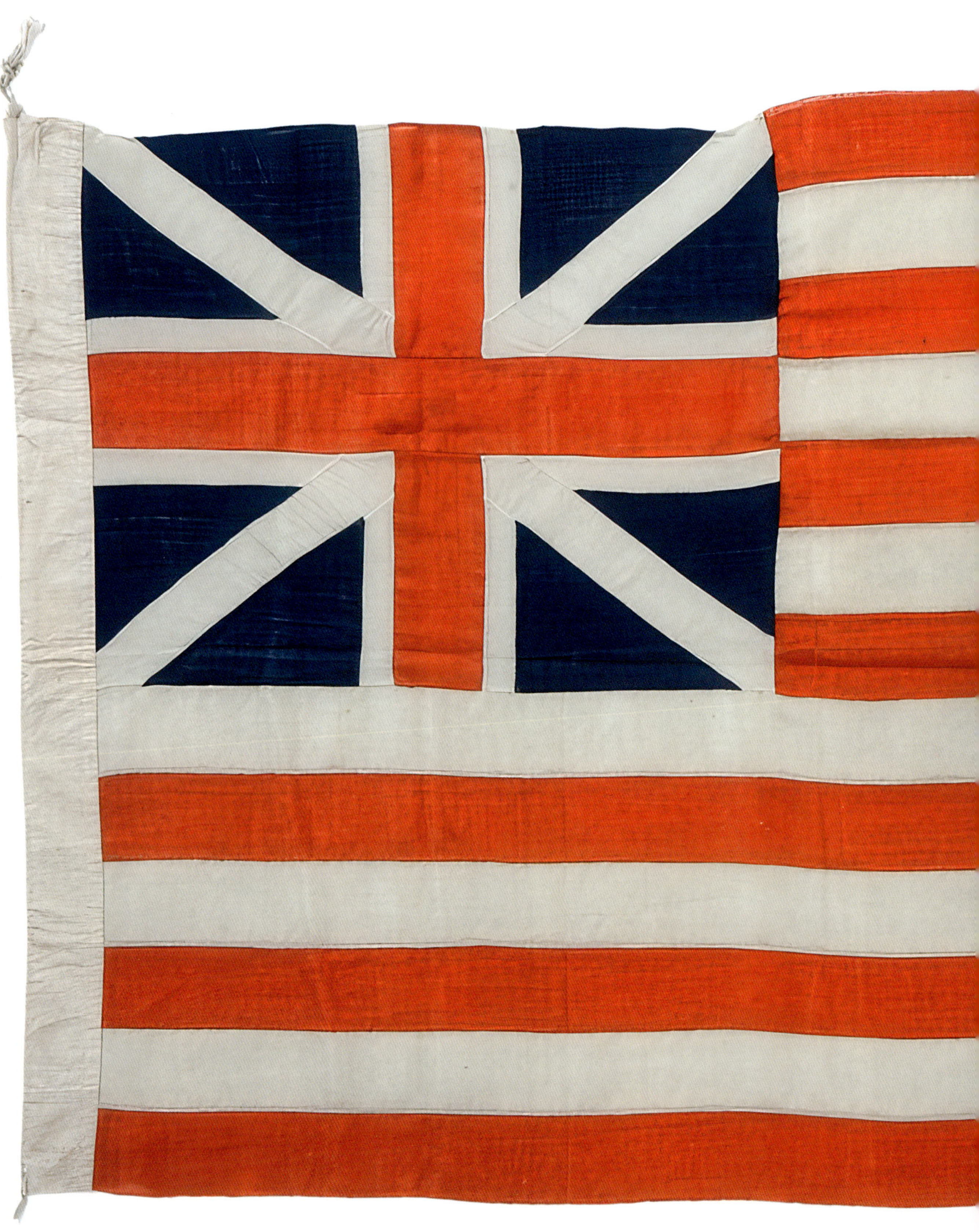

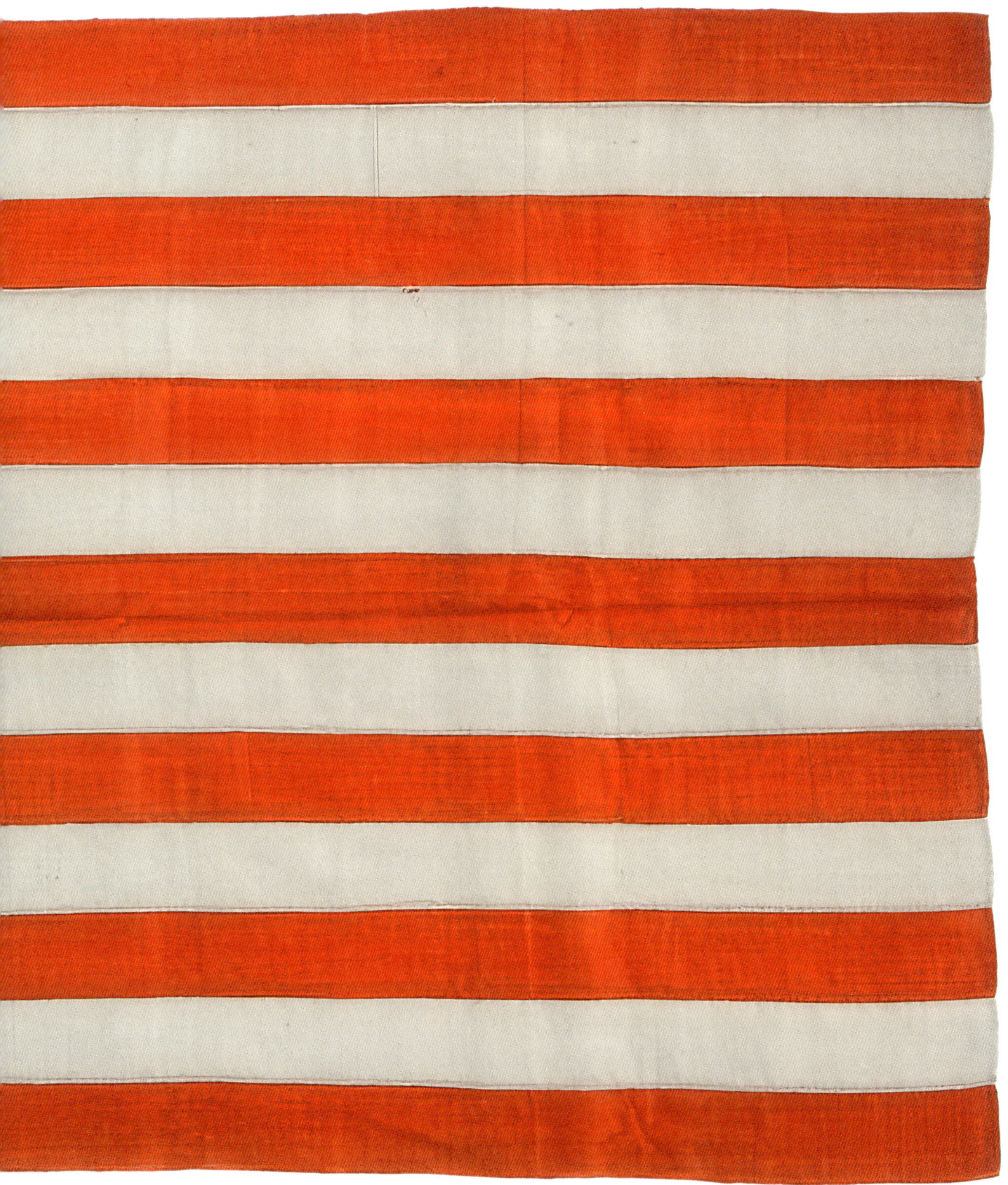

still felt a loyalty to Britain even though they were angry with the way they were ruled.

The Grand Union flag was first flown aboard the *Alfred,* a former merchant ship recommissioned as a colonial warship, on December 3, 1775. Maritime law required that ships display their country of registry. Because the colonies did not have an official flag, the ship flew the Grand Union. (At the time, the *Alfred* was commanded by John Paul Jones, who, during the Battle of Flamborough Head in 1779, when asked by the opposing commander to "strike" his colors, or lower the ship's flag, in surrender, made his famous reply, "I have not yet begun to fight.")

When the Flag Act of 1777 was enacted, the Union Jack featured on the Grand Union flag was replaced with thirteen stars on what became the official American flag, more commonly known as the Betsy Ross flag (page 17).

GADSDEN FLAG

A Snake in the Grass

DATE: December 20, 1775

EVENT LOCATION: USS *Alfred*, Commodore Esek Hopkins's Flagship

CURRENT FLAG LOCATION: Unknown

Christopher Gadsden was a member of the Continental Congress and a general in the Continental army. He designed the flag that bears his name for Commodore Esek Hopkins, who later became commander-in-chief of the Continental navy. Hopkins needed a standard for his flagship, marking in much the same way Washington's Headquarters flag was used to locate Washington as the army's commander (page 5). Hopkins first flew the Gadsden flag on his flagship, the *Alfred* (named for the ninth-century British monarch Alfred the Great), on December 20, 1775, just weeks after John Paul Jones had flown the Grand Union flag on the same ship. Though the Grand Union flag became the unofficial flag of the thirteen colonies, the Gadsden flag became the flag of the Continental Marines (the precursor to the US Marine Corps) during the Revolutionary War.

The Gadsden flag depicts a coiled rattlesnake with its mouth open and rattle elevated, poised to strike, against a yellow background. The words

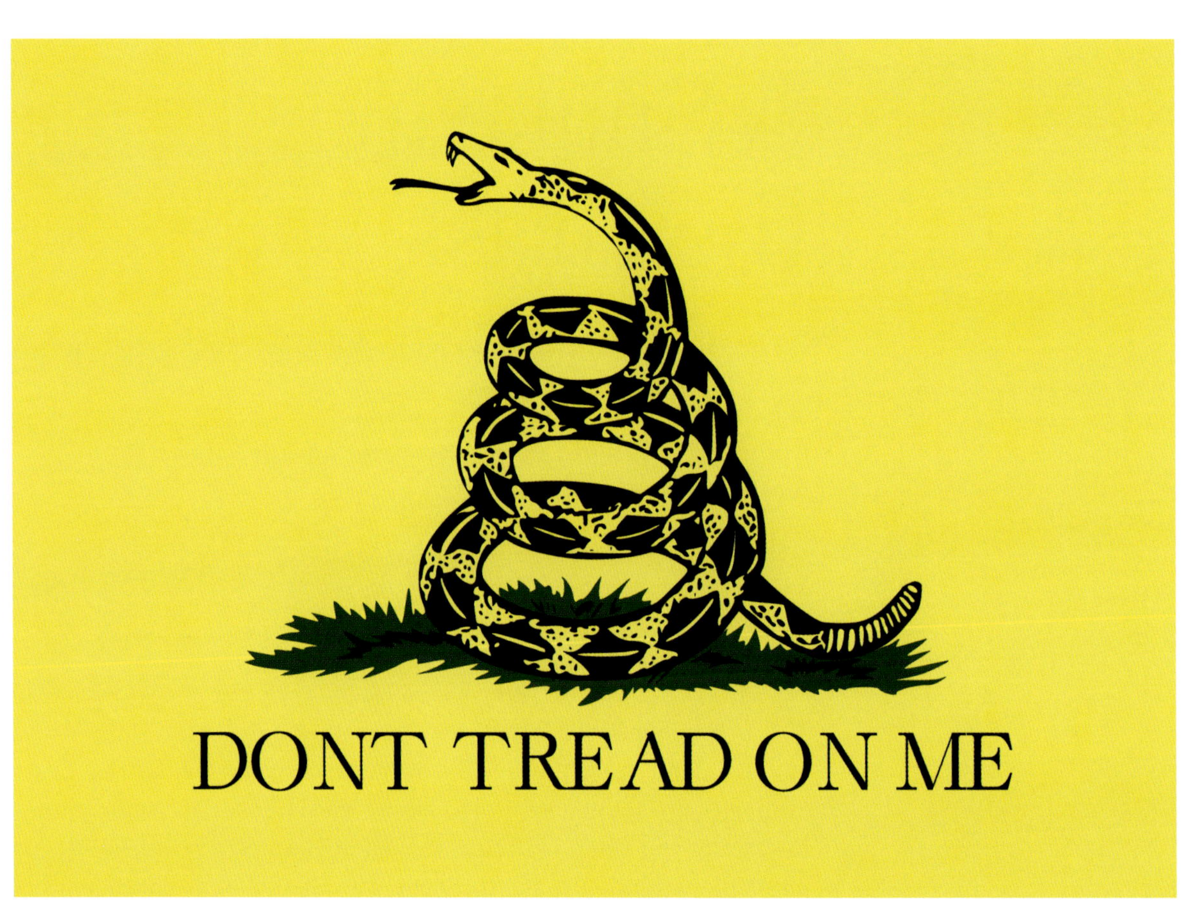
DONT TREAD ON ME

Above: Join, or Die *woodcut by Benjamin Franklin, 1754*

Opposite: *The Gadsden flag featured a rattlesnake that symbolized the vigilance and unity of the settlers during the Revolutionary War, 1775.*

Don't Tread on Me are emblazoned beneath the snake. The idea of using a snake to represent the American colonies came from Benjamin Franklin's woodcut *Join, or Die*. The woodcut print depicts a snake severed into eight pieces, each labeled with abbreviations for the colonies. The illustration was originally aimed at rallying the colonies to help the British fight off the French in the French and Indian War and gain control of the land west of the Appalachian Mountains. The piece took on new meaning when it was published in the *The Constitutional Courant* in response to the Stamp Act of 1765 (page 3). Now the point was that if the colonies were going to thrive and resist British domination, they needed to act in concert. This sense of unity was an essential principle in the flag's design.

No original versions of the Gadsden flag still exist. Its design was unique for its time as it did not use typical symbolism or borrow design elements from existing flags. Its declaration, aimed at the British, sent the message that Americans were united in their resolve to withstand tyranny. The Revolutionary War would test the limits of the patriots' principles and the values symbolized by the Gadsden flag. The following year, in 1776, the United States would declare its independence from Britain, and it would adopt an official flag to represent its freedom while honoring the original thirteen colonies.

MISAPPROPRIATION AND MEANING

★★★

During the Civil War, some Confederate troops began displaying the Gadsden flag to represent their desire to secede from the United States. But they ignored the flag's original symbolic meaning—unity in the rejection of British oppression—and substituted the opposite notion of repressing Blacks under slavery. Their interpretation also ignored Benjamin Franklin's contention that strength lay in a unified aggregation of colonies and, rather, chose the opposite stance of creating a divided nation.

Today, the Gadsden flag continues to be misappropriated. It is used by nationalist, white supremacist, and other alt-right groups as a (mistaken) symbol of separatist power—the exact thing the flag was meant to deter. It's also used as an emblem of protest by groups who are unsatisfied with the duly elected officers of the nation, thus skewing the flag's original meaning as a symbol of dissent against a lack of elected representation.

1776

to

1860

The Origin of the American Flag

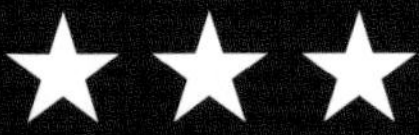

THE SECOND CONTINENTAL CONGRESS APPROVED the Declaration of Independence on July 4, 1776. After breaking away from England, the newly formed country needed an ensign that would identify its military and symbolize its independence. The Flag Act, approved by Congress on June 14, 1777, outlined the design of the new nation's flag: "that the flag of the United States be made of thirteen stripes, alternate red and white; that the union be thirteen stars, white in a blue field, representing a new constellation." The Flag Act of 1777 did not specify the pattern of stars on the blue canton, nor did it address how the flag would change as new states joined the Union. These details would need to considered as the new American banner evolved and as the number of states in the Union grew.

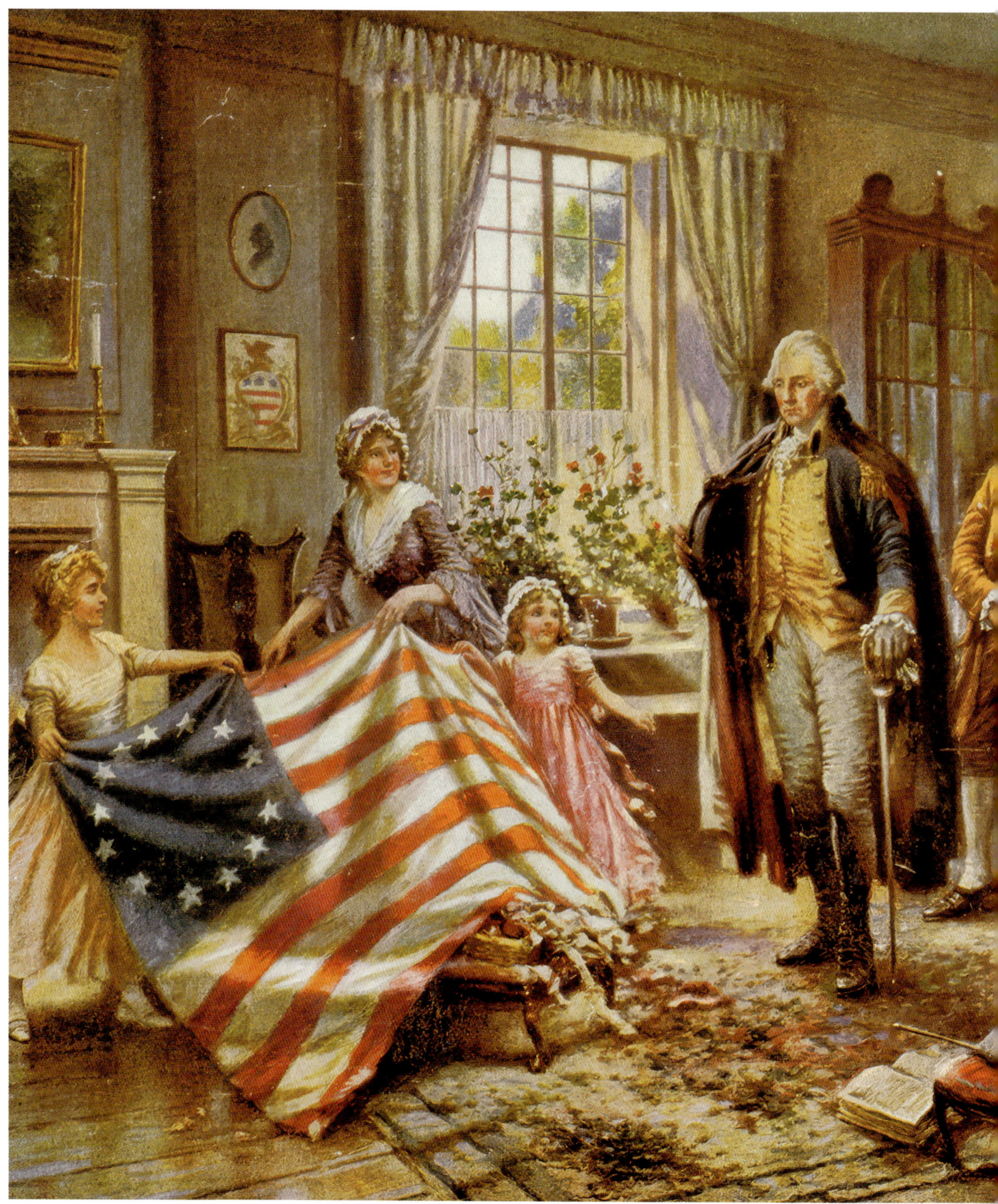

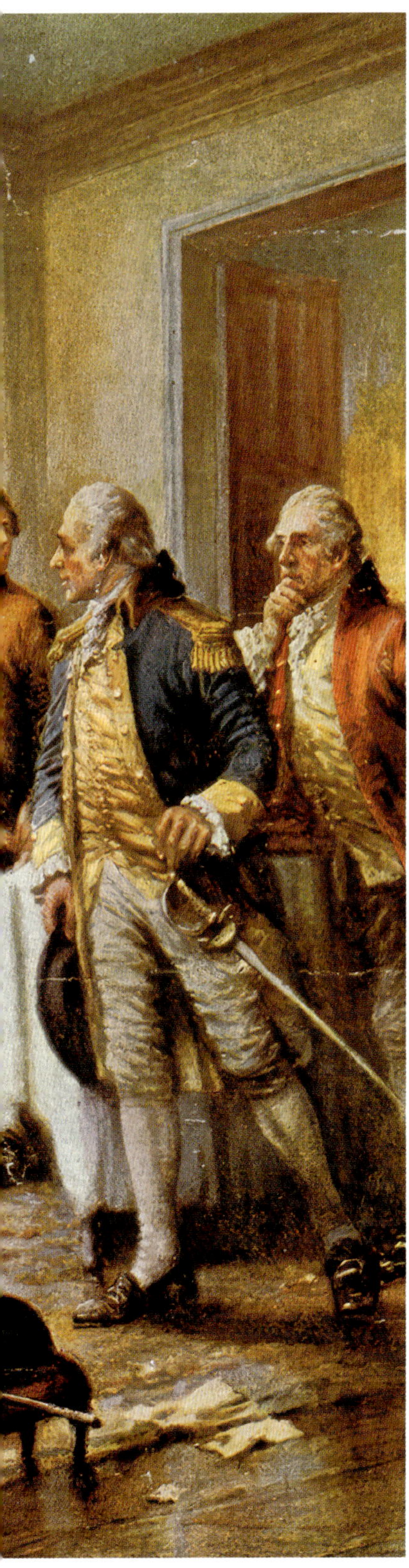

BETSY ROSS FLAG

History or Legend?

DATE: June 1776

EVENT LOCATION: Philadelphia, Pennsylvania

CURRENT FLAG LOCATION: Unknown

Two hundred fifty years ago, the United States adopted its first official ensign, commonly known as the Betsy Ross flag—one of the most recognizable versions. The story of Betsy Ross has been told to schoolchildren across the United States for over a century. However, the history of this banner isn't as clear as the circle of stars on its blue canton.

Betsy and her first husband, John Ross, operated an upholstery business in Philadelphia. When the Revolutionary War began in 1775, John served in the Pennsylvania provincial militia. He died that same year while guarding munitions.

John Ross was George Ross's nephew. Betsy had done seamstress work for George and Martha Washington. Around the time when Betsy is thought to have made the flag, she and the Washingtons both attended Christ Church in Philadelphia and had been assigned adjacent pews. It is feasible that George Ross and George Washington knew Betsy and were

Previous: The Birth of Old Glory *painting by Edward Percy Morgan shows Betsy Ross displaying the flag she made for George Washington, Major John Ross, and Robert Morris, 1917.*

aware of her seamstress skills, which is why they would have chosen her for this task.

Washington, Ross, and Robert Morris (a delegate at the Second Continental Congress) are said to have supplied Betsy with a flag design featuring a circle of thirteen six-pointed stars, which correlates with the six-pointed stars used on Washington's Headquarters flag (page 5). As the story goes, Betsy suggested the use of five-pointed stars instead, demonstrating that one simple cut in folded fabric would yield a five-pointed star.

Betsy reportedly shared her story about the flag with a family friend, Samuel Wetherill, and showed him the star she had made for Washington, Ross, and Morris. When he remarked on the star's significance, Betsy gave it to him. This star was kept in the Wetherill family and was finally rediscovered in 1925. It was displayed at the Free Quaker Meeting House in Philadelphia (where the Rosses were members for a while and where they got to know Wetherill), but it was eventually lost.

The legend behind the Betsy Ross flag was not widely known until the 1870s, when Betsy's grandson, William Canby, made a presentation to the Historical Society of Pennsylvania in Philadelphia about his grandmother's connection to the first official flag of the United States. An 1873 article in *Harper's New Monthly Magazine* further spread Canby's tale of Betsy Ross.

According to Canby and affidavits made by several other of Betsy's relatives, in June 1776, she was approached by three men associated with the Continental Congress: George Washington, Robert Morris, and George Ross, who had supposedly been charged with the creation of an official flag for use by the American armed forces.

The complete history of the Betsy Ross flag will probably never be known. The legend is so large at this point that it would be hard to sway minds to accept otherwise. But there is evidence that she did make flags for the United States government: A receipt made out to Betsy for flag construction from the Pennsylvania Navy Board, dated May 29, 1777, survives in the state archives. And it's believed that Betsy made flags during the Revolutionary War and for many decades after as well.

SIEGE AT FORT STANWIX FLAG

Flag for a Frontier Fort

DATE: August 2–22, 1777

EVENT LOCATION: Fort Stanwix (now Rome), New York

CURRENT FLAG LOCATION: Unknown

The Fort Stanwix flag was raised in August 1777, one month prior to the Flag Act being signed into law. Technically, that meant that the Fort Stanwix flag wasn't an official United States flag, but it may have been the first flag flown by America at a military installation during combat—most likely to indicate that American troops were in possession of the garrison.

Fort Stanwix, located in what is presently Rome, New York, was built by British troops starting in 1758 during the French and Indian War. It took about five years to complete. The fort's position was important for control of the region because it stood near a 6-mile (10 km) portage (known to local Indigenous peoples as the Great Carry) between two water-access routes connecting the Great Lakes to the Atlantic Ocean: the Mohawk River (which led east to the Hudson River and the Atlantic) and Wood Creek (which led west to Lake Oneida and Lake Ontario). The fort was built to protect the portage and resolve disputes over land rights

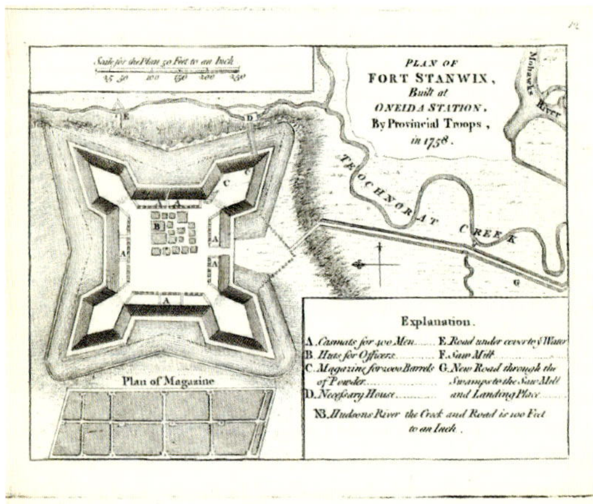

Above: *Plan of Fort Stanwix, 1758, thought to be the site of the first settlers' flag raised in battle at a fort*

Opposite: *Modern view of the reconstructed Fort Stanwix*

between European settlers and the Indigenous tribes in the area. In 1768, the British signed treaties with local Indigenous tribes, which made the fort unnecessary, and it was eventually abandoned.

In July 1776, a little over a year after the start of the Revolutionary War, the US Continental army, under the command of Major General Philip Schuyler, took control of and restored the dilapidated fort, mainly to control the portage. British troops arrived with superior forces and a contingent of Indigenous allies on August 2, 1777, and demanded its surrender. In response, the American troops inside the fort hoisted their flag, fired a cannon on the British camp, and settled in for a siege. The British were unsuccessful in driving out the Americans and were forced to abandon the attack on August 22.

Due to conflicting and incomplete accounts of the siege, there are a number of theories on what the flag at Fort Stanwix looked like. The Flag Act stated that "the flag of the United States be made of thirteen stripes, alternate red and white; that the union be thirteen stars, white in a blue field, representing a new constellation," but the details of the act weren't widely known yet, and it was vague in its description of the specifics, including the placement of the union (canton) on the flag, the number of points on the stars, and the arrangement of the stars on the union. Because the soldiers had limited resources for producing anything, let alone a flag, it is likely the ensign that they made was simple, with red, white, and blue stripes. Some accounts say the soldiers donated their own clothing for the strips of red, white, and blue. Some historians believe the soldiers could have made a version of the Grand Union flag (page 7).

In 1877, newspaper accounts suggested that the flag hoisted at Fort Stanwix was a regimental flag with a painting of two women, a laurel design, a dragon-type figure, and the word *Excelsior*, meaning "ever upward." A year later this design would be adopted as the New York state seal, and it served as the basis for the state flag of New York. Today, the Excelsior regimental flag is housed in the collection of the Albany Institute of History & Art in New York.

Regardless of what it looked like, the raising of the flag at Fort Stanwix began a long tradition of flying the flag wherever United States forces found themselves in battle.

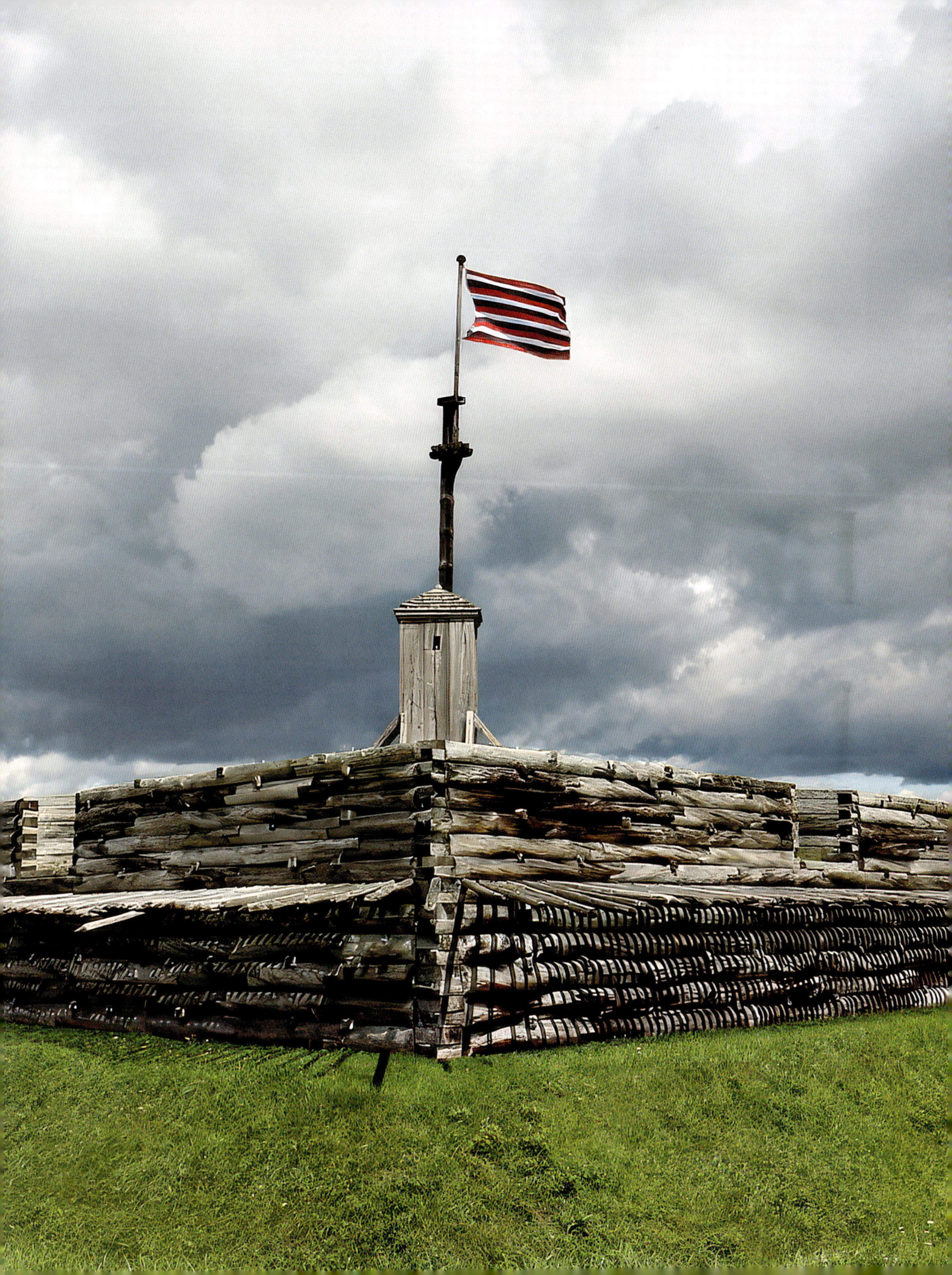

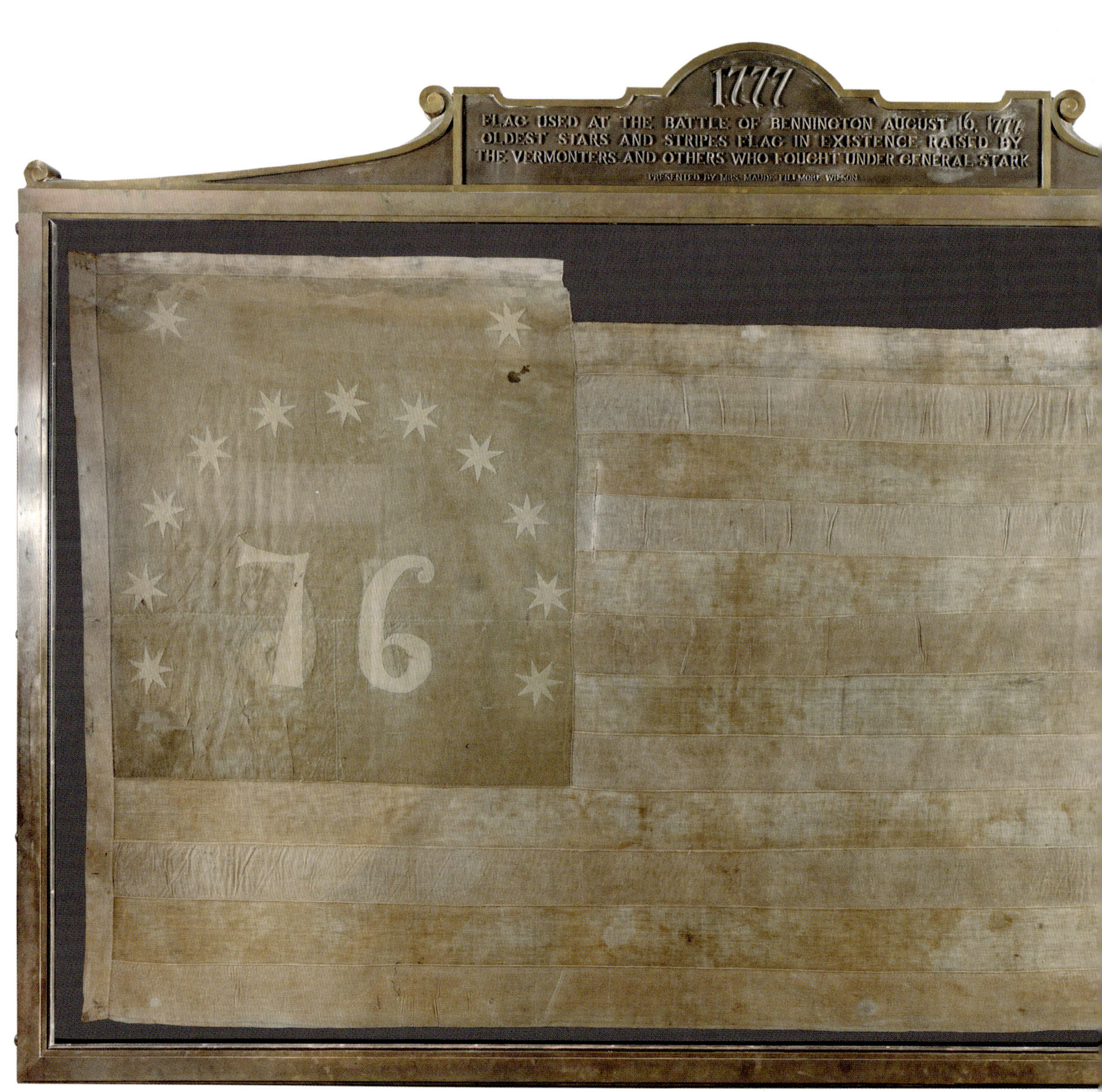
1777
FLAG USED AT THE BATTLE OF BENNINGTON AUGUST 16, 1777
OLDEST STARS AND STRIPES FLAG IN EXISTENCE RAISED BY
THE VERMONTERS AND OTHERS WHO FOUGHT UNDER GENERAL STARK
PRESENTED BY MRS. MAUDE FILLMORE WILSON
76

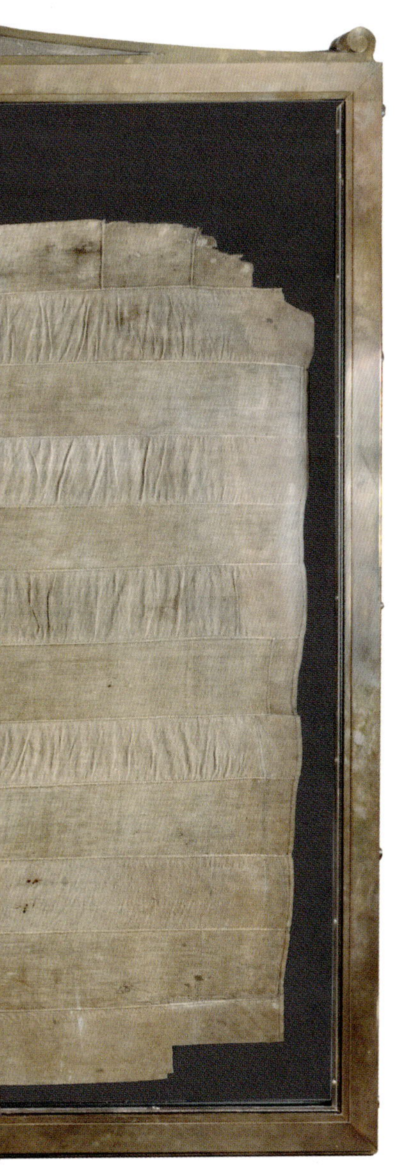

BENNINGTON FLAG

An Underestimated Strength

DATE: August 16, 1777

EVENT LOCATION: Near Walloomsac, New York

CURRENT FLAG LOCATION: Bennington Museum, Bennington, Vermont

The Bennington flag is one of the more well-known flags from the Revolutionary War era. It derives its moniker from the Battle of Bennington in Vermont—considered to be one of the pivotal battles of the war, as it was a major setback for the British. Rather than the more common blue canton with thirteen white stars, seven red stripes, and six white stripes, with red on the upper and lower borders, the Bennington flag sported seven white and six red stripes, with white stripes in the distal positions. It was also made distinct by the "76" emblazoned in the center of the blue canton, beneath an arc of eleven seven-pointed stars, with additional seven-pointed stars in the upper corners of the blue field.

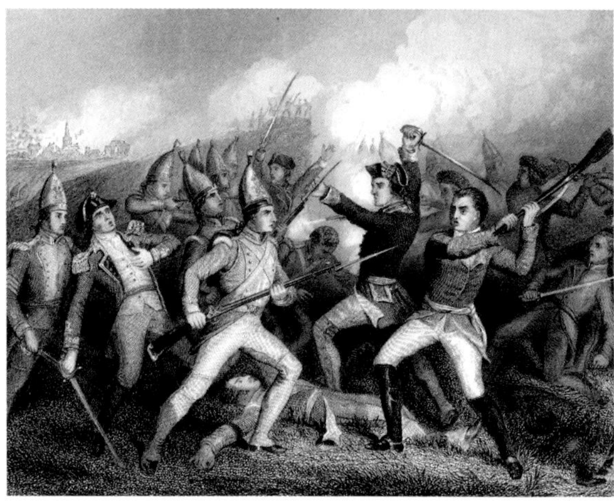

Above: *Illustration of the Battle of Bennington, circa 1777*

Previous: *Bennington flag, early 1800s*

The battle took place not in Bennington but about 10 miles west on a farm near Walloomsac, New York, on August 16, 1777. The British forces, led by Lieutenant Colonel Friedrich Baum, were looking for provisions—horses, food, weapons, and any other goods they could pillage. Baum thought Bennington was lightly protected by the Americans. He didn't know that General John Stark—in command of New Hampshire militia troops—and Colonel Seth Warner—controlling Vermont's Green Mountain Boys—had around 2,000 men in the town. The British numbered around 700, and Stark and his troops quickly overran them. Even as reinforcements arrived for both sides, the rout of the British continued. Between casualties and prisoners, the British lost around 1,000 men. A possibly worse consequence was that many of the Indigenous people who had been working with the British abandoned them, decimating the ranks of their scouting forces and leaving them with limited knowledge of the local terrain for future battles.

The lore of the Bennington flag is that Nathaniel Fillmore, grandfather to Millard Fillmore, the thirteenth president of the United States, carried the flag on the battlefield. According to Fillmore's descendants, the Bennington flag was then handed down through the family and they eventually donated it to the Bennington Museum. As is the case for many early unofficial American flags, the exact history and provenance of the Bennington flag is not fully known. The museum states that the flag's material dates to the early nineteenth century; historians theorize that this flag was made to commemorate 1776 and the revolution in general, rather than the battle of Bennington.

STAR-SPANGLED BANNER

By the Dawn's Early Light

DATE: September 14, 1814

EVENT LOCATION: Fort McHenry, Baltimore, Maryland

CURRENT FLAG LOCATION: National Museum of American History, Washington, DC

Following: *The Star-Spangled Banner, Fort McHenry, Maryland, 1814*

The War of 1812, though one of America's lesser-known conflicts, produced America's national anthem as well as one of the country's most recognizable symbols: the Star-Spangled Banner.

In 1813, Major George Armistead took command of Fort McHenry, at the entrance to Baltimore Harbor. He commissioned two flags: a storm flag, measuring 17 by 25 feet (5.2 by 7.6 m), that would be flown in inclement weather, and a much larger garrison flag, measuring 30 by 42 feet (9.1 by 12.8 m), to be raised in fair weather. The flags would have fifteen stars and fifteen stripes to represent the addition of Vermont and Kentucky into the Union. The gigantic garrison flag's stars are 2 feet in diameter (0.6 m), and the stripes are 2 feet (0.6 m) in width.

The War of 1812 was slogging along on several fronts. In August 1814, negotiations to end the war had begun in Ghent, Belgium. The following month, British troops began the battle for the City of Baltimore. They made an initial ground attack on North Point, near the entrance to

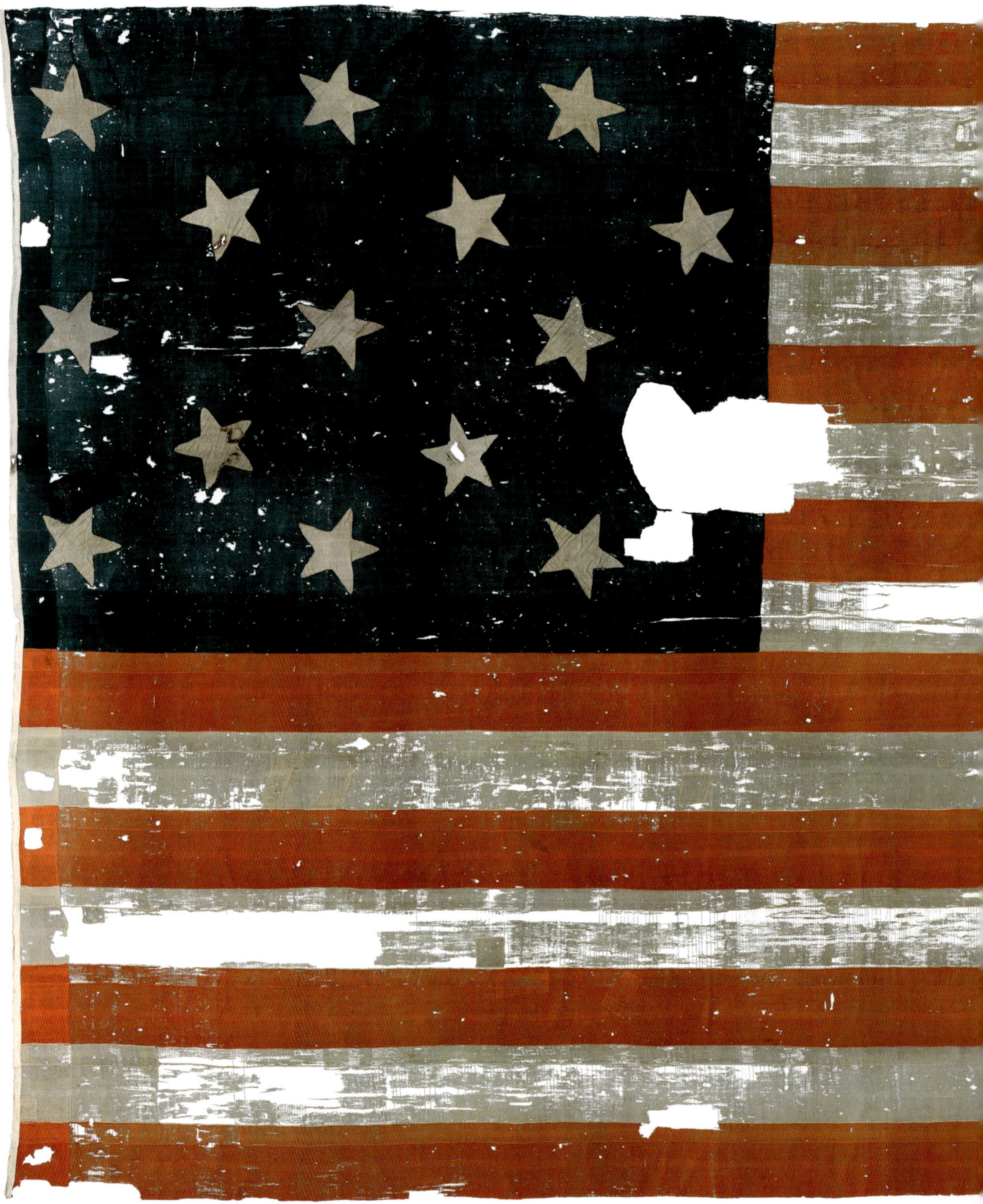

Baltimore Harbor. Traversing up the North Point peninsula, they met resistance from American militia. To advance on Baltimore, the British would have to attack not just by land but also by sea.

Lying at the tip of Whetstone Point, on a wedge-shaped spit of land jutting into the Patapsco River just below the heart of Baltimore, was Fort McHenry. Recently fortified and resupplied, Fort McHenry was a formidable obstacle for the British naval fleet. Early on the morning of September 13, 1814, the British warships directed a fusillade of cannon and rocket fire toward the fort, and they kept it up for twenty-five hours. The weather was stormy; Armistead's men raised the storm flag to show they controlled the fort and kept holding it against the invasion.

Meanwhile, Francis Scott Key, a lawyer in Georgetown, was approached along with American Prisoner Exchange Agent John Stuart Skinner to negotiate the release of an elderly prisoner of war, Dr. William Beanes. Key and Skinner met with British officers aboard a British truce ship, the HMS *Tonnant*, to bargain for Beanes's freedom. Because he had treated several wounded British soldiers, Beanes's release was granted. But Key, Skinner, and Beanes now had knowledge of the strength and position of British forces, and so they were transferred to an American truce ship and required to remain there (behind the British line of attack) until the end of the battle.

It was from this vantage point that Key observed the "rockets' red glare" over Fort McHenry during the British bombardment. In the morning, as the British came to realize that their attack was unsuccessful and began to withdraw, the weather cleared and Armistead ordered the garrison flag to be hoisted. Key was surprised and impressed to see the giant flag flying over the fort. While still on the American truce ship, he began writing his poem, "Defence of Fort M'Henry," and finished it shortly after he and his comrades were released two days later. Key set his poem to a tune that was popular at the time, "Anacreon in Heaven," and it soon became known as "The Star-Spangled Banner" (Honoring the Flag, page 216). (On March 4, 1931, "The Star-Spangled Banner" officially became the national anthem of the United States.)

As for the actual Star-Spangled Banner, meaning the giant garrison flag that was raised upon the victory of US troops at Fort McHenry, in its early life after the battle several souvenir swatches were given away, leaving holes in the flag. One star is missing, as is a segment the length of the fly (the loose end of the flag). The flag's current dimensions are 30 by 34 feet (9.1 by 10.4 m).

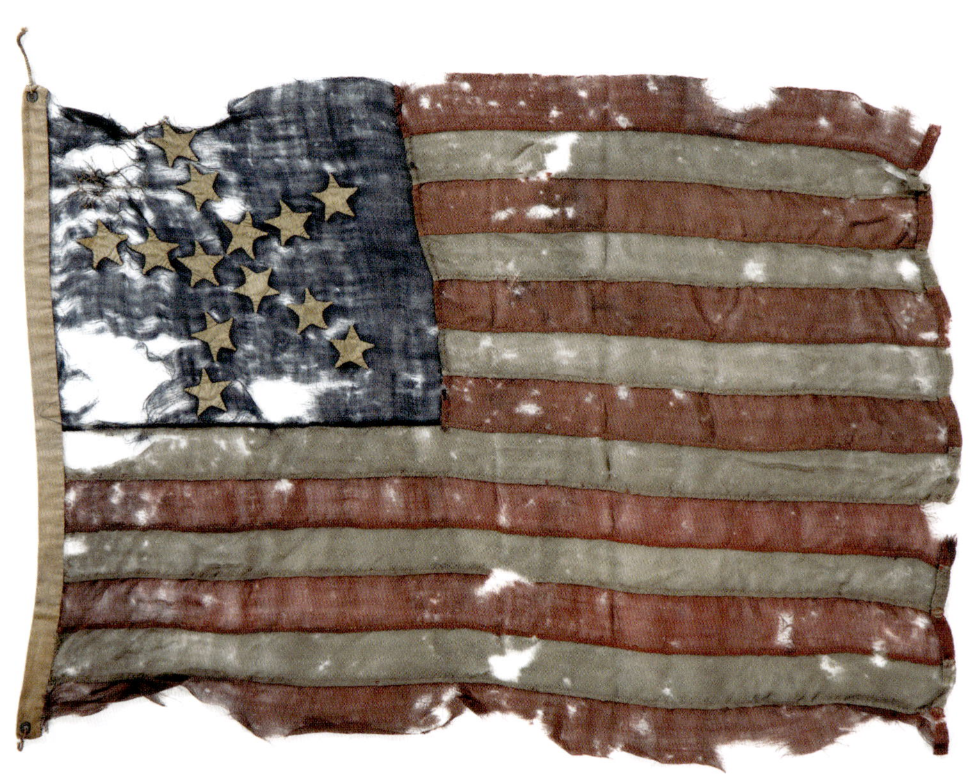

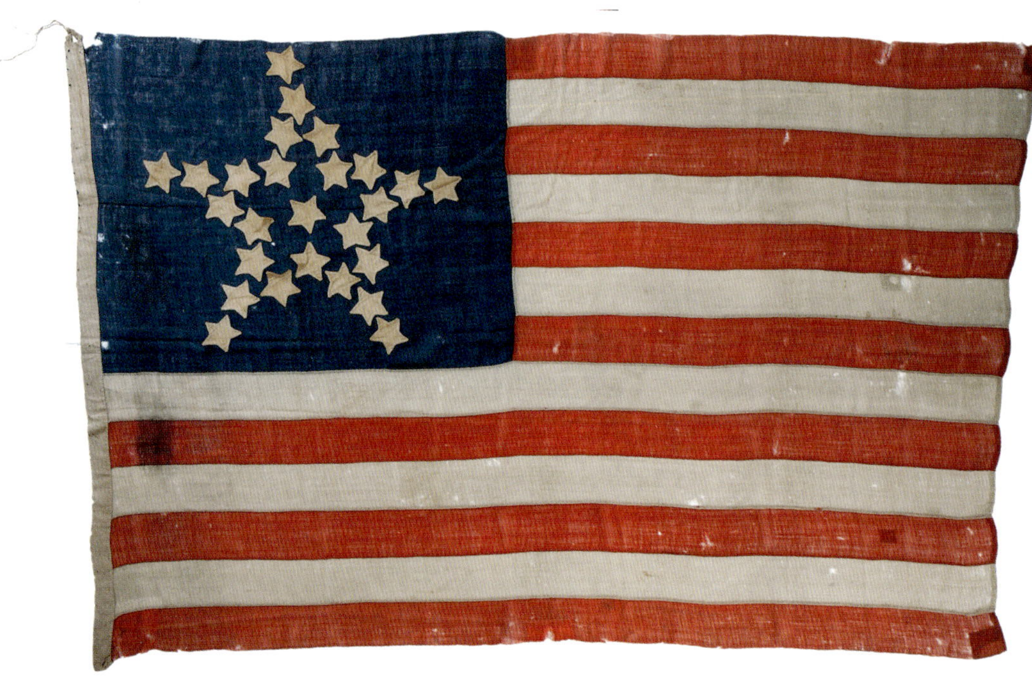

GREAT STAR FLAG (OR GRAND LUMINARY FLAG)

Expanding the Stars and Stripes

DATE: 1818

EVENT LOCATION: n/a

CURRENT FLAG LOCATION: Unknown

Opposite, top: *A thirteen-star Great Star (or Grand Luminary) flag, circa 1790*

Opposite, bottom: *A twenty-six-star Great Star (or Grand Luminary) flag, circa 1837*

Initially, the US flag was designed to have a star and a stripe for every state in the Union. So, when Vermont and Kentucky became the fourteenth and fifteenth states, respectively, Congress designated that the flag should feature fifteen stars and fifteen stripes. This version of the US flag is the only one to have included more than thirteen stripes.

Once Tennessee, Ohio, Louisiana, Indiana, and Mississippi had joined the Union, making twenty states in total, Congress determined that continuing to add a stripe for each state was impractical. The Flag Act of 1818 ordained that the American flag would remain at thirteen stripes, and a star would be added on July 4 following a new state's admission to the Union.

But it did not dictate the pattern of stars, and two main patterns emerged for the twenty-star flag. The first was a traditional arrangement with four rows of five stars each. The second featured the individual stars arranged to make one large star and gave the flag its moniker of the Great Star or Grand Luminary flag.

Opposite: *A thirty-four-star Great Star (or Grand Luminary) flag, circa 1861*

There had been earlier versions of flags using an overall star pattern, and others would follow, but the Great Star twenty-star pattern was the first to come into common use. As the number of states, and therefore stars, grew, the Great Star pattern became less practical.

The twenty-star flag was replaced by versions with the same number of stars as there were states in the Union. With every state that joined, another star was added. Beginning in 1819 and ending in 1877, stars for states twenty-one to thirty-eight of the Union were added to the flag. Several of these flag configurations were also found with the Great Star pattern containing more than twenty stars. In 1890, an additional five stars were added for North Dakota, South Dakota, Montana, Washington, and Idaho, making a forty-three-star flag. Over the next eighteen years, Wyoming, Utah, and Oklahoma were added. With the addition of New Mexico and Arizona in 1912, the number of stars grew to forty-eight in a configuration of six rows of eight stars. Another forty-seven years would pass before a star for Alaska was included, in 1959. Hawai'i's star was added to the flag in 1960 when it became the fiftieth state, giving us our fiftieth star and our current American flag.

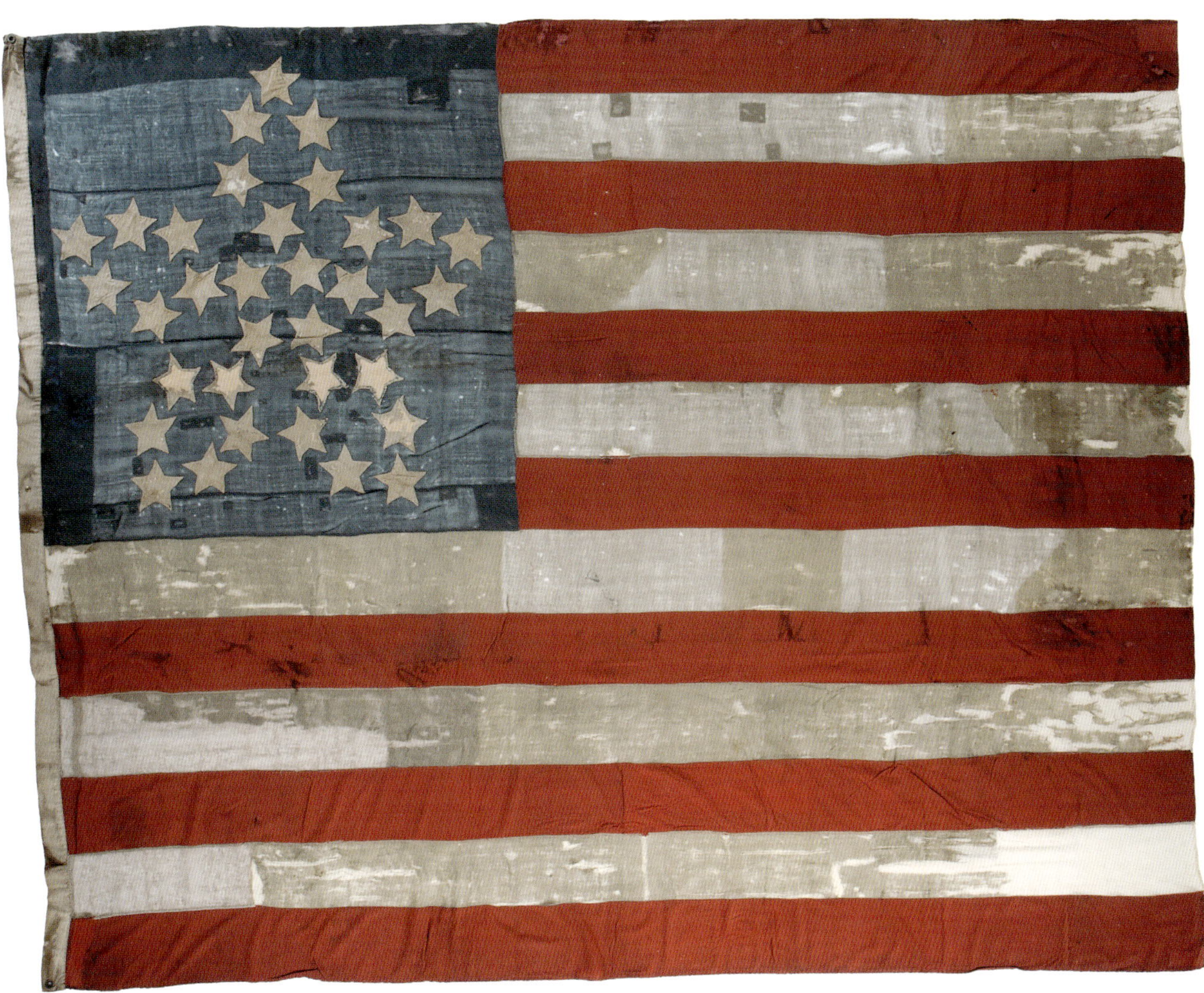

1861

to

1865

The Civil War

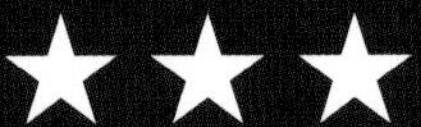

BY THE MID-1800S, THE PRACTICE OF ENSLAVEment was dividing the country between North and South. A war would rise from this discord over human rights, and it would take more American lives than any conflict in the country's history, then and now. The United States flag played a significant role through this era not only as a practical device used in battle but also as a symbolic tool for raising funds, boosting troop morale, and garnering public support for the Civil War.

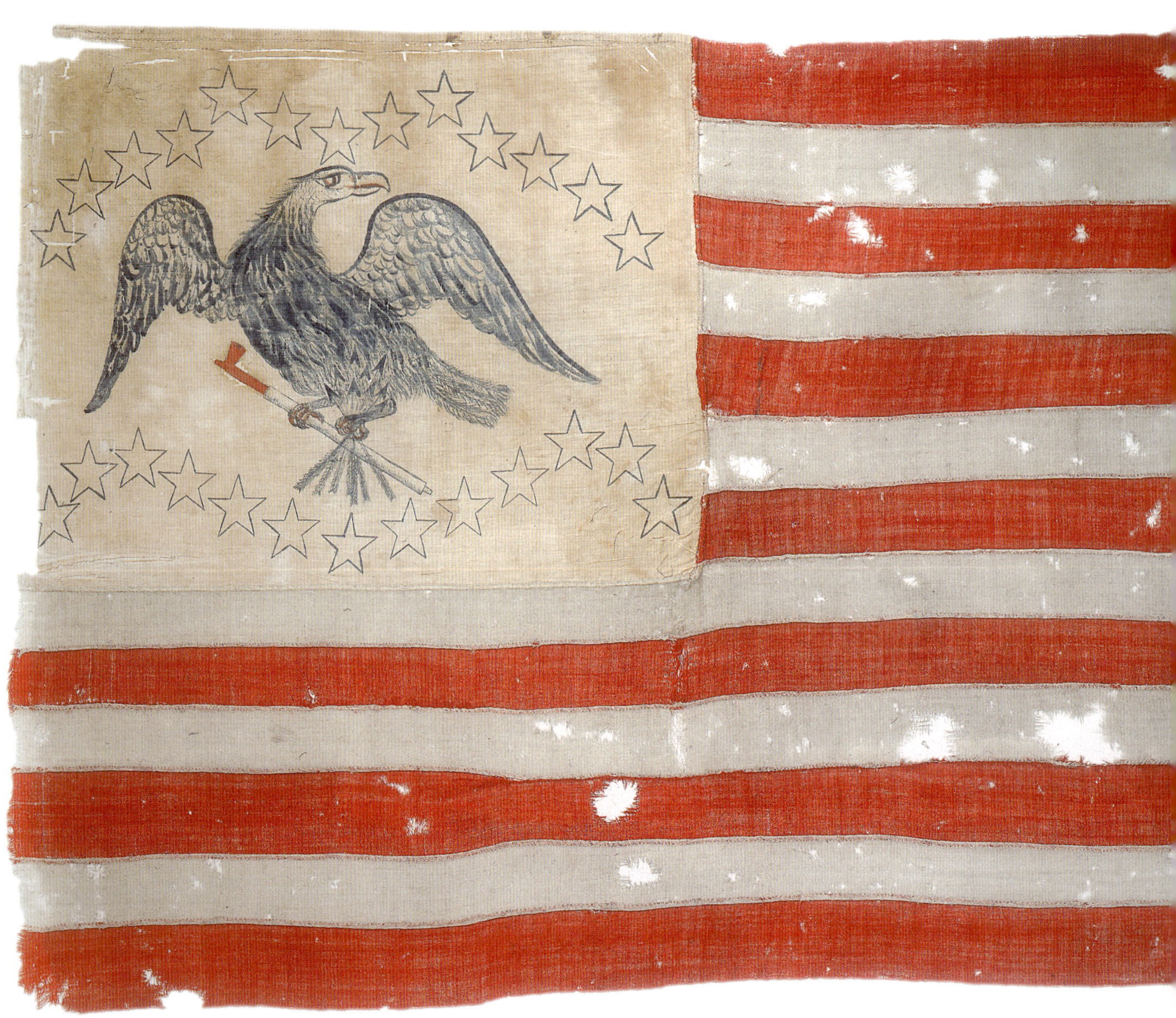

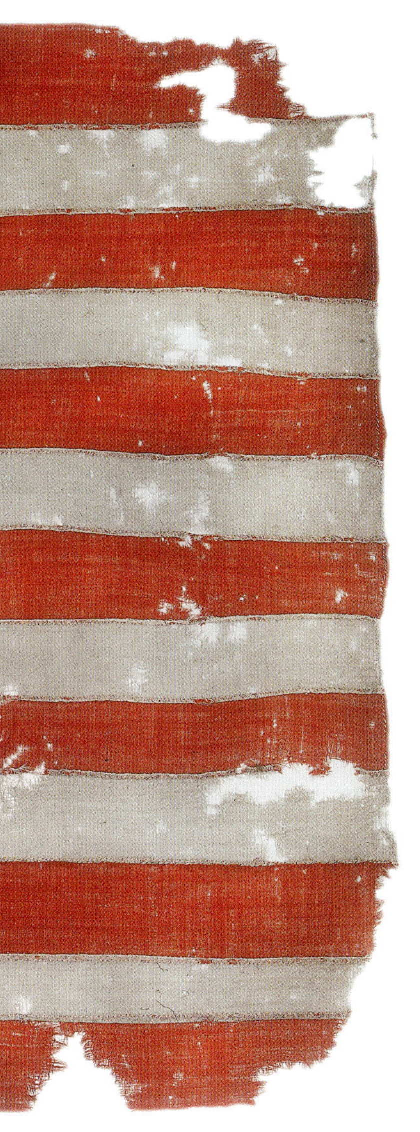

JOHN C. FRÉMONT FLAG

A Paradox in Leadership

DATE: 1842

EVENT LOCATION: Frémont Peak, Wyoming

CURRENT FLAG LOCATION: Autry Museum of the American West, Los Angeles, California

John C. Frémont was an explorer, soldier, and statesman. He was brave and also bullheaded. He was often promoted to high official positions only to later be demoted due to insubordination. He was twice removed from army command positions: once after a conflict of leadership in the newly captured California and again for incompetence when he was commander of the Department of the West during the Civil War.

The pennant that came to be known as the John C. Frémont flag was crafted by his wife, Jessie Benton Frémont. The flag had thirteen red-and-white stripes, and the canton featured an eagle grasping an Indigenous ceremonial pipe on a white background with the outline of twenty-six stars (representing the twenty-six states that were part of the Union at the time).

Jessie's father was western expansionist Thomas Hart Benton, who was elected as an inaugural senator from Missouri. Benton's power in the

Previous: John C. Frémont flag designed by his wife, Jessie, circa 1842

US Senate helped him fund western expeditions—three of which were led by Frémont.

Frémont brought the flag with him on his first trek west in 1842. He climbed a 13,745-foot (4,189 m) mountain (later named Frémont Peak) in the Wind River Range, situated in territory that would become Wyoming, and he flew his flag from the peak. Realizing he would be entering territory not yet belonging to the United States, he needed a flag that was unofficial so it would not signify a territorial claim but still be a symbol of the potential future of the West as American domain. The flag Jessie made fit this purpose precisely.

Frémont's third expedition, which explored California (at the time a holding of Mexico), led to one of the worst massacres of Indigenous people during America's westward expansion. When Frémont and his men arrived in the Sacramento Valley, white settlers informed them that the Indigenous locals were going to attack their settlement. Frémont led his men to the camp of the Wintu tribe along the Sacramento River. Though unprovoked, Frémont's men attacked. The Wintu were hemmed in by the river, with nowhere to run, and their bows and arrows were no match for the long rifles of Frémont's troops. It's estimated that hundreds of the Wintu people were slaughtered. No record of injury or death of any of Frémont's men exists. Frémont and his men instigated at least two other Native American massacres in California, at Klamath Lake and Sutter Buttes.

Hailing from Savannah, Georgia, Frémont was surprisingly an abolitionist. On August 30, 1861, while serving as commander of the Department of the West during the Civil War, he made the Frémont Emancipation. It declared martial law in Missouri and, by effect, freed enslaved people belonging to anyone resisting the Union army.

Frémont's decree caused Abraham Lincoln concern, as the war was still in its early stages. The Civil War was initially dedicated to limiting the expansion of slavery into new states, not necessarily ending the cruel practice entirely. Lincoln feared that if Southerners believed the North's real goal was to free all enslaved peoples, more states would secede from the Union. Less than three months later, Frémont was removed from his position as commander of the Department of the West—not officially for his emancipation order but for incompetence relating to corruption and mismanagement. Still, Lincoln would sign his own Emancipation Proclamation less than fifteen months later, on January 1, 1863, declaring all enslaved people to be free.

Frémont's abolitionist views are at odds with the genocide that he fomented against the Wintu people along the Sacramento River. It can be

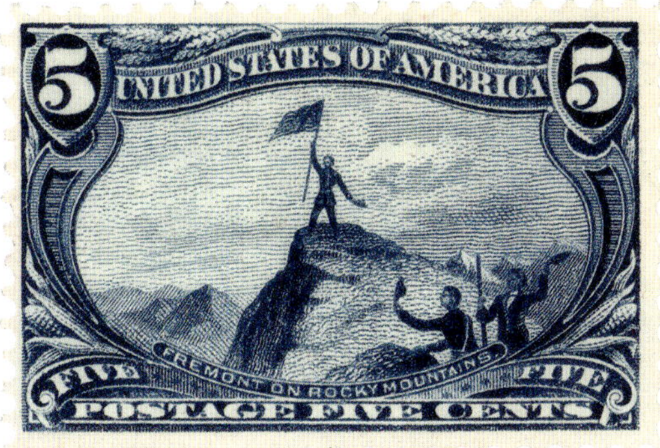

General John C. Frémont stamp from 1898 depicting him planting his flag on his first western expedition, Wyoming, 1842

seen as an example of what John L. O'Sullivan, editor of the *Democratic Review*, had first referred to as "Manifest Destiny" only the year before. Manifest Destiny was the notion that it was inevitable that America would expand its control all the way to the Pacific Ocean, no matter the cost. Under the sway of this concept, violent assaults like the Sacramento River massacre were to play out across the West repeatedly by the hubris of the white troops and settlers.

In March 1862, even after having been removed from command, Frémont was put in charge of the Union army's Mountain Department, covering eastern Tennessee and Kentucky and western Virginia. He later went on to become the Arizona territorial governor from 1878 to 1881.

After the Civil War, Frémont had invested in railroads, which were soon bankrupt due to the Panic of 1873, when financial troubles in Europe spread to the United States' railroad and banking industries. His wife, Jessie, was an author and continued writing books to keep the couple solvent. (Her writing was instrumental in the success of Frémont's widely received reports on his expeditions, several of which she coauthored.)

Frémont died on July 13, 1890, just three months after he had been recommissioned as a major general so he could receive a military pension. The Frémont flag is now part of the Autry Museum of the American West in Los Angeles, California. Historians don't know if the flag held by the museum is the very one that Frémont took on his expeditions or a later copy. It was donated to the museum by his daughter, Elizabeth, in 1905. Though not an official version of the United States flag, the Frémont ensign symbolizes an important yet at times tragic period in American history.

FORT SUMTER FLAG

The First Battle of the Civil War

DATE: April 14, 1861

EVENT LOCATION: Fort Sumter, South Carolina

CURRENT FLAG LOCATION: Fort Sumter Museum, Charleston Harbor, South Carolina

Fort Sumter is perhaps best known as the site where the Civil War began. Positioned at the mouth of Charleston Harbor in South Carolina, the fort was planned after the War of 1812 (page 25), when leaders realized that the country's coastal defenses were lacking. It served to protect the harbor and the city from invasion. It was still under construction when the newly declared Confederate forces demanded that the Union surrender the facility in April 1861. Union leaders refused, and before dawn on April 12, 1861, the rebels began bombarding the fort.

During the battle, the Fort Sumter flag, with thirty-three stars in a unique diamond star pattern, was felled when its pole was hit by a shell. The flag was retrieved and hoisted on another pole at the fort as the assault continued. One report of the incident (recounted in an 1880 *New York Star* article) told of Sergeant Peter Hart nailing the fort's storm flag to a wooden rail and remounting it while the battle raged around him.

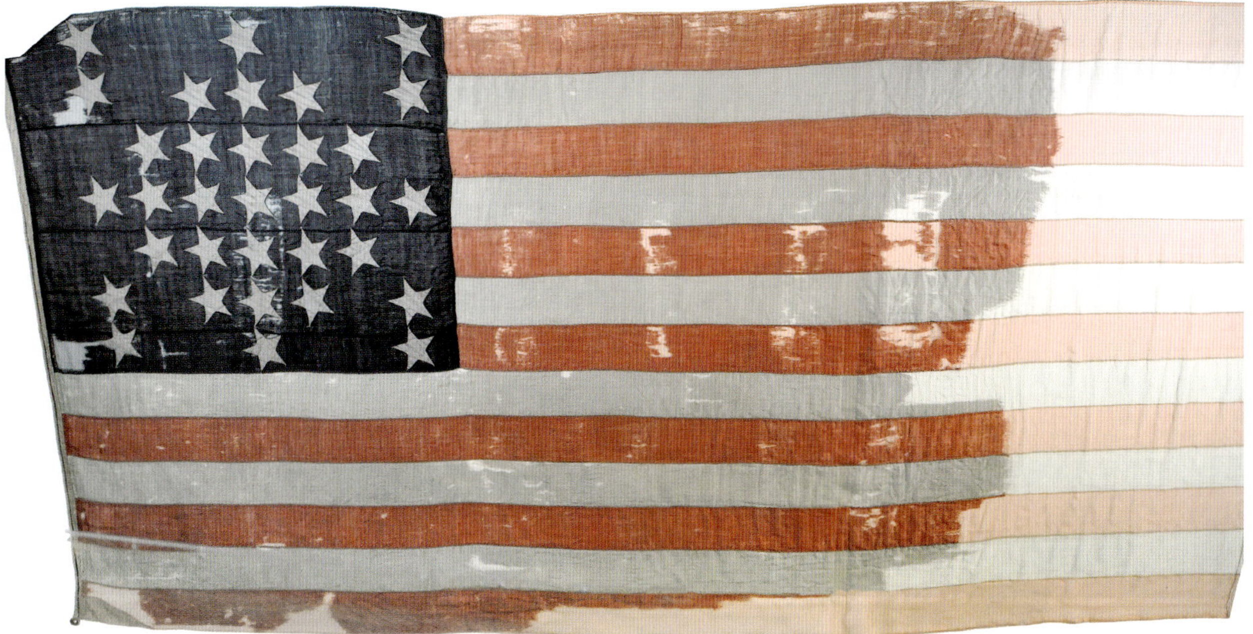

Fort Sumter flag featuring a diamond pattern with two stars in each corner of the canton, South Carolina, 1861

Other accounts say that Lieutenant Norman J. Hall retrieved and raised the banner, burning off his eyebrows in the process.

The United States had been heading for a conflict between the slave states and the free states since the 1850s. Slavery was a pillar of the South's economic system, yet it was also the most prominent issue that divided the North and South. And the federal government was now trying to limit the expansion of slavery as new states were added to the Union.

On December 20, 1860, South Carolina became the first state to secede from the Union. The breakaway state demanded that the United States withdraw from any military installations in South Carolina. The forces at Fort Sumter refused to comply and were cut off from most supplies. By spring of 1861, the soldiers at Fort Sumter were running low on food and necessities, so much so that newly inaugurated President Abraham Lincoln notified the Confederacy that he was sending supply ships to them. The Confederate administration replied by, again, ordering the Union forces to withdraw from the fort. The commander of Fort Sumter, Major Robert Anderson, refused the Confederate commands. This standoff led to the Battle of Fort Sumter, the first battle of the Civil War. After a day and a half of shelling, outnumbered and outgunned, Anderson agreed to abandon the fortress.

Only one Confederate soldier lost his life in the battle, and that was due to a misfiring cannon. There were no casualties on the Union side, but during the surrender ceremony, a spark triggered by a hundred-gun salute set off a pile of cartridges, killing two Union soldiers and wounding four others.

Having removed the Fort Sumter flag during the surrender ceremony, Major Anderson took it with him. The flag was brought from city to city in the North, part of a fundraising campaign to support the war effort. After Confederate general Robert E. Lee's surrender at Appomattox, almost exactly four years after Major Anderson's surrender at Fort Sumter, Anderson returned to Fort Sumter and raised the flag there one final time on April 14, 1865—the same day Abraham Lincoln was shot at Ford's Theatre (page 55).

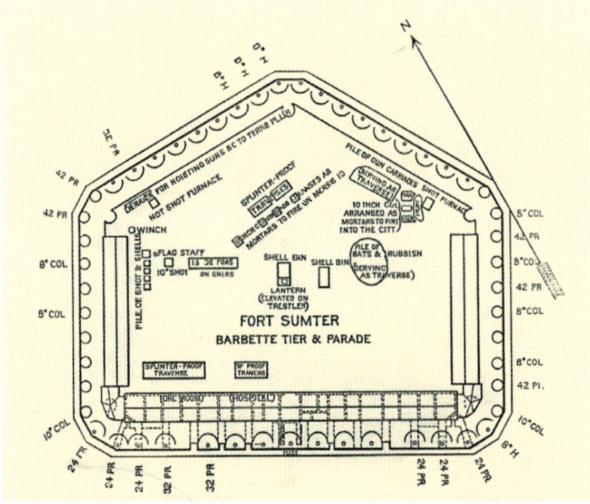

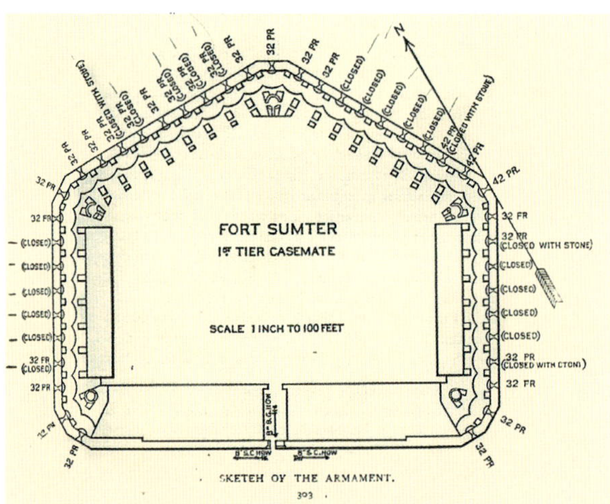

***Below:** Maps of Fort Sumter, showing the layout of cannons during the first battle of the Civil War, 1861*

***Opposite:** Major Robert Anderson, commander of Fort Sumter, returns to the fort to reraise the flag he removed during the surrender four years earlier, 1865.*

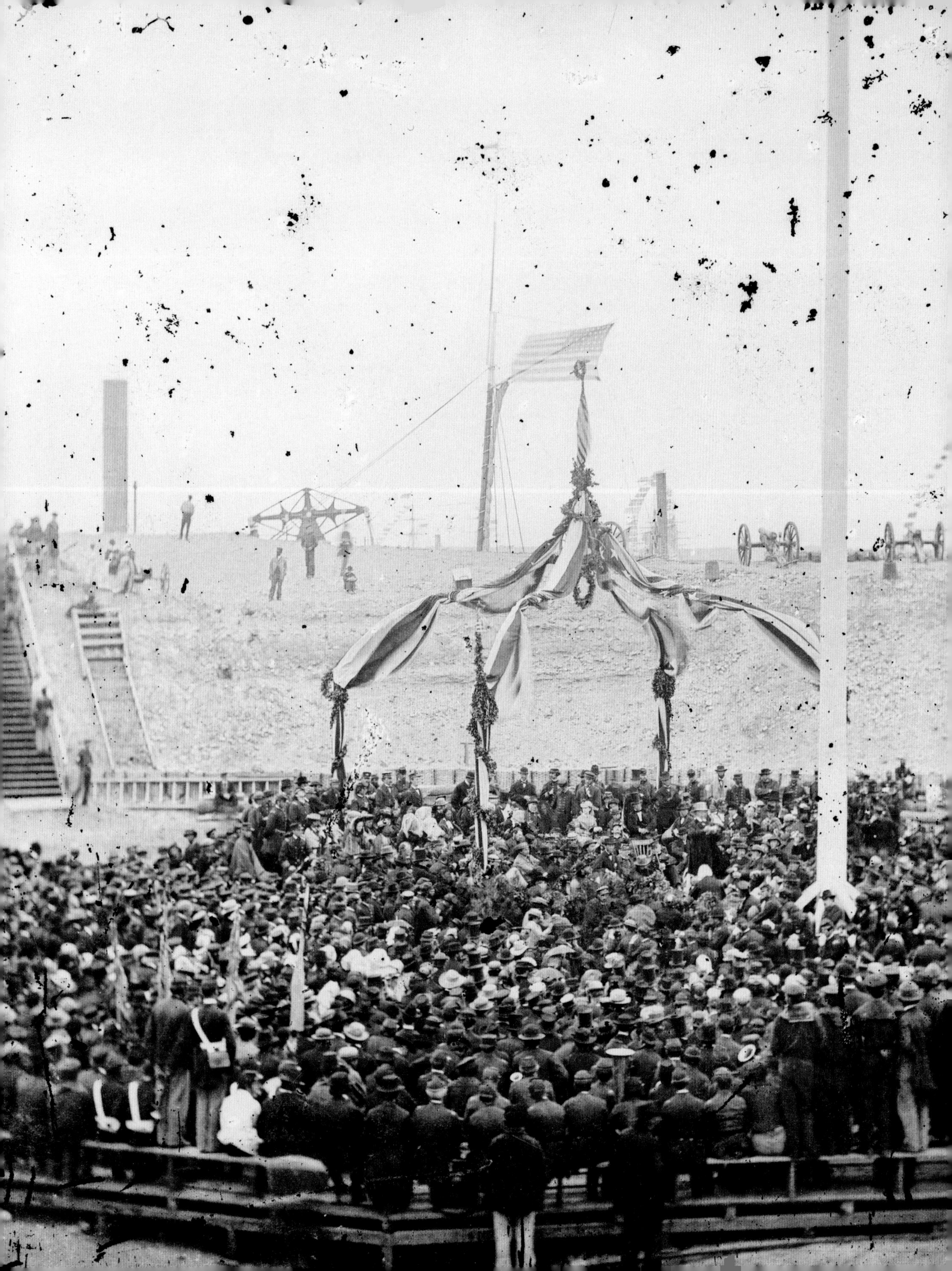

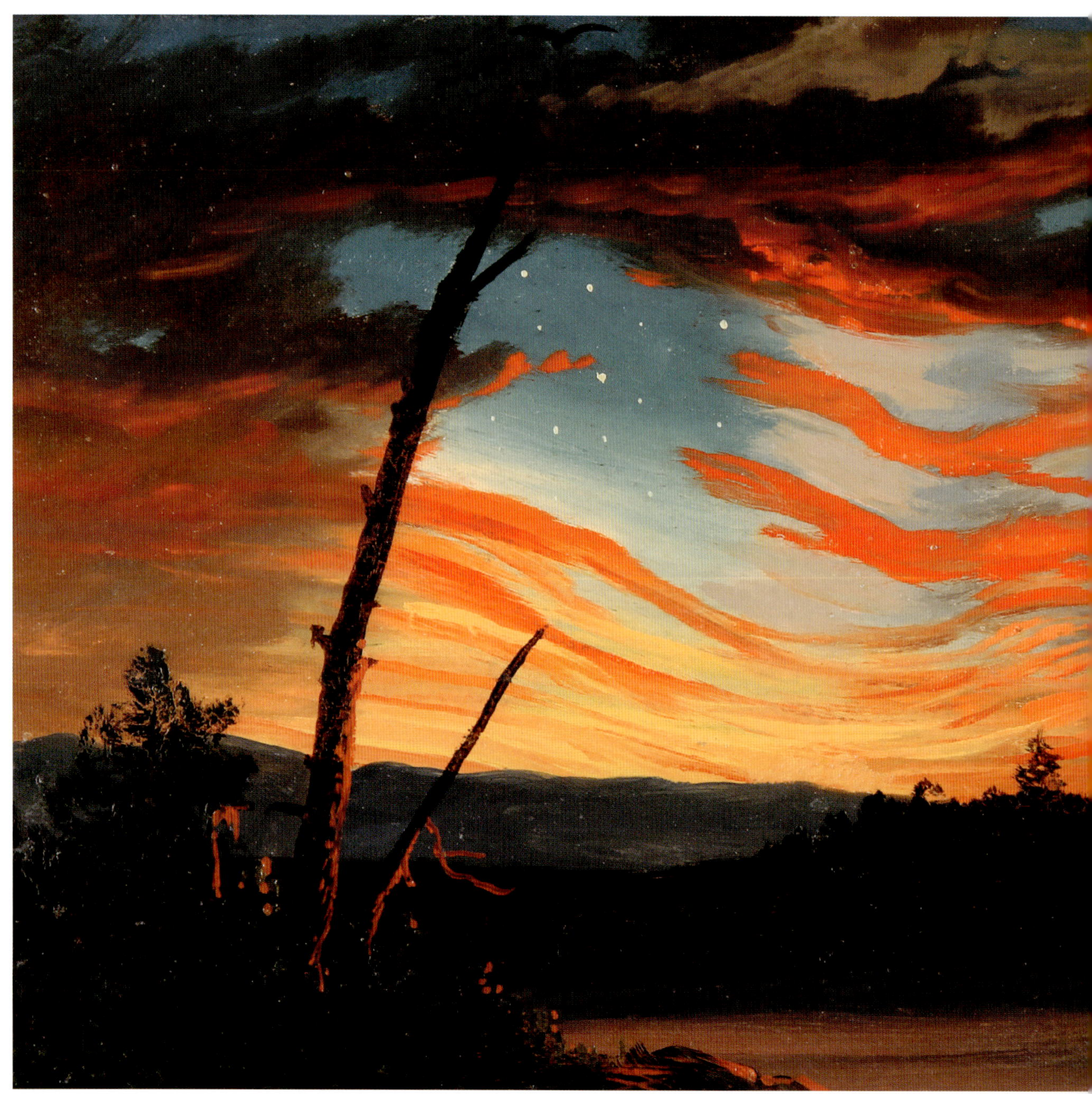

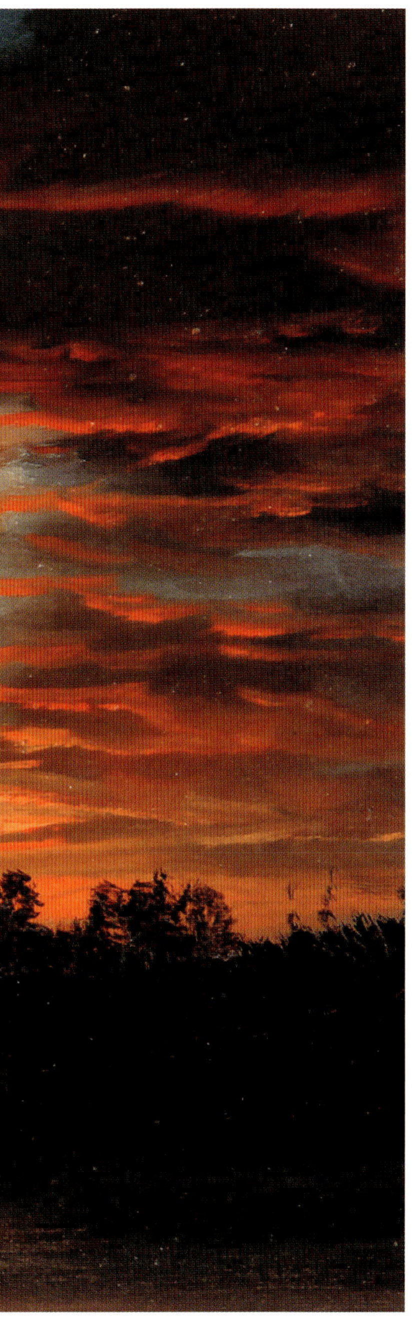

***OUR BANNER IN THE SKY*, BY FREDERIC EDWIN CHURCH**

A Painting to Stir the Nation

DATE: 1861

EVENT LOCATION: Hudson, New York

CURRENT PAINTING LOCATION: Unconfirmed

The surrender of Union troops at Fort Sumter on April 13, 1861 (page 38), was a blow to the North. Even though there had been no direct casualties, the loss of the first battle of the Civil War—and the fact that Confederate forces so easily overwhelmed the Union troops—shook the public's confidence. Frederic Edwin Church, hoping to use his skills as a landscape painter to rouse support for the war, created a noble, patriotic image to rally citizens to the cause of preserving the Union.

Church painted the first of several versions of *Our Banner in the Sky* in the days after the battle for Fort Sumter. The image shows a twilight or morning sky, with bands of high white clouds peeking through bands of crimson stratus clouds. A large dark blue section of sky is visible, with early stars shining through. A single dead tree aligns with the left edge of the blue sky, standing in as a flagpole. The composition reveals a clear representation of a stylized American flag flying in the heavens.

Previous: Our Banner in the Sky *was used to raise morale and funds to support the Civil War, 1861.*

The abstracted image was so popular with the public that it was re-created as a lithograph and sold to support Union soldiers' families.

Church was a member of the Hudson River school of artists, who worked in upstate New York, in the Catskills, and areas farther north into New England. The Hudson River style of painting is distinguished by an almost utopian mix of humankind and nature. The school's landscape works typically include scenes of magnificent wilderness as well as idyllic pastoral settings, where human settlement lies in harmony with the terrain. Emphasis is placed on natural beauty and the dramatic light of the "golden hour"—the hours around dawn and twilight when the sun's light, passing through more of the atmosphere, takes on a warm red/gold quality. By capturing this ephemeral light, the Hudson Valley painters created ethereal scenes and romantic landscapes.

The whereabouts of Church's original oil painting is in question. Several versions thought to be the original are in museums and private collections, but the first one painted by Church remains unconfirmed.

THOMAS HENRY SHEPPARD GETTYSBURG FLAG

A Hidden Loyalty

DATE: July 3, 1863

EVENT LOCATION: Gettysburg Battlefield, Pennsylvania

CURRENT FLAG LOCATION: Dearborn Historical Museum, Dearborn, Michigan

In the 1800s, flags were icons of pride and honor, but they were also functional tools. In a time before radio transmissions, flags carried into battle were used for communication and for locating other friendly forces. Michigan cavalry sergeant and standard-bearer Thomas Henry Sheppard carried his thirty-four-star flag into the Battle of Gettysburg in 1863 to both direct and inspire Union troops.

Sheppard had enlisted in the military in August 1861. A group of women from Marlette, Michigan, near his home north of Detroit in the state's "thumb," made the thirty-four-star US flag to show encouragement for President Lincoln and the Union forces. They gave the flag to Sheppard to carry into battle.

Sheppard saw his first combat in the spring of 1862. He fought for the Union through most of 1862, and in June 1863, he was assigned to the Michigan Brigade under the command of Brigadier General George Armstrong Custer (page 65). The brigade's goal was to locate Confederate Major General James Ewell Brown (Jeb) Stuart and his troops. Stuart was a West Point graduate who had pledged himself to the Confederacy when his home state of Virginia left the Union.

Opposite: Sergeant Thomas Henry Sheppard, with the Gettysburg flag, circa 1890s

Following: *Sheppard's frayed and fatigued Gettysburg flag today*

Stuart's forces skirmished with the Michigan Brigade in Pennsylvania on June 30, 1863, at Hanover and again on July 2 at Hunterstown. Both Stuart's forces and the Michigan Brigade didn't enter the Battle of Gettysburg until the third day of combat, on July 3. Confederate General George Pickett led the main assault on Union lines from the west, while Stuart maneuvered his men to flank the Union troops and began a simultaneous attack to distract and draw Union troops away from Pickett's Charge, as the assault came to be known.

Sergeant Sheppard, carrying the thirty-four-star flag, helped lead the Union charge against Stuart's troops. During the charge, Sheppard was wounded and knocked off his horse behind the Confederate lines. Realizing he would soon be captured, he hid the flag beneath his clothes. Once captured, he was eventually held at more than a half-dozen prison camps.

Sheppard was one of the first prisoners to be sent to Andersonville Prison, which would become notorious for the cruel treatment of the men held there. Nearly a third of the prisoners died. With their losses at Gettysburg and Vicksburg in the summer of 1863, it became clear that the Confederate Army could not win the war. When General William Tecumseh Sherman's Union troops captured Atlanta a year later, the Confederates soon began moving prisoners out of Andersonville knowing it, too, would soon fall into Union hands. Sheppard ended up in the Millen Stockade at Camp Lawton near Millen, Georgia. On November 20, 1864, after 505 days in captivity, he was released in a prisoner exchange. Sheppard had kept the flag hidden on his person the entire time.

CIVIL WAR-ERA FLAGS

★★★

At the beginning of the Civil War, there were thirty-four states in the Union. Kansas had been the most recent addition on January 29, 1861. Yet according to the Flag Act of 1818 (page 29), a star for a new state was not added to the American flag until the July 4 following that state's incorporation. Because of this, Union flags were often out of step with the actual number of states during the Civil War. When the war began at Fort Sumter on April 12, 1861, Union forces were still using thirty-three-star flags; the thirty-fourth star representing Kansas wouldn't be official until July 4, 1861.

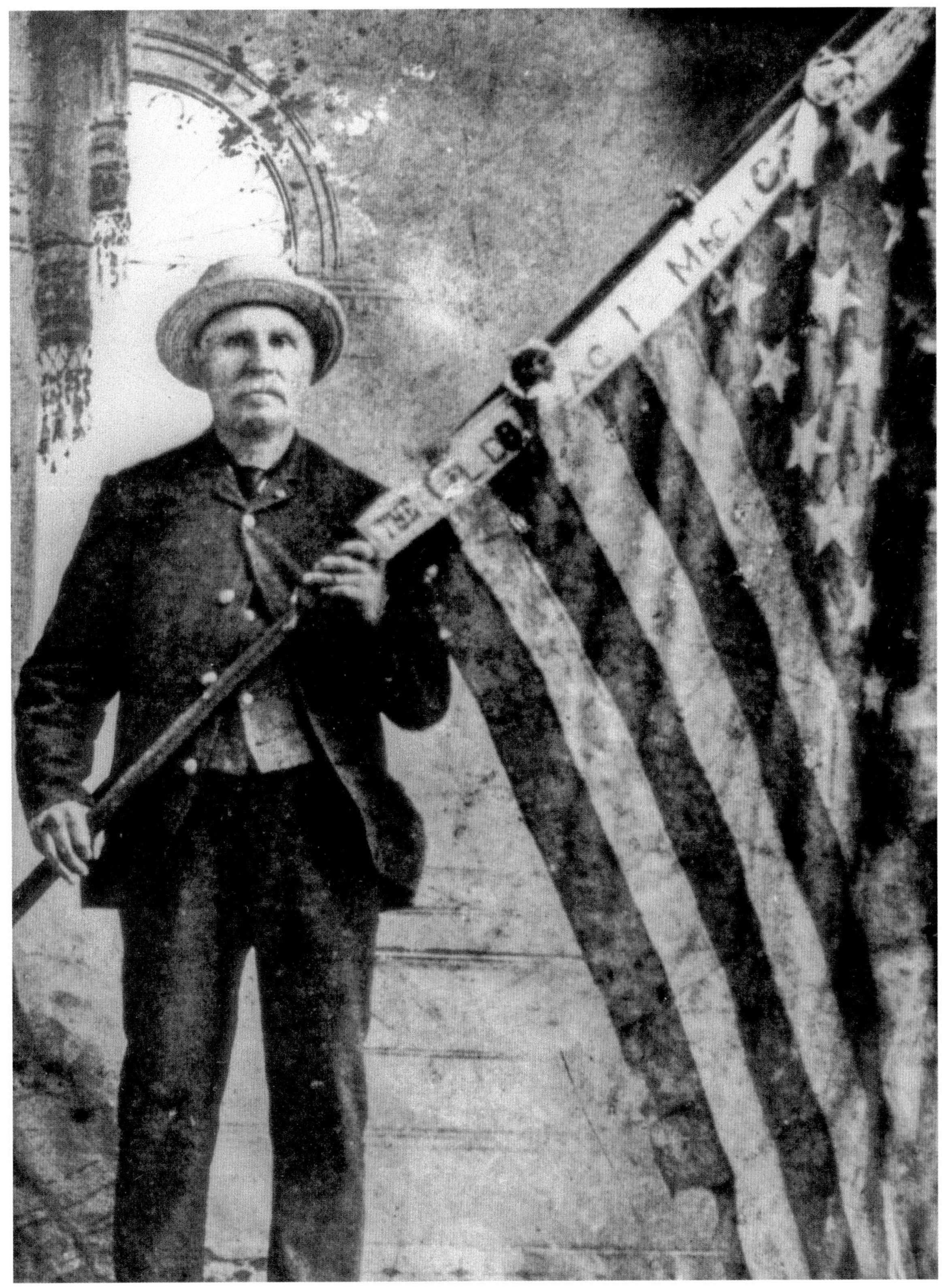

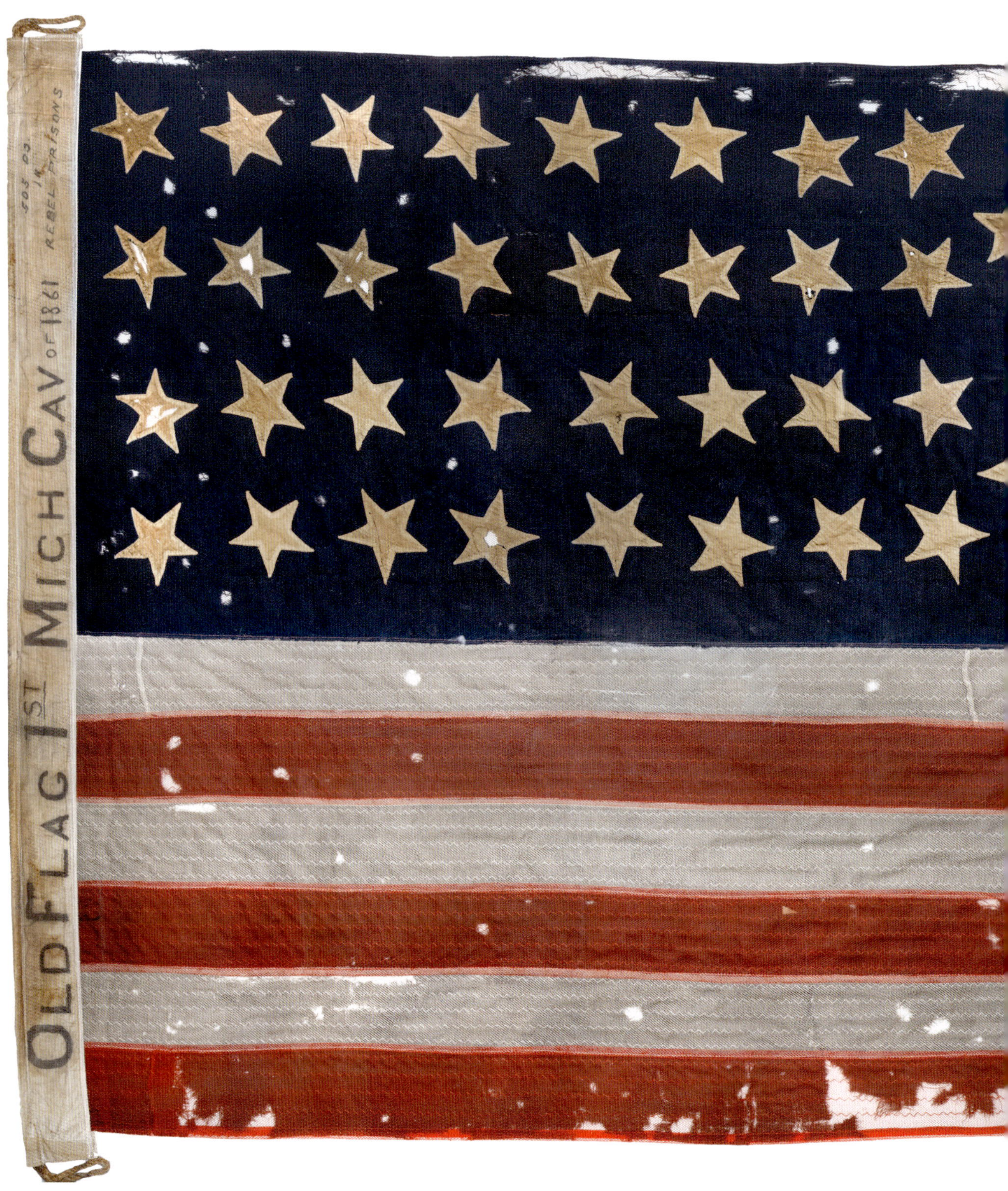
OLD FLAG 1ST MICH CAV OF 1861
REBEL PRISONS

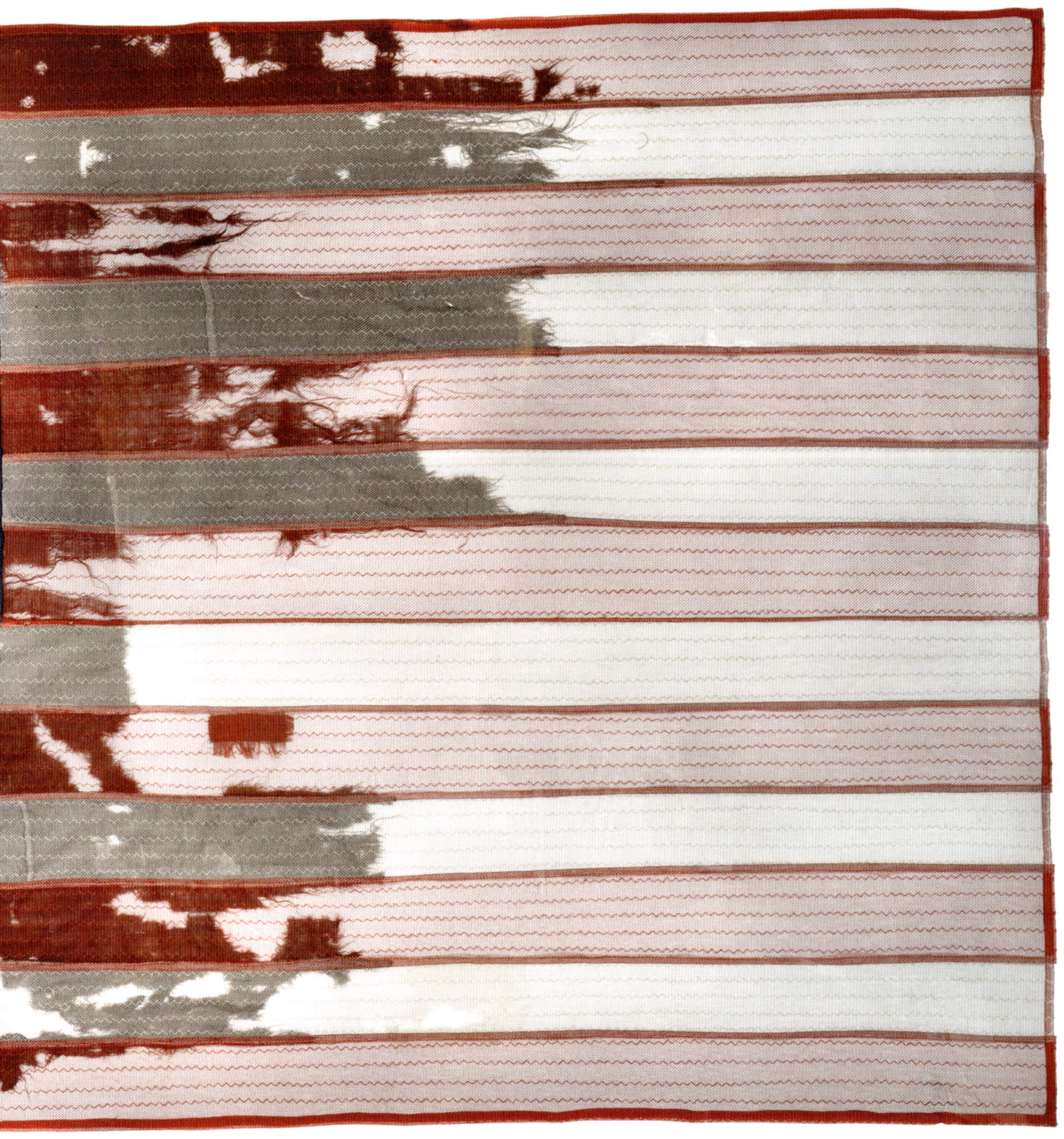

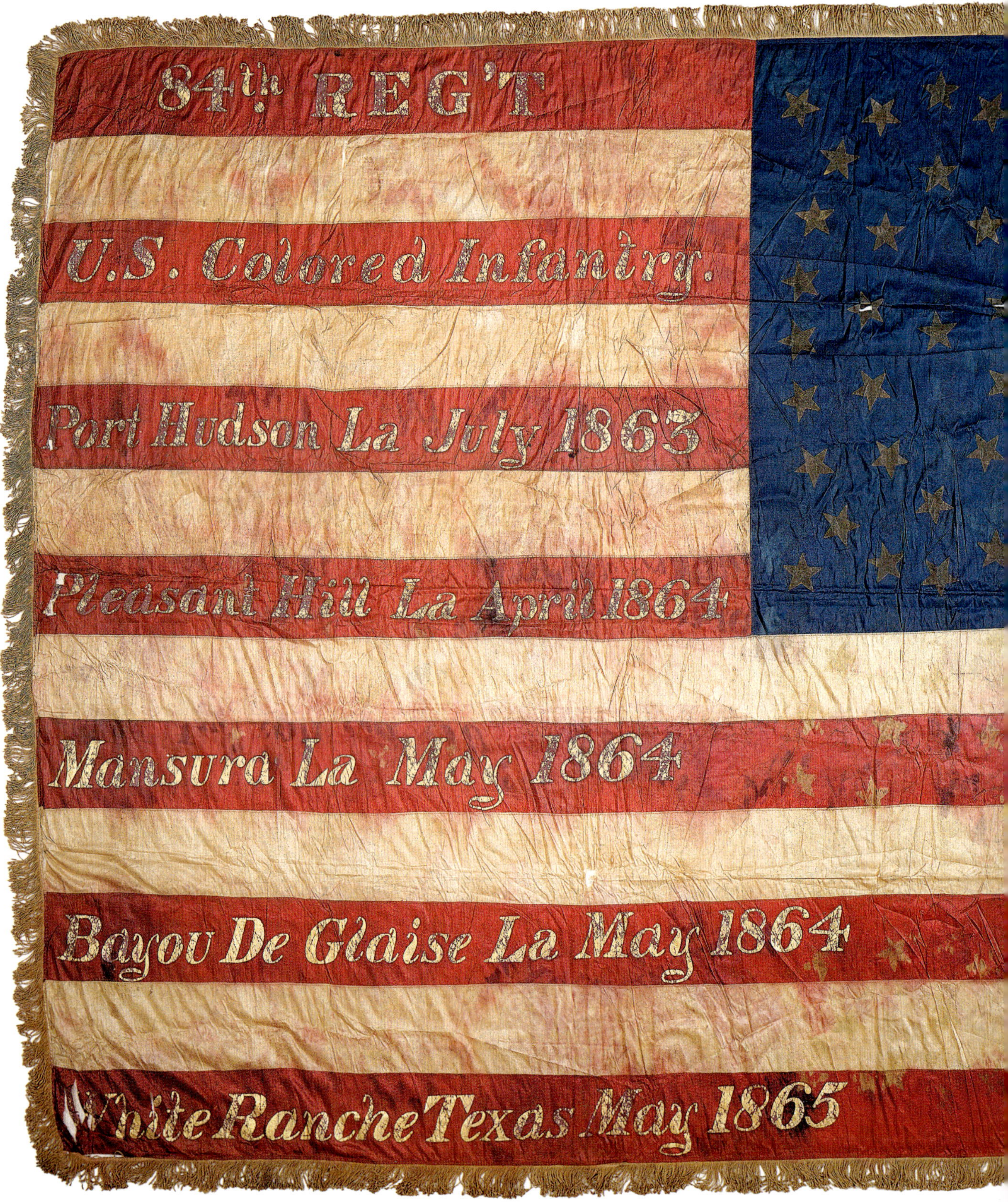
84th REG'T
U.S. Colored Infantry.
Port Hudson La July 1863
Pleasant Hill La April 1864
Mansura La May 1864
Bayou De Glaise La May 1864
White Ranche Texas May 1865

EIGHTY-FOURTH REGIMENT OF INFANTRY FLAG

Fighting for Freedom and Respect

DATE: 1863–1865

EVENT LOCATION: Civil War battlefields

CURRENT FLAG LOCATION: National Museum of American History, Washington, DC

The Second Militia Act of 1792 required the conscription of "each and every free able-bodied white male citizen of the respective States, resident therein, who is or shall be of age of eighteen years, and under the age of forty-five years," to "provide for the National Defence" when called upon. Even though many Black citizens volunteered to serve in the Union military, this law was still in effect in 1861, which meant Black Americans were forbidden from joining the armed forces.

On July 17, 1862, Congress passed the Second Confiscation Act, which freed enslaved people owned by those in the Confederate military or government. The Militia Act of 1862 also passed, allowing people of African descent to enroll in the armed forces "for the purpose of constructing entrenchments, performing camp service, or other labor, or any military or naval service for which they are found competent."

Previous: *Flag of the Eighty-Fourth Infantry Regiment, one of the first groups of Black Union troops to fight in combat, circa 1864*

Opposite: Men of Color *recruitment broadside, Philadelphia, Pennsylvania, 1863*

This meant that free Blacks could serve in the military, though only in limited roles.

It wasn't until President Abraham Lincoln signed the Emancipation Proclamation on January 1, 1863, that all Black American men were allowed to serve in the US military, and their direct recruitment commenced. Even still, prejudice and ignorance meant that Black troops were initially relegated to mostly noncombat duty: guarding facilities and charged with labor tasks, like building bridges and fortifications.

Several events made Union commanders more amenable to having Black soldiers enter combat. One such incident was the Battle of Port Hudson, in Louisiana, where one of the first Black troops was used in combat, when the First and Third Louisiana Native Guard regiments were sent into the battle. Control of the Mississippi River was equally crucial to the Union and the Confederacy for moving soldiers and supplies. In 1862, the Union began a push from both the north and the south to try to gain control of the entire length of the waterway. Moving north from New Orleans, Union forces drove the Confederates from Baton Rouge in late April of 1862. By August of that year, the last remaining Confederate strongholds on the Mississippi River were Vicksburg, Mississippi, and Port Hudson, Louisiana.

The Confederate fort at Port Hudson lay on the outside of a bend of the Mississippi River, atop a bluff about 75 feet (23 m) above the water, and was heavily fortified. The Union navy shelled Port Hudson from the river on March 13, 1863, but the high position of the Confederate cannons and the narrow pinch of the river bend prevented Union forces from making any headway, and so they returned to Baton Rouge. Nearly two months later, on May 11, 1863, Black soldiers from the Third Regiment of the Louisiana Native Guards began building bridges across the river for another assault. Union troops crossed the river and began moving equipment and supplies into position. On May 27, Union troops made two ground attacks on Port Hudson, from the north and the east. The first groups charged through a ravine that bulged into the Confederate lines and put them in the enemy's crossfire. The terrain, vegetation, and crossfire stymied their advance. The second set of assault groups met the same fate.

Brigadier General William Dwight, overseeing the assault, realized his men were not going to advance. He ordered the First and Third Louisiana Native Guard regiments to go into battle. These all-Black regiments were made up of a few free men of color and mostly escaped slaves. They had never before been sent into combat—but forward they charged. Though they were no more successful than the other Union troops at

MEN OF COLOR

TO ARMS! TO ARMS!

NOW OR NEVER

This is our golden moment! The Government of the United States calls for every Able-bodied Colored Man to enter the Army for the

Three Years' Service!

And join in Fighting the Battles of Liberty and the Union. A new era is open to us. For generations we have suffered under the horrors of slavery, outrage and wrong; our manhood has been denied, our citizenship blotted out, our souls seared and burned, our spirits cowed and crushed, and the hopes of the future of our race involved in doubt and darkness. But now our relations to the white race are changed. Now, therefore, is our most precious moment. Let us rush to arms!

FAIL NOW, & OUR RACE IS DOOMED

this the soil of our birth. We must now awake, arise, or be forever fallen. If we value liberty, if we wish to be free in this land, if we love our country, if we love our families, our children, our home, we must strike *now* while the country calls; we must rise up in the dignity of our manhood, and show by our own right arms that we are worthy to be freemen. Our enemies have made the country believe that we are craven cowards, without soul, without manhood, without the spirit of soldiers. Shall we die with this stigma resting upon our graves? Shall we leave this inheritance of Shame to our Children? No! a thousand times NO! We WILL Rise! The alternative is upon us. Let us rather die freemen than live to be slaves. What is life without liberty? We say that we have manhood; now is the time to prove it. A nation or a people that cannot fight may be pitied, but cannot be respected. If we would be regarded *men*, if we would forever silence the tongue of Calumny, of Prejudice and Hate, let us Rise Now and Fly to Arms! We have seen what Valor and Heroism our Brothers displayed at Port Hudson and Milliken's Bend, though they are just from the galling, poisoning grasp of Slavery, they have startled the World by the most exalted heroism. If they have proved themselves heroes, cannot WE PROVE OURSELVES MEN?

ARE FREEMEN LESS BRAVE THAN SLAVES

More than a Million White Men have left Comfortable Homes and joined the Armies of the Union to save their Country. Cannot we leave ours, and swell the Hosts of the Union, to save our liberties, vindicate our manhood, and deserve well of our Country. MEN OF COLOR! the Englishman, the Irishman, the Frenchman, the German, the American, have been called to assert their claim to freedom and a manly character, by an appeal to the sword. The day that has seen an enslaved race in arms has, in all history, seen their last trial. We now see that our last opportunity has come. If we are not lower in the scale of humanity than Englishmen, Irishmen, White Americans and other Races, we can show it now. Men of Color, Brothers and Fathers, we appeal to you, by all your concern for yourselves and your liberties, by all your regard for God and humanity, by all your desire for Citizenship and Equality before the law, by all your love for the Country, to stop at no subterfuge, listen to nothing that shall deter you from rallying for the Army. Come Forward, and at once Enroll your Names for the Three Years' Service. Strike now, and you are henceforth and forever Freemen!

E. D. Bassett,	Rev. J. Underdue,	P. J. Armstrong,	Rev. J. C. Gibbs,	Elijah J. Davis,
William D. Forten.	John W. Price,	J. W. Simpson,	Daniel George,	John P. Burr,
Frederick Douglass,	Augustus Dorsey,	Rev. J. B. Trusty,	Robert M. Adger,	Robert Jones,
Wm. Whipper,	Rev. Stephen Smith,	S. Morgan Smith,	Henry M. Cropper,	O. V. Catto,
D. D. Turner,	N. W. Depee,	William E. Gipson,	Rev. J. B. Reeve,	Thos. J. Dorsey,
Jas. McCrummell,	Dr. J. H. Wilson,	Rev. J. Boulden,	Rev. J. A. Williams,	I. D. Cliff,
A. S. Cassey,	J. W. Cassey,	Rev. J. Asher,	Rev. A. L. Stanford,	Jacob C. White,
A. M. Green,	James Needham,	Rev. Elisha Weaver,	Thomas J. Bowers,	Morris Hall,
J. W. Page,	Ebenezer Black,	David B. Bowser,	J. C. White, Jr.,	J. P. Johnson,
L. R. Seymour,	James R. Gordon,	Henry Minton,	Rev. J. P. Campbell,	Franklin Turner,
Rev. William T. Catto,	Samuel Stewart,	Daniel Colley.	Rev. W. J. Alston,	Jesse E. Glasgow.

A Meeting in furtherance of the above named object will be held

And will be Addressed by

U. S. Steam-Power Book and Job Printing Establishment, Ledger Buildings, Third and Chestnut Streets, Philadelphia.

Port Hudson, the Native Guards' bravery and fearless assault made many on the Union side take notice.

Not that all prejudice was wiped away. Major General Nathaniel P. Banks, who was in charge of the Department of the Gulf, which included Louisiana, for the Union, was one of the more bigoted officers in the army. When a truce was called at Port Hudson on May 28, the day after the Union attack, Banks had his men remove the fallen white soldiers from the field of battle but left the Black soldiers' bodies where they lay.

Eventually, after a long siege, the Confederates surrendered Port Hudson, ceding control of the Mississippi River to the Union. The prejudice and injustices put on display during the battle for the fort served as examples of the outright hostility Black soldiers faced across the Union army. Nevertheless, Black soldiers continued to enlist, fight, and die for the Union cause.

In the spring of 1864, Black units within the Union army were restructured. Since the Battle of Port Hudson, the Louisiana Native Guards had been renamed the Corps d'Afrique, and now they became the Eighty-Fourth Regiment of Infantry for the US Colored Troops.

The Eighty-Fourth Regiment flag, created after the Battle at Port Hudson, is roughly square, measuring 72 by 78 inches (1.8 by 1.9 m). (Technically it is considered a banner rather than a flag due to its square shape; flags are more distinctly rectangular, and longer on the horizontal axis than the vertical.) It features the same red-and-white stripes as the American flag but has a gold fringe along its top, bottom, and fly side, and the unit's identification, "84th REG'T," is emblazoned across the top red stripe. The banner was carried in battle at Louisiana. The major campaigns the unit fought are listed on the flag: Port Hudson, Louisiana, July 1863; Pleasant Hill, Louisiana, April 1864; Mansura, Louisiana, May 1864; Bayou De Glaise, Louisiana, May 1864; and White Ranche, Texas, May 1865 (the last took place after Lee's surrender at Appomattox). The battle at White Ranche was one of the last in the Civil War. The Eighty-Fourth regiment's flag commemorates the bravery and honor exhibited by these men.

LINCOLN ASSASSINATION FLAG

A Flag of Care

DATE: April 14, 1865

EVENT LOCATION: Ford's Theatre, Washington, DC

CURRENT FLAG LOCATION: Columns Museum of the Pike County Historical Society, Milford, Pennsylvania

In the spring of 1865, the Civil War was nearly over. Although it took until November for all Confederate troops to surrender, Robert E. Lee's surrender to Ulysses S. Grant at Wilmer and Virginia McLean's home in Appomattox Court House, Virginia, on April 9, 1865, marked the fall of the South. Abraham and Mary Todd Lincoln had already attended Ford's Theatre in Washington, DC, nine times during his presidency, but on April 14, 1865, a mere five days after that surrender, with the end of the long and brutal war firmly in sight, a night out at the theater must have felt extraordinary.

On the morning of April 14, when John Wilkes Booth learned that President Lincoln would be attending the play *Our American Cousin* that evening, he realized that this was the opportunity he'd been waiting for. Though not a cast member of the current production, Booth had performed at Ford's Theatre, including in one of the plays the Lincolns had previously attended. He was well known to the theater, which would give him access without arousing much suspicion. This allowed him to slip into Lincoln's theater box without any alarm. Upon entering, he shot

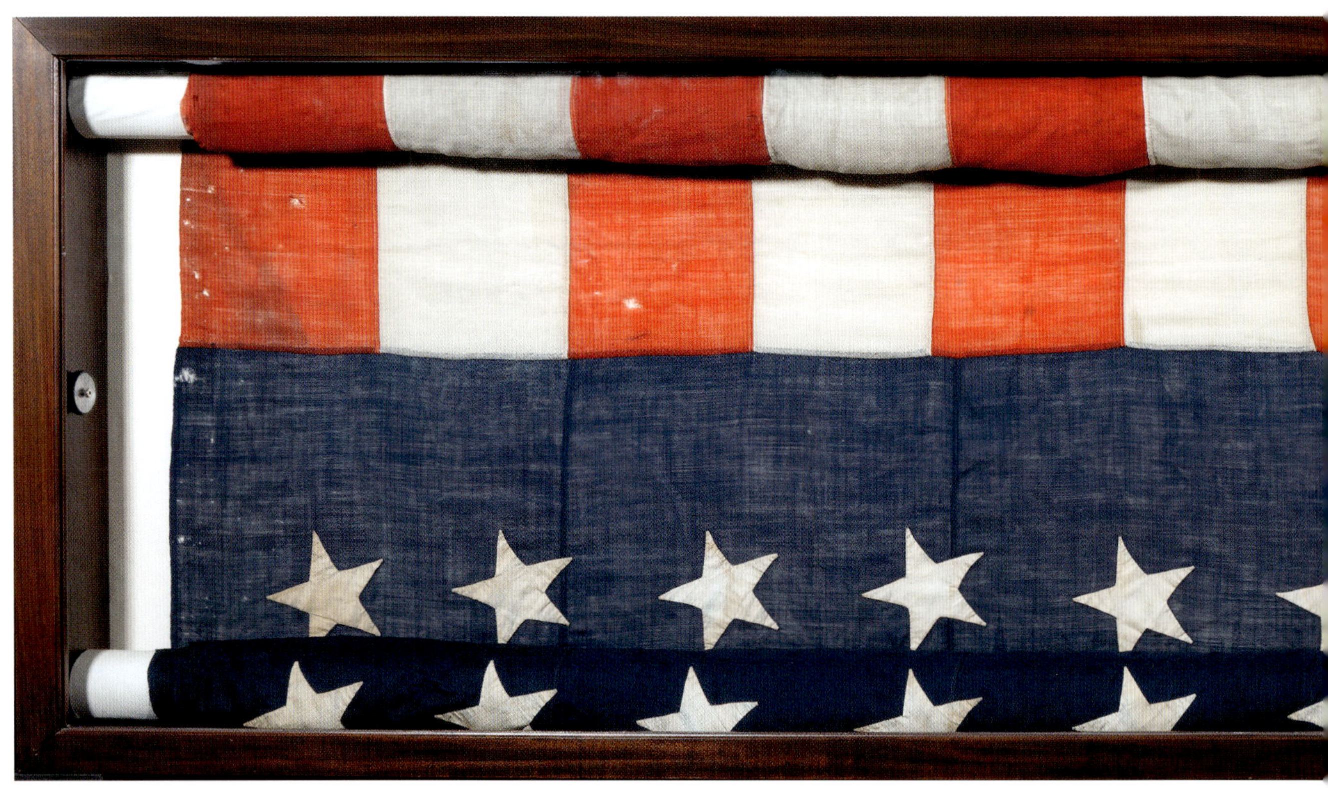

Section of the flag used to cradle President Lincoln's head after John Wilkes Booth shot him in Ford's Theatre in Washington, DC, 1865

Abraham Lincoln in the back of the head during one of the play's louder laugh-lines. Booth then vaulted onto the stage, breaking his leg when he landed. He fended off those who attempted to stop him, fled through a side door, and rode away on a waiting horse.

Booth had knocked down actress Laura Keene on his way out the door of the theater. Keene got up, took the stage, and pleaded for calm and order. Lincoln, mortally wounded, was laid on the floor. Soon after, according to many reports, Keene made her way to the president's box. She took his head in her lap. Once Keene left, someone took one of the five flags that had been borrowed from the Treasury Department to decorate the theater box and slipped it under Lincoln's head, presumably to try to make him more comfortable. The doctors attending the president agreed that Lincoln would not survive a carriage ride back to the White House, and so he was transported to the home of William Peterson,

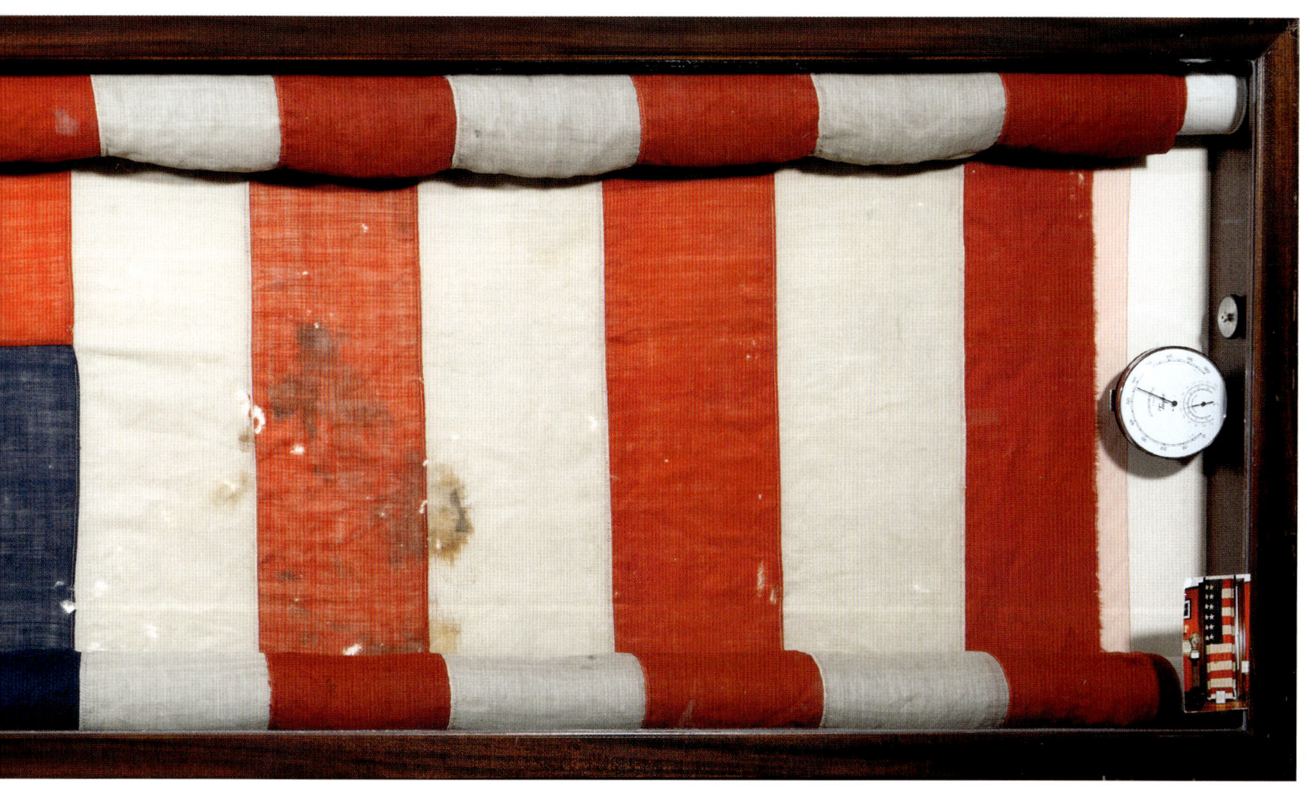

a tailor who also ran a boardinghouse in his home, which was directly across the street from the theater. A group of soldiers carried Lincoln to the Peterson house. They laid him down in a bedroom. The next morning, April 15, 1865, at 7:22 a.m., Lincoln took his last breath.

According to Ford's Theatre, the flag used to cradle Lincoln's head, which became known as the Lincoln flag, was saved by another actor in the play, Thomas Gourlay. Lincoln had been carried to the Peterson house with the flag still under his head. When the flag was given to Gourlay to return to the theater, he took it home instead. He later gave it to his daughter, Jeannie Gourlay, who had an acting role in the play on the evening of the assassination. Jeannie in turn willed the flag to her son, V. Paul Struthers, upon her death. He donated it to the Pike County Historical Society in Milford, Pennsylvania, where it currently resides.

1866

to

1941

Expansion, Immigration, and Depression

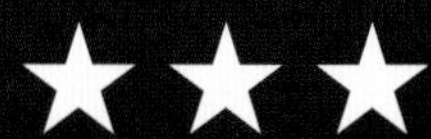

AFTER THE CIVIL WAR, THE AMERICAN FLAG became a symbol for the reconciliation and reconstruction to come. Meanwhile, the country's attention turned to westward expansion. The newfound prominence of the United States on the world stage brought millions of immigrants, for whom the flag represented a promise of freedom and a chance for success. That hope for prosperity was short-lived, however, as the world entered the worst economic period in modern history: the Great Depression.

GOLDEN SPIKE FLAG

East Meets West

DATE: May 10, 1869
EVENT LOCATION: Promontory, Utah
CURRENT FLAG LOCATION: Unknown

The end of the Civil War in 1865 (page 55) meant that the United States was once again unified. However, many rifts and societal challenges remained. Despite these divides, the American flag was now displayed at homes and businesses more than ever—at least in the Union states. Union soldiers brought home flags. The flag flew prominently at parades to memorialize the end of the war and at yearly commemorations. The flag was also more often present at other public events, like celebrations of national holidays, political rallies, and veterans' funerals. Before the Civil War, the flag had mostly been used by the military and the government. After the war, it found use in ceremonies and remembrances both public and private, across the country. One of those was the Meeting of the Rails.

A mere four years after the end of Civil War hostilities, a major event would unify the country, if not north and south, then at least east and west: the completion of the nation's first transcontinental railroad. The joining of the Union Pacific railway (approaching west from Council Bluffs, Iowa) and the Central Pacific railway (progressing east from Sacramento, California) near Promontory Summit in Utah meant

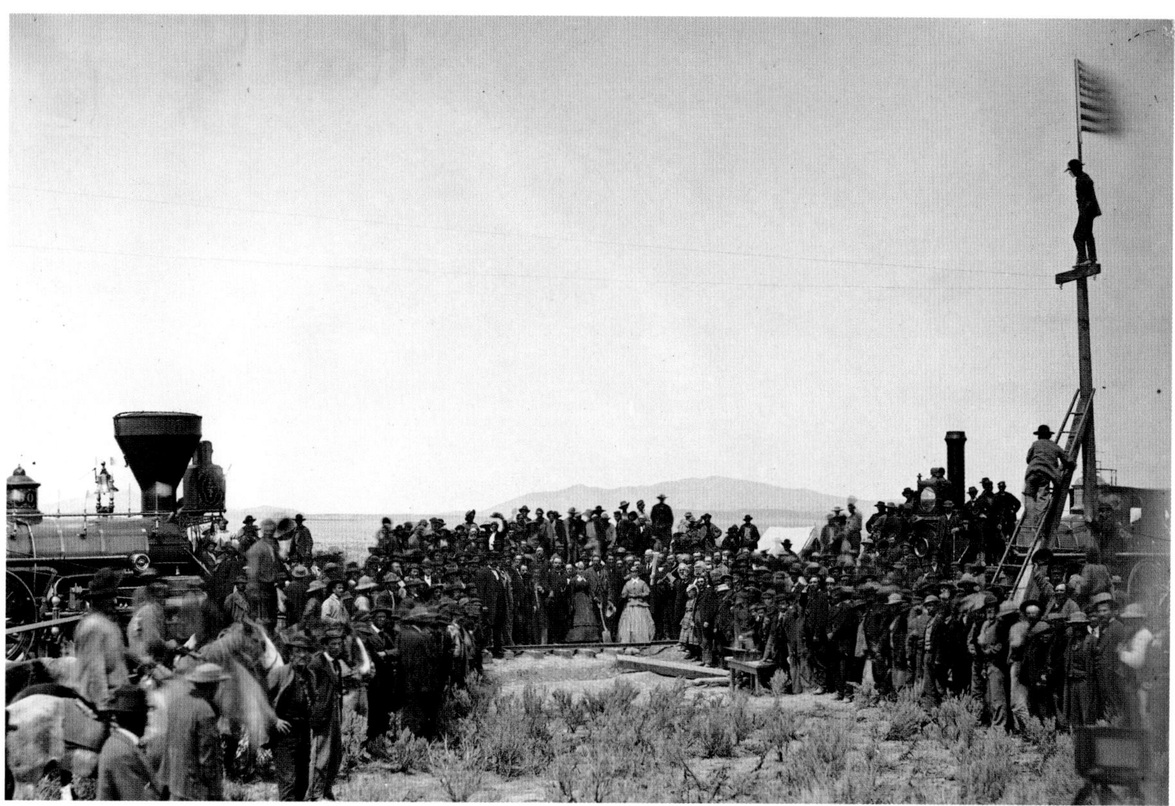

Above: One of Andrew J. Russell's photographs of the Golden Spike Ceremony near Promontory Summit, Utah Territory, May 10, 1869

Following: The Golden Spike, post-ceremony, photograph by Andrew J. Russell, May 10, 1869

that instead of taking months, people and goods could be moved across the country in weeks or days. The transcontinental railroad would help open the western United States and territories to further emigration and settlement and assist in fulfilling the nation's "Manifest Destiny" of expanding westward (page 37).

Joining the Union Pacific and Central Pacific railroads was a major technological and engineering feat. Building a railroad through the Sierra Nevada and other mountain ranges and canyons was a challenging task. Dynamiting mountainsides, drilling and blasting tunnels, and constructing enormous wooden trestles to span canyons and chasms all required engineering prowess and skilled labor. The work was taxing and dangerous. Most of the work was done by Irish and Chinese immigrants and Latter-day Saints—Mormons who had settled Utah in the 1840s. At one point during the construction, Chinese workers made up more than three-quarters of the workforce. Over 1,000 Chinese railroad workers died during the construction.

A ceremony to drive the last spike into place and celebrate the Meeting of the Rails was held on Monday, May 10, 1869. Dignitaries, of

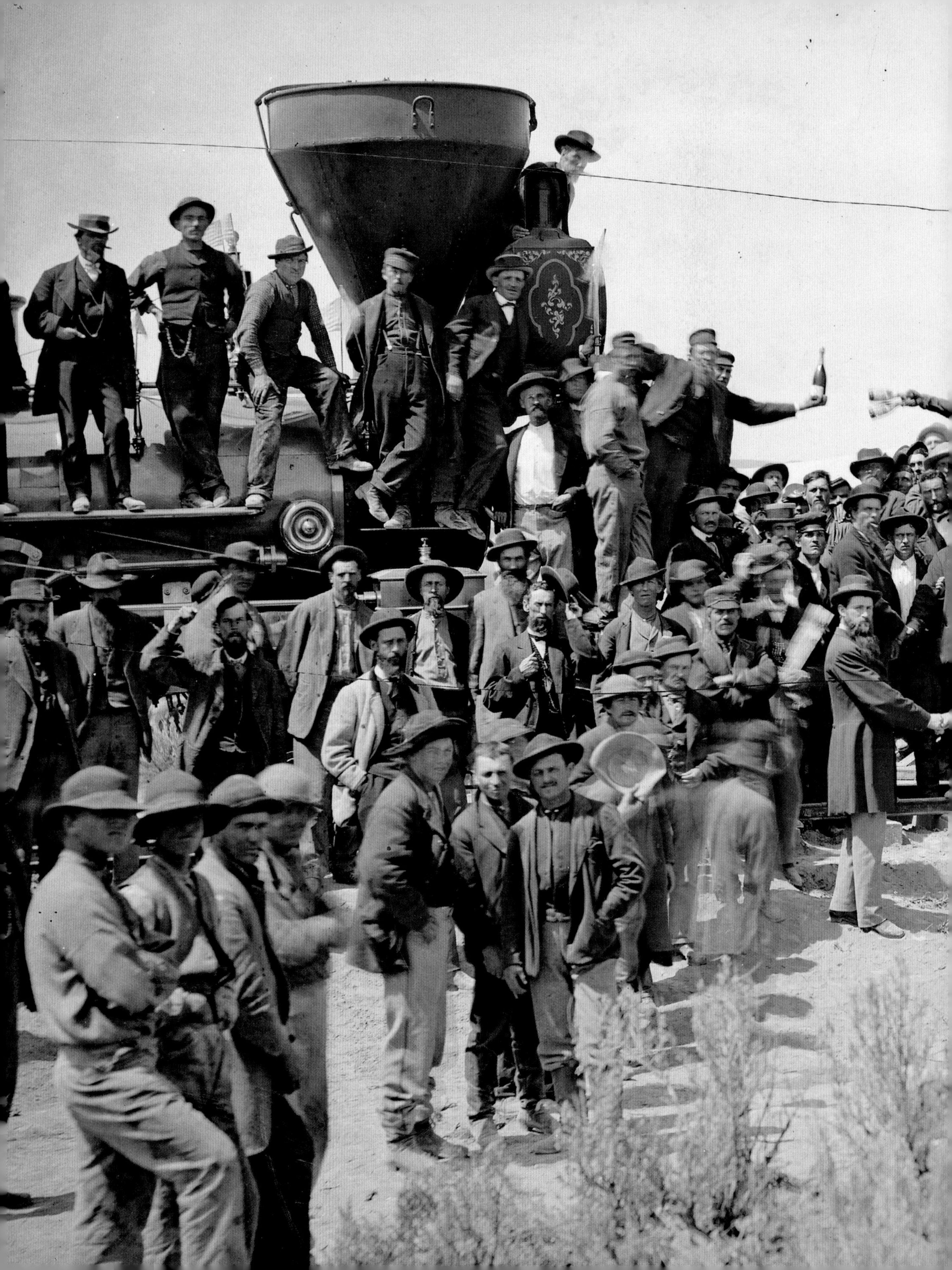

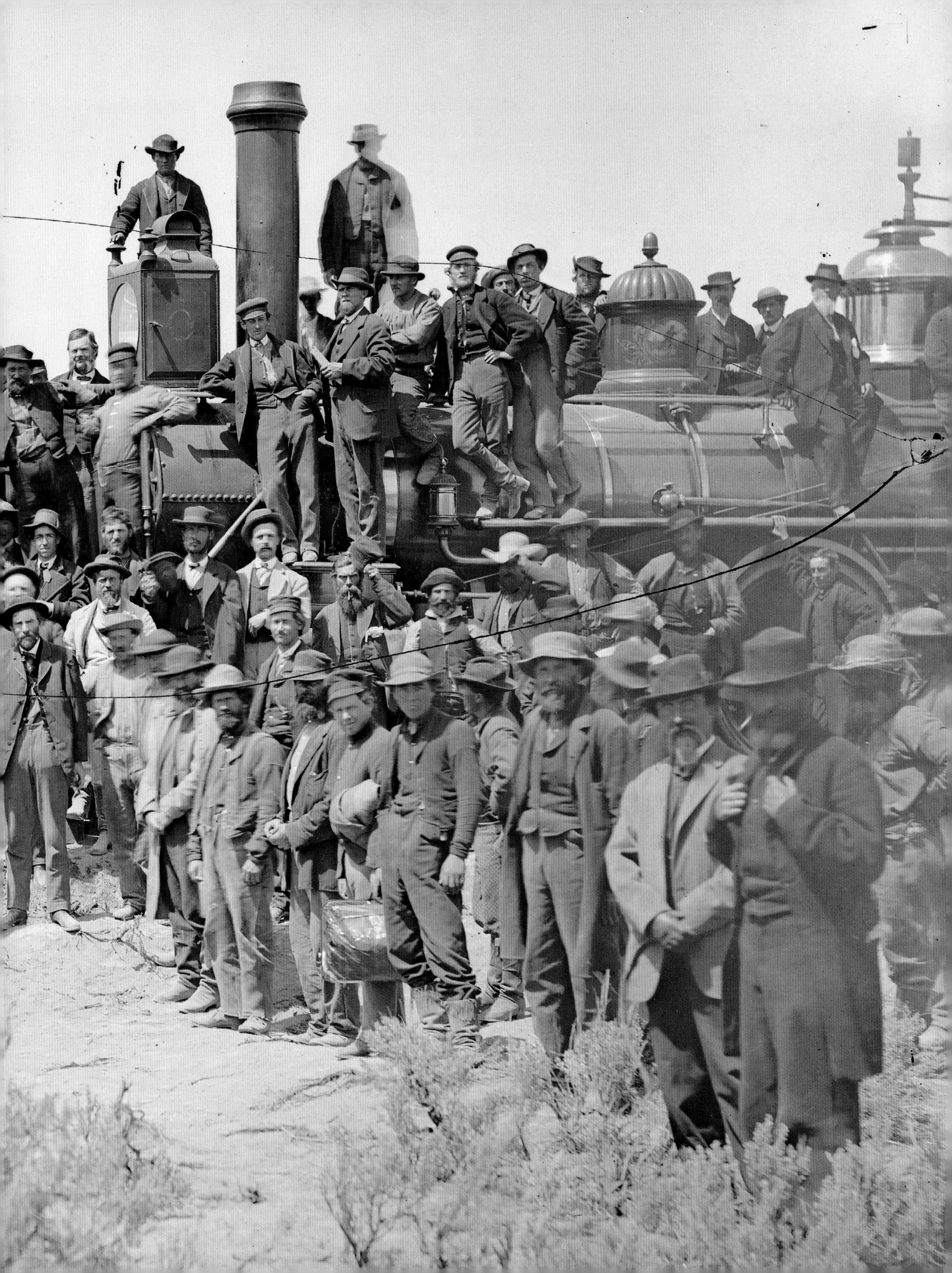

course, arrived, including Leland Stanford, president of the Central Pacific Railroad, and Thomas C. Durant, vice president of Union Pacific. Reporters and photographers were also present, including noted Civil War photographer Andrew J. Russell.

Photographs of the event show that American flags were in attendance as well, marking the celebration of American achievement with a patriotic fervor. But there is no clear record of which versions of the flag were hung for the festivities. The long exposure times required for the photographs of that era make most of them too blurry to tell. One image shows the flag unblurred, but it's partially wrapped around the flagpole with only part of the canton visible. Based on the number of visible stars, it is almost certainly a thirty-seven-star flag that was approved on July 4, 1867, nearly two years earlier.

The driving of the Golden Spike—the final spike that joined the two sets of rails, which was literally made of gold—is considered to have been one of the first events to be reported live around the country, if not the world. The spike was wired to a telegraph so that when it was struck with the specially made, silver-plated maul, it activated telegraphs that were wired to bells that rang around the country.

After the festivities, the dignitaries retired to one of the railcars for a luncheon. It was there that Russell took one of his most famous photographs. The two trains that met at Promontory for the celebration, the Union Pacific's *Engine 119* and the Central Pacific's *Jupiter*, were moved nearly nose-to-nose. The train workers, railway laborers, and other observers crowded around. George Booth, the *Jupiter*'s engineer, hung off the front of his train holding a bottle of champagne, and engineer Sam Bradford clung to the front of his *Engine 119* holding two champagne glasses. Russell captured the joyous moment. The dignitaries, dining in their railcar, missed being a part of the definitive image from the celebration.

***EVENTS LEADING TO THE BATTLE OF THE LITTLE BIG HORN,* BY STEPHEN STANDING BEAR (MATÓ NÁJIN)**

Two Perspectives on an Epic Battle

DATE: June 25–26, 1876

EVENT LOCATION: Little Bighorn Battlefield, Wyoming

CURRENT PAINTING LOCATION: Brinton Museum, Big Horn, Wyoming

The Battle of Little Bighorn took place beside the meandering waters of the Little Bighorn River in Montana on June 25, 1876. It was here that the Seventh Cavalry, led by Lieutenant Colonel George Armstrong Custer, suffered one of the US Army's most dramatic losses to Native American forces during the Great Sioux War of 1876.

The battle is illustrated in an 1899 painting by Stephen Standing Bear (Mató Nájin), a Minneconjou Lakota who, at the age of sixteen, fought in the encounter. The main portion of the painting shows the battle scene, with slain soldiers and horses on the ground. Across the very top, a line of cavalry soldiers marches with three company guidons (military versions of the American flag that signify a specific company, troop, or platoon and often have a swallowtail shape on the fly side). Just below them are two wounded soldiers, also with guidons. The two-dimensional perspective adds to the chaotic nature of the scene. The geometric design and bright colors of the Indigenous people's clothing and body painting

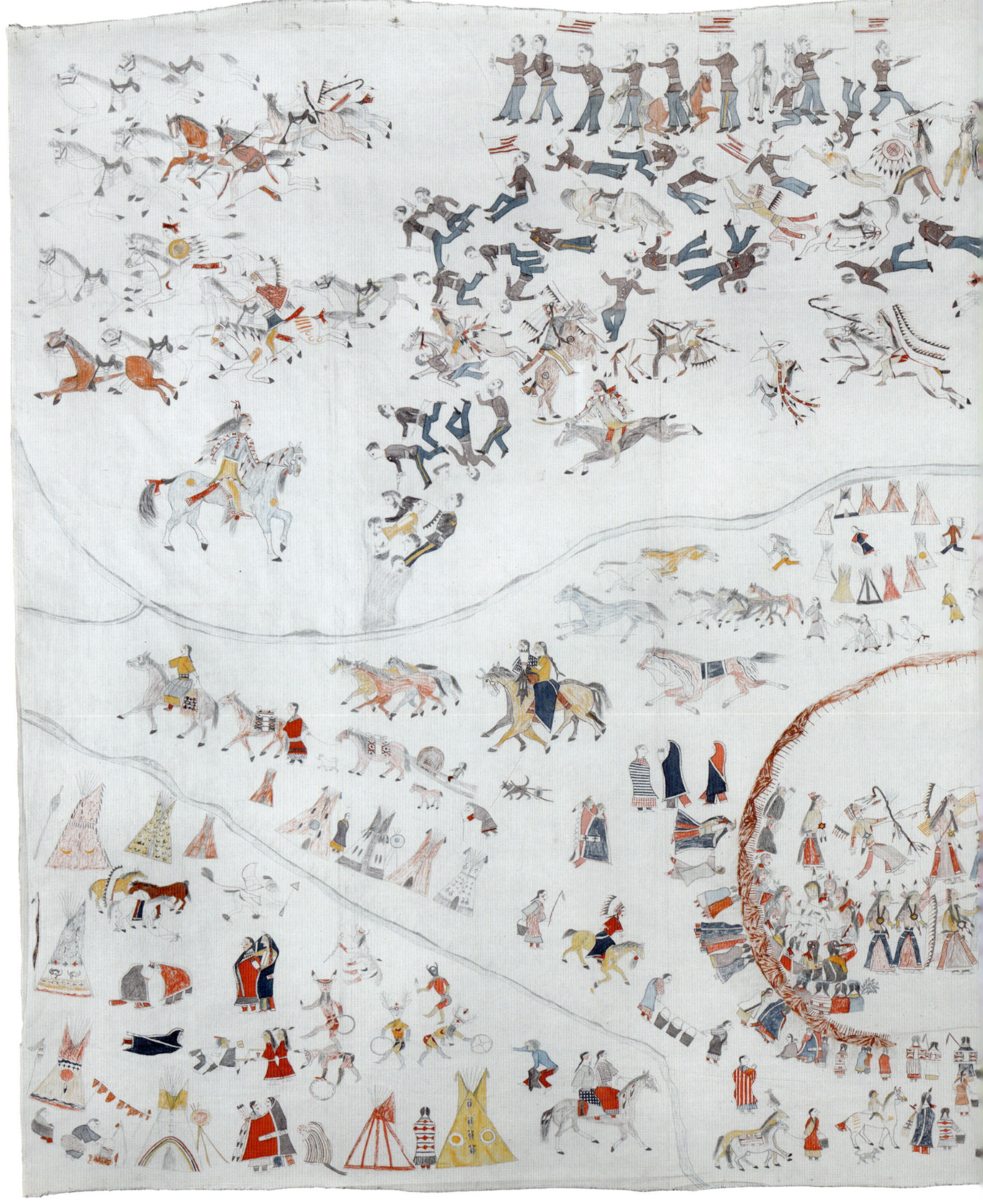

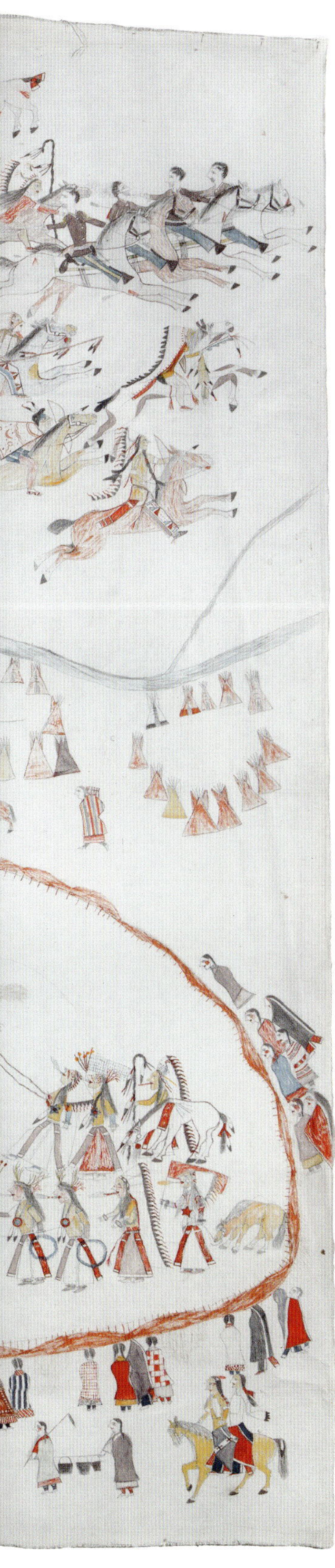

contrast greatly against the more plain character and tones of the cavalry's military uniforms.

The battle began when the cavalry troops attacked the Indigenous people. But the government's initial account characterized the Lakota and Cheyenne warriors as the aggressors and a "savage" massacre of the cavalry. In that vein, on March 31, 1895, almost twenty years after the incident, Charles C. Colbrath wrote an article, "Memento of a Massacre," in the *Detroit Free Press* about a cavalry guidon retrieved by a burial party after the fighting. Colbrath had served under Custer but did not participate in the Battle of Little Bighorn.

Known to the Lakota Sioux people of the northern Great Plains as the Battle of the Greasy Grass and in popular culture as Custer's Last Stand (a title that, even in defeat, puts the emphasis on the US cavalry), the Battle of Little Bighorn was a crucial event in the early summer of 1876, just a bit more than a week shy of the nation's one hundredth birthday. It was a humiliating defeat for the cavalry's forces and served to further energize the army's efforts to gain control of the West from the Indigenous tribes. It also set in motion a period of vengeful reprisals against the tribes.

If you visit the battleground today, located a few miles southeast of Crow Agency, Montana, you will observe a peaceful series of rolling hills dotted with marble markers where both Seventh Cavalry soldiers and Lakota and Cheyenne peoples—and even the combatants' horses—fell. The Battle of Little Bighorn was born in part from the US government's goals of claiming the Black Hills and the gold they contained for development by settlers and reducing the Lakota and Cheyenne's territory and confining them to reservations. Over time, historians have come to regard the event with a more balanced viewpoint. The engagement is generally considered to have been a grave miscalculation by Custer. To Custer's men who carried them into battle, the guidons were icons of patriotic loyalty and honor. But to the Indigenous people at the battle, the flags symbolized invaders.

Opposite: *Stephen Standing Bear's (Mató Nájin) painting* Events Leading to the Battle of the Little Big Horn, *ca 1899*

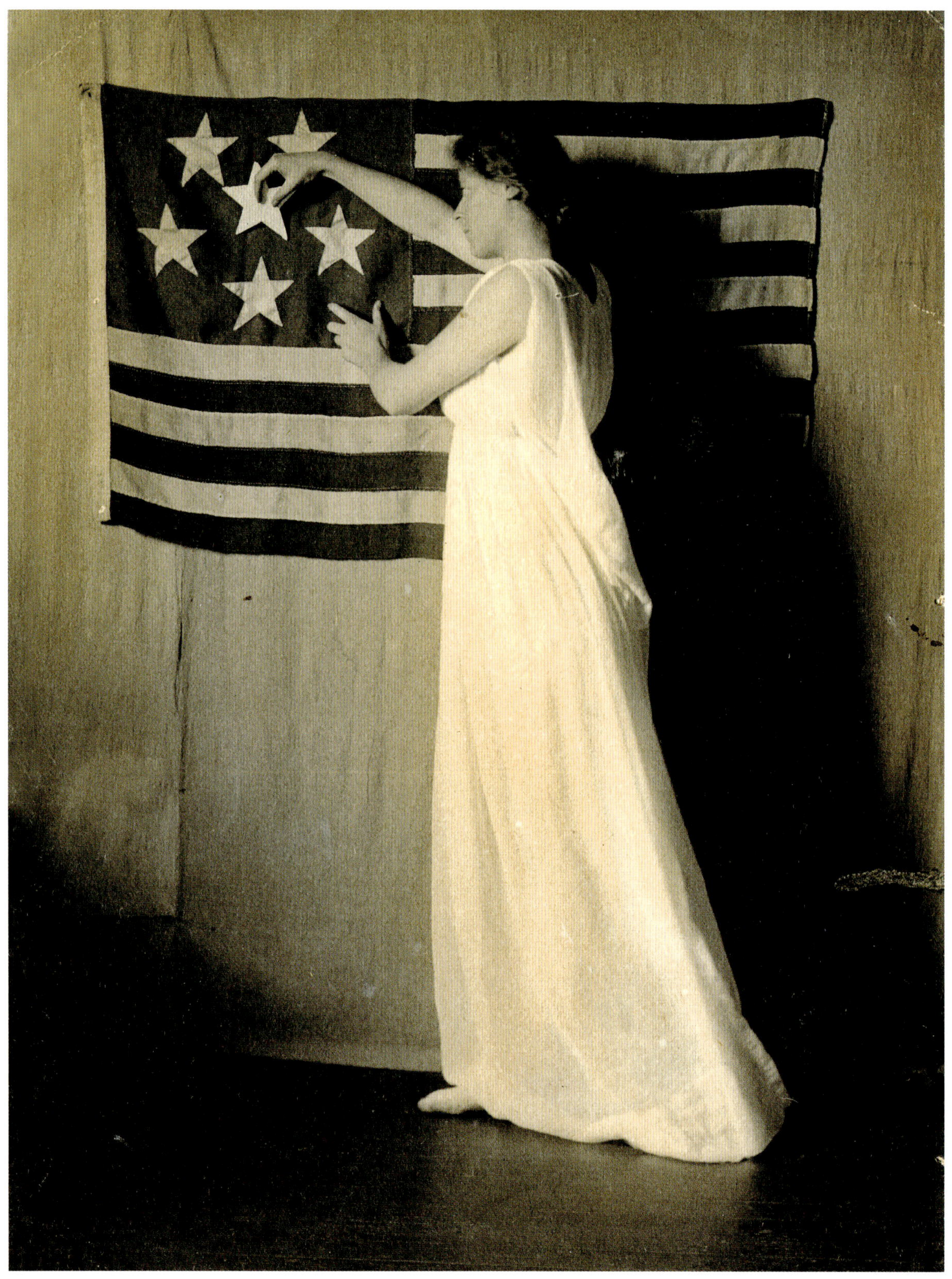

FOUR-STAR SUFFRAGETTE FLAG

A Flag of Suffrage

DATE: circa 1900

EVENT LOCATION: n/a

CURRENT FLAG LOCATION: National Museum of American History, Washington, DC

Opposite: A woman adds a sixth suffrage star to the flag to indicate California's adoption of women's voting rights.

Women have had the right to vote in the United States for only a little more than 100 of the country's 250-year history. Going back to around 1900, suffragettes made American flags with four stars on the canton in support of the first four states (Wyoming, Utah, Colorado, and Idaho) to grant women the right to vote and to demonstrate their frustration with the lack of progress toward achieving those rights nationwide.

The four-star suffragette flag helped draw attention to the disparity between the states. Though it's not an official American flag, this suffrage banner is a genuine symbol of support for democracy, in this case in reference to equality for women and the basic democratic right to have a say in determining who leads the nation.

There were other versions of women's suffrage flags as well. One of the more well known is the medallion flag, which carried forty-eight stars of varying sizes in a concentric medallion pattern on the front-side canton and six stars on the back-side canton representing the six states that (at the time the flag was designed) had legalized voting rights for women.

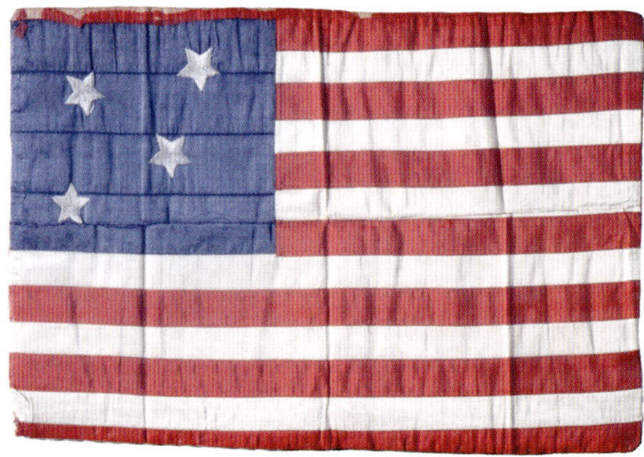

Above: *The four-star suffragette flag, circa 1900*

Opposite: *The front (top) and back (bottom) of a suffrage flag with various size stars, circa 1912*

The first time women were allowed to vote in America was in the late 1700s, when women were voting in New Jersey. The caveat was that they had to own property to qualify to vote. In many cases, property deeds were solely in the name of a woman's husband, which disqualified her from participating at the polls. This limited right to vote for women in New Jersey lasted only until 1807, when their rights were revoked.

Full, legal voting rights for women in the United States were granted in Wyoming in 1869, and then in Utah in 1870. Colorado granted women the right to vote in 1893, followed by Idaho in 1896. These four states became known as the "free states" for women's suffrage and were the impetus behind the four-star suffragette flag. As more states approved women's right to vote, more stars were added to the flag. Finally, after decades of struggle and petitioning, the Nineteenth Amendment was ratified on August 26, 1920, codifying the right of women to vote in the United States.

There are contemporary efforts to again limit women's voting rights. In 2025, legislation (the SAVE Act) was introduced in Congress that would require anyone voting to prove their citizenship by presenting identification documents, such as a birth certificate or passport, which match their name as listed on the voter registration roll. This would impact women voters much more than men. It would mean that any person who married and took their partner's last name or changed their name in any other fashion could have difficulty proving their identity. A person who registered to vote with their married name could not use a birth certificate to prove their identity. A person who registered to vote with their maiden name might not be able to use their passport to prove their identity. A study conducted by the Brennan Center for Justice suggests that the SAVE Act could disenfranchise more than twenty million eligible American voters who simply lack the required documents to prove citizenship.

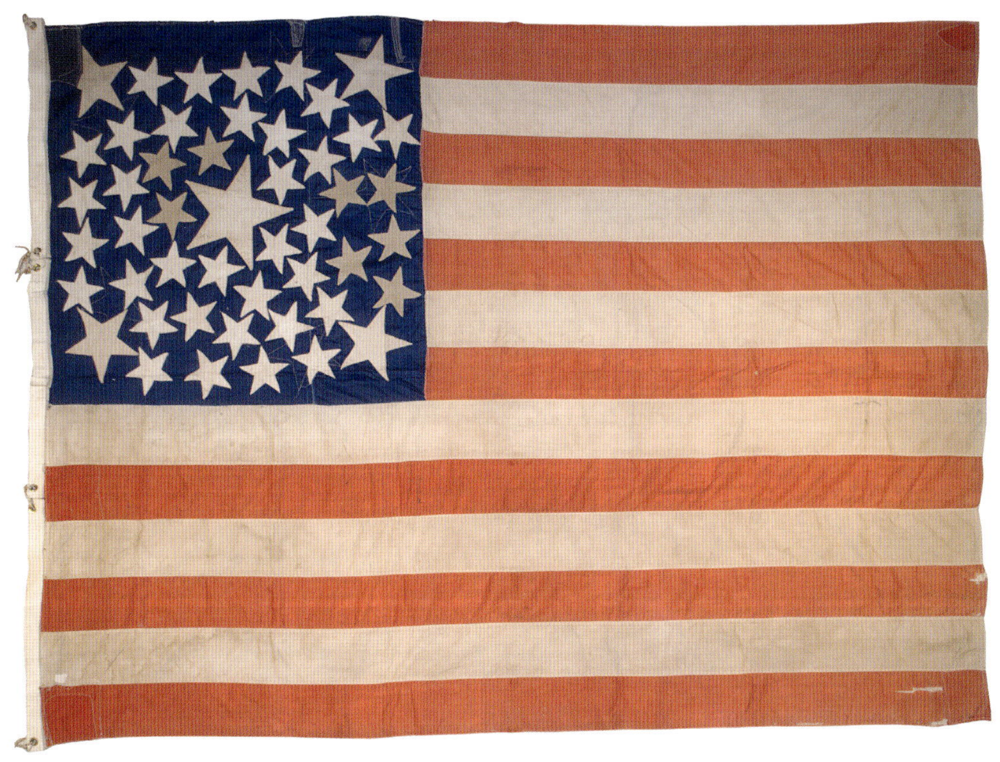

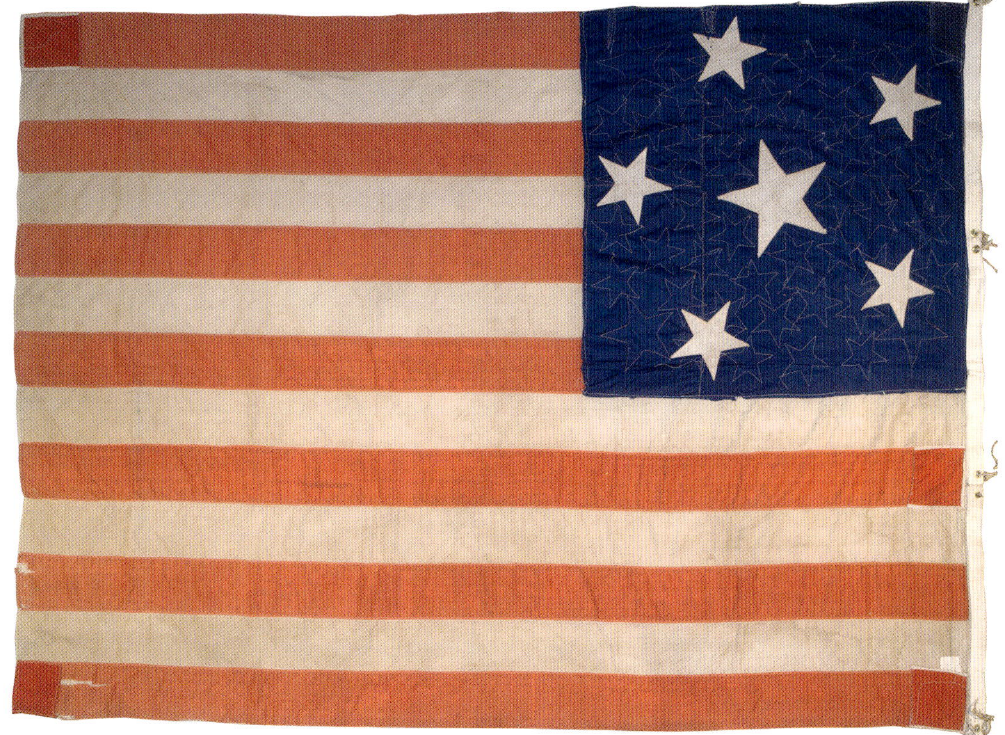

TWENTY-FOURTH INFANTRY REGIMENT FLAG

"Remember the *Maine*!"

DATE: July 1, 1898

EVENT LOCATION: San Juan Heights, Puerto Rico, Spanish-American War

CURRENT FLAG LOCATION: Fort Douglas Military Museum, Salt Lake City, Utah

On February 15, 1898, the USS *Maine* exploded in Havana Harbor, killing more than 260 sailors. This event became the impetus for the start of the Spanish-American War. The *Maine,* an armored cruiser, had been sent to Havana to safeguard American resources during the Cuban War of Independence. Much like the American colonies wanted independence from England, Cuba and other Spanish dependencies wanted to be free of Spain's rule. In January 1898, riots of Spanish supporters broke out in the western part of Havana. American diplomats in Cuba requested protection for US citizens living in Cuba. The US government sent the *Maine* to assist.

The cause of the explosion remains a mystery, but it led to a major uproar in the United States and ultimately to America's entry into what became the Spanish-American War. "Remember the *Maine*! To hell with Spain!" became the outcry of the American people. It forced President William McKinley, twenty-fifth president of the United States, to demand Spain's departure from Cuba, which led to both sides declaring war in late

Following, left: *Twenty-Fourth Regiment, US Infantry flag, Battle of San Juan Heights, Cuba, July 1, 1898*

Following, right: *Teddy Roosevelt (standing center) and his Rough Riders, after capturing Kettle Hill, July 1, 1898*

April of 1898. Because Spain's holdings at the time included Puerto Rico, Guam, and the Philippines, it meant that the United States was fighting in both the Atlantic and the Pacific—a harbinger of what was to come in World War II. It is also the reason the Philippines, until shortly after World War II, Puerto Rico, and Guam became territories of the United States after the nation's victory over Spain.

One of the major engagements of the war was the Battle of San Juan Hill in Puerto Rico. The conflict took place on the San Juan Heights, which consisted of San Juan Hill and Kettle Hill. Among the troops who fought that day were four groups of Black soldiers—the "Colored" Ninth and Tenth Cavalry and the Twenty-Fourth and Twenty-Fifth Infantry. That day, the Twenty-Fourth Infantry carried the American flag up San Juan Hill. The words *24th Regiment U. S. Infantry* were embroidered in its middle red stripe. The flag was donated to Fort Douglas, the former home of the Twenty-Fourth Infantry, by the daughter of Major Jay Milton Thompson who had been a member of the Twenty-Fourth.

The Black soldiers, moving determinedly up San Juan Hill against tenacious Spanish defenses, helped turn the tide of the battle. One of their fellow combatants, Rough Rider Frank Knox, said, "I never saw braver men anywhere." Yet little had changed since the Civil War with regard to how Black troops were treated. The Black units got very little official credit for their valiant efforts in the battle. Instead, it was Teddy Roosevelt's mounted charge up Kettle Hill with his Rough Riders that is remembered.

Many members of the Ninth and Tenth Cavalry and Twenty-Fourth and Twenty-Fifth Infantry earned commendations for their fearless fighting at San Juan, including Edward L. Baker Jr., who received the Medal of Honor for rescuing a stranded wounded soldier. But their efforts were overshadowed by those of the Rough Riders. The white troops' heroics were lauded, and those of Black soldiers were diminished when the story of the battle was initially reported. Even Roosevelt disparaged the Black troops' efforts at San Juan Hill. But his view was challenged by his own cavalry. Reflecting on the performance of the Black soldiers, Lieutenant John J. Pershing wrote, "They fought their way into the hearts of the American people."

The American flag that the Twenty-Fourth Infantry carried up San Juan Hill now resides at the Fort Douglas Military Museum in Salt Lake City, Utah, where the Twenty-Fourth Infantry was stationed when they were sent to Cuba.

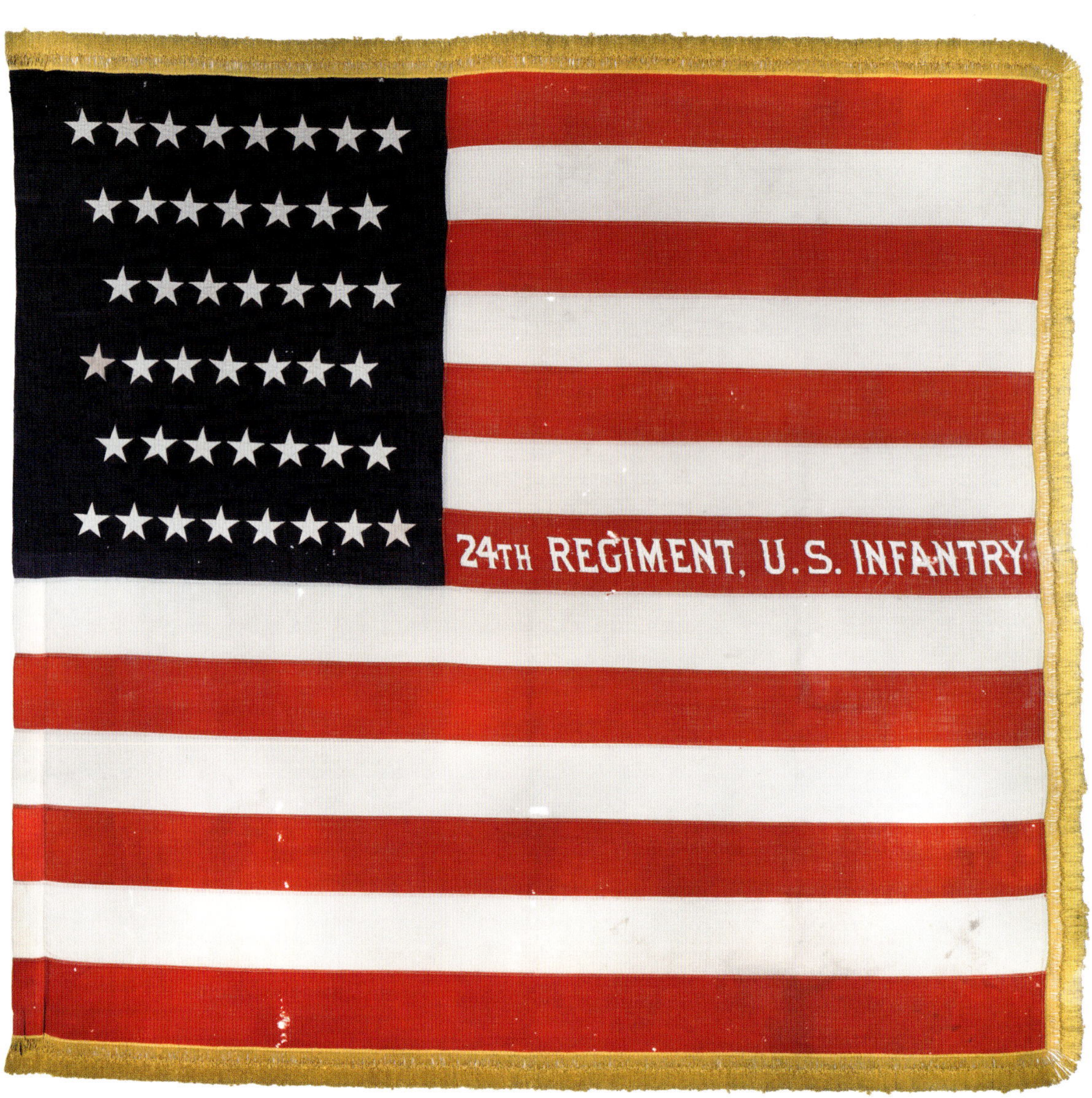
24TH REGIMENT, U.S. INFANTRY

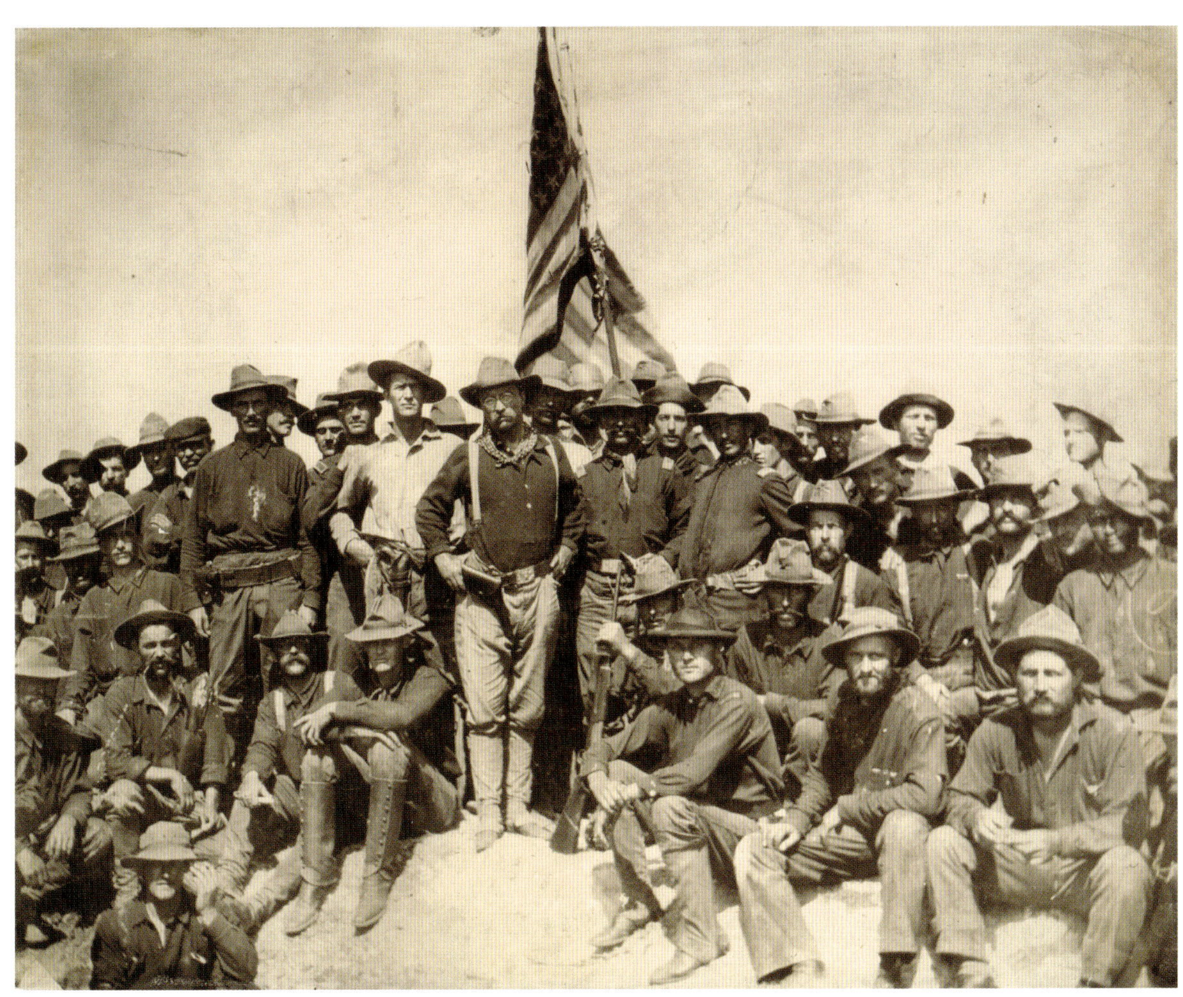

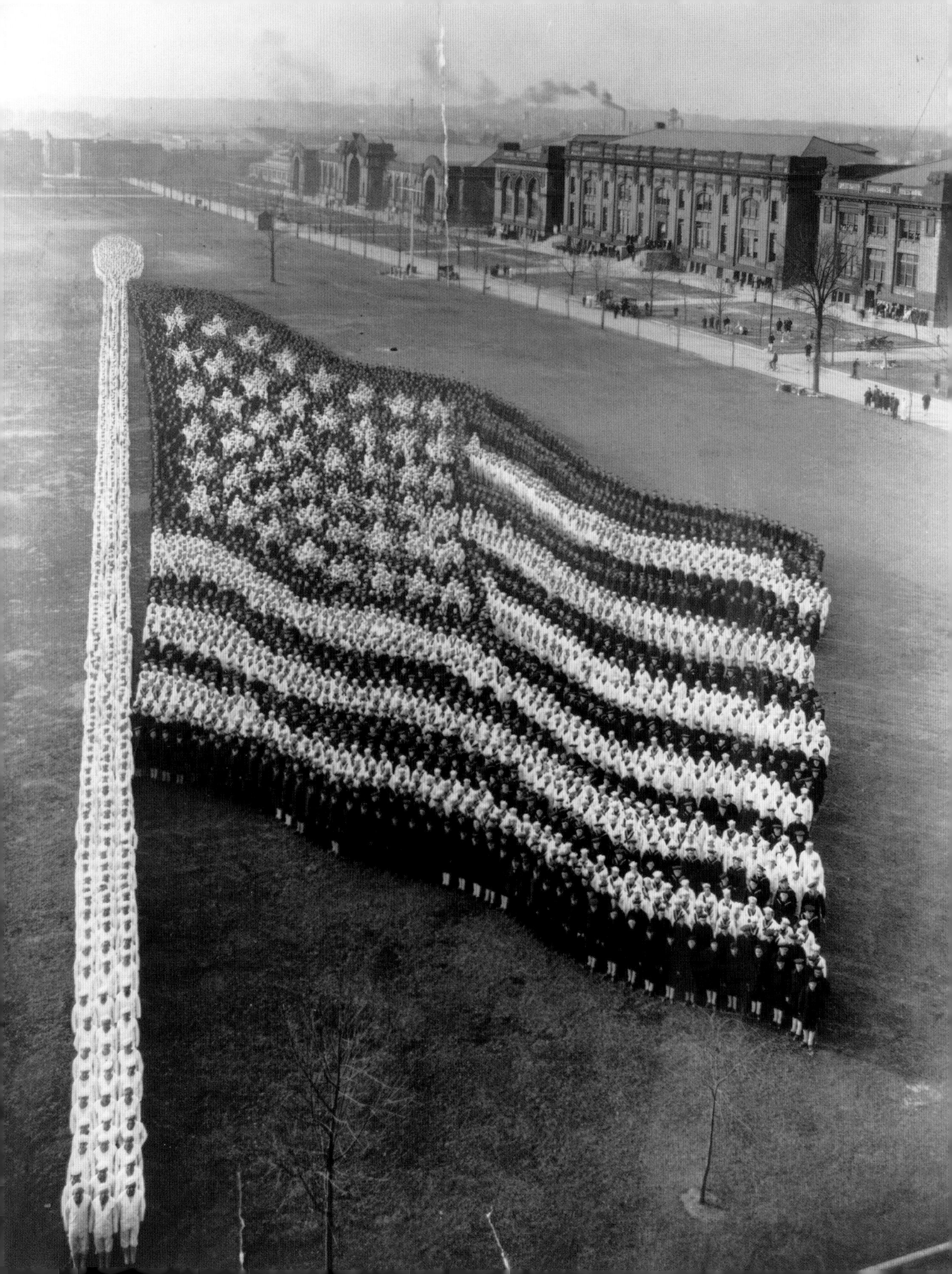

A LIVING TRIBUTE TO THE FLAG

The Flag Formed by 10,000 Naval Recruits

DATE: 1915–1921

EVENT LOCATION: Naval Training Station, Great Lakes, Illinois, and others

CURRENT FLAG LOCATION: n/a

Opposite: *"Living Flag" made up of 10,000 sailors at the Naval Training Station in Great Lakes, Illinois, 1917*

In the early 1900s, the US military commissioned a series of patriotic photographs to build morale and support for the country's possible entry into World War I. Photographer Arthur Mole and his assistant, John Thomas, had large groups of soldiers and sailors stand together to form different patriotic symbols, such as the US flag, the Liberty Bell, or an emblem of a service branch.

Mole, an immigrant from England, was a commercial photographer based in Zion, Illinois. Prior to this commission, beginning in 1913, Mole had created smaller versions of these "living photographs," but these new larger designs required at least a week of preparation and tens of thousands of service members. Their clothing colors had to be coordinated with the tones needed to accurately reproduce the object's values

Opposite: Thousands of soldiers from Fort Riley, Kansas, form the "Service Flag," which is displayed in homes of those serving in the US military, 1918.

in the black-and-white photograph, and their positioning on the ground had to match the line of perspective from the camera. One of the most notable images is the "Living Flag," which was taken in a field at the Naval Training Station in Great Lakes, Illinois, where 10,000 sailors formed the shape of a US flag flying on a pole. The recruits wearing white made up the stars, stripes, and flagpole, and those in navy blue formed the blue canton and the red stripes.

To create these dramatic images, Cole and Thomas first laid out the design on the ground-glass screen (the glass at the back of a camera onto which the lens projects the image so the photographer can see it) of their 11-by-14-inch (roughly 28 by 36 cm) view camera. Cole, working from an 80-foot (24 m) platform, used a megaphone and a white flag on a pole to direct the positioning of the soldiers. On the day the photograph was made, Thomas and his assistants worked at ground level for hours corralling the men into the desired formation. The key was to use many more men in the background to account for the larger scale as the perspective receded from the camera. In the foreground, there might be a few dozen soldiers, but in the distant background, thousands would be needed to give the illusion of a matching size. For example, in the *Living Flag*, the flagpole consists of approximately 550 men, while the little ball at the top of the pole is, on its own, made up of more than 300 men. The effort required the men to remain in place for extended periods, a challenge in and of itself, and even more so when the shoots occurred in the warmer months of the year; many men fainted.

Cole and Thomas made around thirty of these living photographs over eight years. Along with the US flag, their subjects included President Woodrow Wilson, the Service Flag (which families of service members would hang in the windows of their homes), the insignia of the 27th Division, the Allied flags (Britian, France, Italy, and the United States), the shield from the Great Seal of the United States, Uncle Sam, the American eagle symbol, and the Statue of Liberty. Other military units around the world copied their efforts with their own living-symbol images.

These photographs were, in part, intended to demonstrate the strength and size of the American forces available for entry into World War I. Since mass communication technologies like television and the internet weren't available in the early 1900s, photographs, which could be widely reproduced in newspapers, in magazines, and as postcards, were among the few ways to visually influence large audiences. While these images might seem quaint by today's standards, they carried powerful messages at the time, demonstrating the nation's preparedness and determination to defend democracy.

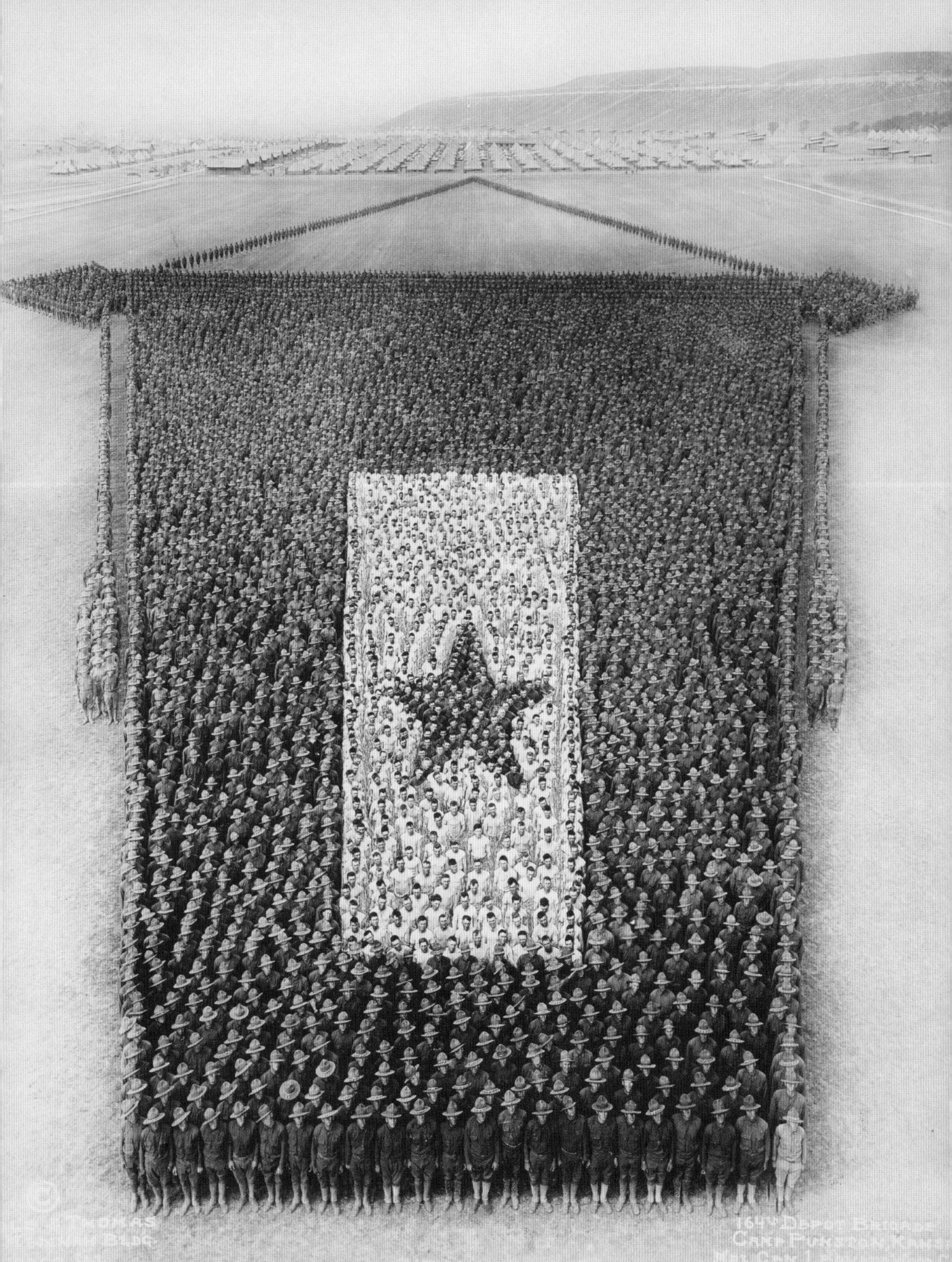
164th Depot Brigade
Camp Funston

WAKE UP AMERICA PARADE FLAGS

The War to End All Wars

DATE: April 19, 1917
EVENT LOCATION: New York City
CURRENT FLAG LOCATION: Unknown

On April 19, 1917, shortly after the United States entered World War I, the city of New York celebrated Wake Up America Day, part of an effort to boost recruitment for the military. The event was planned to coincide with the 142nd anniversary of the battles at Lexington and Concord that initiated the Revolutionary War. Boy Scouts waving a mass of American flags ran down Fifth Avenue in a parade attended by some 60,000 people. The flags they held had forty-eight stars laid out in six rows of eight stars, a version approved five years earlier with the addition of New Mexico and Arizona as the forty-seventh and forty-eighth states.

Though the parade was well attended, only a few hundred men signed up for service in the week following the march. This led to Congress approving the Selective Service Act on May 18, 1917. The act meant that men between the ages of twenty-one and forty-five were required to register for military service.

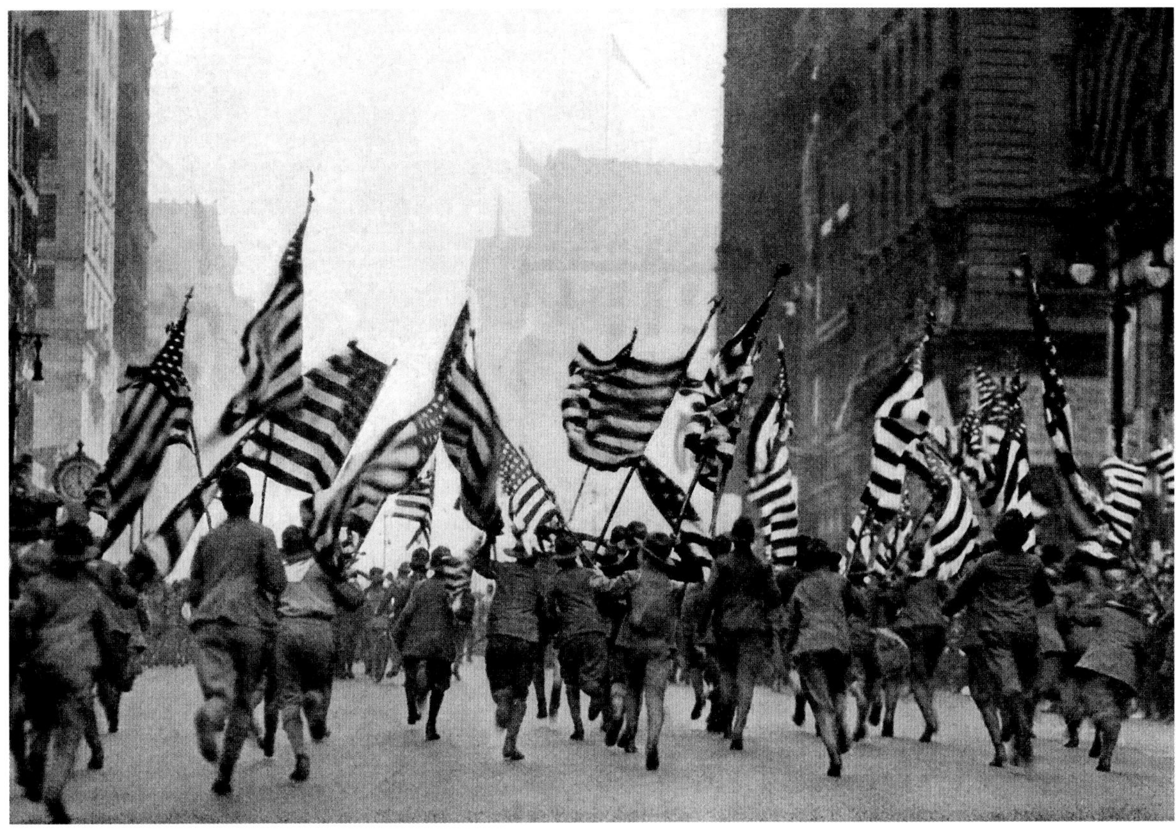

Boy Scouts running with American flags during the Wake Up America parade, New York City, April 19, 1917

The United States had made a great effort to avoid joining World War I. But the sinking of the *Lusitania* pushed America into the fray. On May 7, 1916, eighteen-year-old seaman Leslie Morton was the bow lookout on the British ocean liner and noticed what appeared to be two torpedoes headed for the starboard side of the passenger vessel. The German U-boat SM U-20 had fired on the ship. Morton called out, but it was too late; the torpedoes struck the ship.

The *Lusitania* began listing badly to starboard after it was hit. The ship almost immediately lost electrical power and steam propulsion. With the power out, Captain William Thomas Turner gave the order to abandon ship. The ship's tilt made deployment of the lifeboats difficult. Many passengers and crew ended up in the water, including the captain. Others were trapped below deck. The ship sank in eighteen minutes, less than 12 miles (19 km) off the Irish coast. The ship's occupants had numbered 1,962. About one-third were crew and two-thirds were passengers.

Only 761 people survived, including just 31 of the 159 Americans on board that day.

The German attack on the *Lusitania,* coupled with sinking of other merchant and passenger ships by U-boats, eventually tipped the scales for the United States. On April 6, 1917, eleven months after the sinking of the *Lusitania,* America declared war on Germany. American troops joined the Entente powers in repelling the Central Powers. With the Treaty of Versailles, the war ended on November 11, 1918. That date was then celebrated annually as Armistice Day.

"The war to end all wars," as World War I was called, turned out to be an overly idealistic slogan. Unfortunately, the Treaty of Versailles's harsh financial penalties for Germany (over half a trillion dollars, when adjusted for inflation) and the ruined state of its economy laid the groundwork for World War II. The forty-eight-star flags carried en masse down Fifth Avenue by a charging pack of Boy Scouts in 1917 would be carried by American troops through the battles of not just World War I but also World War II and the Korean War. In 1954, after the conclusion of the Korean War, Armistice Day was changed to Veterans Day in the United States, to honor the service of soldiers from every war.

ELLIS ISLAND FLAG

A Flag of the American Dream

DATE: 1892–1954

EVENT LOCATION: Ellis Island, New York

CURRENT FLAG LOCATION: Unknown

Beginning in the mid-1800s, conflict, famine, oppression, and economic hardship affected people all over the world. This turmoil led to millions of immigrants arriving on America's shores in the late nineteenth and early twentieth centuries.

Many viewed America as a land of freedom and economic opportunity. At the same time, American industries began to grow rapidly. A large number of skilled, and unskilled, workers were needed to help expand the country's economic growth. In 1850, just under 10 percent of the US population was born abroad. By 1890, that figure rose to nearly 15 percent. (Census data from 2022 estimated the percentage of immigrants in the United States at around 13.9 percent.)

While immigration was previously managed at the state level, the growing influx of newcomers forced America to adapt, and the Immigration Act of 1891 was placed under the federal government for the first time. On January 1, 1892, Ellis Island, in New York Harbor, became

__Opposite:__ The Inspection Room, where doctors examined immigrants at Ellis Island, New York, New York, circa 1910s

the main entry point and primary reception station for immigrants for over thirty years.

Those arriving in New York were greeted by the Statue of Liberty. Once on Ellis Island, they could see the ensign of their newly adopted country in the immigration facilities. There could be no more meaningful symbols of freedom and opportunity than the "Lady of the Harbor" and the American flag to these passengers, most of whom hoped to become naturalized citizens someday.

America benefited from this creative alchemy through the combination of diverse thoughts, experiences, and ideas from different traditions working together, leading to some of the nation's greatest achievements in science, medicine, and the arts.

With the passage of the Emergency Immigration Act of 1921 and the National Origins Act of 1924, immigration to the United States began to decline. Ellis Island became an expensive facility to operate. By the late 1940s, the government started closing parts of the site, and operations ended entirely in November 1954.

The ebb and flow of immigration was affected by many factors and events as the United States expanded and evolved. Changing laws and attitudes towards immigrants have, over time, both limited and increased the demand to come to America. Foreign wars drove emigres to our shores. Domestic war (specifically the Civil War) reduced the influx. Currently, the same pressures—poverty, lack of opportunity, and violence—that drove Europeans and others to America during the early 1900s are still influencing immigration trends.

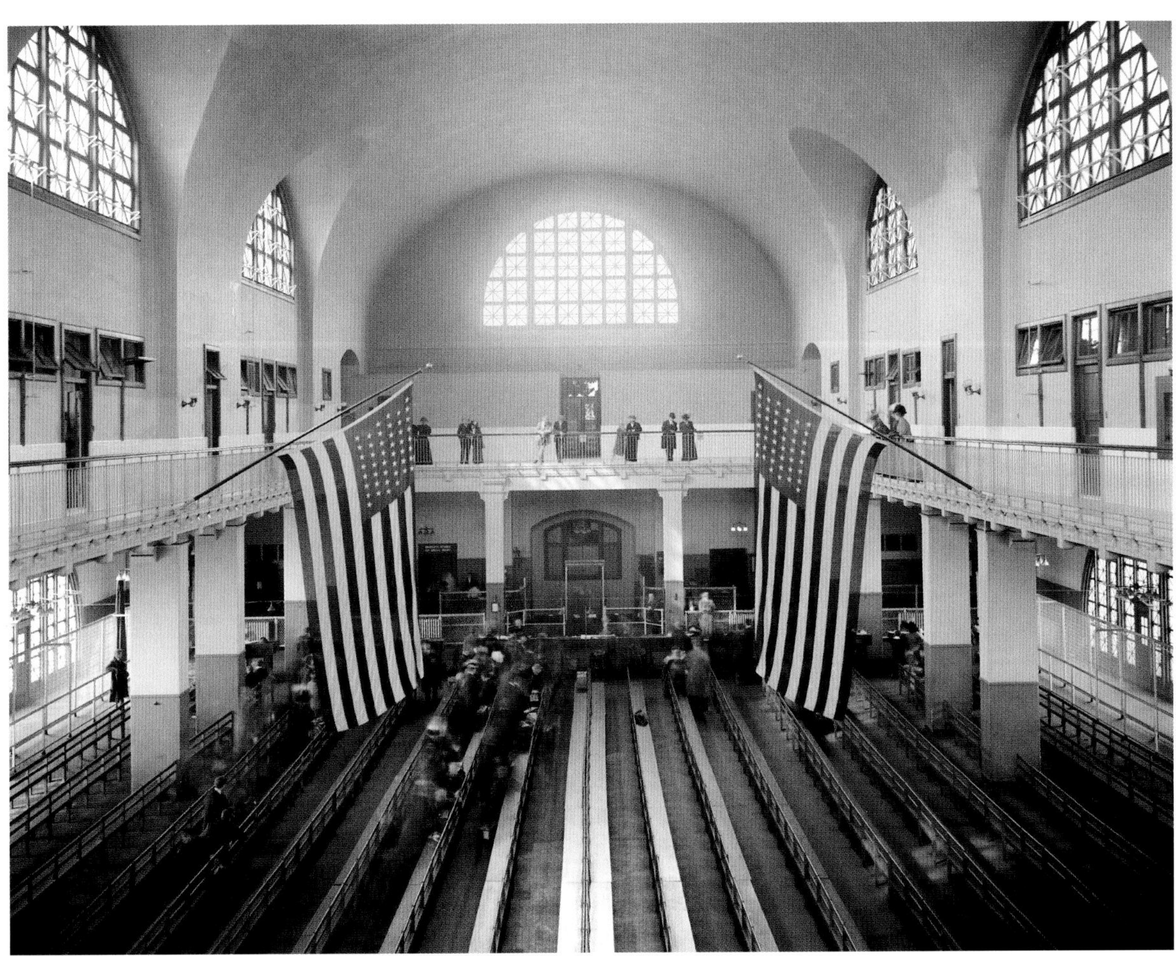

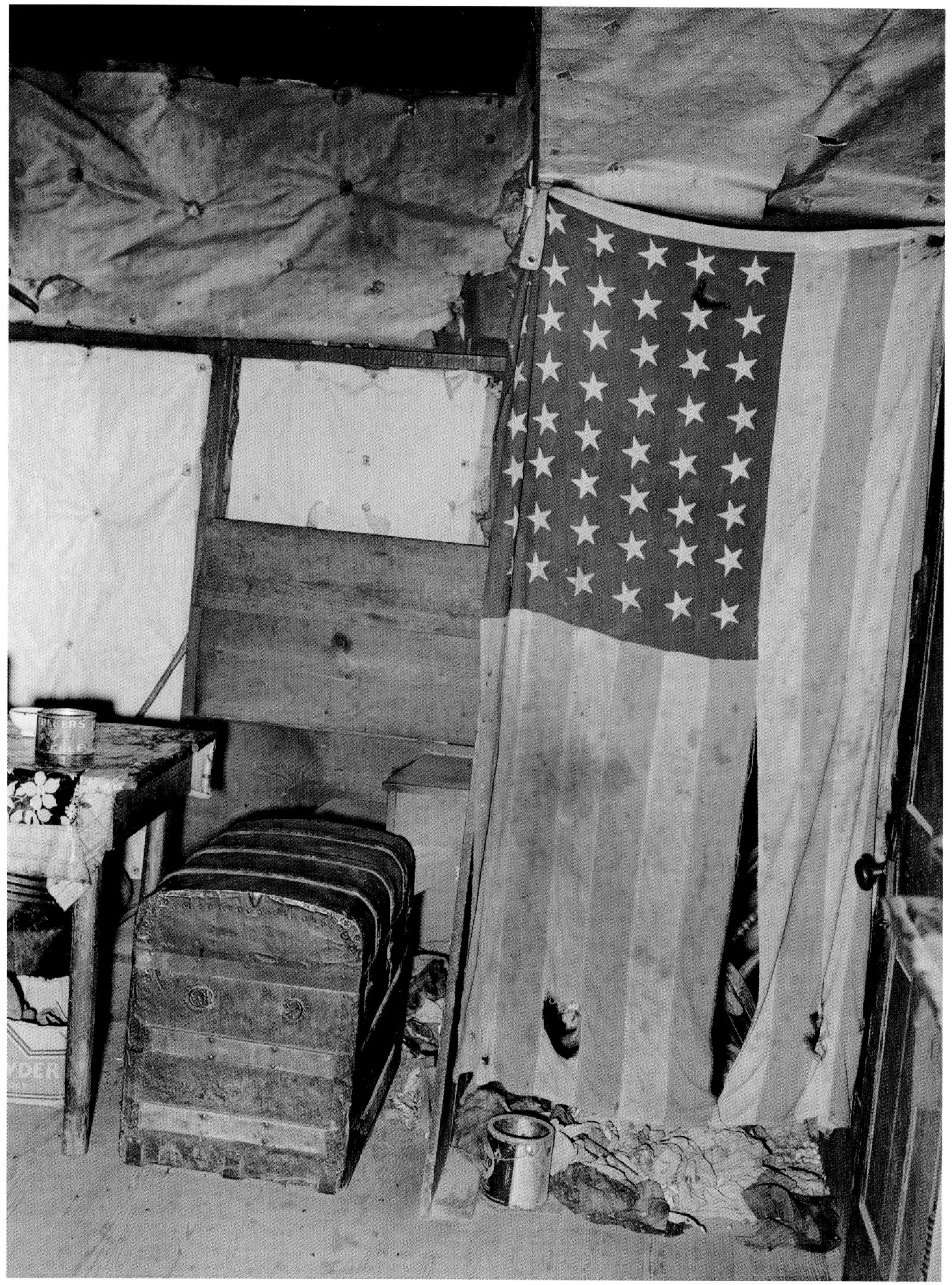

GREAT DEPRESSION–ERA FLAG

Trying Times

DATE: June 1939

EVENT LOCATION: Wagoner County, Oklahoma

CURRENT FLAG LOCATION: Unknown

Opposite: Interior of a Negro Farmworker's Home, *Wagoner County, Oklahoma, Farm Securities Administration (FSA) photo, 1939*

The Farm Securities Administration (FSA) was created in 1937 as part of President Franklin D. Roosevelt's New Deal programs, which aimed for unemployment relief, economic recovery, and financial system reform. Along with assisting farmers who were suffering from both the Great Depression's economic woes and the loss of production from a series of severe droughts that hit the Great Plains (and further depressed the economic fortunes of America), the FSA recruited photographers to document the effects of these factors on Americans.

At the time, financial pressures and drought were forcing many city dwellers and farmers alike to migrate west or south to California, Florida, and other states where the economic possibilities and wetter weather promised work. Many migrants lived in their cars—if they had them. Others camped in tents or found shelter wherever they could. Those lucky enough to find agricultural work were often lodged in small wood houses with unfinished interiors and little in the way of amenities. Occupants would often insulate the flimsy walls with newspapers, blankets, and cloth.

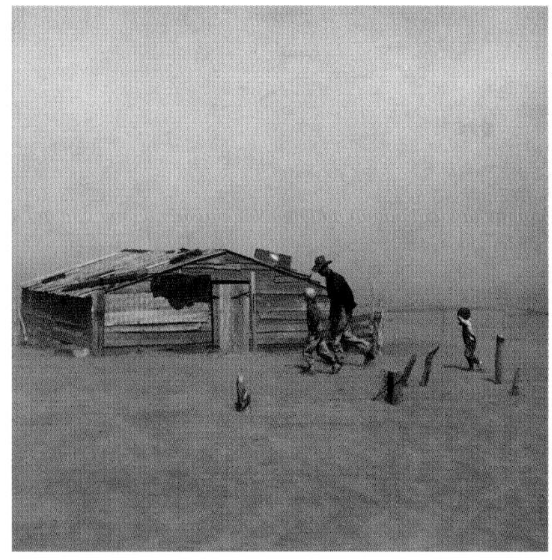

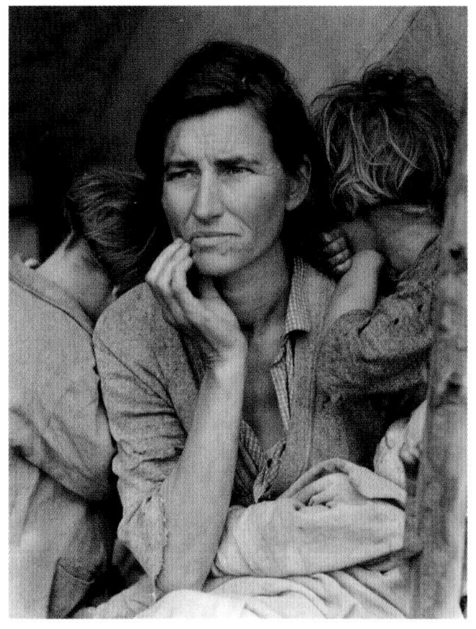

Top: Farmer and Sons Walking in the Face of a Dust Storm, *Cimarron County, Oklahoma, FSA photo, 1936*

Bottom: Migrant Mother, *Nipomo, California, FSA photo, 1936*

In a 1939 photo of one of these homes, FSA photographer Russell Lee captured the scene inside a farm worker's shack lined with cardboard and containing a few items: a trunk, a small table, and a few cans. Most notable is the American flag that is used to conceal a storage area. The torn and heavily soiled flag is no longer a symbol of national pride but a functional curtain cordoning off a closet. For the occupants of the home, it was perhaps fitting; desperation, not patriotism, was the mood of the times, and it might have seemed as if the country had abandoned them.

After a post–World War I boom in the 1920s, the American economy had begun to cool. The government was partly to blame. Government financial policies, including increasing interest rates and tightening the money supply, were intended to slow the rise in already overvalued stock prices. When the stock market crashed in October 1929, many investors who had borrowed money against their shares' values were forced to sell everything, which precipitated a further drop in stock prices.

On top of that, by 1934, the full effects of severe, prolonged drought stretched from the northern Gulf Coast to the northern plains, with the worst effects felt in the Dust Bowl, encompassing parts of Colorado, Kansas, Nebraska, New Mexico, Oklahoma, and Texas. In all, the Great Depression, as it became known, triggered by the intertwining factors of economic meltdown and long-term drought, would last ten years.

The FSA photographers who traveled the country during this time created a poignant record of the worst widespread economic conditions in American history. Led by Roy Stryker, the FSA photographers included Esther Bubley, John Collier Jr., Marjory Collins, Jack Delano, Walker Evans, Theodor Jung, Dorothea Lange, Russell Lee, Carl Mydans, Gordon Parks, Louise Rosskam, Arthur Rothstein, Ben Shahn, John Vachon, and Marion Post Wolcott, among others. The group produced iconic images of the era: *Migrant Mother* by Lange, *American Gothic* by Parks (page 105), and *Farmer and Sons Walking in the Face of a Dust Storm, Cimarron County, Oklahoma* by Rothstein, as examples. The project also produced one of the first extensive photographic records of Black life in America.

By focusing on individuals and their suffering, the FSA imagery helped build empathy for those most affected by the Great Depression.

WONDER WOMAN'S FLAG-MOTIF OUTFIT

A Role Model for Women in World War II

DATE: 1941

EVENT LOCATION: New York City

CURRENT COMIC LOCATION: National Museum of American History, Washington, DC

Wonder Woman was introduced to American comic book audiences in 1941, in the eighth issue of the DC Comics series *All-Star Comics,* less than eight weeks before the bombing of Pearl Harbor (page 94). At the time, comic books offered very few female lead characters. It had been only twenty years since the signing of the Nineteenth Amendment (page 70) gave women across the country the right to vote, and it would be another twenty years before the women's liberation movement took root. As a female protagonist, Wonder Woman played to the hopes of women who wished for more than a role as wife and homemaker. Over time, and through various iterations of the character, Wonder Woman was portrayed as a fierce warrior, a sophisticated woman, and a compassionate leader.

Opposite: *Title page to "Wonder Woman" from* All-Star Comics *#8, October 1941. © & ™ DC Comics.*

In part, *All-Star Comics* #8 tells Wonder Woman's origin story as Diana, daughter of Queen Hippolyta, who is raised on Paradise Island (later referred to as Themyscira), a country of Amazon women from ancient Greek mythology. Diana becomes "Wonder Woman" through a contest of athletics and skill. American fighter pilot Steve Trevor crashes his plane on the island and Wonder Woman is tasked with helping him return to America and fighting alongside him to defeat the Nazis. For this journey, Wonder Woman is given an outfit that's styled to resemble the American flag—a red torso top with a golden eagle and a blue skirt with white stars. Her ensemble reflected her commitment to America—once she leaves Paradise Island, she can never return.

By 1941, when Wonder Woman made her patriotic debut, America had helped win World War I and survived the Great Depression. In the months and years to come, Wonder Woman's steely strength would be exemplified by women all around the country—and the world—who stepped into nontraditional roles to help defeat the Axis powers in World War II.

Wonder Woman has evolved over time, reinvented in pop culture media every few decades. In 1975, the *Wonder Woman* TV series premiered, starring Lynda Carter, whose costume maintained the American flag symbology of her predecessor from the 1940s. In 2017, Wonder Woman debuted in the movies, starring Gal Gadot; her superhero costume had evolved, avoiding any direct reference to the American flag, but the key elements of a red corset, golden eagle emblem, and blue skirt remained.

There exists a paradox between Wonder Woman's liberated personality and power and her sexualized attire, of course. The objectification of her character is at odds with her knowledge, skill, and ability. The American flag motif of her superhero costume adds another dimension to her already complex image. Nevertheless, when we look at Wonder Woman through the lens of 1940s norms, she was well ahead of her time. She was also just in time to inspire and support the women the nation would need to defeat the Germans, Italians, and Japanese, not in comic books, but in real life.

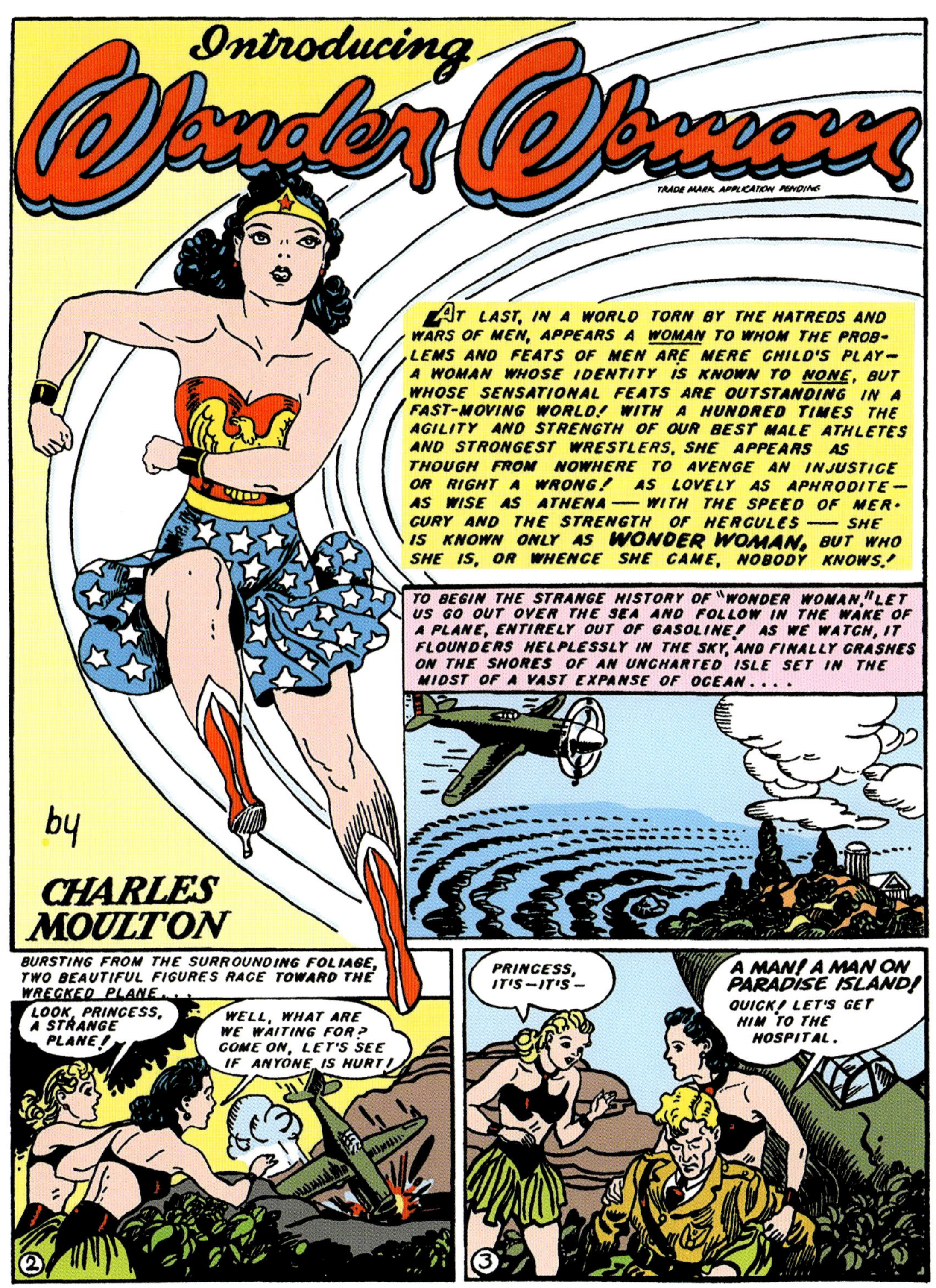
Introducing
Wonder Woman
TRADE MARK APPLICATION PENDING
AT LAST, IN A WORLD TORN BY THE HATREDS AND WARS OF MEN, APPEARS A WOMAN TO WHOM THE PROBLEMS AND FEATS OF MEN ARE MERE CHILD'S PLAY— A WOMAN WHOSE IDENTITY IS KNOWN TO NONE, BUT WHOSE SENSATIONAL FEATS ARE OUTSTANDING IN A FAST-MOVING WORLD! WITH A HUNDRED TIMES THE AGILITY AND STRENGTH OF OUR BEST MALE ATHLETES AND STRONGEST WRESTLERS, SHE APPEARS AS THOUGH FROM NOWHERE TO AVENGE AN INJUSTICE OR RIGHT A WRONG! AS LOVELY AS APHRODITE— AS WISE AS ATHENA — WITH THE SPEED OF MERCURY AND THE STRENGTH OF HERCULES — SHE IS KNOWN ONLY AS WONDER WOMAN, BUT WHO SHE IS, OR WHENCE SHE CAME, NOBODY KNOWS!
TO BEGIN THE STRANGE HISTORY OF "WONDER WOMAN," LET US GO OUT OVER THE SEA AND FOLLOW IN THE WAKE OF A PLANE, ENTIRELY OUT OF GASOLINE! AS WE WATCH, IT FLOUNDERS HELPLESSLY IN THE SKY, AND FINALLY CRASHES ON THE SHORES OF AN UNCHARTED ISLE SET IN THE MIDST OF A VAST EXPANSE OF OCEAN....
by
CHARLES MOULTON
BURSTING FROM THE SURROUNDING FOLIAGE, TWO BEAUTIFUL FIGURES RACE TOWARD THE WRECKED PLANE...
LOOK, PRINCESS, A STRANGE PLANE!
WELL, WHAT ARE WE WAITING FOR? COME ON, LET'S SEE IF ANYONE IS HURT!
2
PRINCESS, IT'S—IT'S—
A MAN! A MAN ON PARADISE ISLAND!
QUICK! LET'S GET HIM TO THE HOSPITAL.
3

1941

to

1945

World War II

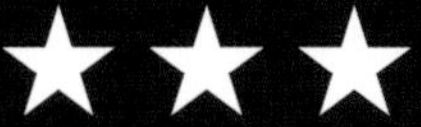

BY THE START OF WORLD WAR II, THE FORTY-eight-star American flag had been in use for twenty-nine years. During the war, that flag would come to symbolize the brave acts of servicepeople around the globe. It would also serve as a reminder that the incarceration of Japanese Americans, who were citizens of the United States, was a tragic stain on the country's record of civil rights.

FLAG FROM THE USS *ARIZONA*

A Day of Infamy

DATE: December 7, 1941

EVENT LOCATION: Ford Island, Pearl Harbor, Hawai'i

CURRENT FLAG LOCATION: Arizona Capitol Museum, Phoenix, Arizona

From the bottom of Pearl Harbor in Hawai'i, oil still rises slowly from the fuel bunkers of the USS *Arizona*, which was sunk more than eight decades ago. The sheen of oil on the surface of the harbor's water is a grim reminder of the 2,403 sailors, soldiers, and civilians who died when the Japanese attacked the United States' ships and military installations on Hawai'i on December 7, 1941 in what would become the first battle of World War II. Of those, 1,177 died on the *Arizona*.

Shortly after the attack, an American flag was retrieved from either Captain Franklin van Valkenburgh's barge or Rear Admiral Isaac Kidd's gig (both killed during the attack) on the USS *Arizona*. A salvage team working on the sunken ship found the flag and gave it to tugboat captain Joseph Dowdy, who was friends with the crew. Dowdy recounted the story of the flag's provenance in a letter he wrote to the Hawai'ian American Legion, to whom he donated the flag. The flag is soiled with oil from the battleship, another tragic artifact from that fateful December day. The shape of the oil stain echoes that of the explosive cloud captured in photographs and on film when the *Arizona*'s forward munitions magazine detonated after it was hit by a Japanese bomb.

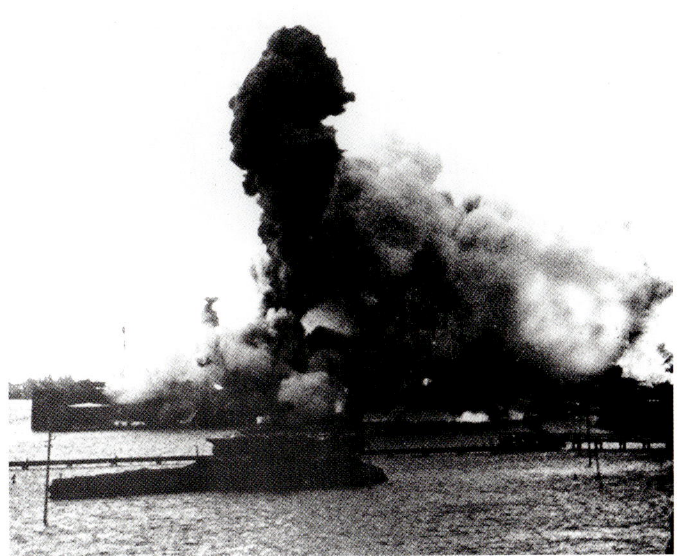

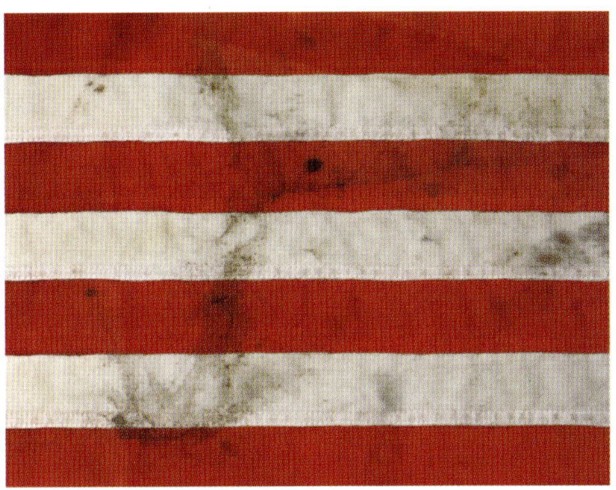

Above, left: *Forward magazines exploding on USS* Arizona*, after being struck by a Japanese armor-piercing bomb, Pearl Harbor, Hawai'i. December 7, 1941*

Above, right: *Detail of the oil stain on the flag retrieved from the USS* Arizona

In the 1980s the Hawai'ian American Legion gifted the flag to the Phoenix American Legion, which then gave it to the state of Arizona. The USS *Arizona* flag is now displayed in the Arizona Capitol Museum in Phoenix.

The long chain of events that would lead to the attack on Pearl Harbor had begun ten years earlier. In 1931, Japan began its military aggression in China by attacking Manchuria and installing a Japan-friendly government. America was competing with Japan for influence and trade in the Asia-Pacific region. With the island territories of Hawai'i, Guam, Midway, the Philippines, and others, the United States had a solid foothold in the Pacific. Japan believed that to be the dominant power in the region, it would have to capture those territories.

By 1937, China and Japan were in all-out war. In December 1937, Japanese troops took the city of Nanjing, massacred hundreds of thousands of Chinese civilians and soldiers, and raped thousands of Chinese women. Yet the Rape of Nanjing, as the horrific assault came to be known, did not provoke much response from the US government, which was more concerned with protecting its own national interests. Japan's geography

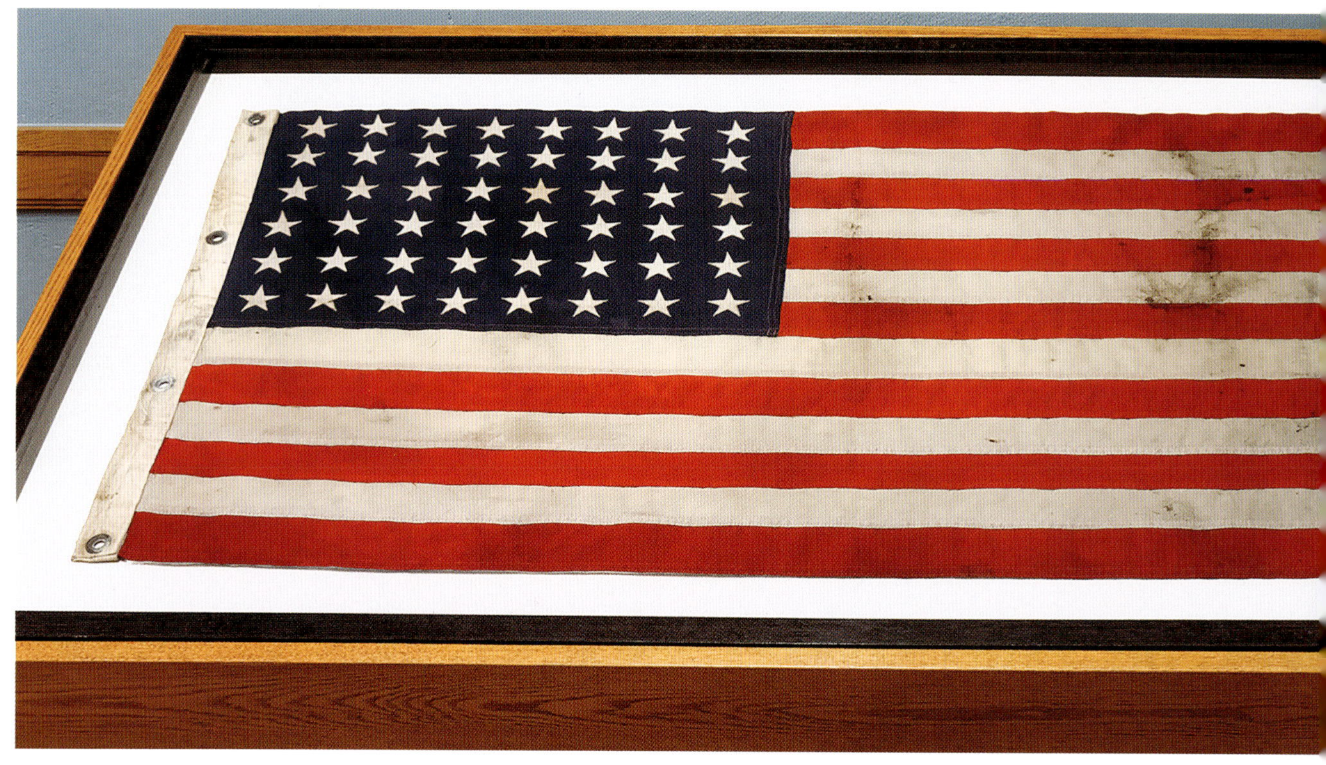

Flag retrieved from the deck of the USS Arizona *after it was sunk, Pearl Harbor, Hawai'i*

as a small island nation meant it lacked several critical resources on its home soil—namely oil for fuel and iron ore for steel. In mid-1940, the United States scaled back the supply of raw materials being sent to Japan for use in the war against China. This raised tensions between the countries. Partly because of the loss of access to vital raw materials, Japan devised a plan (known as the Southern Operation) to take control of the western Pacific. The goal was to attack and capture the American and Allied strongholds and resource-rich territories in the western Pacific and destroy the American fleet at Pearl Harbor.

Over the next year, Japan began moving into parts of Indochina to gain access to resources for the essential raw materials the United States was no longer providing. The United States froze Japanese assets on July 26, 1941, and shortly after put in place an embargo on fuel shipments to Japan.

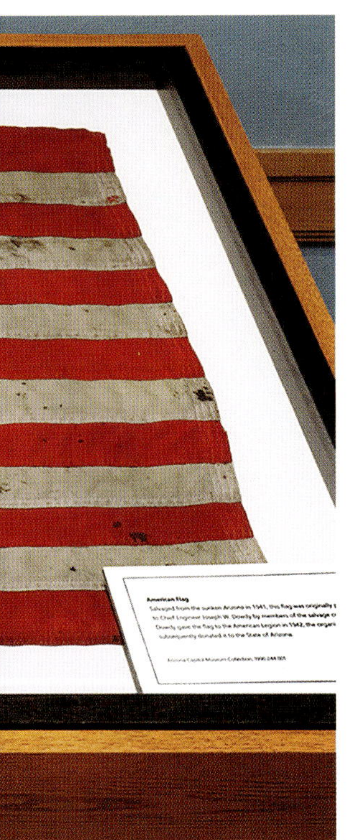

The two countries still tried to reconcile their differences. In the ensuing negotiations, the United States sought Japan's complete withdrawal from China. Japan requested guaranteed delivery of raw materials, specifically aviation fuel. Both countries balked at the other's demands. Those talks were stalled in early December of 1941.

On December 7, 1941, the Japanese embassy in Washington, DC, was supposed to deliver a message withdrawing from the negotiations thirty minutes prior to the attack on Pearl Harbor—a de facto declaration of war. Slow communications between Japan's foreign ministry and the Japanese embassy meant that Japan's message was delivered to US Secretary of State Cordell Hull after the air raid had occurred instead.

To execute the attack, more than 400 planes from six Japanese aircraft carriers were launched in two waves, an hour apart, starting at 6:00 a.m., from a point 230 miles (370 km) north of Hawai'i. The first wave of torpedo, dive, and horizontal bombers—protected by Zero fighters—arrived at Pearl Harbor at 7:55 a.m. The entire attack lasted almost two hours. The Japanese sank six of eight battleships, including the *Arizona*, that were docked at Ford Island in the harbor. Numerous other ships were sunk or damaged. The raid destroyed 188 aircraft.

US commanders in the Pacific were caught off-guard by the attack. Though the general feeling was that the United States would eventually enter the war with Japan, most military leaders believed that Japan would attack the Philippines before they tried for Hawai'i. Several warning signs that could have averted the devasting attack were missed. Luckily, the aircraft carriers stationed at Pearl Harbor were out on maneuvers, and the Japanese planes were never able to find them.

The attack on Pearl Harbor pulled the United States into war with all three Axis powers: Japan, Germany, and Italy. President Roosevelt declared war against Japan the next day, on December 8. Three days later, on December 11, Germany and Italy declared war on the United States.

In the week following Pearl Harbor, Japan also attacked other US holdings in the Pacific. Japanese forces shelled Midway Island on December 7, 1941, but the American troops there were able to maintain control. Japanese forces captured Guam on December 10 and Wake Island on December 23. They launched an attack on the Philippines on December 8, 1941, and the final surrender by American and Philippine forces occurred on the island of Corregidor in Manila Bay on May 6, 1942.

The USS *Arizona* flag commemorates the sacrifice of those who fought and died in the battle. The *Arizona* itself remains a solemn memorial to those who perished in the attack.

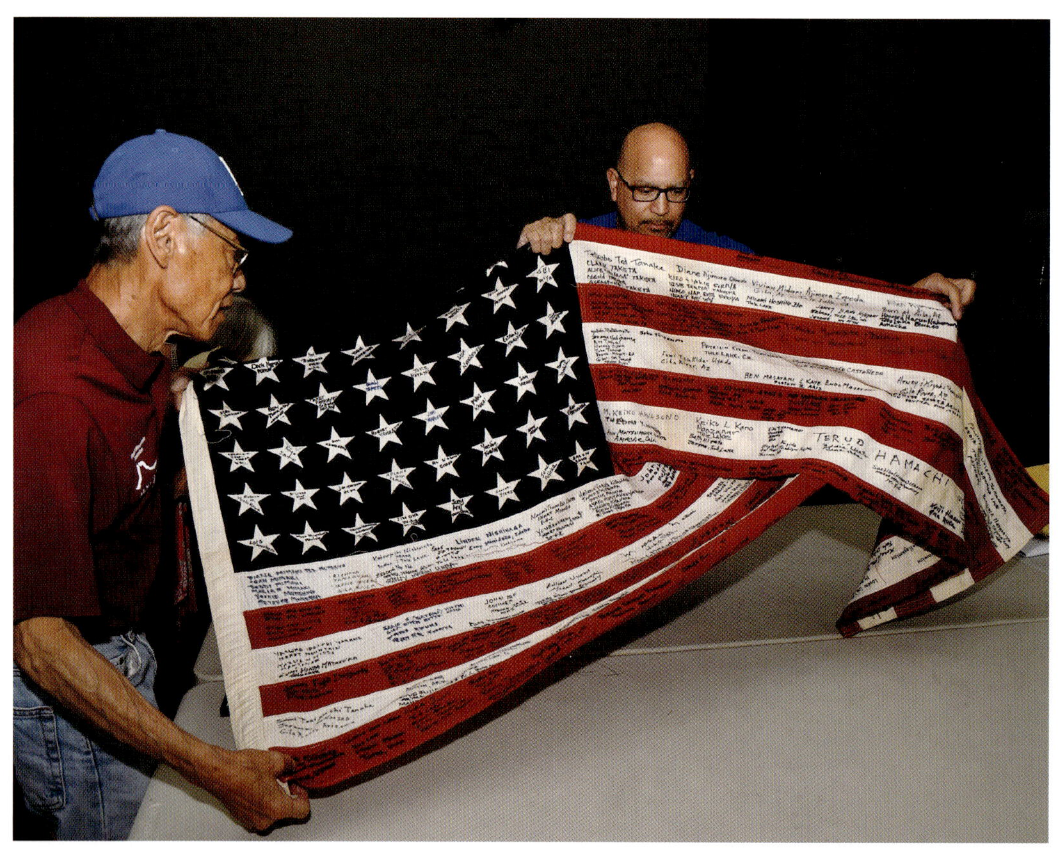

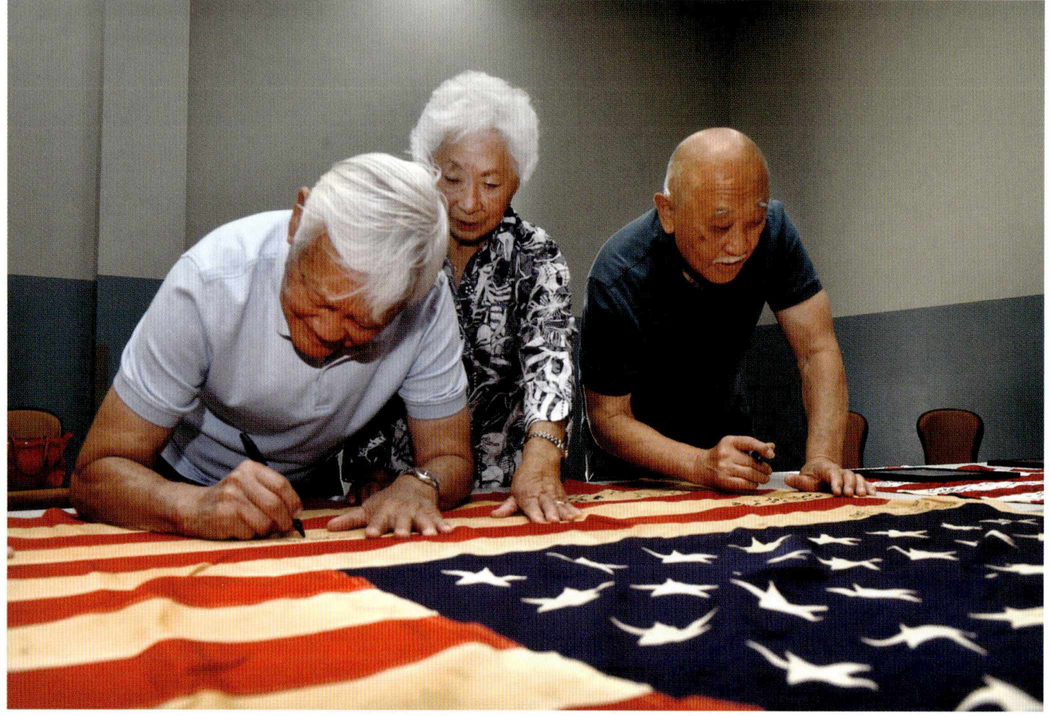

FLAG SIGNED BY JAPANESE INTERNMENT SURVIVORS

A Dark Stain

DATE: February 19, 1942–March 30, 1946

EVENT LOCATION: Japanese internment camps

CURRENT FLAG LOCATION: Japanese American Museums of San Jose and Los Angeles, California

Opposite, top: *The forty-eight-star American flag signed by survivors of Japanese internment camps is held by Dale Kumitomi, who was born at the Heart Mountain, Wyoming, internment camp, and Santa Clara County Superior Court Judge Johnny Cepeda Gogo, Camarillo, California, June 28, 2021*

Opposite, bottom: *Shigeru "Shig" Yabu, Irene Yabu, and Prentiss Uchida, internment camp survivors, sign a forty-eight-star American flag in Camarillo, California, June 28, 2021.*

On February 19, 1942, President Franklin Delano Roosevelt signed the unprecedented Executive Order 9066. It was like no other approved by an American leader up to that time. The order allowed the military to declare certain areas of the United States, like the West Coast, off-limits to "any or all persons." Beginning on March 24, 1942, the military started rounding up and evicting West Coast residents of Japanese ancestry—citizens and noncitizens alike. They were sent to concentration camps in Arizona, Arkansas, California, Colorado, Idaho, Utah, and Wyoming on the pretext of protecting national security and preventing espionage.

After the bombing of Pearl Harbor, emotions in the country were running high. It was logical to be concerned that Japan might have spies and operatives in the United States (which they did). Still, Japanese Americans weren't allowed due process to contest their incarceration. They were rounded up regardless of whether or not they were US citizens. They had only a few days to pack what they could carry. They were forced to leave their homes and businesses abandoned—many never to return.

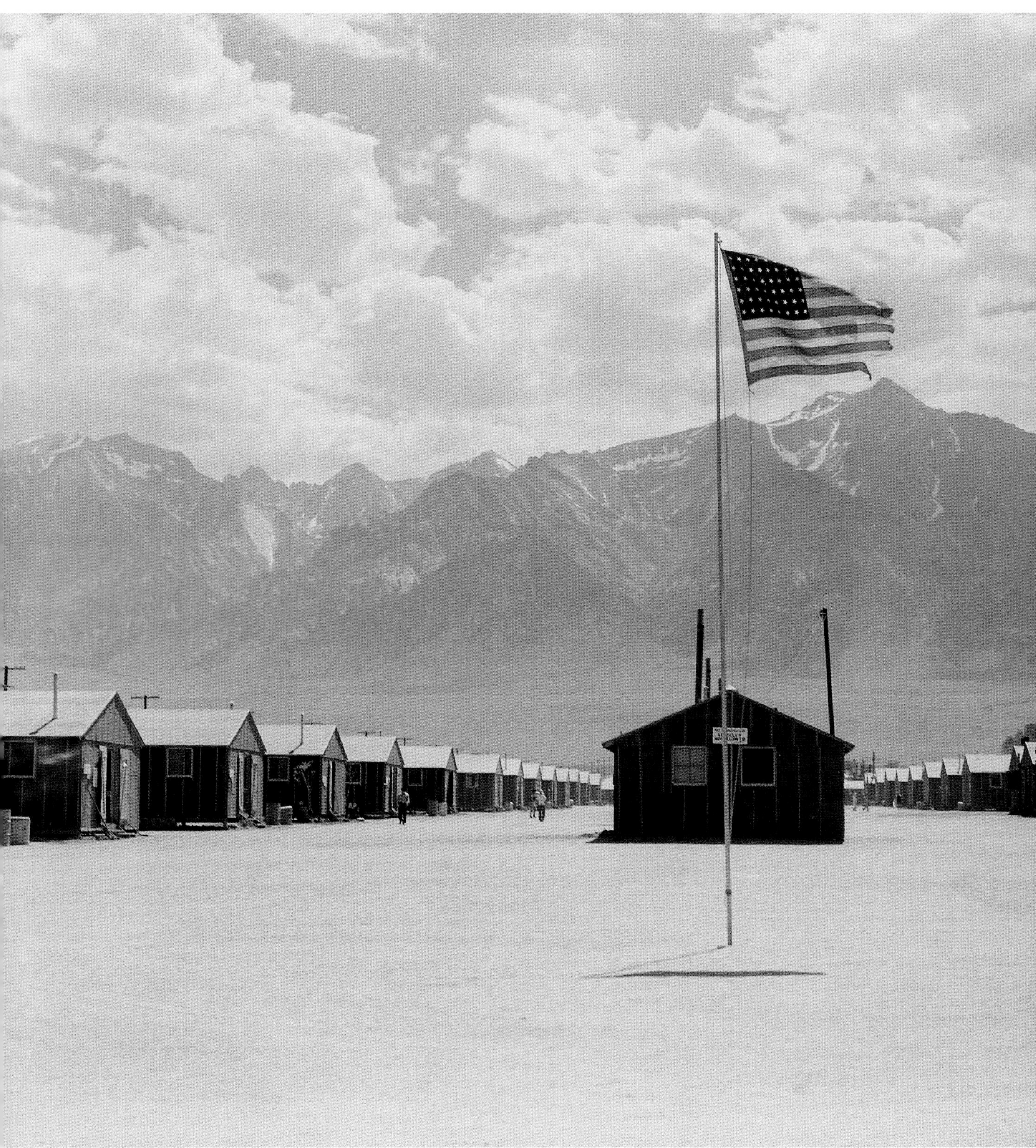

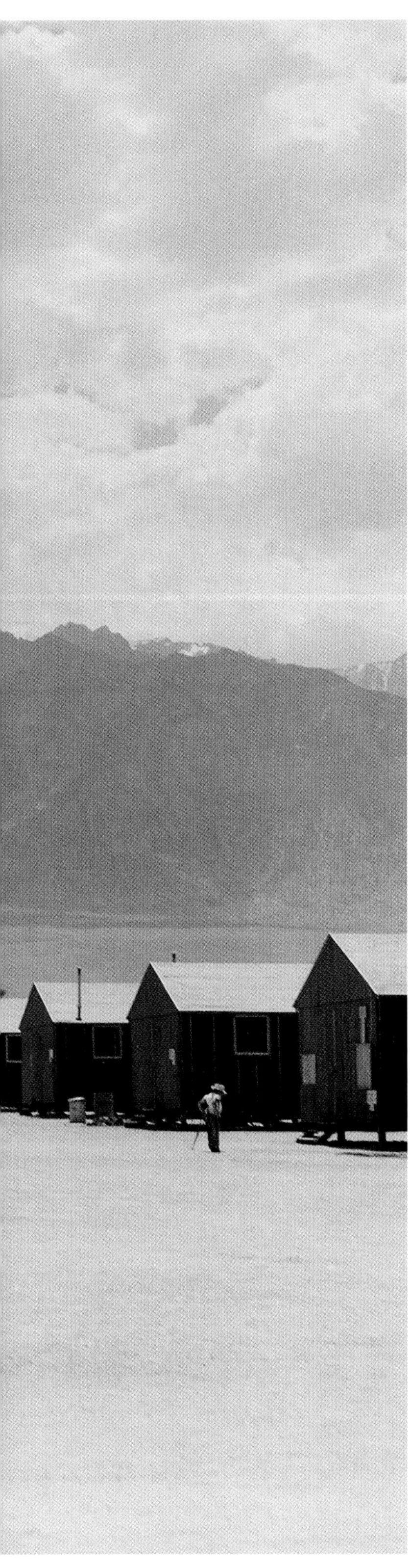

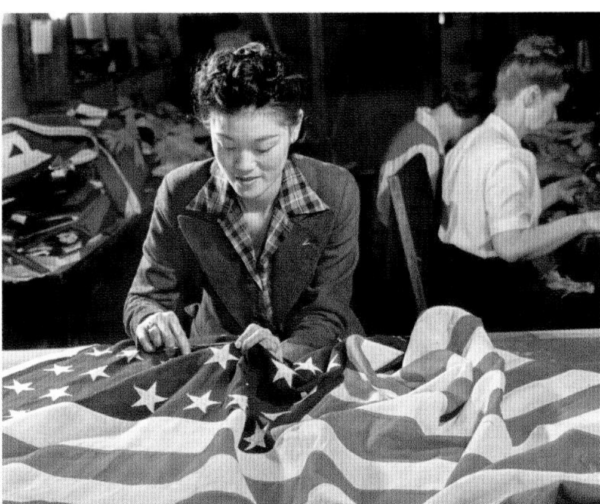

Opposite: *Flag flying at Manzanar Japanese Internment Camp, Manzanar, California, July 3, 1942*

Left: *Former internee, Mrs. Yoshiye Abe, making American flags in a Denver factory, 1942–1945*

Roughly 125,000 people were incarcerated, most in "relocation centers"—a slightly less troubling label for what were, in effect, concentration camps. Two-thirds of those incarcerated were American citizens. Many had been born in the United States.

Fred Toyosaburo Korematsu was born in Oakland, California, in 1919 to parents who had immigrated from Japan. He was proud to be an American, but growing up, he faced discrimination in school and later in the workplace. After Japan's attack on Pearl Harbor (page 94), Korematsu, at twenty-two, was fired from his job as a welder due to his Japanese ancestry.

Korematsu refused to comply with Executive Order 9066. He felt it violated his rights as a citizen (and indeed, the Fifth Amendment outlines a citizen's right to a fair trial before any judgment may be passed on guilt or innocence). Initially Korematsu hid out, but he was arrested on May 30, 1942. The American Civil Liberties Union took Korematsu's case, which eventually ended up before the United States Supreme Court. The Court's ruling on December 18, 1944, is considered one of the low points in American jurisprudence. The verdict in *Korematsu v. United States* upheld Korematsu's conviction for ignoring Executive Order 9066, and the judgment gave de facto permission for the government to continue incarcerating individuals without a fair trial.

In contrast to that ruling, on the same day, the Court released its ex parte decision in the case of Mitsuye Endo, another Japanese American contesting her incarceration in the camps. The Court found that the US War Relocation Authority did not have the power to incarcerate citizens who had demonstrated their loyalty to the United States. Endo was considered trustworthy because she had never been to Japan, she had worked for the California state government, and her brother was serving in the US military.

The Japanese American concentration camps were prisons fenced in with barbed wire. The camp perimeter included guard towers with soldiers instructed to shoot anyone who ventured past the wire. There were seven reported instances of guards firing on and killing detainees. Housing conditions in the camps were not much better than the tarpaper shacks that sprang up during the Great Depression (page 87). The residential barracks were 120 feet (37 m) wide and 200 feet (61 m) long. In their barracks, each family was allotted a minimum of 200 square feet (19 m^2) and a maximum of 480 square feet (45 m^2), depending on the number of members—roughly equivalent to the size of a living room. The buildings were arranged in "blocks"—sets of fourteen barracks with a separate mess hall, a recreation building, laundry facilities, and showers and latrines for men and women. Made from uninsulated wood and heated with coal stoves, the facilities had limited amenities. Still, the camp detainees were resilient, forming churches, schools, and teams for sports like baseball. They created communities in their new surroundings and found purpose even in captivity.

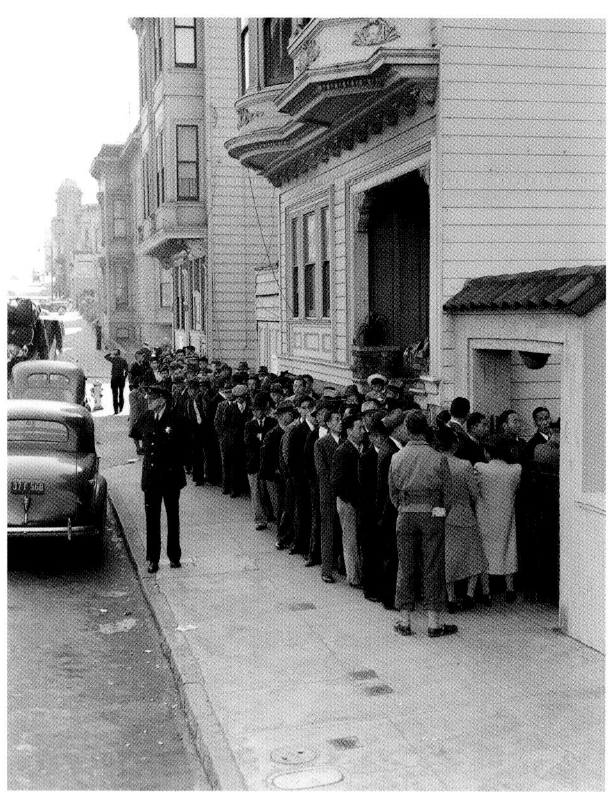

Japanese Americans line up to register in San Francisco before being sent to internment camps for the duration of the war, 1942

The last Japanese American concentration camp closed about four years after Roosevelt signed Executive Order 9066. Many camp internees who returned to the West Coast found their homes and businesses taken. Some moved to other parts of the country. Others struggled, having no resources to begin again. Over time, some reparations were authorized by the federal government, but it was too little, too late.

First celebrated in California in 2011 as Fred Korematsu Day of Civil Liberties and the Constitution, it is observed on January 30 to honor Korematsu's efforts to advance civil rights. In 2018, Judge Johnny Cepeda Gogo of the Santa Clara County Superior Court of California met Korematsu's daughter while he was promoting the day of remembrance (now celebrated in six other states as some form of Fred Korematsu Day). Judge Gogo wanted to find a way to honor the suffering and sacrifice of the internees of the Japanese American concentration camps and bring attention to the prized, yet tenuous nature of American civil liberties. He told the *Palo Alto Weekly*: "What I hope people learn is that we as American citizens have to be vigilant in protecting our constitutional rights because as we've seen during World War II, the government made a decision to bypass the Constitution and mass incarcerate over 120,000 Japanese Americans and Japanese nationals in the United States, primarily on the West Coast, without the due process of law."

Judge Gogo purchased several forty-eight-star American flags—the flag in use at the time of the Japanese American internment camps—and sent them around the United States to have them signed by surviving camp detainees. He donated the signed flags to museums; one went to the Japanese American Museum of San Jose, and one went to the Japanese American Museum of Los Angeles. Currently the flags contain more than 500 signatures of those who were imprisoned based on Executive Order 9066.

DEMONSTRATED LOYALTY

★★★

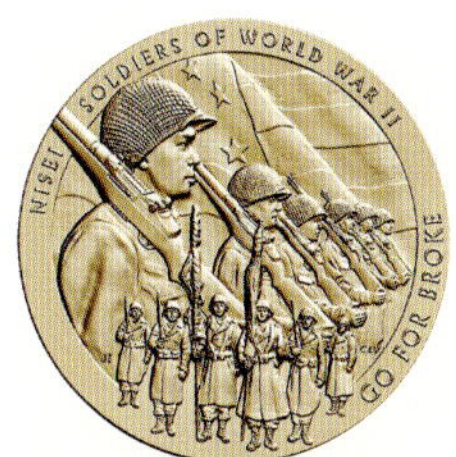

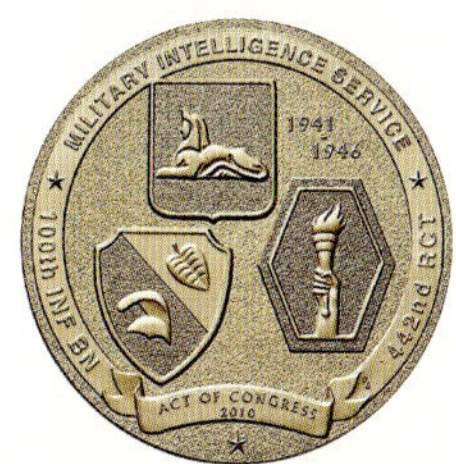

Nisei Soldiers of World War II Congressional Gold Medal, front (top) and back, 2011

Some 1,500 Japanese Americans living in the United States were arrested shortly after the bombing of Pearl Harbor on suspicion of being spies. However, the FBI and the Department of Justice did not truly consider the general population of Japanese Americans to be a significant threat to the country's security. Just as the attacks on 9/11 induced unwarranted threats and assaults on Muslim Americans and others of Middle Eastern ancestry, after the bombing of Pearl Harbor in 1941, the public was leery of Japanese Americans. Some in the media fanned these fears, which helped justify the confinement of Japanese Americans in concentration camps.

The truth is that many Japanese Americans served valiantly in the United States army and other branches of the service during World War II—so much so that three units were awarded the Congressional Gold Medal for their service on November 2, 2011.

The 100th Infantry Battalion (part of the 442nd Regimental Combat Team) fought on the beaches of Anzio, Italy, in spring of 1944 and led the push to capture Rome. They received the Presidential Unit Citation.

To this day, the 442nd Regiment is the most highly decorated unit in American military history. More than 4,000 second-generation Japanese Americans (known as Nisei) made up the unit, and they earned more than 4,000 Bronze Stars and an equal number of Purple Hearts. The unit received seven Presidential Unit Citations between 1944 and 1946.

More than a thousand Japanese American servicemen helped translate and interpret Japanese military radio transmissions and interrogations of Japanese prisoners of war in the Pacific Theater. Their service is believed to have considerably shortened the length of the war with Japan and saved innumerable lives.

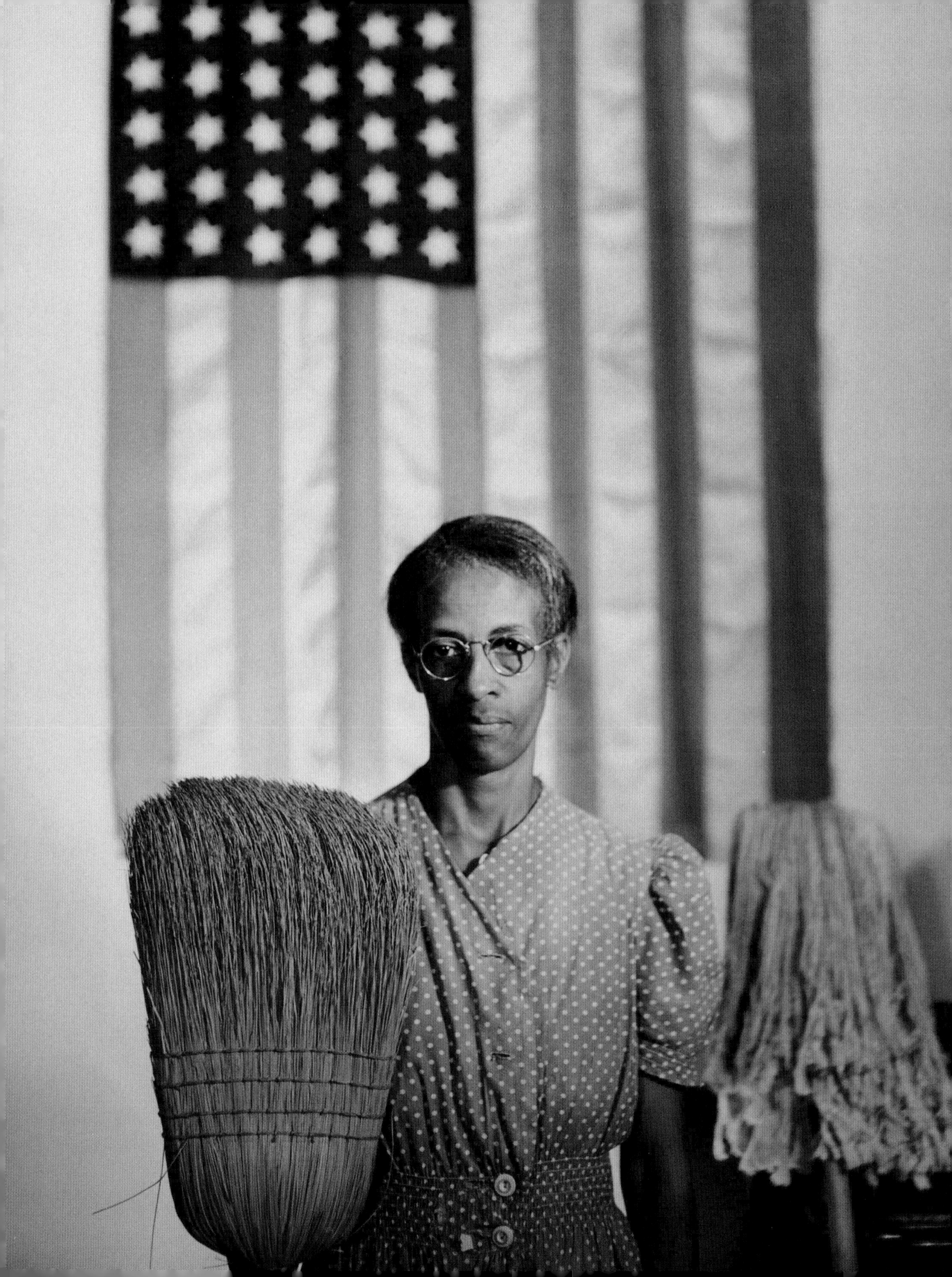

AMERICAN GOTHIC, BY GORDON PARKS

American Gothic

DATE: 1942

EVENT LOCATION: Farm Securities Administration, Washington, DC

CURRENT FLAG LOCATION: Unknown

Opposite: American Gothic, *FSA Headquarters, August 1942*

Gordon Parks was a largely self-taught photographer who became a modern-day renaissance man in the latter half of the twentieth century through his filmmaking, music, writing, poetry, and photography. As a Black youth growing up in Kansas in the 1920s, his desire to achieve was initially met with discrimination. His mother died when he was fourteen. The youngest of fifteen children, he was sent to live with an older sister in Minnesota. After a series of jobs, he found work as a waiter and porter on the North Coast Limited Railroad. He became interested in photography by looking at images in magazines discarded by rail passengers. He was intrigued by the images of Depression-era migrant workers as well as fashion photographs in these periodicals.

On one rail trip to Seattle, he photographed the waterfront area of the city. Returning to Minneapolis, he had his film processed by a Kodak lab. When he picked up his processed photographs, a Kodak employee complimented his photographic work and offered to give him an exhibition. This showing of his work steered Parks into producing fashion photographs for local stores in Minneapolis. In 1942, Parks received a Julius Rosenwald Fellowship (a grant program geared toward African American

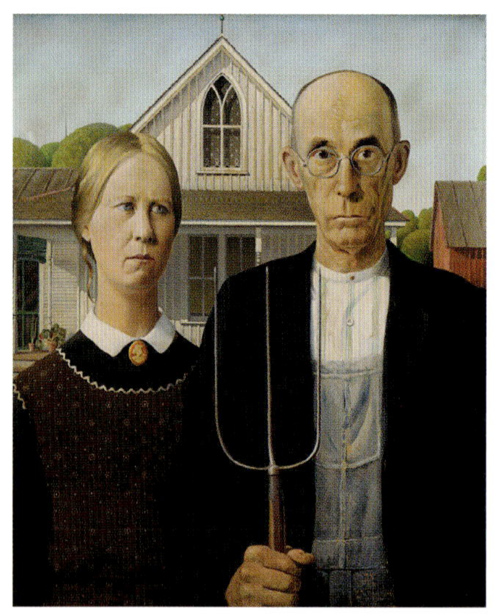

American Gothic, painting by Grant Wood, Chicago Art Institute, Chicago, Illinois, 1930

artists, authors, and scholars, along with non-Blacks working in the field of race relations). This in turn led Parks to work for the Farm Securities Administration (FSA) that same year. The photographers of the FSA were documenting the effects of the Great Depression and Dust Bowl on farmers and rural towns for the United States government (page 87).

Parks moved to Washington, DC, to work for the FSA. As he began exploring the city, he found that, even in the nation's capital, Blacks were treated as second-class citizens. Parks befriended Ella Watson, a cleaning woman at the FSA headquarters. Watson introduced Parks to the Black community in Washington, and he began documenting the lives of the people.

One of Parks's most important photographs, *American Gothic*, is of Watson in the FSA headquarters holding a broom and mop in front of a forty-eight-star American flag. The photograph references Grant Wood's painting of the same title, which is a tableau of an Iowa farmer and his daughter in front of their gothic-style farmhouse.

There are several differences between Wood's and Parks's *American Gothic* works—a key one being fiction versus documentation, respectively. The incongruence between the subjects in the two pieces is also palpable in the lighting, backgrounds, and implements they clutch. The farmer's pitchfork in Wood's painting alludes to a life of hard work, but in the background is a bright, clean house with potted plants on the porch, a barn painted a deep shade of red, and green trees beyond, displaying seemingly reasonable living circumstances. In Parks's photograph, in contrast, Watson's broom and mop denote manual labor and the low reward found in occupations open to Black Americans in the 1940s. The harsh lighting portrays a tough existence, overshadowed by a vivid flag that represents a life and livelihood still out of reach for most Blacks at the time—and, to some extent, still today.

One similarity exists in that all three subjects possess the same dour countenance. And though the farmer stares straight at the viewer, the farmer's daughter and Watson have almost the exact same expression: flat, tight lips and eyes cast slightly down and to the side.

Park's photograph exposed the dichotomy between the standard of living for white citizens compared with Black citizens during the mid-twentieth century. The whereabouts of the flag shown in Parks's *American Gothic* are unknown, but the photograph can be found in the Library of Congress and numerous art and history museum collections.

D-DAY LANDING FLAG

The Greatest Armada

DATE: June 6, 1944

EVENT LOCATION: Utah Beach, Normandy, France

CURRENT FLAG LOCATION: National Museum of American History, Washington, DC

As daylight broke on June 6, 1944, Lieutenant Howard Vander Beek looked to the aft of his boat, *Landing Craft Control 60* (*LCC 60*). Behind him, he saw hundreds of other landing crafts and ships, a small portion of the more than 7,000 watercraft joining the invasion of Normandy—a day that would soon be known simply as D-Day. Then he turned back to his job: shepherding tanks and soldiers ashore.

Vander Beek later described the landing scene: "At some time I looked astern and saw what lay at sea behind us: the greatest armada the world had ever known, the greatest it would ever know. I must have been overwhelmed by the sight as I clung to the rail for a moment to take in the magnitude of that assembled fleet: many great, gray ships majestically poised in their positions; larger numbers of unwieldy landing vessels heaved by the heavy sea; and countless numbers of smaller amphibious craft tossed mercilessly by the waves."

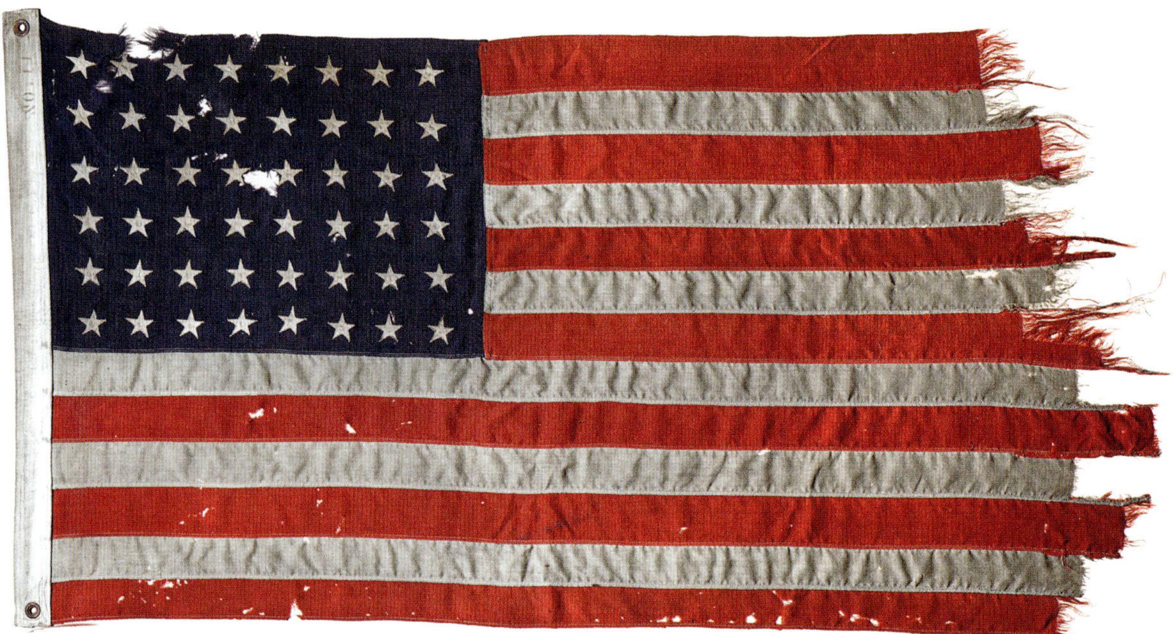

Flag that flew on Landing Craft Control 60 *on D-Day, June 6, 1940*

Vander Beek was an executive officer on *LCC 60*. LCCs were used to orchestrate the positioning of landing craft carrying troops and vehicles to the beaches. When the D-Day armada's first-line LCCs were sunk by German mines and shelling and others foundered, Vander Beek's vessel became the primary director of the landing craft and swimming tanks (dual-drive tanks that incorporated flotation screens and propellers for seaborne travel). The rough seas of that day were too much for some of the swimming tanks, and a few sank to the bottom.

Vander Beek directed landing craft until he was relieved that afternoon. He noted the morale boost that seeing the American flags gave his crew in his 1995 memoir, *Aboard the LCC 60*: "Flashes of color lifted our spirits, particularly those of the American flag waving majestically over the beach. Knowing that it had been raised by men whom we had led in the assault fed our pride."

When the D-Day landing was over, Vander Beek made a point of retrieving the American flag that had flown from the *LCC 60*. He carried the banner with him for the remainder of the war and kept it for the rest of his life. When he died in 2014, the flag was purchased at auction for $514,000 by Dutch art collector Bert Kreuk. Kreuk donated the flag to the National Museum of American History.

IWO JIMA FLAGS

A Tale of Two Flags

DATE: February 23, 1945

EVENT LOCATION: Mount Suribachi, Iwo Jima, Japan

CURRENT FLAG LOCATION: National Museum of the Marine Corps, Triangle, Virginia

Following: *Raising the flag on Mount Suribachi, Iwo Jima, Japan, February 23, 1945*

Joe Rosenthal's photograph of US Marines raising the American flag at the summit of Mount Suribachi on the Japanese Island of Iwo Jima is one of the most iconic images from World War II. It has been featured in news articles, posters, stamps, and even the Marine Corps War Memorial in Washington, DC—a massive 78-foot-tall (24 m) bronze sculpture depicting the event. Yet the manner in which Rosenthal captured the photograph, and some confusion over the sequence of events that led to the flag raising, has led to unnecessary controversy about this quintessential image.

In early 1945, a little more than three years after Japan attacked Pearl Harbor (page 94), the Japanese island of Iwo Jima was the site of one of the fiercest battles in world history. Why was an island less than 12 square miles (31 km^2) in size such an important military target?

Iwo Jima's location, less than 700 hundred miles (1,127 km) south of Japan's mainland, made it an ideal base for Allied troops to launch

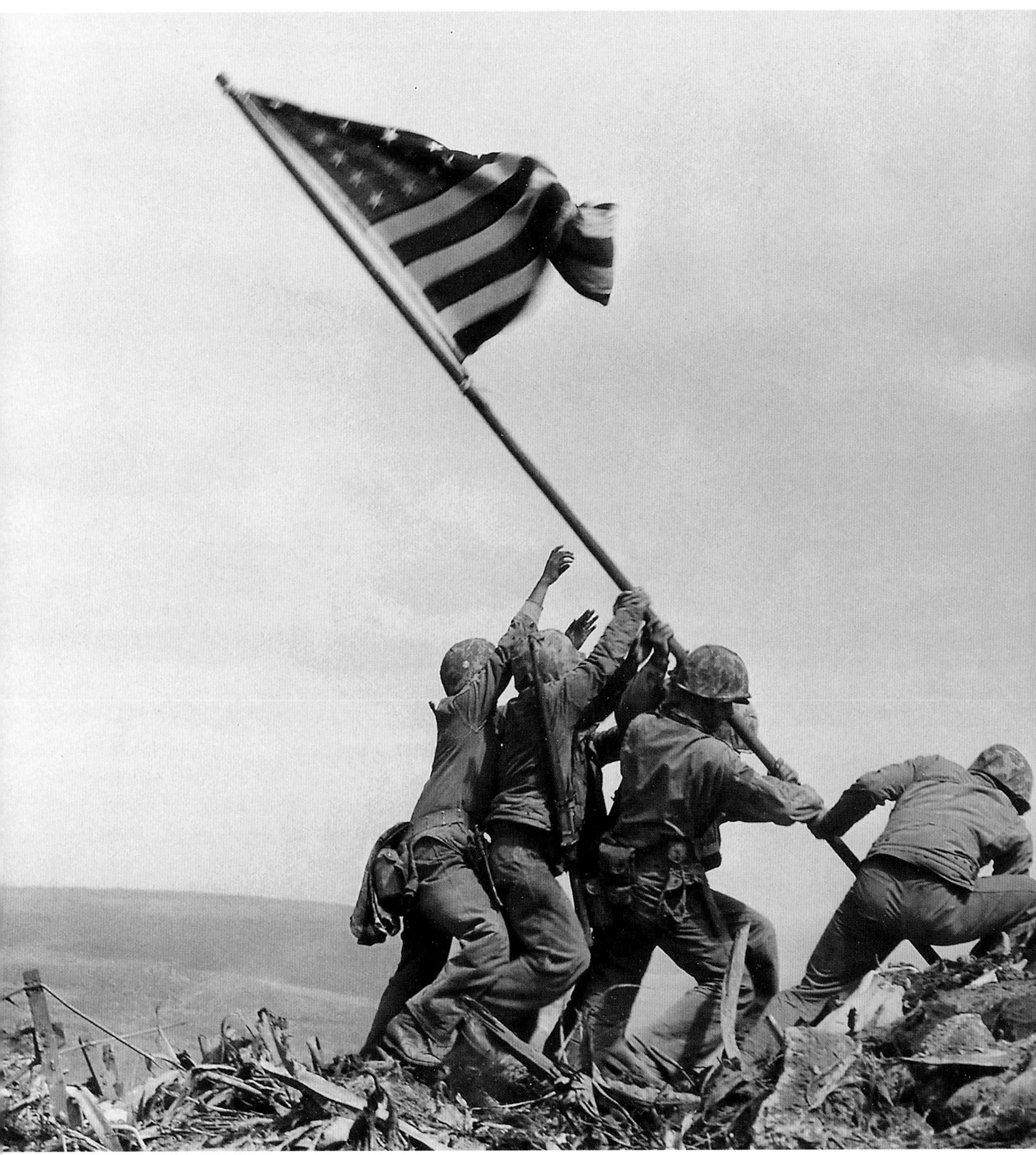

assaults. It also provided a critical foothold in the Allied effort to retake Pacific and Oceania islands that had been conquered by the Japanese. And it was one of a handful of islands in that part of the Pacific that were large and flat enough to support aircraft landing strips. It lay nearly alone in 2.5 million square miles (6.5 million km^2) of ocean, providing the only safe runways within thousands of miles.

The Japanese also realized the military importance of Iwo Jima. Along with affording a base of operations well east in the Pacific Ocean, Iwo Jima allowed the Japanese an observation point and facility for launching air patrols to track Allied bombers heading for mainland Japan. Japanese forces on the island had spent nearly a year preparing to be invaded. Iwo Jima's fortifications, bunkers, and tunnels were so well constructed and concealed that most survived the initial bombardment from US ships. Marine commanders had requested ten days of shelling of the island, but due to logistical concerns only three were allotted. Bad weather during those three days limited the navy's barrage even further.

Once the invasion began, American commanders determined that taking the highest point on the island, Mount Suribachi, would reduce the enemy's ability to direct fire against landing forces. American troops captured Mount Suribachi on the fifth day of the battle, February 23, 1945. Even so, the battle for Iwo Jima would continue for another month.

When the Americans reached the summit of Mount Suribachi, 554 feet (169 m) above sea level, they raised a small—54 by 28 inches (137 by 71 cm)—American flag. When the troops and sailors saw it, they began shooting in the air and blowing ships' horns in celebration.

Associated Press photographer Joe Rosenthal had been photographing the invasion for several days when he learned about the detachment of forty men that had headed up Mount Suribachi to raise the American flag. Rosenthal went up to photograph the flag raising. On the way, he ran into marine photographers Private Bob Campbell and Sergeant Bill Genaust and convinced them to climb to the summit with him. Then the three men ran into Marine Corps combat photographer Staff Sergeant Louis Lowery, who had photographed the flag being raised and was on his way down from the summit. Rosenthal noted in a February 1955 article for *Collier's Magazine* that upon hearing this news, he'd nearly turned around. But the three persevered.

Rosenthal and his companions were in for a surprise. They would soon learn that Colonel Chandler Johnson had asked for the flag that had been hoisted to be replaced with a bigger one, measuring 96 by 56 inches (244 by 142 cm). The troops' response to the original flag's raising had been so powerful that the US commanders hoped a larger flag would be

Opposite: *Two soldiers with the flag looking to the northwest from the summit of Mount Suribachi, 1945*

seen by more troops and have an even greater effect on morale. (Colonel Johnson commanded the Second Battalion, Twenty-Eighth Marine Regiment that captured Mount Suribachi. Johnson was killed on Iwo Jima one week later.)

As Rosenthal, Campbell, and Genaust reached the summit, they saw a group of Marines preparing to raise the replacement flag. Rosenthal hastily positioned himself to get a good vantage point. He saw the flag starting to rise out of the corner of his eye and quickly pushed the shutter release. He didn't think he got much of a photograph, so he took a couple of others, including one in which he asked the Marines to pose around the flag they had just raised.

The rest is history. When Rosenthal returned to Guam, where he was based, and before he even knew which photo everyone was so excited about, someone asked him if he had posed the image. He said yes, thinking they meant the one of the troops standing around the already raised flag. This mistaken comment birthed the erroneous story that Rosenthal had made the soldiers re-create the flag raising and pose for the now famous image. Adding to the confusion was the fact that Rosenthal had photographed the second flag raising on Mount Suribachi that morning.

From his perspective, Rosenthal understood why the image was important, but he considered his role in its creation minor. He believed that the soldiers who stormed the beaches of Iwo Jima and the men who captured Mount Suribachi deserved the credit.

Because of the two flag raisings, there has been some mix-up regarding the identity of the Marines in the photograph. Current opinion holds that the men who raised the flag were Corporal Harlon Block, Corporal Harold P. Keller, Private First Class (PFC) Ira Hayes, PFC Harold Schultz, PFC Franklin Sousley, and Sergeant Michael Strank.

Block, Sousley, and Strank (along with Marine photographer Bill Genaust) all died on Iwo Jima in the following days. Through Rosenthal's photograph, these individuals exemplify the bravery and sacrifice of all those who fought for and served the United States in World War II.

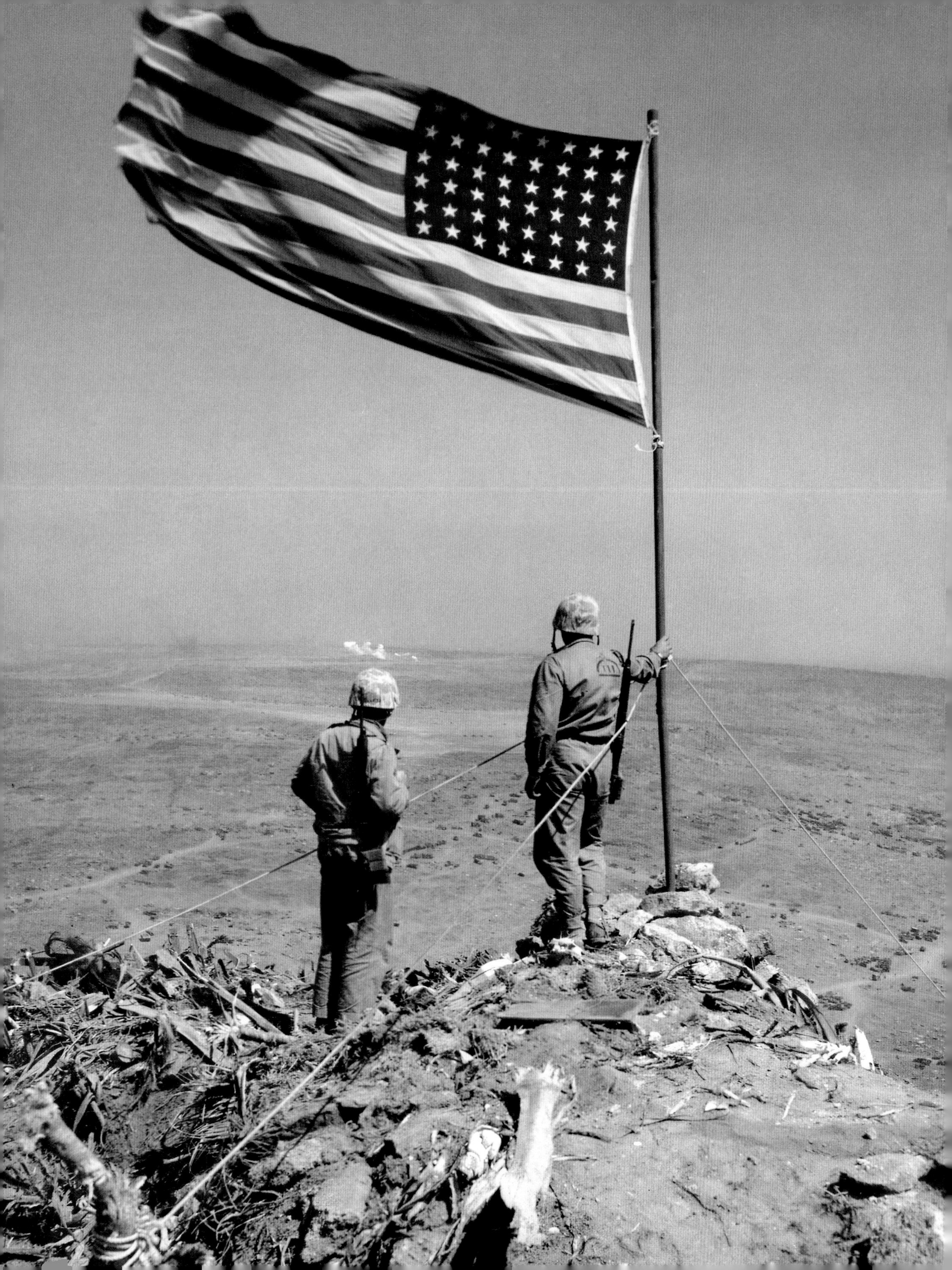

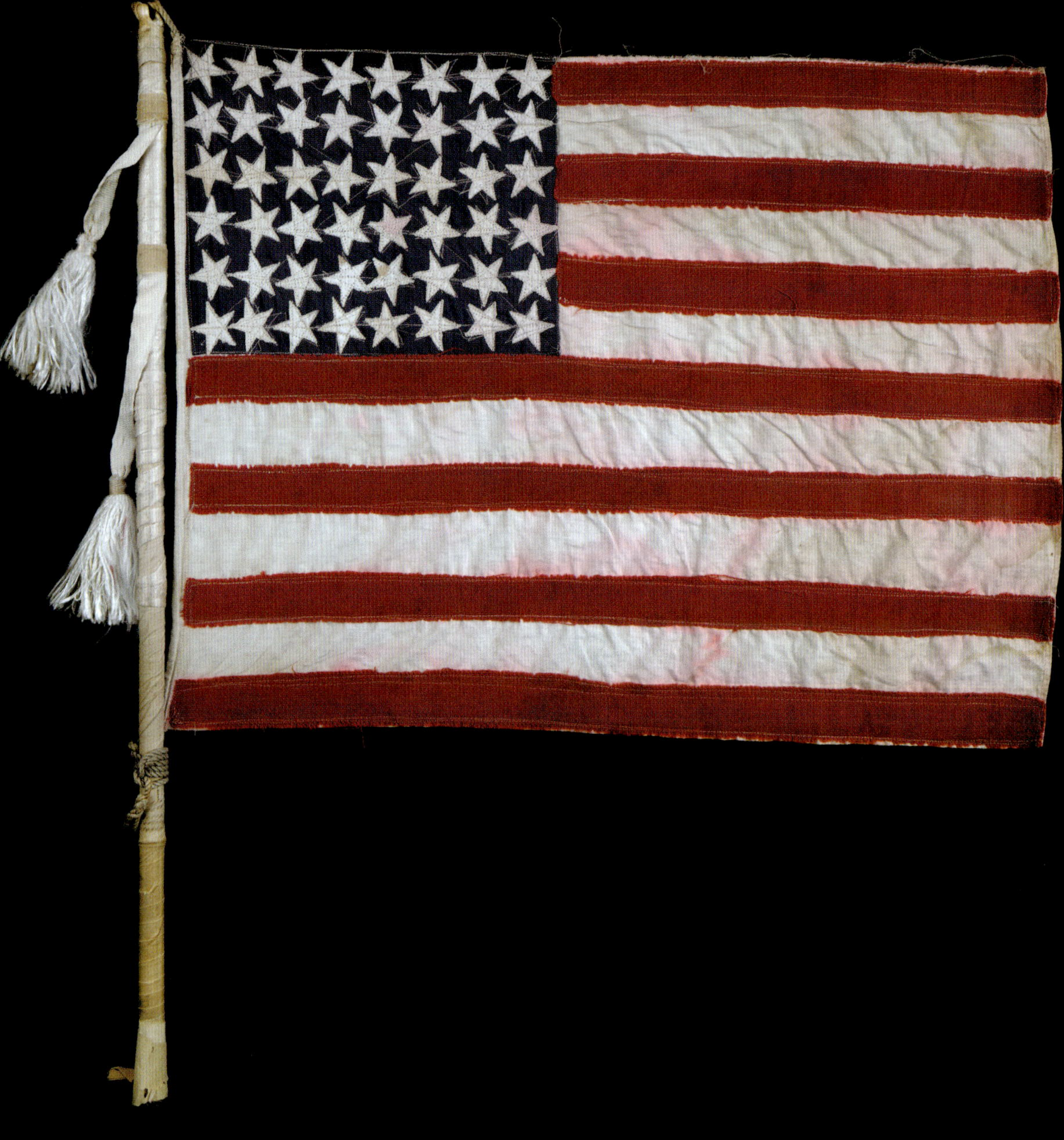

PRIVATE JOSEPH O. "JOSE" QUINTERO POW FLAG

One Flag and Two Soldiers

DATE: August 15, 1945

EVENT LOCATION: Niigata Labor Camp 5B, Japan

CURRENT FLAG LOCATION: National Museum of American History, Washington, DC

Opposite: *Flag made by Joseph Quintero while a POW at the Niigata Labor Camp 5B in Japan, 1945*

It was August 15, 1945. The news of Japan's surrender was broadcast over a radio set up for the guards to hear. Though the prisoners of war at Niigata Labor Camp 5B could not understand much Japanese, the few bits of information they garnered—coupled with the guards' solemn and doleful body language—told the story. An interpreter confirmed the news. Emperor Hirohito had surrendered—World War II was finally over. The official armistice would be signed aboard the USS *Missouri* on September 2, 1945. The prisoners knew nothing of the new, devastating weapons the Americans had unleashed on Hiroshima and Nagasaki. They would later learn that the city of Niigata had been on the list of possible atomic bomb targets if the Japanese had not surrendered.

Private First Class Joseph O. "Jose" Quintero was one of the POWs being held at Niigata. Upon hearing the news of the end of the war, he grabbed the small American flag he had clandestinely made and ran outside, waving it in jubilation. Just as he did, he heard an approaching plane heading toward the camp. He quickly realized it was an American bomber, and that its crew might mistake the POW camp for a military installation.

Just a few days earlier, on August 10, President Truman had paused the bombing of Japan by Allied forces to allow the Japanese government time to respond to the Allies' demand for unconditional surrender. Owing to a lack of appropriate response from Japan, and hoping to avoid the need to drop an atomic bomb on Tokyo to end the war, President Truman had ordered conventional bombing to resume on August 14, the day before the Japanese surrendered.

Not knowing whether the bomber crew had heard the news of the armistice, Quintero climbed on top of one of the camp buildings, still waving his flag. The guards could have killed him just for having the flag; he and his fellow prisoners had taken a great risk in making it and keeping it hidden. But now he waved it at the sky, trying to catch the bomber crew's attention. He watched as the plane opened its bomb bay doors. Then he saw the pilot waggle the plane's wings, signaling that he understood there were American prisoners on the ground.

This daring act may have saved the lives of prisoners—and yet it was only one of Quintero's many brave accomplishments during the war. Quintero had enlisted in the army in January 1941, eleven months before the United States entered World War II. By 1942, he was in the Pacific Theater, serving in the Philippines on the island of Corregidor. He earned a Silver Star for his efforts in defending the island. When Corregidor fell to the Japanese, he was captured and held there in Cabanatuan Camp No. 2 as a prisoner of war. He was later taken by boat to Japan. On that voyage, he developed appendicitis. With no medical assistance from his captors, Quintero endured an appendectomy performed by an army doctor—a fellow POW—on the boat. There was no sterilization, anesthesia, antibiotics, painkillers, or surgical tools; the doctor used a razor blade and two spoons to remove his appendix. Quintero somehow survived the procedure.

While in the Niigata POW camp, Quintero decided to make an American flag as a symbol of optimism and resilience. He had witnessed the American flag being lowered after the surrender on Corregidor and hoped to see the colors restored there one day. Quintero befriended a Canadian prisoner who mended the Japanese soldiers' uniforms and sewed bedding for the camp hospital from worn-out clothing and other textile scraps. The Canadian had access to a sewing machine, and he provided some of his remnants of red, white, and blue material for Quintero to construct the flag.

In total, Quintero spent more than four years in POW camps—nearly the entire duration of World War II. After being repatriated to Texas, he moved to Albuquerque, New Mexico. He loaned his flag to National Guard Lieutenant General Edward Baca. Baca had served in Vietnam, eventually rising to the rank of general, and was chief of the National Guard Bureau—the first Latino to serve in this role. Shortly after assuming his duties, Baca awarded Quintero the New Mexico Medal of Valor with Palm. After the ceremony, Quintero permanently gifted Baca the flag he'd made in Niigata. He charged Baca with telling the prisoners' story around the United States, using the flag as a symbol of their resolve to survive and triumph.

Quintero succumbed to Parkinson's disease on November 12, 2000. He was buried in the Santa Fe National Cemetery in New Mexico.

Baca honored Quintero's request, and more. He delivered presentations with the flag in all fifty states and around the world. Before his death in 2020, Baca promised to donate Quintero's flag to the Smithsonian National Museum of American History. His estate made good on his promise, and the flag is now included in the museum's permanent collection.

1946

to

1969

Postwar Prosperity and Disparity

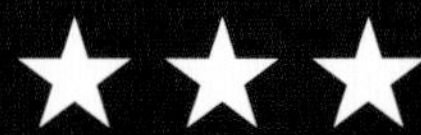

WORLD WAR II PUSHED AMERICA INTO A NEW phase of social discourse. Both women and people of color had stepped up to do their part in preserving democracy around the world. After the war, the American flag would become a symbol of the civil rights movement and the fight for women's rights and equality. The flag became a fixture in popular culture in post–World War II America.

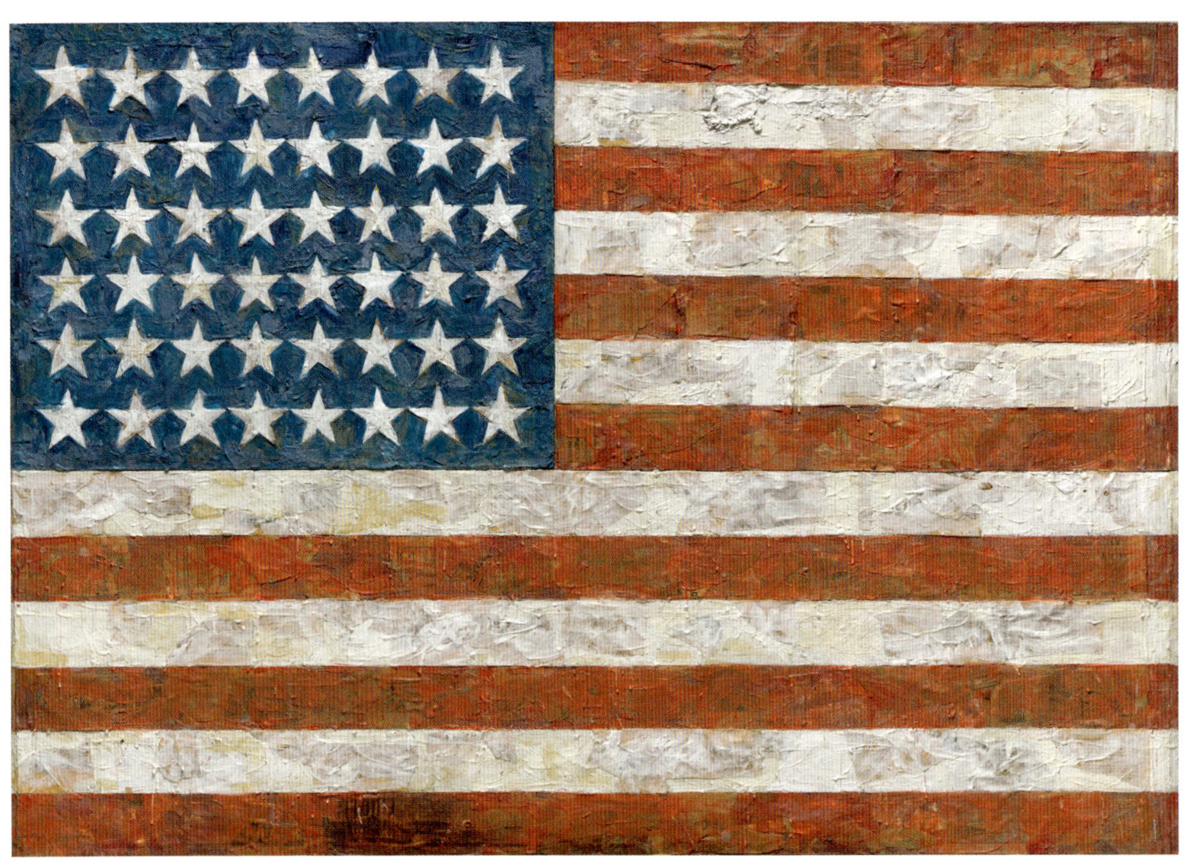

FLAG, *THREE FLAGS*, AND *FLAGS* BY JASPER JOHNS

Jasper Johns's American Flag Artwork

DATE: 1954–1955

EVENT LOCATION: New York City

CURRENT PAINTING LOCATION: Museum of Modern Art, New York City

Opposite: Flag, *Jasper Johns, encaustic painting and newspaper collage, 1954–1955*

Jasper Johns was one of the twentieth century's most influential painters. His use of common objects as subject matter influenced modern painting and helped birth the Pop Art movement in America. He is a student of semiotics—the study of symbols and signs and their implementation and interpretation. In 1954, Johns made the dramatic decision to destroy all his existing work (seven years' worth) and start afresh.

Not long after, Johns had a dream where he saw himself painting the American flag, and he decided to do so. In 1955, he finished *Flag*. With this piece, he turned the symbol of America into a pivotal work of modern art. Using the encaustic method, Johns applied pigment combined with hot wax to strips of newspaper, which allowed some of the newsprint's text to bleed through to the surface. The pigment-embedded wax retained the

Right: Three Flags, *Jasper Johns, encaustic painting, 1958*

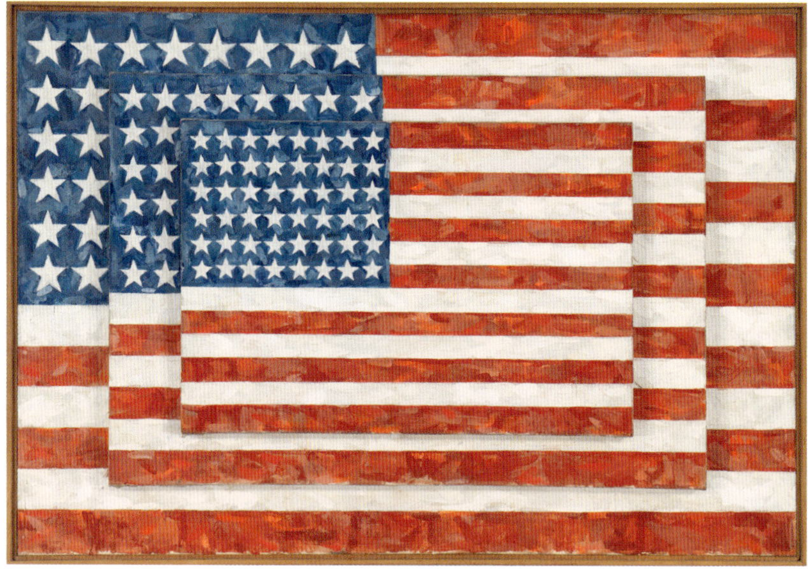

evidence of his brushstrokes. This effect gives the painting a depth and texture that traditional oil or acrylic paint don't afford. The newspaper text—though mostly illegible—hints at the many layers of history and meanings the American flag carries.

But what was the meaning of the painting? Johns left the interpretation of *Flag* up to individual viewers to determine from their own experiences and perspectives. Speaking about his work, Johns stated, "Everyone is of course free to interpret the work in his own way. I think seeing a picture is one thing and interpreting it is another." When asked if the work was a painting or a flag, Johns replied, "Both."

In his art, Johns often portrayed common, basic objects like letters, numbers, and bull's-eyes in new ways, presenting viewers with the opportunity to look at ordinary objects as extraordinary things of beauty and intrigue. By blurring the line between works of art and everyday objects, Johns forced viewers to consider representationalism juxtaposed with symbolism.

Flag was a harbinger of the Pop Art movement of the late 1950s and 1960s, led by artists like Roy Lichtenstein, Robert Rauschenberg, and Andy Warhol. Critics agree that *Flag* is one of the twentieth century's most important works of modern art. By removing the American flag from its usual context and treating it as an ordinary object to be reproduced as if in a still life or genre painting, Johns allows viewers to discard the patriotic burden the flag normally carries and lets them study the design, texture, and depth of the piece.

Johns produced dozens of artworks with American flags as their main elements. His *Three Flags*, created using the same encaustic painting method, features three paintings of the American flag mounted over one another in ever decreasing size. Johns again asks viewers to pay attention to the object and not its political or historical significance.

Johns created another series composed of inverted chroma flags, including *Flags* (where the red, white, and blue colors are replaced with green, black, and orange, respectively). These were designed so that when viewers stared at the work for thirty seconds and then turned to look at a white wall or surface, the latent image of a flag, with the opposite colors—red, white, and blue—would appear. This effect is due to the brain's effort to "color compensate"—to neutralize any color by adding the opposite color to the observer's vision. If you've ever worn heavily tinted green ski googles or sunglasses, you may have experienced the same effect when you removed them. Your brain was compensating for the overabundance of green light by adding magenta to your vision; when you removed the green glasses, the world may have looked pink for a short time before your eyes readapted to the unfiltered light. The reversed color scheme removes the patriotic bias normally triggered by the flag; the experience becomes a visual escapade rather than just a literal viewing of an American flag.

Though Johns's approach to the American flag appears to remove its political aspect, in truth he emphasized the use of the flag as political motivator with works like the *Moratorium* poster, which features the green, black, and orange inverted-color flag. *Moratorium* was commissioned by the Leo Castelli Gallery of Los Angeles to commemorate the Vietnam moratorium marches in 1969 (page 153). These protests were held in Washington, DC, New York, Detroit, Boston, Miami, and other sites around the country in response to the rising death toll of American soldiers in Vietnam. (During Richard Nixon's first year as president, more than 10,000 US service members were killed in Vietnam. That number equaled almost one-third of the 34,000 American troops killed in the previous ten years of the war.)

Johns's *Flag*, *Three Flags*, and *Flags* paintings stand out as symbols of the conflict between America's patriotism and the nation's complex relationship with the world.

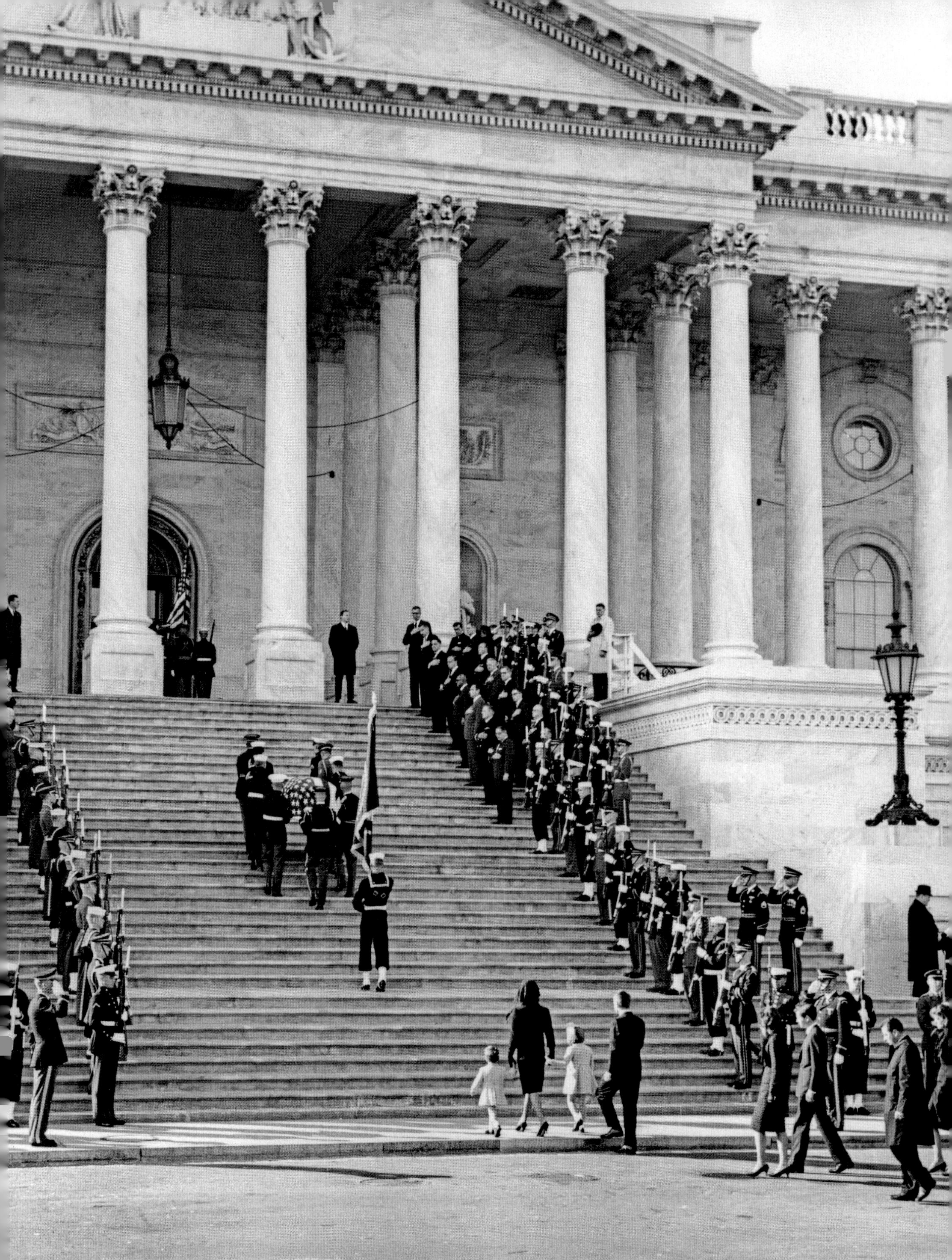

PRESIDENT KENNEDY'S CASKET FLAG

The End of Camelot

DATE: November 23–25, 1963

EVENT LOCATION: East Room of the White House, US Capitol, St. Matthew's Cathedral, and Arlington National Cemetery

CURRENT FLAG LOCATION: John F. Kennedy Presidential Library and Museum, Boston, Massachusetts

***Opposite:** Jacqueline Kennedy with her children and Attorney General Robert F. Kennedy, follow the flag-draped casket of President John F. Kennedy as they ascend the steps of the US Capitol, Washington, DC, November 24, 1963.*

Grassy knoll, Dealey Plaza, Book Depository, magic bullet—all are phrases that would become fodder for an array of conspiracy theories that grew after President John Fitzgerald Kennedy was assassinated on November 22, 1963, in Dallas, Texas. But it would take weeks and months for these phrases to catch the attention of ordinary citizens. Over the years, the theories of what really happened on that day have eclipsed the pain that was so palpable in the nation immediately after Lee Harvey Oswald gunned down America's thirty-fifth president.

The nation was grief-stricken after the death of JFK. A public viewing was scheduled in the Capitol Rotunda, and Kennedy's coffin—draped in the American flag—was placed on the same catafalque that had been used to support Abraham Lincoln's casket, also in the Capitol Rotunda, nearly a hundred years earlier (page 55). In less than twenty-four hours,

Below: Pallbearers lift the casket flag at the graveside services for the funeral of President John F. Kennedy, Arlington National Cemetery, Virginia, November 25, 1963.

a cortege of more than a quarter of a million mourners, many openly weeping, walked past Kennedy's casket to pay their respects.

The events surrounding the assassination are clouded with politics and intrigue. In the late 1950s and early 1960s, the Democratic platform was becoming more liberal, and conservative Southern Democrats were not pleased—especially with the push for racial equality and civil rights. President Kennedy was scheduled to speak to the Citizens Council at the Dallas Trade Mart that November afternoon. His real purpose for visiting the city that day was to calm a feud between Texas's governor, the conservative Democrat John Connally, and liberal Democrat Ralph Yarborough, US senator from Texas. (Ten years later, Connally would switch parties and join the Republicans.)

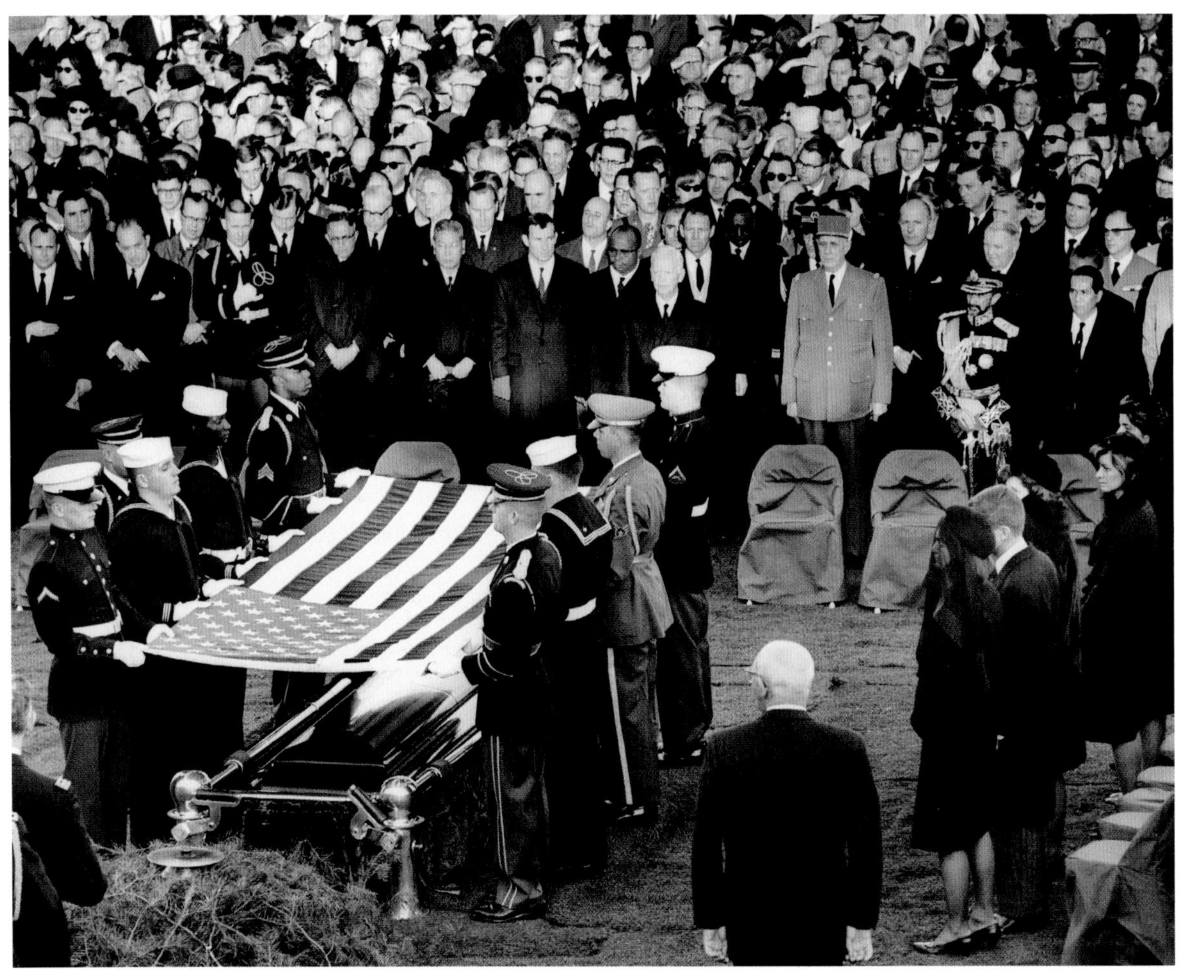

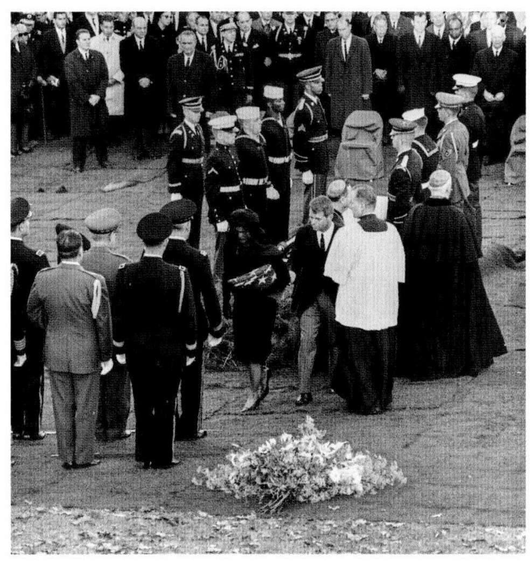

Top: *Jacqueline Kennedy (holding the flag) and US Attorney General Robert F. Kennedy depart President John F. Kennedy's graveside service, Arlington National Cemetery, Virginia, November 25, 1963.*

Bottom: *John F. Kennedy funeral flag, 1963*

President Kennedy, First Lady Jacqueline Kennedy, Governor Connally, and Connally's wife, Nellie, were all riding in an open convertible as part of a motorcade through downtown Dallas, heading to the Trade Mart. Kennedy was already preparing his reelection campaign and wanted to be visible to the crowds of onlookers. At 12:30 p.m. on November 22, 1963, Lee Harvey Oswald shot both Connally and Kennedy from the sixth-floor window of the Texas School Book Depository, where he worked. Oswald, a communist, had defected to Russia for a time and had ties to Cuba as well. His connections to communist regimes later led to speculation that the Soviets or Cubans were involved in the assassination. No conclusive proof has ever confirmed those theories.

Connally survived his injuries, but Kennedy was mortally wounded. He was pronounced dead at 1:00 p.m., a half hour after the shooting. Kennedy's body was placed aboard *Air Force One* to be flown back to Washington, DC. On board, just before takeoff, Lyndon Johnson was sworn in as the thirty-sixth president, with Jackie Kennedy at his side, her husband's blood still staining her clothing. The nation was in shock.

Back in Washington, an autopsy was performed. Then, on November 23, Kennedy's flag-draped casket was moved to the East Room of the White House, where he lay in repose with an honor guard at hand until the following morning, when the casket was moved by caisson to the Capitol Rotunda. The Rotunda viewing ended on November 25, and a funeral procession commenced from the Capitol to the White House. As Kennedy's coffin was carried down the Capitol steps for the procession, John Jr. raised his hand in salute to his father. It was his third birthday.

Again, Kennedy's flag-shrouded casket was moved by caisson. From the White House, the procession proceeded on foot about a mile to St. Matthew's Cathedral for the funeral service. An estimated one million mourners lined the route from the Capitol to St. Matthew's. After the service, Kennedy was buried in Arlington National Cemetery with full military honors. An honor guard composed of members from each branch of the armed services acted as pallbearers and ceremoniously removed the American flag from his casket, folded it, and delivered it to Jacqueline at the graveside. The flag was later donated by Kennedy's estate to the

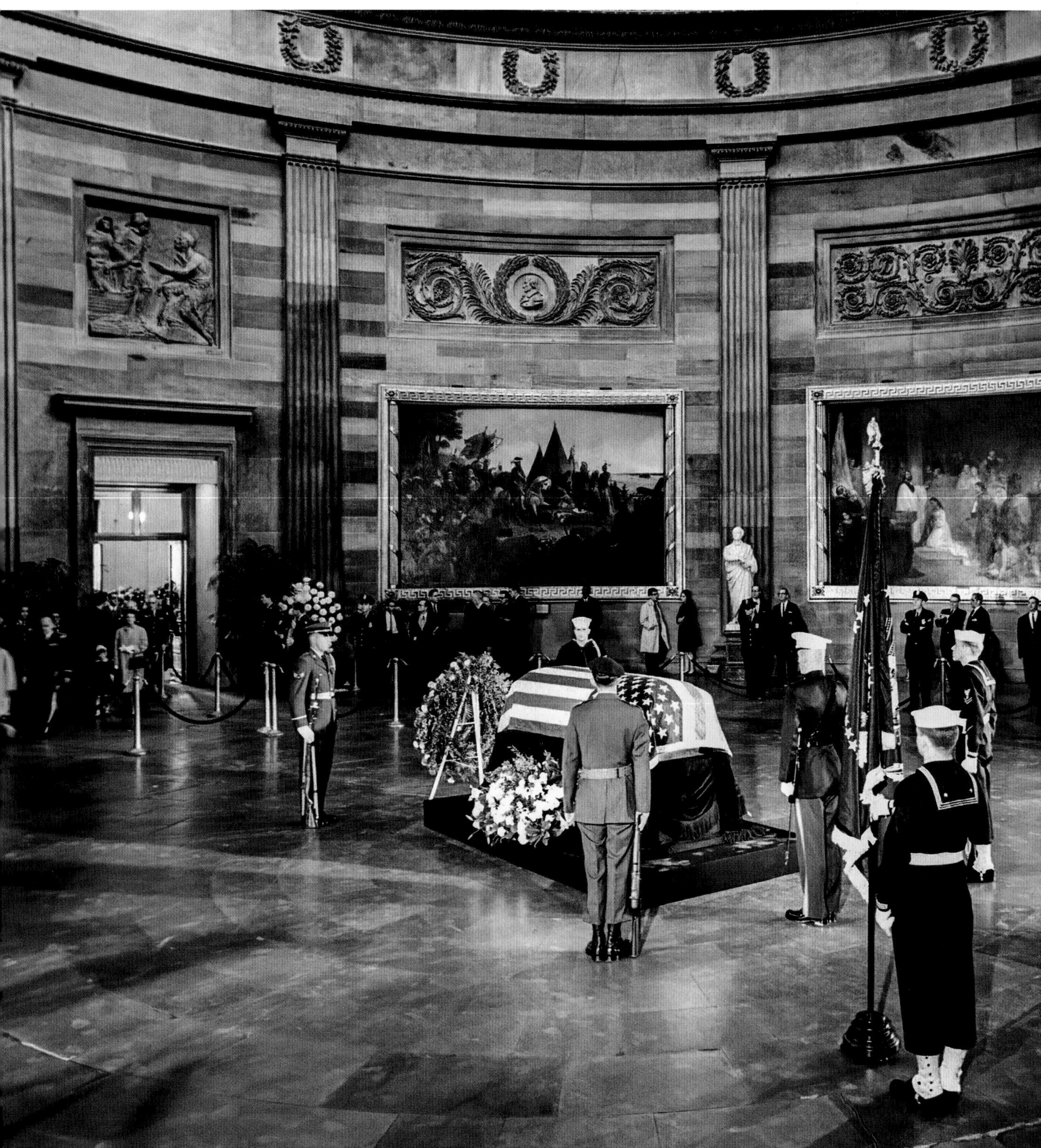

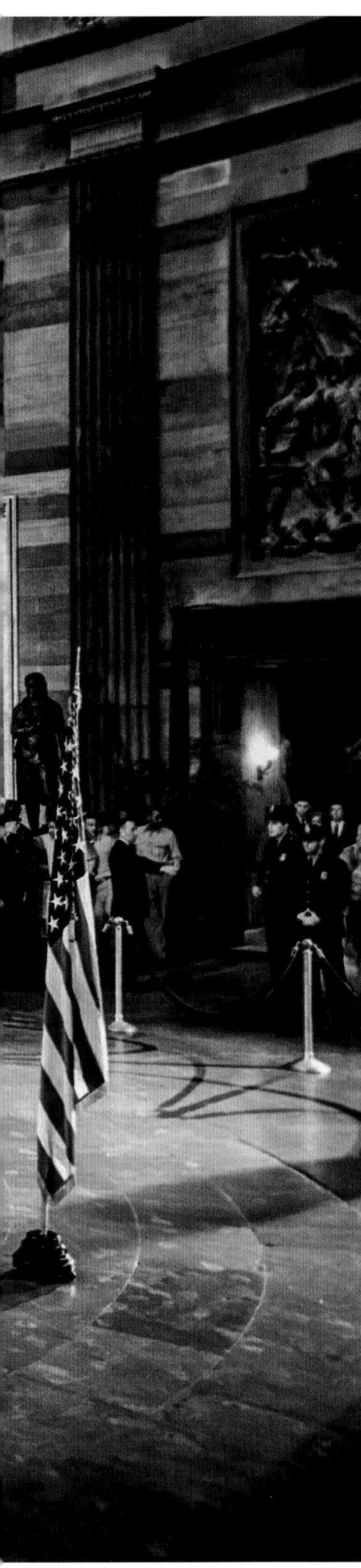

Kennedy Presidential Library in Boston, Massachusetts, where it is housed to this day.

It had been sixty-two years since a sitting president (William McKinley) had been assassinated. The nation was awakened out of a post–World War II dream to a new paradigm of modern American life. Kennedy's tenure as president had been seen as a kind of Camelot—a golden age, akin to the mythical grandeur of King Arthur's court and his Knights of the Round Table, when the world seemed to be both secure and prosperous. Never mind that the United States nearly entered a nuclear war with the Soviets in October 1962, when U2 spy planes detected the construction of nuclear missile launch complexes in Cuba, just a hundred miles from American soil. Even so, America had seemed to be on the right track.

John F. Kennedy's death brought an end to Camelot. A series of political assassinations hastened the shattering of the dream—and indeed, had begun even before JFK's assassination with the murder of civil rights activist Medgar Evers, who'd been gunned down in his driveway five months earlier, on June 12, 1963. On February 21, 1965, another proponent of civil liberties, Malcolm X, was killed by three gunmen while preparing to speak to the Organization of Afro-American Unity at the Audubon Ballroom in New York City. Civil rights leader Martin Luther King Jr. was shot on a hotel balcony in Memphis on April 4, 1968. Just two months later, on June 5, 1968, JFK's brother, Robert (Bobby) Kennedy, was mortally wounded at a presidential campaign rally in Los Angeles. It felt as if the world was spinning off its axis. If our nation's political leaders weren't safe, how could the average American feel secure?

One constant throughout this series of devastating losses was the presence of the American flag. It draped across caskets; it fluttered at gravesides; it flew at ceremonies and celebrations honoring those who died. That tradition of flying the flag in the face of tragedy stands even to this day. It is a reminder that the United States has been through difficult trials in the past, and it gives hope that the nation can survive far into the future.

Opposite: *President John F. Kennedy's casket in the Rotunda of the US Capitol, Washington, DC, November 24, 1963*

ANTHONY QUIN FLAG

A Symbol for Voters' Rights

DATE: June 17, 1965
EVENT LOCATION: Governor's Mansion, Jackson, Mississippi
CURRENT FLAG LOCATION: Unknown

The sight of a white Mississippi Highway Patrol officer, Hughie Kohler, tearing an American flag out of the hands of a five-year-old Black boy, Anthony Quin, is frightening. It also demonstrates the symbolic power of the American flag. Photographer Matt Herron took the photograph on June 17, 1965, at the Governor's Mansion in Jackson, Mississippi. Quin was there with his mother, Aylene "Mama" Quin, to protest the election of five congressmen from districts in the state that prevented Black citizens from voting.

Aylene Quin had been active in the National Association for the Advancement of Colored People (NAACP) since the 1950s and aided the Student Nonviolent Coordinating Committee (SNCC—pronounced *snick*) during the 1960s. Composed mainly of Black college students, SNCC organized and promoted nonviolent protests to fight racial discrimination and segregation. Clandestine meetings of SNCC were held at South of the Border, the restaurant Quin owned. During the Freedom

Following, left: *Protesting the seating of five congressmen from districts that did not allow Blacks to vote, Mrs. Aylene Quin of McComb, Mississippi, holds a sign reading* NO MORE POLICE BRUTALITY, *Governor's Mansion, Jackson, Mississippi, June 17, 1965.*

Following, right: *Mississippi highway patrolman Hughie Kohler tears an American flag out of the hands of Anthony Quin, five, son of Mrs. Aylene Quin, Governor's Mansion, Jackson, Mississippi, June 17, 1965.*

Summer of 1964, Quin helped locate food and housing for civil rights activists in the area and participated in demonstrations. Her assistance to the civil rights movement led to her home being bombed in September 1964. Thankfully, no one was harmed in the explosion. Quin didn't let the attack deter her efforts. Her continued dedication to civil rights inspired her to participate in the protest at the Mississippi Governor's Mansion the following June.

Matt Herron was a versatile photographer who specialized in photojournalism and documentary photography. It is not a coincidence that Herron was at the Governor's Mansion that day. He worked closely with SNCC to document the racial injustices occurring in the South during the 1960s.

By the mid-1960s, the American flag had become an evocative symbol for the civil rights movement—a call for the nation to live up to its ideals of freedom and equality. So the image of a white trooper wresting the American flag out of the hands of a Black child at a protest for voters' rights was particularly compelling—a glaring symbol of the violent suppression of Black votes and Black liberty. As heart-wrenching as Herron's image is, it was also a harbinger of the turning tide of the civil rights movement in the mid-1960s. Why was a heavily armed adult so threatened by a young child and his flag? Had the American flag become such a bold symbol of civil rights that it threatened the power of conservative Southerners? Slowly, slowly, the tide of American opinion began to turn.

Though much progress has been made in securing civil rights for all Americans over the past sixty-plus years, recent events have shown that there is still much more to be done. Even today, white supremacists still carry the Confederate flag, with all of the hateful principles it stands for, and they fly it side by side with the American flag as an emblem of "patriotic" pride. There is sad irony in the fact that hate groups have latched on to the American flag as a symbol of their ideology when it once was a powerful icon of resistance against their contemptible ideals and beliefs.

Anthony Quin and Matt Herron reunited in 2014 for an exhibition, *And the Children Shall Lead Them,* a display of civil rights photography in Jackson, Mississippi, in recognition of the fiftieth anniversary of Freedom Summer, the effort to register Black voters in Mississippi in 1964. Quin died of pancreatic cancer in 2015 after earning three college degrees, including a PhD in education administration. Herron died in 2020 at the age of eighty-nine when the glider plane he was flying crashed. Their lives are linked in this iconic image from the civil rights movement.

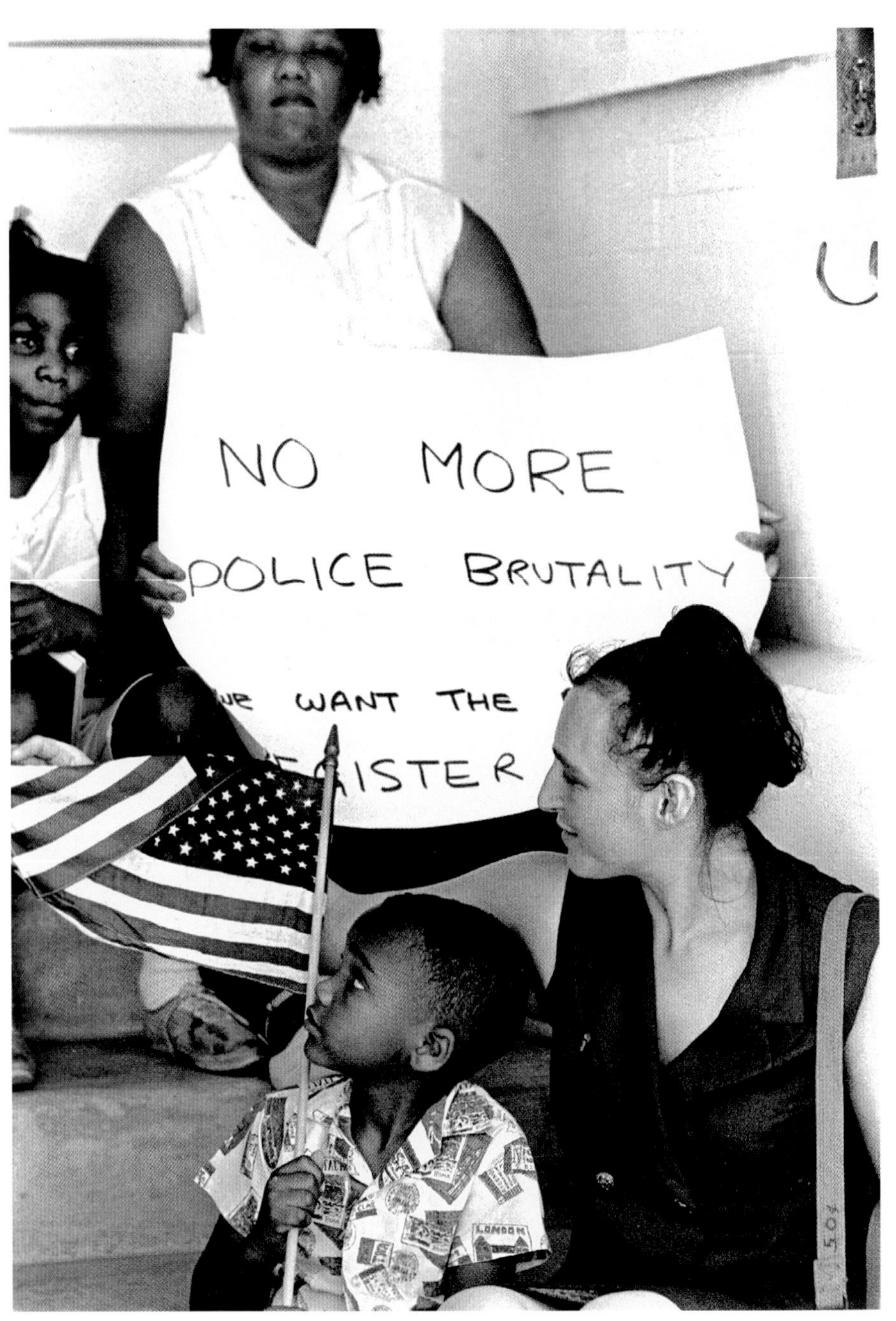
NO MORE
POLICE BRUTALITY
WANT THE
LONDON

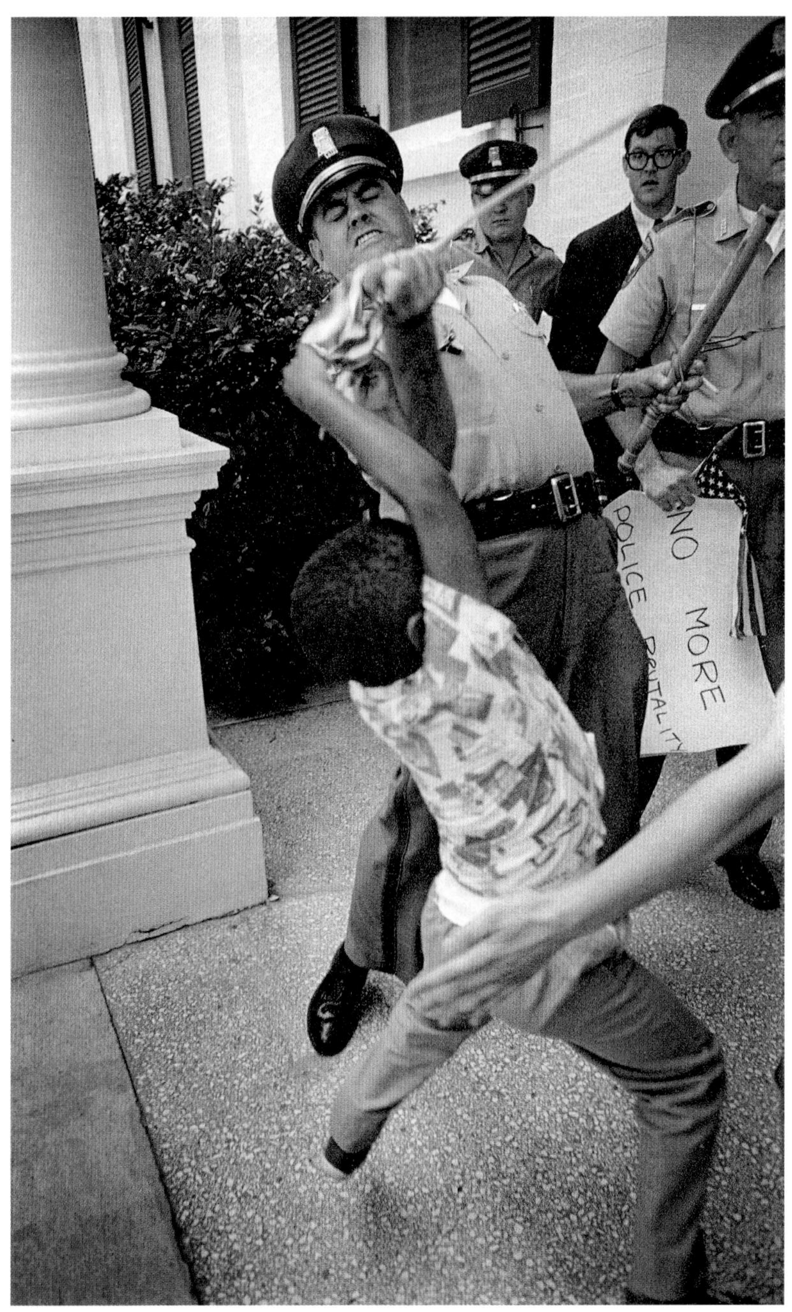
NO MORE
POLICE

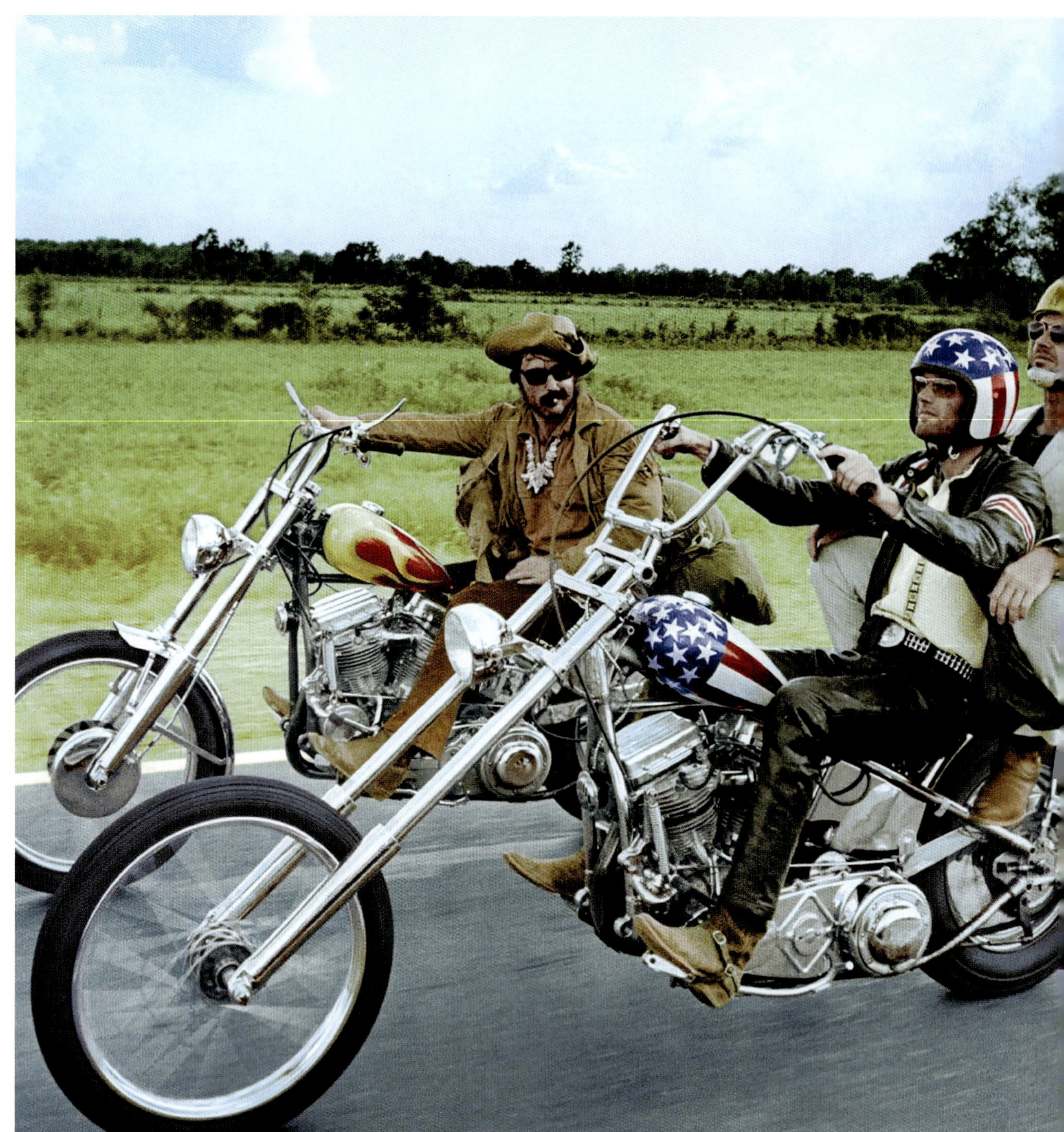

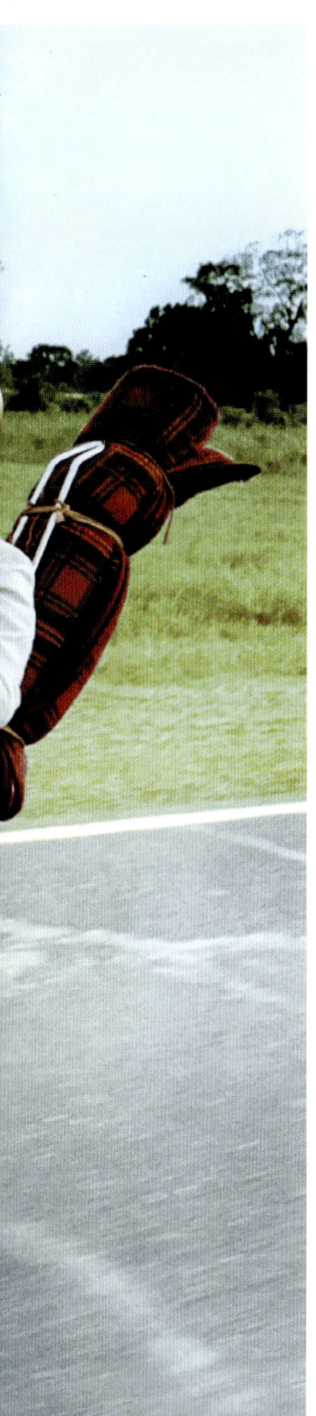

EASY RIDER'S CAPTAIN AMERICA FLAGS

Fear of the Free

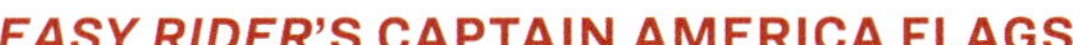

DATE: July 14, 1969
EVENT LOCATION: n/a
CURRENT FLAG LOCATION: Private collection

Actor and director Dennis Hopper's 1969 film *Easy Rider* is an antiestablishment rejection of cultural and social norms of the mid-twentieth century. The movie chronicles the journey of two motorcycle-riding renegades, played by Hopper and Peter Fonda, who smuggle cocaine into the United States from Mexico and sell it to a dealer in Los Angeles. They hide the money they received in the American-flag-themed gas tank of Fonda's Harley-Davidson chopper and head for Mardi Gras in New Orleans.

Easy Rider is thick with metaphor and meaning. Fonda's and Hopper's character names, Wyatt (Fonda) and Billy (Hopper), are derived from those of Wyatt Earp (the lawman most famous for the shootout at the O.K. Corral in Tombstone, Arizona, in 1881) and Billy the Kid (the famous young outlaw and gunslinger). Wyatt also goes by the nickname Captain America, and the American flag motif of his motorcycle, helmet, and jacket emphasize this connection. On their ride eastward, Wyatt and Billy interact with a cross section of Americans, including prostitutes, hippies, small-town law enforcement officers, farmers, malicious locals, and even an ACLU lawyer, George Hanson, played by Jack Nicholson.

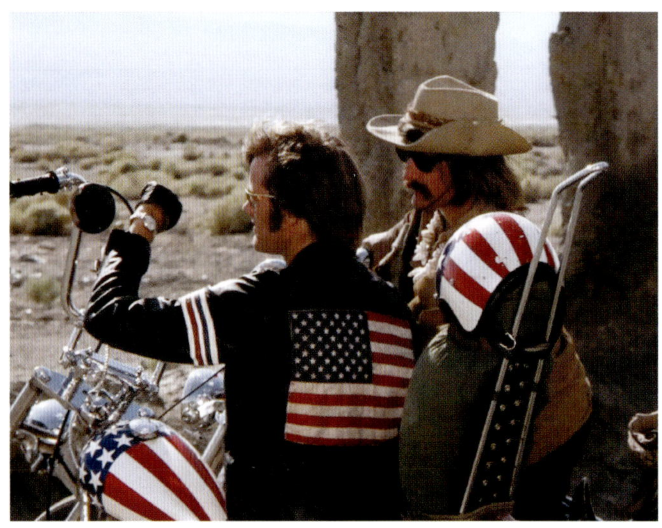

Wyatt and Billy's long hair, choppers, and defiant attitude are not appreciated by most of the people they encounter in rural America in the 1960s—much as was the reality at the time. Hanson informs them that it's not their looks, bikes, or attitudes. It's that the free-wheeling duo reminds others of their own lack of freedom.

Spoiler alert: In the final climactic scene of *Easy Rider*, Wyatt and Billy are out riding their Harleys when Billy is shot by locals in a pickup truck they pass. He goes down, ending up on his back in a ditch with his bike in the road.

Above: *Wyatt (Peter Fonda) with his flag motif gas tank, helmet, and jacket—and Billy (Dennis Hopper) on their motorcycles, 1969*

Previous: *Dennis Hopper, Peter Fonda, and Jack Nicholson on their Easy Rider chopper motorcycles, 1969*

Wyatt turns around to help Billy. He pulls his jacket and helmet from the top of his bike's sissy bar. He tosses the American flag–patterned helmet into the grass next to Billy. He takes his jacket, which has an embroidered American flag on the back, and covers Billy with it so that the flag is facing the camera. Wyatt tells Billy he is going for help. As he rides down the highway, the pickup truck has turned around. We see Wyatt approaching, and the scene cuts to the pickup as the passenger leans over and shoots out of the driver's window.

The next shot shows Wyatt's bike launched into the air with the front fork and wheel detached. The bike lands, and its American flag–painted gas tank explodes. The scene cuts to an aerial view above the wreckage, and we see Wyatt lying on the shoulder and the motorcycle engulfed in flames as the camera rises higher and higher.

The flag designs on Wyatt's jacket, helmet, and gas tank are a nod to the concept of freedom—and how its meaning differs depending on your perspective. They also reference the graphic novel character Captain America, who serves as Wyatt's alter ego. Captain America first appeared in comic books a little less than a year before the United States entered World War II. His origin story holds that Captain America was part of an experimental military program designed to create a super-soldier to fight the Axis powers of World War II: Germany, Japan, and Italy. His superhero outfit echoes the design elements of the American flag, consisting of a tunic with red-and-white stripes on the midriff and a blue upper torso containing a large, single white star. Captain America's round shield features a single white star in a field of blue, surrounded by three concentric rings of red, white, and red.

Below: *The patch from Peter Fonda's* Easy Rider *jacket, 1969*

Wyatt's use of the moniker Captain America is a paradox to his uninhibited, drug-smuggling lifestyle. Wyatt can also be seen as a foe of the Vietnam War—the opposite of Captain America's role in warfare. While Captain America serves others, Wyatt, though mostly harmless, serves only himself. Still, he flaunts the American flag on his clothing and motorcycle as if claiming it for himself. The intolerant rural folks he encounters are forced to take offense at Wyatt wearing the American flag.

Easy Rider was released mid-1969, at a time when the country was turning against the Vietnam War. It premiered just a few days before the United States landed the first humans on the moon and effectively won the Space Race. Billy and Wyatt's freewheeling lifestyle exemplified a new era where, through grassroots efforts, young Americans helped end a war and moved the country toward a more progressive future.

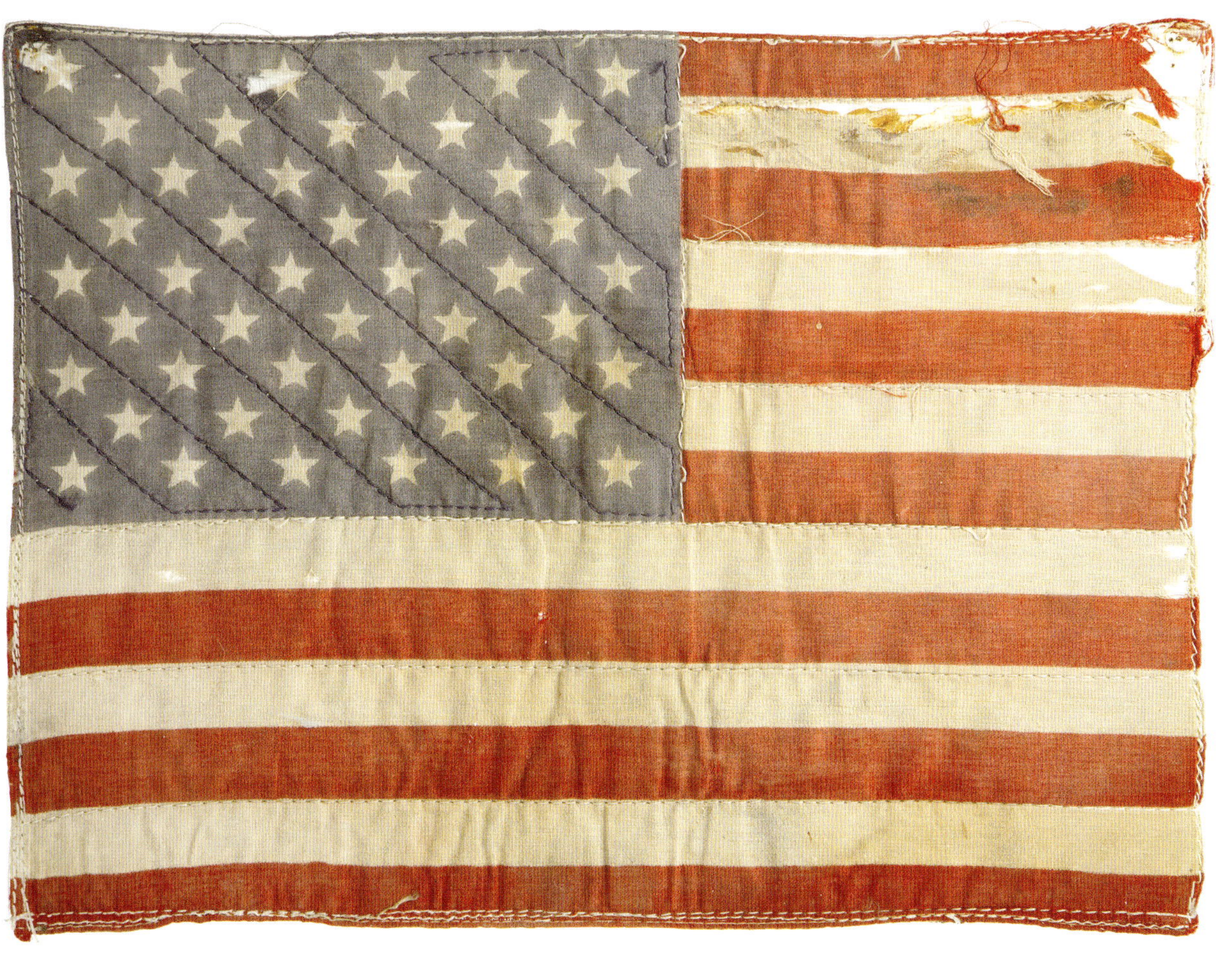

1969

to

1975

The Cold War and Vietnam

BY THE LATE 1960S, AMERICA WAS CAUGHT UP in the Vietnam War and the Cold War. Most Americans understood the threat from the Communist Soviet Union, but the reasons behind the war in Vietnam were murkier. At the same time, the American flag came to symbolize both the nation's pride in its technological and daring space exploration efforts, as well as an increasing opposition to the war in Southeast Asia.

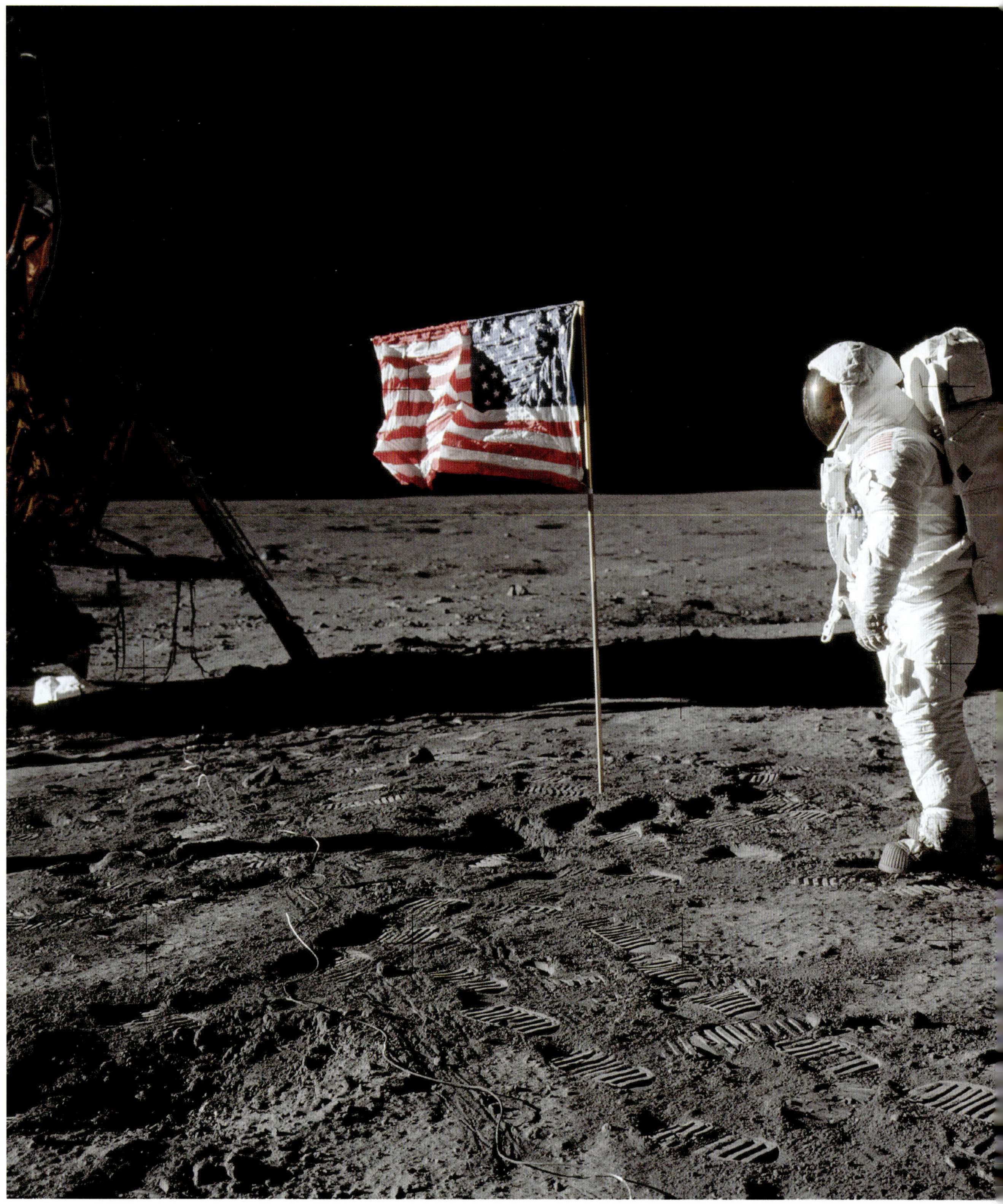

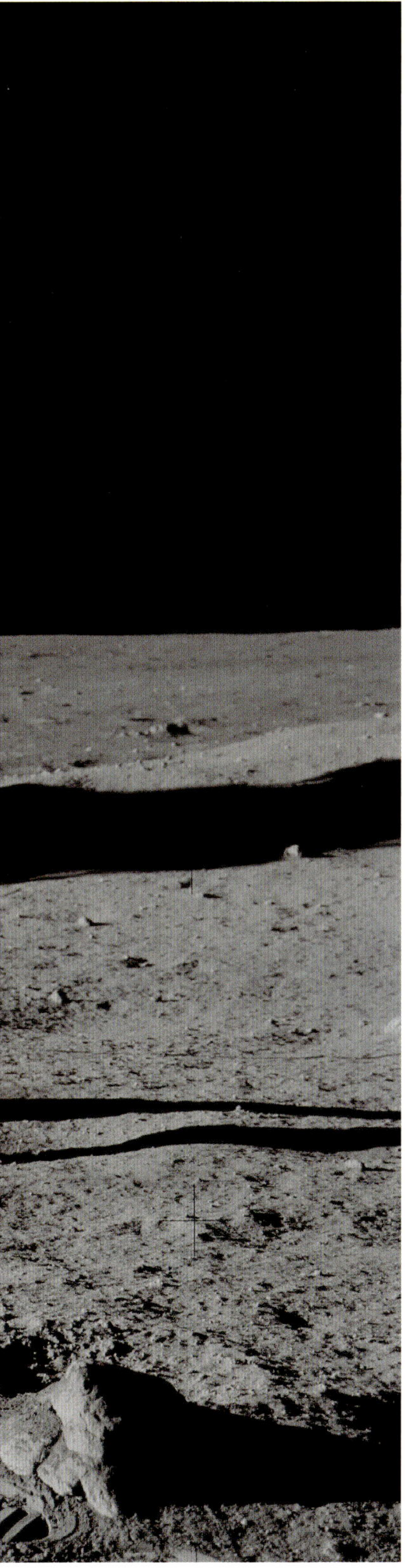

APOLLO 11 MOON FLAG

Six Flags over the Moon

DATE: July 20, 1969

EVENT LOCATION: Tranquility Base, Sea of Tranquility, the moon

CURRENT FLAG LOCATION: Tranquility Base, Sea of Tranquility, the moon

It was a simple act, planting a flag on a pole a few inches into the soil. However, the technical and political hurdles that would need to be overcome in order to achieve this seemingly straightforward task were daunting, if not impossible. In 1961, when President John F. Kennedy declared that the United States would land a man on the moon and return him safely by the end of the decade, the country had a total of fifteen minutes of crewed spaceflight experience (Alan Shepard's Mercury *Freedom 7* suborbital flight).

To reach the moon and return safely, technology that did not exist—and whole areas of materials science—would need to be developed or expanded. Skills and techniques, like orbital rendezvous, would need to be mastered. President Kennedy's nine-year timeline only made the task that much more challenging. Once the Mercury and Gemini programs had been successful and it appeared that there was a chance (though still slim) that the United States might reach the moon before Kennedy's

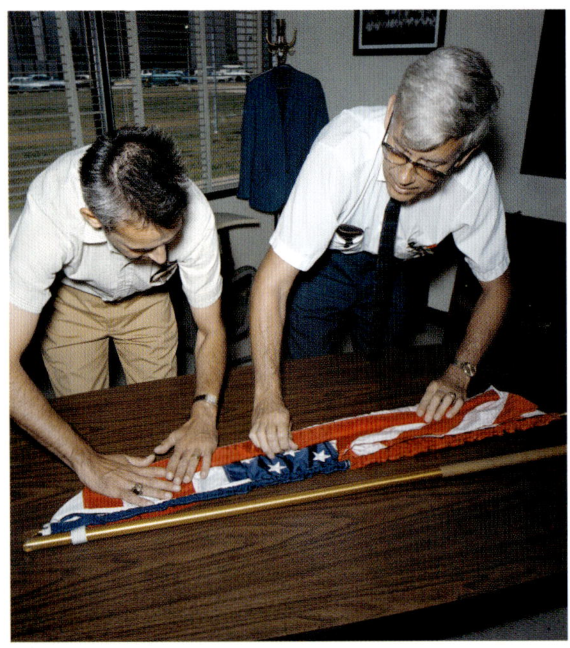

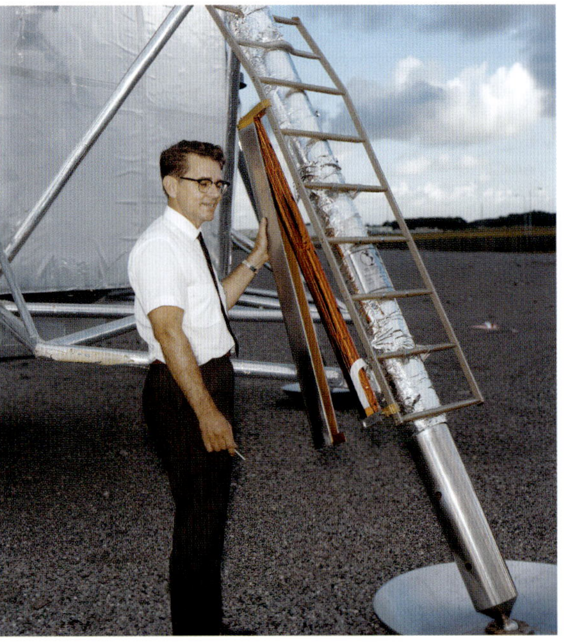

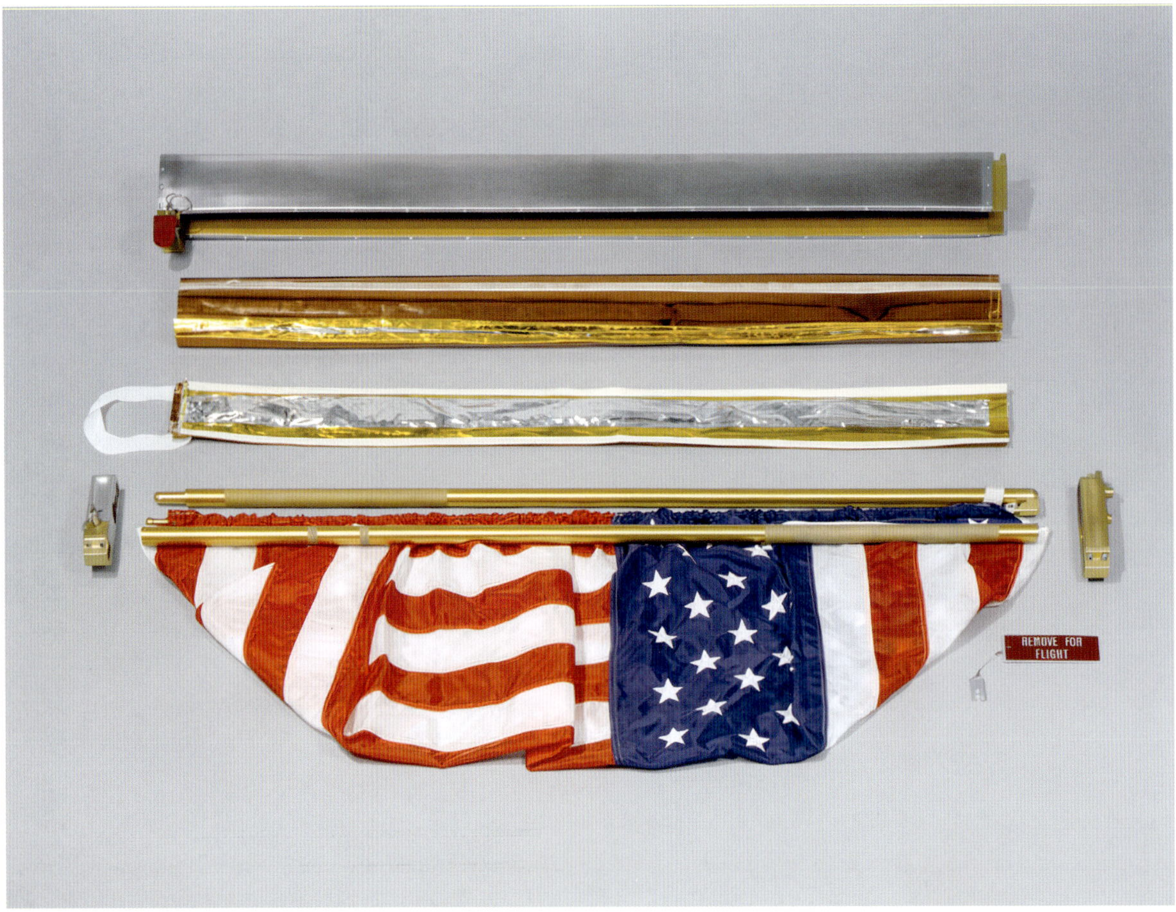

Previous: Buzz Aldrin on the moon with the American flag during the Apollo 11 lunar excursion, July 20, 1969

Opposite, clockwise from top left: William E. Drummond (NASA Parachute Support Section) and Jack Kinzler (Chief of NASA's Technical Services Division) fold the Apollo 11 flag in preparation for stowing it on the Lunar Module, NASA's Johnson Space Center, Texas, 1969; Dave McCraw (Technical Services deputy division chief, NASA's Manned Spacecraft Center) demonstrates the removal of the flag shroud from the Lunar Module ladder, NASA's Johnson Space Center, Texas, 1969; Apollo 11 flag assembly, NASA's Johnson Space Center, Texas, 1969.

deadline, serious consideration had to be given to what the astronauts who traveled to the moon would do while they were on the surface. Even by 1966, whether or not they would plant a flag (and what type) were not major considerations.

It had long been customary for any explorer to plant the flag of their home nation on newly discovered territory (page 36). Planting a flag was meant to symbolize that the explorer claimed that area in the name of their country. On January 27, 1967 (tragically, the same day that the Apollo 1 fire took the lives of American astronauts Roger Chaffey, Gus Grissom, and Edward White), the United States, the United Kingdom, the Soviet Union, and forty-three other countries signed the Outer Space Treaty. Eventually, 114 countries would sign on to the treaty. Article II of the treaty states: "Outer space, including the moon and other celestial bodies, is not subject to national appropriation by claim of sovereignty, by means of use or occupation, or by any other means." What would planting a flag on the moon symbolize to the rest of the countries of the world that were considering this agreement? Would it even be legal? It would have to be seen by the world as a symbolic flag raising, not an assertion of ownership of the moon by the United States. Some even suggested planting a United Nations flag instead of an American flag to avoid any confusion.

Less than five months before the planned Apollo 11 lunar landing, Thomas O. Paine, NASA's acting administrator, created a committee to address these concerns. The committee consulted with several government organizations, including the Library of Congress, the Smithsonian Institution, and the NASA Historical Advisory Committee. Most of these agencies and institutions recommended that the astronauts plant the American flag on the moon. To address the political concerns, the committee also recommended the following wording for the plaque attached to the leg of the Lunar Module (LM): "Here men from the planet Earth first set foot upon the moon July 1969, A.D. We came in peace for all mankind."

Once the committee had made its decision, only three months remained until the Apollo 11 mission's launch. Jack A. Kinzler, chief of NASA's Technical Services Division, was tasked with creating a flag that wouldn't be a fire or other hazard and could somehow appear to "fly" in the moon's airless environment. The design was completed in a few days. It used an off-the-shelf nylon American flag modified with a sleeve along the top to allow a rod to be inserted so the flag could appear to fly, even though, in reality, it was simply hanging from the rod. Then the team had to find a safe place to stow the flag on the LM to protect it from the 2,000°F (1093°C) heat that would be generated by the module's descent engine.

They determined that an insulated stainless-steel container located on the left side of the LM's ladder would protect the flag and not interfere with any systems on the spacecraft. (Flags were subsequently carried this way on the Apollo 12, 13, and 14 missions.)

On July 20, 1969, two and a half years after the signing of the Outer Space Treaty, Neil Armstrong and Buzz Aldrin planted the American flag about forty-five minutes into their walk on the surface of the moon. Armstrong took a photo of Aldrin by the flag—one of the most famous photographs from the Apollo program.

Armstrong and Aldrin carried a duplicate American flag to the surface of the moon (that was not flown) and returned it to Earth. Today, it is on display in the lobby of the Olin E. Teague Auditorium at NASA's Johnson Space Center. You can see the tight folds left in the fabric from being compacted for spaceflight.

When the Apollo 11 astronauts launched from the moon to return to the *Columbia* (the spacecraft that would take them home), Armstrong saw the flag they'd planted get knocked down by the blast of the LM's ascent engine. On Apollo missions 12, 14, 15, 16, and 17, flags were planted farther from the LM to avoid the exhaust from blastoff and ensure they would remain standing. Between 2009 and 2011, the Lunar Reconnaissance Orbiter (LRO), a NASA satellite orbiting and mapping the moon, photographed all the Apollo lunar landing sites. At that time, the flags of Apollo 12, 16, and 17 appeared to still be standing. The images confirmed that the Apollo 11 flag was no longer standing. The fate of Apollo 14 and 15's flags remained unclear. Made of ordinary nylon, the flags have likely faded and may have disintegrated due to ultraviolet radiation and the extreme heat and cold on the moon's surface since the LRO images were taken.

Although it may no longer be standing, the planting of the Apollo 11 American flag on the surface of the moon was the culmination of a decade's work by hundreds of thousands of individuals. As it turned out, instead of alienating other countries, planting the American flag on the moon symbolized not only the nation's dramatic achievement but also, for a moment, the alignment of humanity's dreams of reaching the stars.

AMERICAN PEACE SYMBOL FLAG

Woodstock Peace Symbol Flag

DATE: August 15–18, 1969

EVENT LOCATION: Woodstock Music Festival, Bethel, New York

CURRENT FLAG LOCATION: Bethel Woods Center for the Arts, Bethel, New York

***Following:** Peace flag carried at the Woodstock Music Festival, Max Yasgur's farm near Bethel Woods, New York, August 15–18, 1969*

The mud puddles formed quickly in the pastures of Max Yasgur's dairy farm, the site of one of the largest music festivals in history. Woodstock, as the event came to be known, had been billed as "three days of peace and music" but stretched to four due to the heavy rains on that mid-August weekend in 1969 just outside Bethel, New York. At its peak attendance, an estimated 400,000 to 500,000 people settled into the muddy landscape to enjoy performances from some of the era's most popular musicians—Joan Baez, the Who, Santana, Jimi Hendrix, and many others.

Though the peace symbol wasn't the official emblem of Woodstock (a white dove perched on the neck of a guitar served that role), many concertgoers wore or displayed the now aptly named peace symbol during the event. Mark Shustak, a Woodstock attendee, brought a peace symbol flag to the festival. He and his companion wrapped themselves in it to keep dry from the downpour. (Similar flags were being used in antiwar

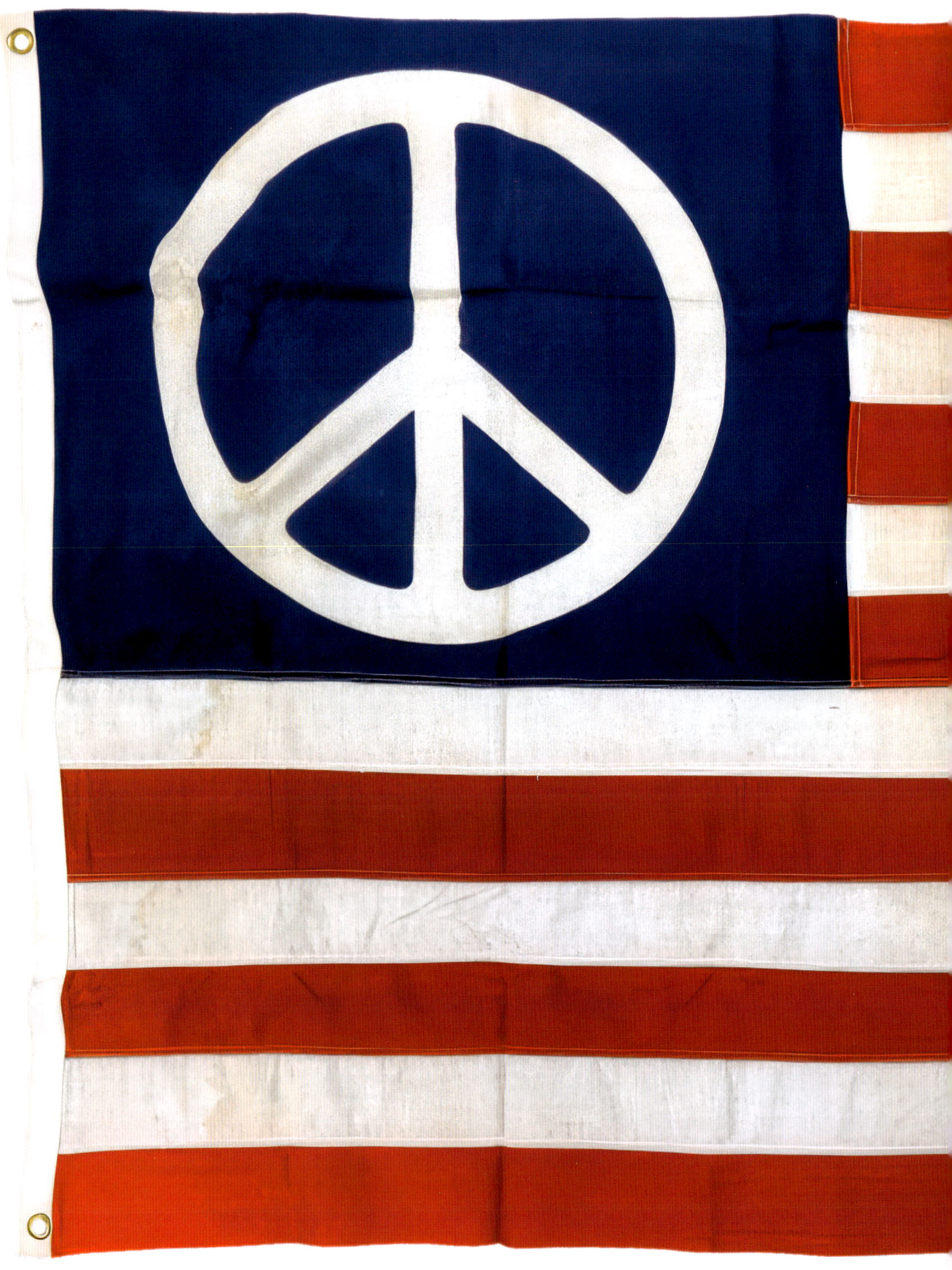

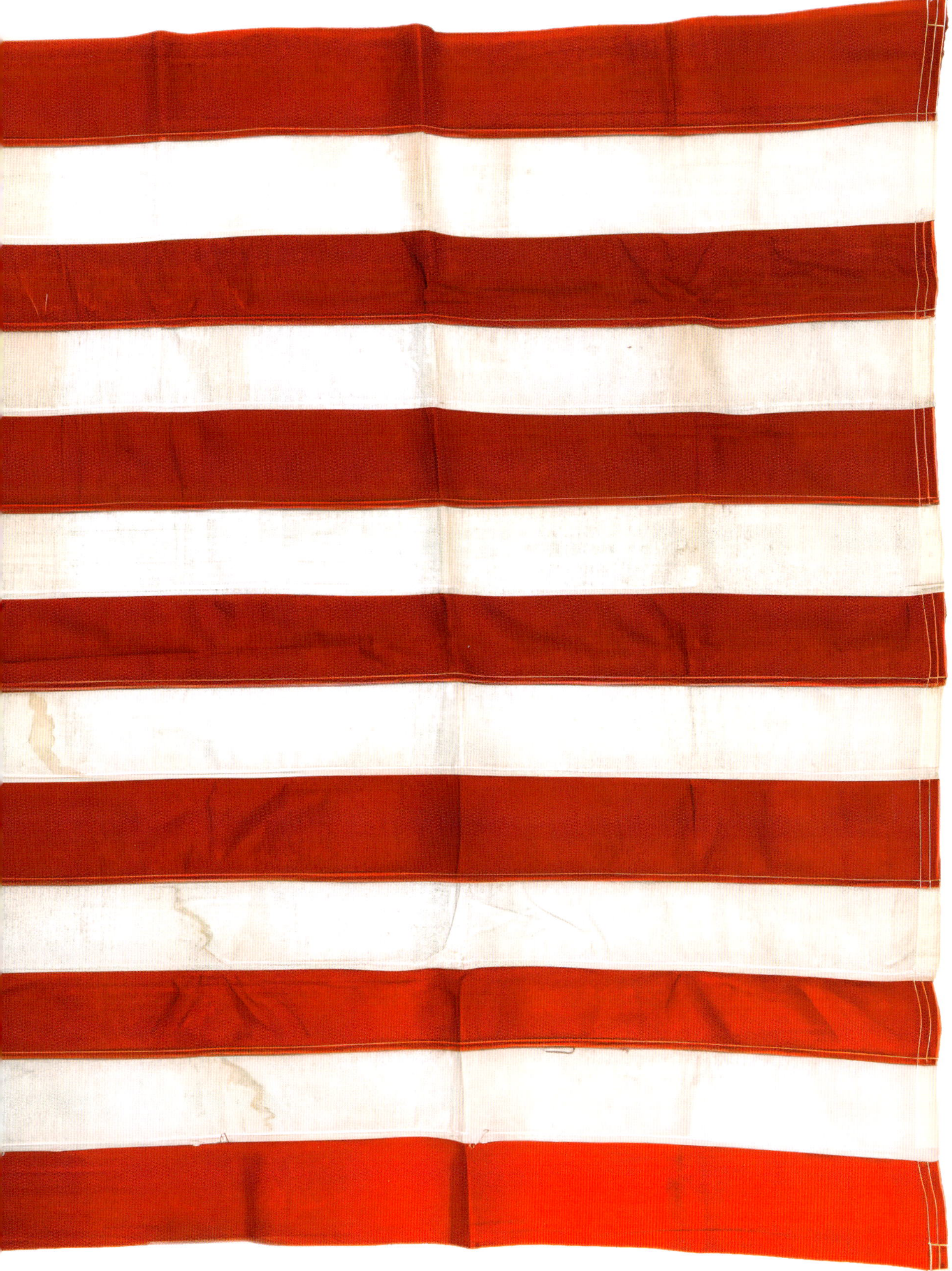

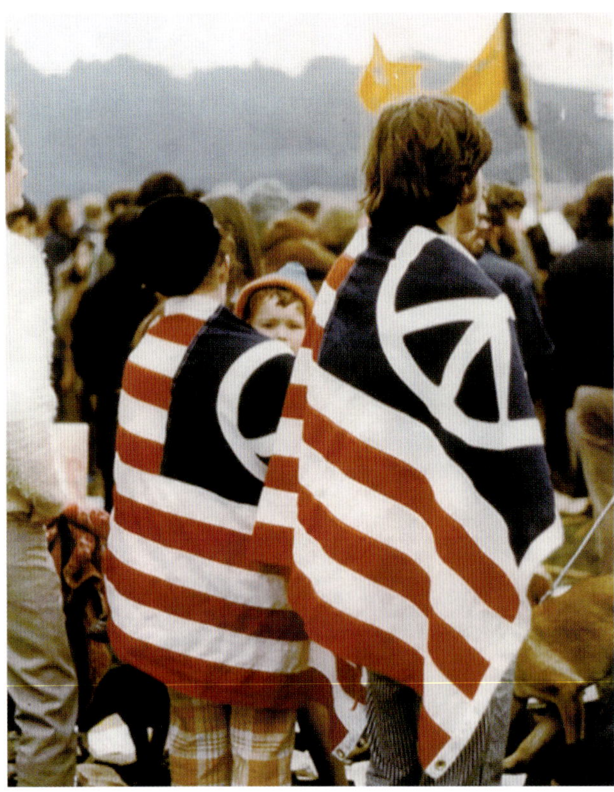

Family wrapped in peace flags at an anti–Vietnam War protest in San Francisco, California's Golden Gate Park, November 15, 1969

protests around the United States.) Shustak would gift his flag to the Bethel Woods Center for the Arts in New York (at the site of the Woodstock Festival), where it is currently on display.

The peace symbol was created in 1958 by British designer Gerald Holtom for the Campaign for Nuclear Disarmament (CND), a movement that grew in response to the development of nuclear weapons. Following the United States' utilization of two atomic bombs to force Japan to surrender and end World War II, the CND hoped to deter the further development and production of nuclear warheads and the safe destruction of those already produced.

The original design was based on standard semaphore code with flags representing the letters *N* and *D*—an acronym for "nuclear disarmament." The semaphore *N* is signaled by holding a flag in each hand with the arms aimed downward at an angle, creating an upside-down *V* shape. The letter *D* is designated by holding the right-hand flag straight up and the left-hand flag straight down, creating a vertical line. Holtom combined these two patterns, overlapping the vertical line with the upside-down *V* and enclosing them in a circle, with the ends of the lines touching the circle's perimeter. The symbol quickly came to represent more than just nuclear disarmament. Most notably, the anti–Vietnam War movement adopted it as a message of peace.

Eleven years later, in 1969, concert promoters Joel Rosenman and John Roberts envisioned an open-air music and art festival in the Catskills area of upstate New York. Originally anticipated to draw 50,000 music fans, the Woodstock Music and Arts Festival drew nearly ten times that many attendees. The concert was to be held near the town of Woodstock, New York, before residents there rejected the idea. After several other towns in the Catskills region similarly declined to host the festival, Woodstock was eventually held on Yasgur's farm near Bethel, New York.

COLONEL JOHN A. DRAMESI POW FLAG

A Clandestine Flag Ritual

DATE: 1967–1973

EVENT LOCATION: Hanoi, North Vietnam

CURRENT FLAG LOCATION: Richard Nixon Presidential Library and Museum, Yorba Linda, California

On May 10, 1969, Colonel John A. Dramesi and fellow prisoner of war Captain Edwin Lee Atterberry, both of the US Air Force, escaped through a hole in the roof of the Cu Loc Prison in Hanoi, Vietnam—known to the POWs as "the Zoo." After traveling only three miles, they were recaptured the next day. As punishment, Dramesi and Atterberry were tortured for more than a month. Atterberry died during the ordeal, but Dramesi survived. Because of the escape attempt, many of the Zoo's other prisoners were also punished, as were those at other prisons. This caused the senior American officers who were captives to prohibit any escape attempts that didn't meet strict criteria, (such as having outside help) out of fear that they would cause reprisals against the remaining POWs.

Dramesi had originally been captured during his fifty-ninth bombing mission over North Vietnam, on April 2, 1967. His F105 aircraft was damaged by enemy fire and he was forced to eject. After parachuting into the

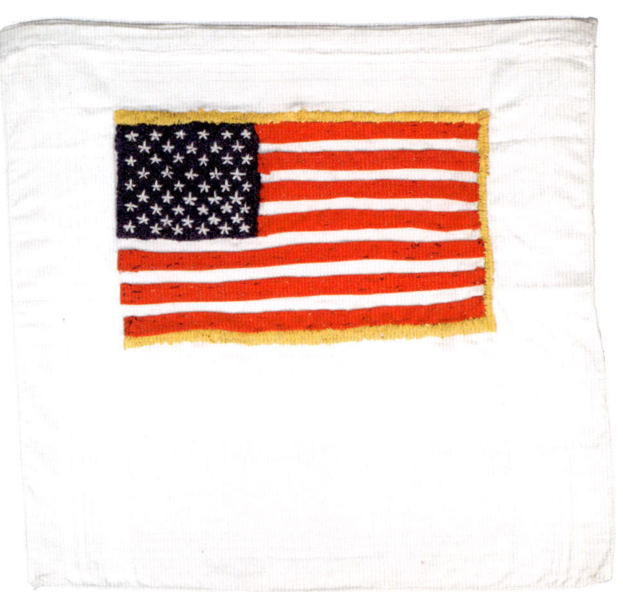

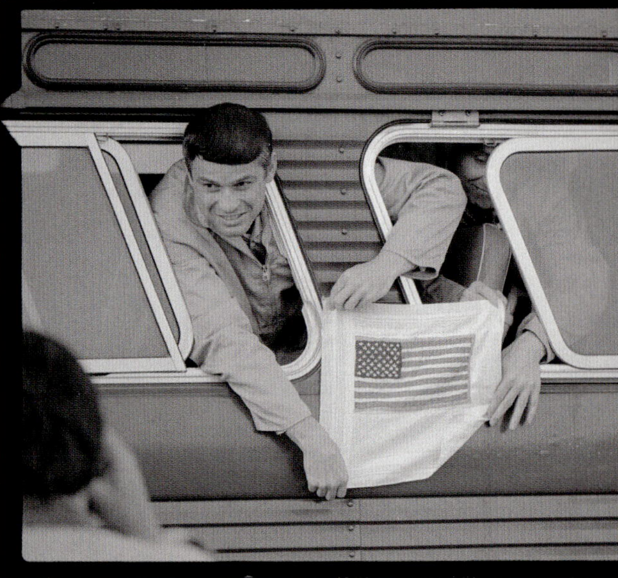

Above, left: *John Dramesi Vietnam War POW flag, made in the Hoa Lo (Hanoi Hilton) Prison, Hanoi, North Vietnam, 1971*

Above, right: *USAF Colonel John Dramesi waves his flag made during captivity in North Vietnam, Clark Air Force Base, Philippines, March 4, 1973.*

Vietnamese landscape, Dramesi hid his parachute, grabbed his survival gear, and headed uphill away from his landing spot. Soon he could hear voices and gunfire near where he had landed. He kept climbing and took cover in the brush near the top of a ridge. Using a radio, he contacted the three Douglas AE-1 Skyraider planes (known by their call sign, "Sandies") that escorted the combat search and rescue (CSAR) helicopter assigned to pick him up. But before the CSAR helicopter reached Dramesi, North Vietnamese soldiers surrounded him. He fired at them, but he was shot in the right leg and taken prisoner.

In the prison camps, POWs worked out elaborate communication systems among themselves: tapping, sweeping rhythms, using their toes and feet to sign Morse code, and more. They were typically forbidden from communicating between prison cells. The "tap code" was developed in Hoa Lo Prison (known as the "Hanoi Hilton") and used a five-by-five grid of letters ("C" was sometimes used in place of "K"). The prisoners would first tap out the line number, then tap out the letter position in that line. Prisoners also sent coded messages to loved ones through letters. The military and the CIA clandestinely provided materials that allowed further communication from and with the prisoners, such as invisible ink carbon paper, microdots, and film sometimes hidden in dried fruit sent to the camp. They even attempted to send parts to construct a shortwave radio.

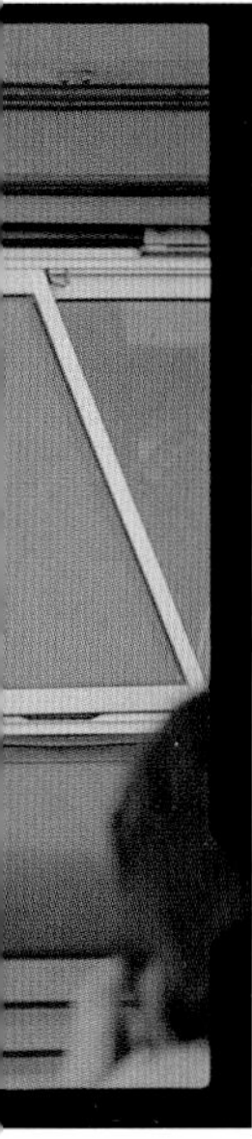

In 1971, while still held captive, Dramesi began making a small American flag from scraps of cloth and thread embroidered onto a handkerchief. His fellow POWs donated the materials, and the project took a little over a week. Dramesi kept the flag hidden from his Vietnamese captors for more than a year. He and the other POWs would salute the flag in the evening, leave it displayed overnight, salute it in the morning, and return it to its hiding place (in some mosquito netting) before the guards returned. In his 1975 memoir, *Code of Honor*, Dramesi noted, "It seemed to me there was a necessity to reaffirm our identity, to be able to see and touch that which was American, to again be reminded that we were American fighting men." Much like Joseph Quintero, who sewed an American flag while a prisoner of war in Japan during World War II (page 115), Dramesi found that the flag, as a symbol of American pride, helped the POWs maintain their inner strength and will to live.

Dramesi was torn between his desire to keep trying to escape, based partly on his strong belief in the US military's Code of Conduct (page 210), and his respect for his commanding officer's orders. The Code of Conduct outlines how soldiers should act in conflict and otherwise. Article III states:

> *If I am captured I will continue to resist by all means available. I will make every effort to escape and aid others to escape. I will accept neither parole nor special favors from the enemy.*

Yet in Dramesi's situation, Article III conflicted with Article IV, which states,

> *If I become a prisoner of war, I will keep faith with my fellow prisoners. I will give no information or take part in any action which might be harmful to my comrades. If I am senior, I will take command. If not, I will obey the lawful orders of those appointed over me and will back them up in every way.*

The signing of the Paris Peace Accords on January 27, 1973, signaled the beginning of the end of American participation in the Vietnam War and a way home for the POWs. Dramesi was released on March 4, 1973, having spent nearly seven years in captivity. On May 24, Dramesi and his fellow POWs were honored by President Nixon at a White House dinner. The next day, Dramesi presented President Nixon with the flag he had made while in captivity.

By August, most American troops had withdrawn from Vietnam. Less than two years later, in April 1975, Saigon fell to the North Vietnamese army, and the war was over (page 155).

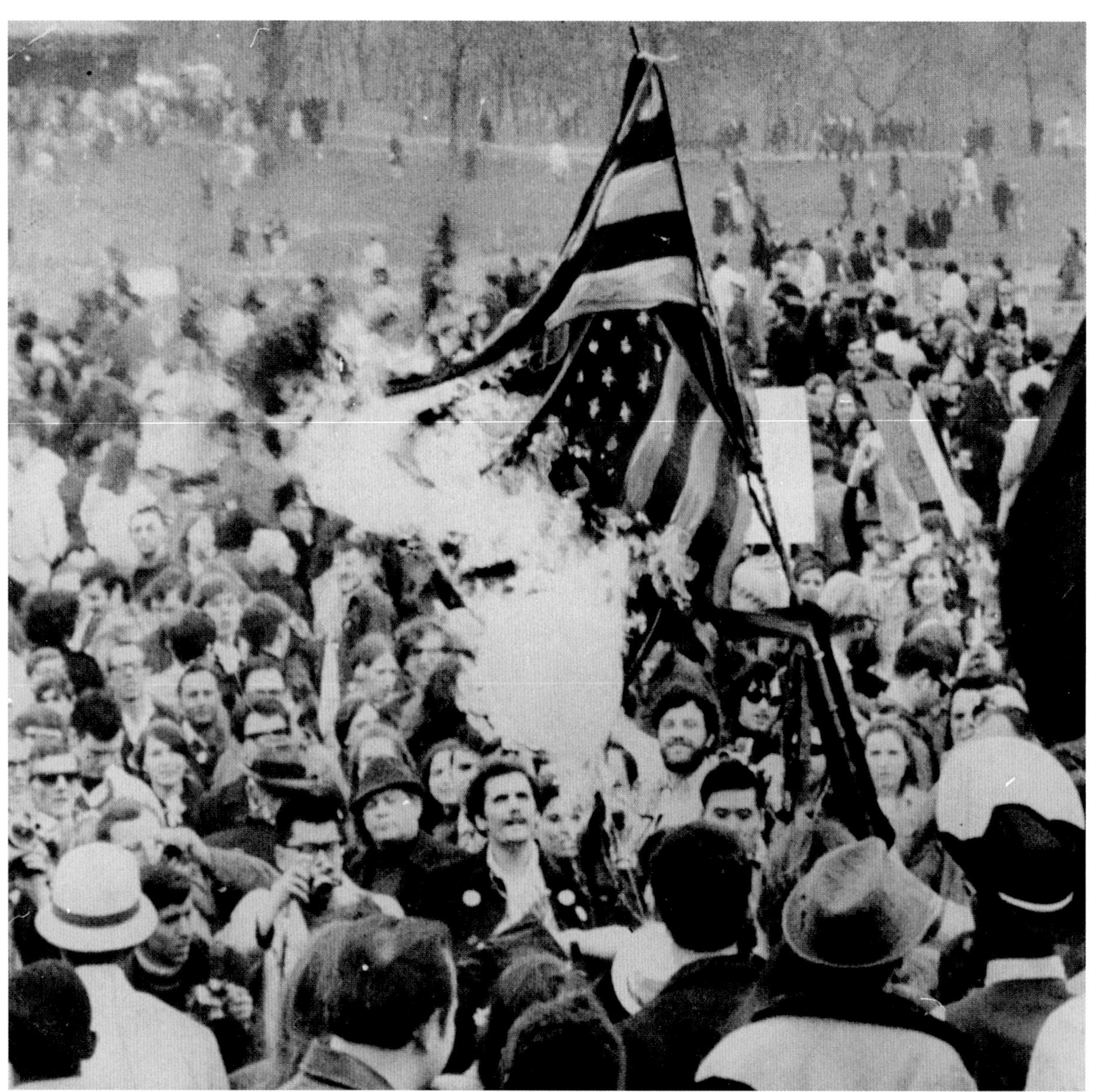

VIETNAM WAR PROTEST FLAGS

The Flag in Flames

DATE: 1960s–1970s

EVENT LOCATION: n/a

CURRENT FLAG LOCATION: Destroyed

***Opposite:** An American flag burns in Sheep Meadow, Central Park as war protestors march to the UN in opposition to the war in Vietnam, New York City, April 15, 1967.*

The American Civil War was the first conflict extensively documented in photographs. Photographers like Timothy O. Sullivan, Alexander Gardner, and Mathew Brady mainly recorded battle aftermaths because long exposures blurred any movement, preventing capturing combat action. Despite this, it was the first time the world's viewers, including families of soldiers, saw the war's carnage.

Much had changed a hundred years later, during the Vietnam War era. Reporters and photographers were often embedded with troops on the ground, covering the war up close and on a much larger scale. Technology for recording still and moving images had improved dramatically by the 1960s, and images of the harsh reality of war could be viewed in newspapers, magazines, and TV news broadcasts, often within hours of their creation. The immediacy and intimacy of the imagery coming out of Vietnam made Americans consider the costs and benefits of the war much more closely.

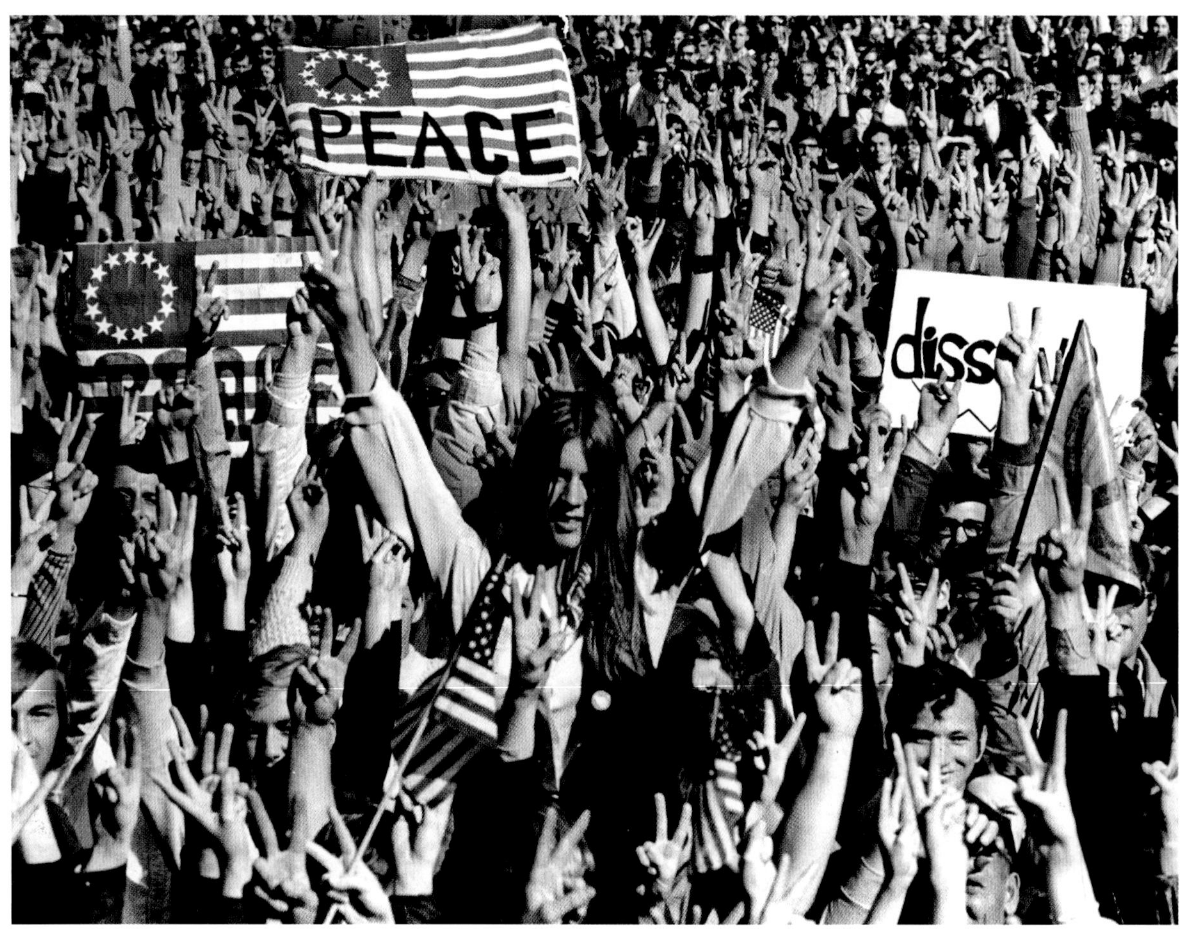

The largest demonstration in Boston's history happened on Vietnam Moratorium Day, October 15, 1969, with an estimated 100,000 protestors demanding an end to the Vietnam War.

The Vietnam War was the United States' effort to rein in the spread of communism in Southeast Asia. After years of war and conflict between the French and the communist Vietnamese forces, the Geneva Accords of 1954 recognized North Vietnam as a communist entity and South Vietnam as a Western-backed democratic regime. This agreement set the stage for the Second Indochina War (more commonly known as the Vietnam War in the United States). War begets war.

After the Geneva Accords, the United States began supplying South Vietnam with financing and military aid to stop the further spread of communism into Southeast Asia based on the "domino theory"—that if a country fell into communism, it would soon take neighboring nations with it into the communist fold. Over the next two decades, the United States was dragged further and further into a conflict that—through the draft process and the terrible toll on American GIs—would slowly turn the nation against the war.

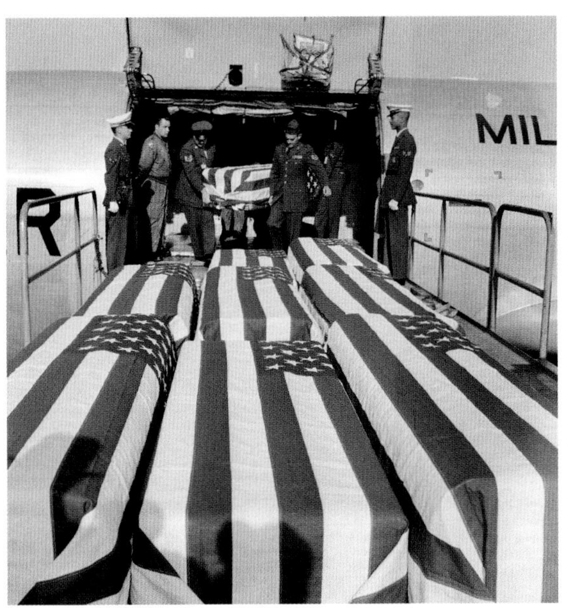

Flag-draped caskets of nine US servicemen killed in Vietnam are unloaded from a USAF transport plane, February 11, 1965.

By the mid-1960s, antiwar protests were being held in major cities across the country, driven in part by the factual portrayal of the brutality of combat by journalists in Vietnam. Students formed a large part of the protesters. They were joined by feminists and other liberal groups. Civil rights activists participated in the antiwar rallies as well, concerned that a disproportionate number of the young men fighting and dying in Vietnam were Black, Latino, and other non-white minorities.

There were pro-war rallies too. They were not as large and plentiful as the antiwar protests, but many Americans believed that the communists were a credible threat to the survival of the United States. Both groups of protesters carried American flags in their marches; both believed that the banner stood for their principles and goals.

Though the Vietnam War would drag on until 1975, the protests of the late 1960s and early 1970s would influence President Richard Nixon's policies and approach to Vietnam and eventually help end America's official involvement in the war by 1973 (page 151).

American flags were often burned at antiwar protests. On the one hand, burning an American flag in protest can be seen as an insult to everyone who has fought for the United States and its freedoms. Conversely, the right of American citizens to burn the flag—the right to freely stand up and demonstrate their disapproval of the government and its actions—is one of the many constitutional rights the brave men and women of our military fight to preserve.

The First Amendment of the US Constitution states that the American people have the right to object to the government and their elected representatives—even though the people themselves elected the representatives of the government they are now protesting.

In 1984, a protester, Gregory Lee Johnson, burned a flag at the 1984 Republican National Convention in Dallas. He was charged and convicted under a Texas law that banned burning the flag, sentenced to one year in prison, and fined $2,000. In 1989, the Supreme Court sided with Johnson, and his conviction was overturned based on the First Amendment. The Court also struck down the Texas law and similar laws in forty-seven other states.

In response, Congress passed the Flag Protection Act of 1989, which prohibited desecration of the American flag, including burning it.

Opposite, top: *Joan Baez performing at an anti-draft demonstration, Central Park Band Shell, New York City, 1968*

Opposite, bottom: *An army veteran clutches an American flag at an anti–Vietnam War protest in Boston, 1969.*

The federal law, which mirrored the Texas law, was later overturned by the Supreme Court. The Court again based its decision on the right of free speech granted by the First Amendment of the Constitution.

Many people still believe that it should be illegal to burn an American flag, but repeatedly, the courts of the land have upheld the right to burn the flag based on the principle that symbols, even that of the nation's flag, should not take precedence over rights. Criminalizing the right to burn the American flag would be a direct affront to the freedoms the flag represents.

ENDING THE VIETNAM WAR

★★★

The peace flag symbolized the disdain many Americans had for a war being fought halfway across the world, whose purpose and endgame appeared unclear. In 1970, the deaths of four students at Kent State University in Ohio at the hands of National Guard troops called in to quell anti–Vietnam War demonstrators added to the pressure President Richard Nixon felt to end the war. Two years later, after failed attempts to force the North Vietnamese to negotiate in good faith, Nixon found himself swept up in the early stages of the Watergate scandal. He tried to get the warring parties to sign a negotiated peace prior to the 1972 presidential election. That effort failed when the South Vietnamese leader, Nguyen Van Thieu, would not agree to concessions included in the agreement. Peace negotiations broke down in mid-December 1972.

Nixon threatened to resume heavy bombing of North Vietnam with B-52 aircraft if the North did not resume peace talks. The North Vietnamese refused, and Operation Linebacker II (also referred to as the Christmas Bombing) commenced three days later. The combined pressure of the peace movement in America and the continued bombing of Hanoi and other cities in North Vietnam brought all sides back to the negotiating table. In early 1973, a peace agreement was signed, allowing the United States to withdraw from the war. The peace did not last. The North and South Vietnamese forces continued to fight until North Vietnamese forces overran Saigon, in South Vietnam, on April 30, 1975, ending the war and uniting Vietnam under communist rule. Peace was finally achieved, but only after decades of struggle and at the cost of millions of lives.

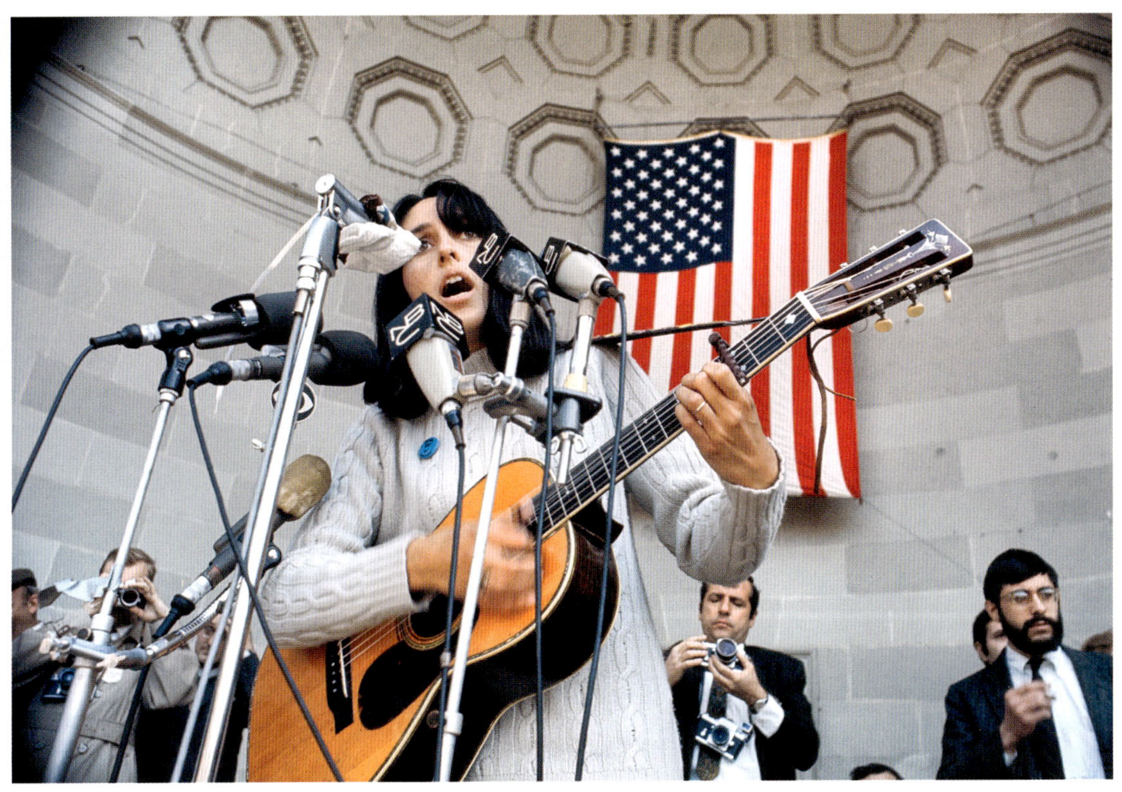

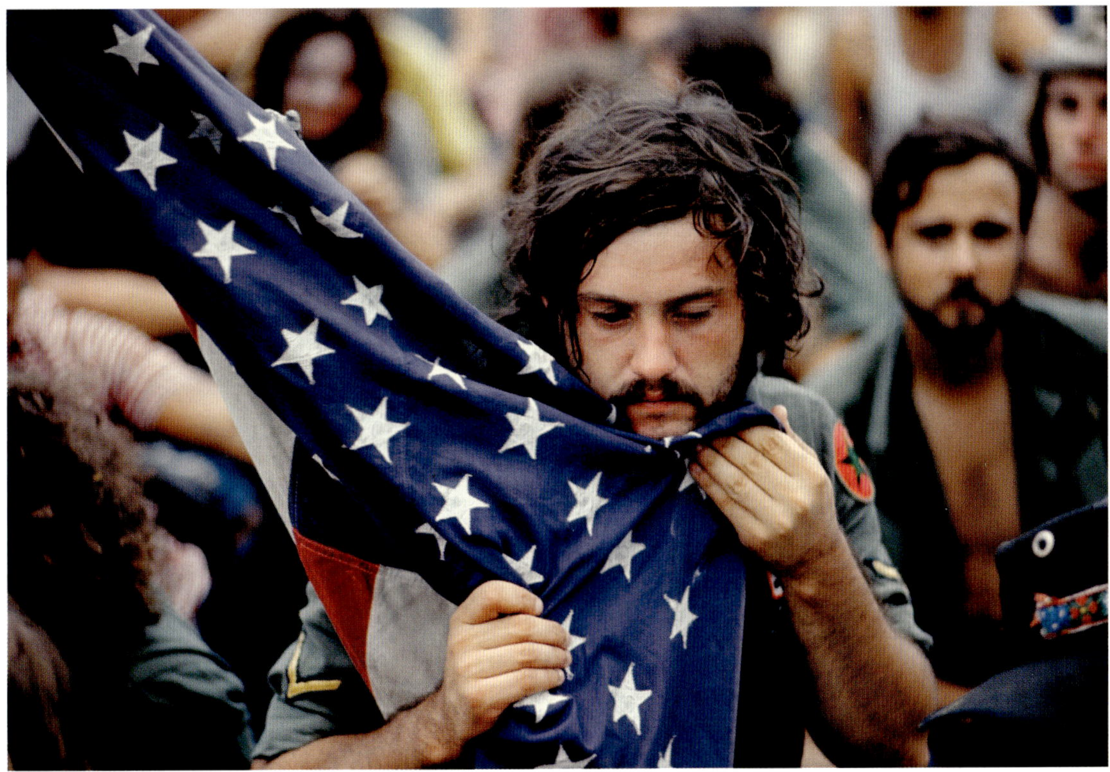

1976

to

2000

Tragedies and Miracles

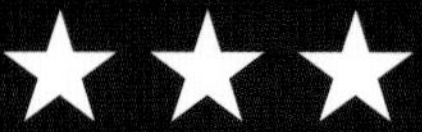

AS THE UNITED STATES BEGAN ITS THIRD CENTURY of existence, the final quarter of the twentieth century saw some progress in civil rights and growing conflict in the Middle East. The world was growing smaller as advances in communications and transportation fed the globalization of economies. The American flag came to be seen as a symbol of oppression by nations whose governments and resources had been used to support the growth of the American economy. America witnessed terrible tragedies on its home soil and abroad. The nation also saw great successes, including some in which the flag played a supporting role.

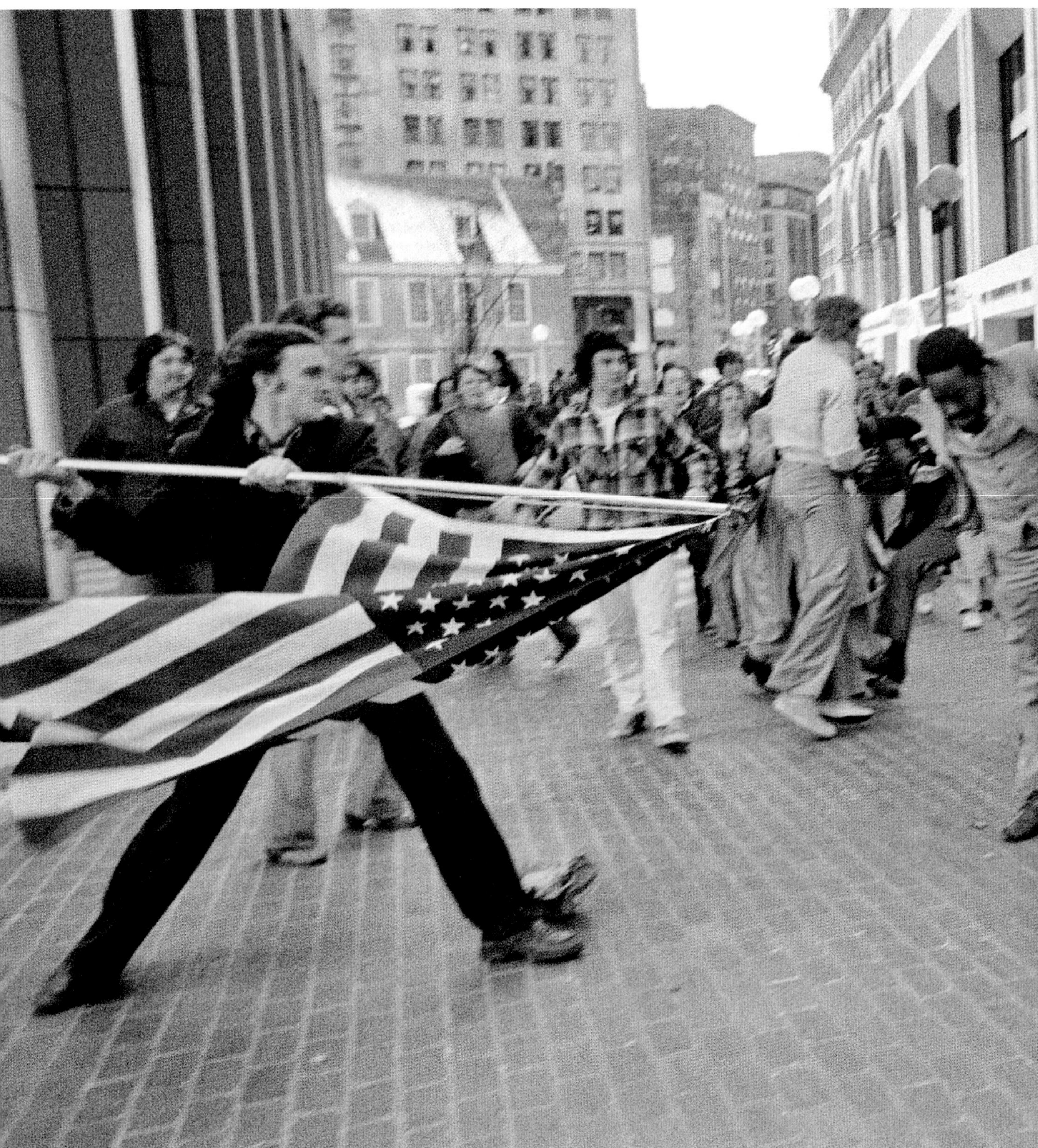

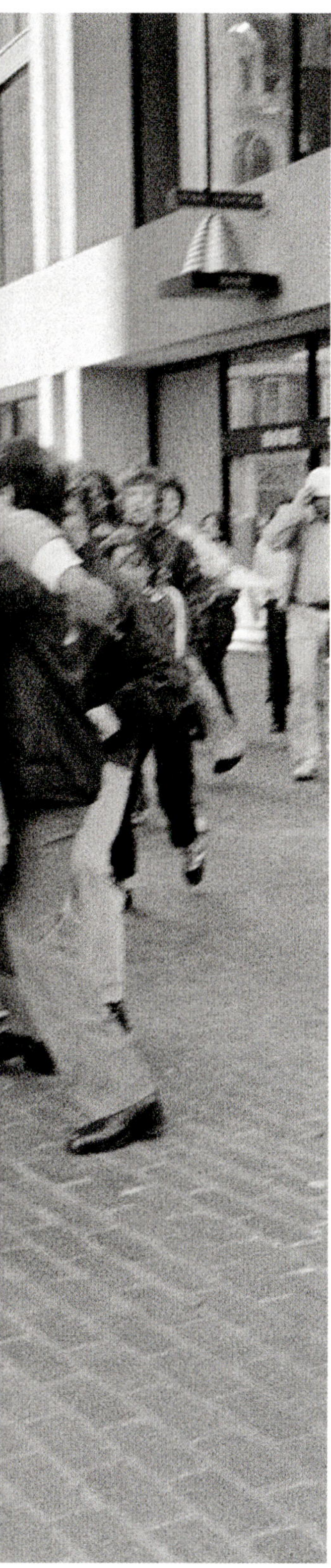

THE SOILING OF OLD GLORY

A Balancing Act

DATE: April 5, 1976

EVENT LOCATION: Boston City Hall Plaza, Boston, Massachusetts

CURRENT FLAG LOCATION: Unknown

After the gains of the civil rights movement of the 1960s, America's large cities faced a challenge: how to make public education more equitable for non-white students. In 1965, the state legislature of Massachusetts passed the Racial Imbalance Act, which declared that any school with a majority of non-white students was considered to be racially imbalanced and required those schools to desegregate or risk losing their state funding—permanently. The Boston School Committee (the governing body of the Boston Public Schools) refused to comply, and several members of the committee were eventually held in contempt of court. The judge in the case, Wendell Arthur Garrity Jr., ultimately supervised a plan created by the Massachusetts State Board of Education that bused students outside their neighborhoods to better integrate Boston's schools.

In the spring of 1976, after two years of court-ordered desegregation busing in Boston, tempers had gotten hot. The nearly daily protests around Boston by anti-desegregation activists boiled over on the morning of April 5 at Boston City Hall Plaza. Stanley Forman, a photographer

Previous: The Soiling of Old Glory, *photographed by Stanley Forman, during an anti-desegregation busing protest in Boston, April 5, 1976*

for the *Boston Herald American*, was documenting the protest, as he had been doing for months.

On that morning, Ted Landsmark, a Black community activist lobbying for better minority representation in the building trades, was going to a meeting at city hall. Unaware of the protest, he turned the corner into the plaza just as the demonstrators were heading toward him. They began shouting racial slurs and beating and kicking him. As Forman photographed the scene, one protester, high school student Joseph Rakes, swung an American flag attached to a pole at Landsmark. Forman captured the rage on Rakes's face and Landsmark's jump backward to avoid being hit. In the photo, it looks like Rakes was trying to stab Landsmark with the flag. (Later, Rakes said he was angry because he was being forced to attend a different school than the one that friends he grew up with attended. Rakes was convicted of assault with a deadly weapon and received a two-year suspended sentence.)

Forman's photograph, which came to be titled *The Soiling of Old Glory*, won the Pulitzer Prize for Spot Photography in 1977. It captured a moment of hate and frustration in the ongoing struggle for civil rights in the United States. The image also foreshadowed the use of flags as weaponry at the January 6, 2021, Capitol insurrection (page 197).

AMERICAN PRIDE FLAG

Pride and Prejudice

DATE: June 25, 1978
EVENT LOCATION: San Francisco, California
CURRENT FLAG LOCATION: GLBT Historical Society Museum, San Francisco, California

The Rainbow Flag (a series of horizontal stripes in rainbow colors) was first displayed publicly on June 25, 1978, for San Francisco's Gay Pride Day. Designed by Gilbert Baker, Lynn Segerblom, and James McNamara, the original flag consisted of eight horizontal stripes in pink, red, orange, yellow, green, turquoise, indigo, and violet. The layout was later simplified to feature six colors: red for life, orange for healing, yellow for sunlight, green for nature, blue for harmony and peace, and violet for spirit.

Pride events had taken on particular significance for the gay community in the 1970s after the events of the Stonewall riots. On June 28, 1969, New York City police officers raided the Stonewall Inn, at the time an illegal gay bar in Greenwich Village in Manhattan. Prior to that, most efforts by the New York police to shut down the gay bar industry were

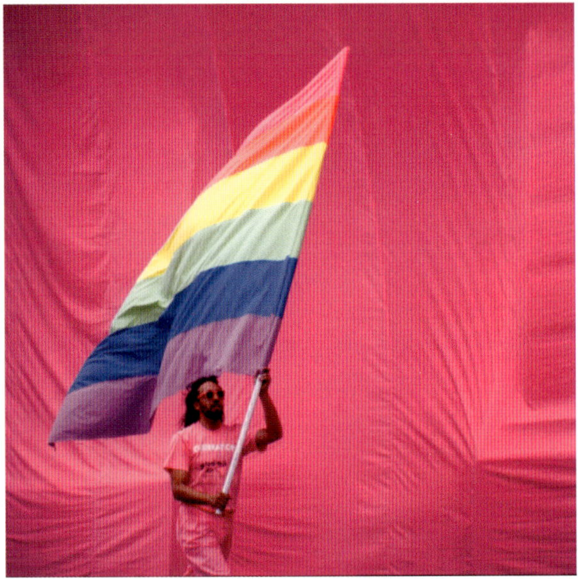

Above, left: *The original Rainbow Flag design, which consisted of eight color stripes, circa 1978*

Above, right: *Gilbert Baker with a contemporary Rainbow Flag, 1989*

Opposite: *Mile-long Rainbow Flag created by Gilbert Baker in 1994 and carried down First Avenue in Manhattan, New York, to commemorate the 25th anniversary of the Stonewall riots*

half-hearted attempts with consequently few arrests. Police typically came early in the evening, when patrons would be few in number, and were often bribed to inform gay bars of upcoming raids, allowing staff and bar-goers to prepare and avoid arrest. On this night, however, officers arrived with no warning and much later in the evening (a little after 1:00 a.m.), taking everyone in the Stonewall by surprise. Patrons refused to cooperate with the police. Minor scuffles broke out.

As the police waited for transport wagons for those being arrested, a mob of angry onlookers from the community grew outside the inn. Eventually things became violent, and fighting escalated between the police and the mob, which by now greatly outnumbered the officers. A fire was started in the Stonewall Inn. More fighting and chases ensued on Christopher Street and the surrounding area. It took police almost three hours to gain control of the neighborhood.

For the next few nights, riots continued. Though not the first uprising by the gay community, the Stonewall riots brought attention to the discrimination against and mistreatment of the gay community. Exactly a year later, on June 28, 1970, one of the largest gay pride demonstrations held to that point, the Christopher Street Liberation Day, took place. Similar marches were held in Chicago and Los Angeles, signaling an

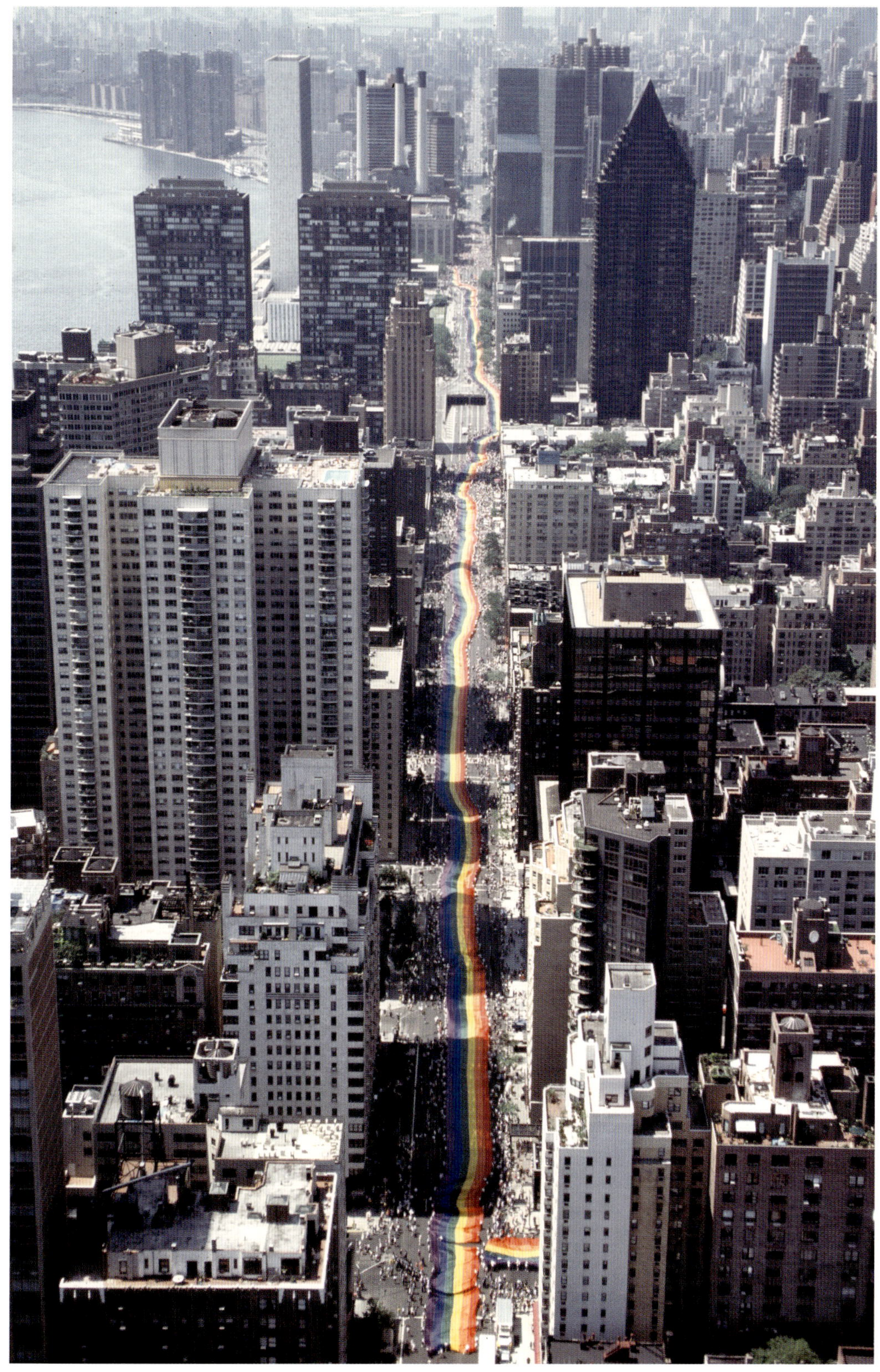

Protesters hold a pro-LGTBQIA+ rights flag outside the US Supreme Court on April 25, 2015, Washington, DC.

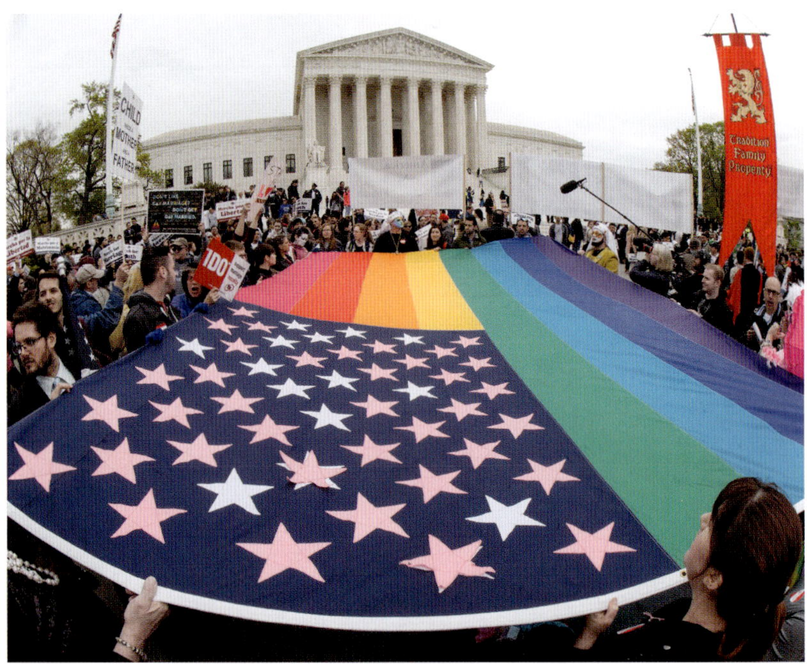

elevation in the frustration and visibility of the gay community. It was a sea change moment for the pride movement.

The pride constellation flag, created by Eddie Reynoso in 2009, adds the blue canton with stars from the American flag to the traditional Pride flag, tying the movement to more than two centuries of American history. Reynoso's original pride constellation flag had forty-six white stars and four pink stars representing the four states that had approved gay marriage at that time: Connecticut, Iowa, Massachusetts, and Vermont.

For each new state that approved gay marriage, one white star on the pride constellation flag was replaced with a pink one, in a manner similar to the addition of stars to the suffragette flag as states approved women's voting rights (page 69.) With the Supreme Court ruling in *Obergefell v. Hodges* in June 2015, gay marriage was established as national law in the United States and all the remaining white stars were replaced with pink stars.

Recent political rhetoric and events have raised alarms for the LGBTQIA+ community. Today, the Pride flag remains a symbol of not only gay pride but also the LGBTQIA+ community's determination to retain the rights they have fought for so bravely.

IRAN HOSTAGES FLAG

A Flag of Service and Suffering

DATE: 1979–1981

EVENT LOCATION: American Embassy, Tehran, Iran

CURRENT FLAG LOCATION: Private collection of Doug Sperling

On November 4, 1979, hundreds of students demonstrating at the American embassy in Tehran, Iran, broke through the gates of the compound and took sixty-six Americans hostage. Fourteen were released over the next few months. The rest were held for 444 days, until Ronald Reagan was sworn in as the fortieth president of the United States on January 20, 1981.

Historic events never occur in a vacuum. They are ramifications from the past, and they portend the future in the same fashion. The Iran hostage crisis stands as an example. In the early part of the twentieth century, Reza Shah Pahlavi had risen rapidly through the ranks of Iran's military to become the country's minister of war. In 1921, while the king, Ahmad Shah Qajar, was out of the country being treated for an illness, Pahlavi led a military coup and pronounced himself the new shah (the title *shah* is taken from *shahanshah,* "king of kings"). But Pahlavi struggled to respond to the rapidly changing world order and Iran's internal strife during his tenure.

In September 1941, fearing that Iran would side with the Nazis and supply them with critical oil resources, Britain and Russia invaded Iran and forced Pahlavi from power into exile. His son, Mohammad Reza Pahlavi, became the shah. The British and Russian occupation succeeded in keeping Germany from getting oil from Iran. After the war, Mohammad Reza Pahlavi began to modernize Iran, and the economy grew. People began to move from the countryside to the major cities, sparking further economic and social development.

In 1953, Prime Minister Mohammad Mosaddegh nationalized British oil investments in Iran, in opposition to Pahlavi, who it looked like might be ousted. American and British interests deemed Iranian oil too important to allow any interference with Pahlavi's cooperation, so the two countries backed a successful coup to remove Mosaddegh. This short-term fix caused long-term issues. The new shah became increasingly obsessed with controlling every aspect of the country. By 1979, Iran was brewing with turmoil. The citizens were frustrated with the shah's rule. The shah clamped down on any opposition. Many Iranians blamed the West—especially the United States—for the shah's ability to restrict their life. Eventually the shah's policies and his iron-fisted rule brought the Iranian people together in the Iranian Revolution. On January 17, 1979, the shah sought exile, first in Egypt and later in Morocco.

With the shah gone, the revolutionaries turned their ire toward the United States, the country they felt had aided the shah in his tyrannous rule. Their disdain for America was on display on February 14, 1979, when members of Fadaiyan-e-Khalq (Organization of Iranian People's Fedai Guerrillas) stormed the American embassy in Tehran. To prevent further violence, Ambassador William H. Sullivan surrendered to them. Iranian authorities were able to return control of the embassy to the Americans in a few hours and Sullivan was released.

Pressured by Henry Kissinger (who had been secretary of state under Presidents Nixon and Ford) and other conservatives, President Jimmy Carter allowed the shah to travel to the United States in October 1979 for treatment of chronic lymphocytic leukemia. This was the final straw for the revolutionaries. On November 4, they seized the embassy, marking the beginning of the Iran hostage crisis.

David J. Sperling was serving as defense attaché for the US Embassy in Cairo, Egypt, when the unrest in Iran began. His son, Doug Sperling, was a student at the Cairo American College (an international high school) at the time of the embassy takeover. One of Doug's teachers, Roberta Smith, knew one of the hostages, Bill Keough. Keough had previously been the superintendent of the American School in Tehran. In 1979, he was working

Right: *Letter written by Bill Keough, one of the hostages, May 17, 1981*

Following: *A newspaper flag signed by twenty of the Iranian hostages from the US Embassy in Tehran, 1981*

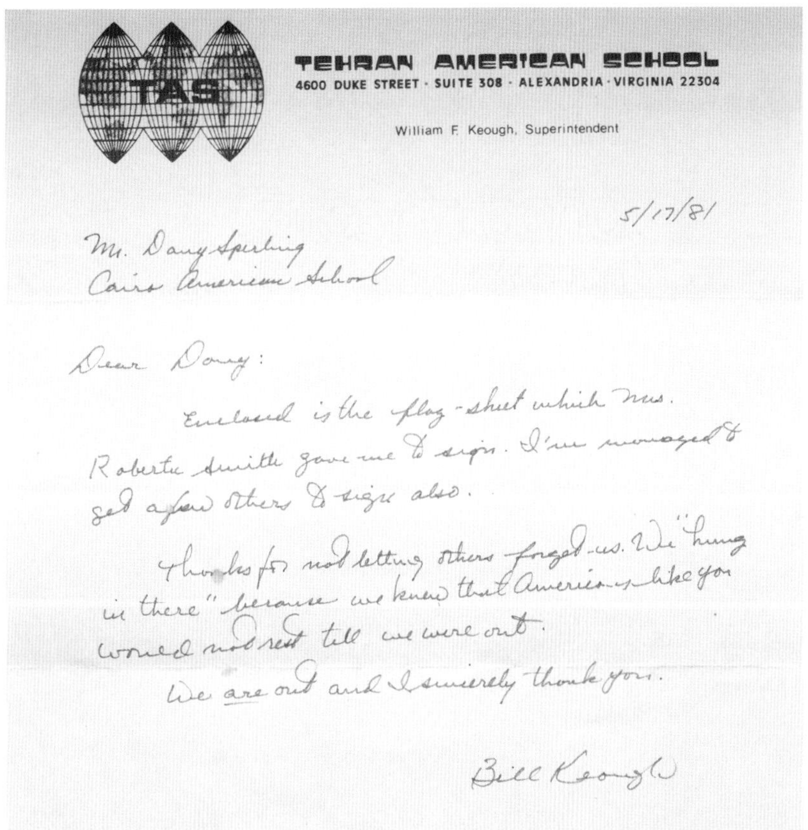

TAS

TEHRAN AMERICAN SCHOOL
4600 DUKE STREET · SUITE 308 · ALEXANDRIA · VIRGINIA 22304

William F. Keough, Superintendent

5/17/81

Mr. Doug Sperling
Cairo American School

Dear Doug:

Enclosed is the flag-sheet which Mrs. Roberta Smith gave me to sign. I've managed to get a few others to sign also.

Thanks for not letting others forget us. We "hung in there" because we knew that Americans like you would not rest till we were out.

We are out and I sincerely thank you.

Bill Keough

in Pakistan but had returned to Tehran to retrieve student records. He just happened to be at the embassy when the Iranian students took over the compound.

Doug had saved a copy of a page depicting an American flag that was published in his hometown paper, the *Pensacola News Journal*, on December 9, 1979, with the words "Free Our Hostages" printed beneath it. In 1981, after the hostages had been released, Doug gave the printed flag to Smith so she could get it to Keough. He was able to have it signed by many of the hostages and then returned it to Sperling. Keough included a letter that read, in part, "Thanks for not letting others forget us. We 'hung in there' because we knew Americans like you would not rest till we were out. We *are* out and I sincerely thank you."

The simple paper flag that the Iran hostages signed symbolizes the service, bravery, and suffering they endured. It should also remind us that all our government's actions have consequences. Understanding that our interactions with other nations will shape our relationships and events in the years to come is critical to ensuring the security and longevity of the United States.

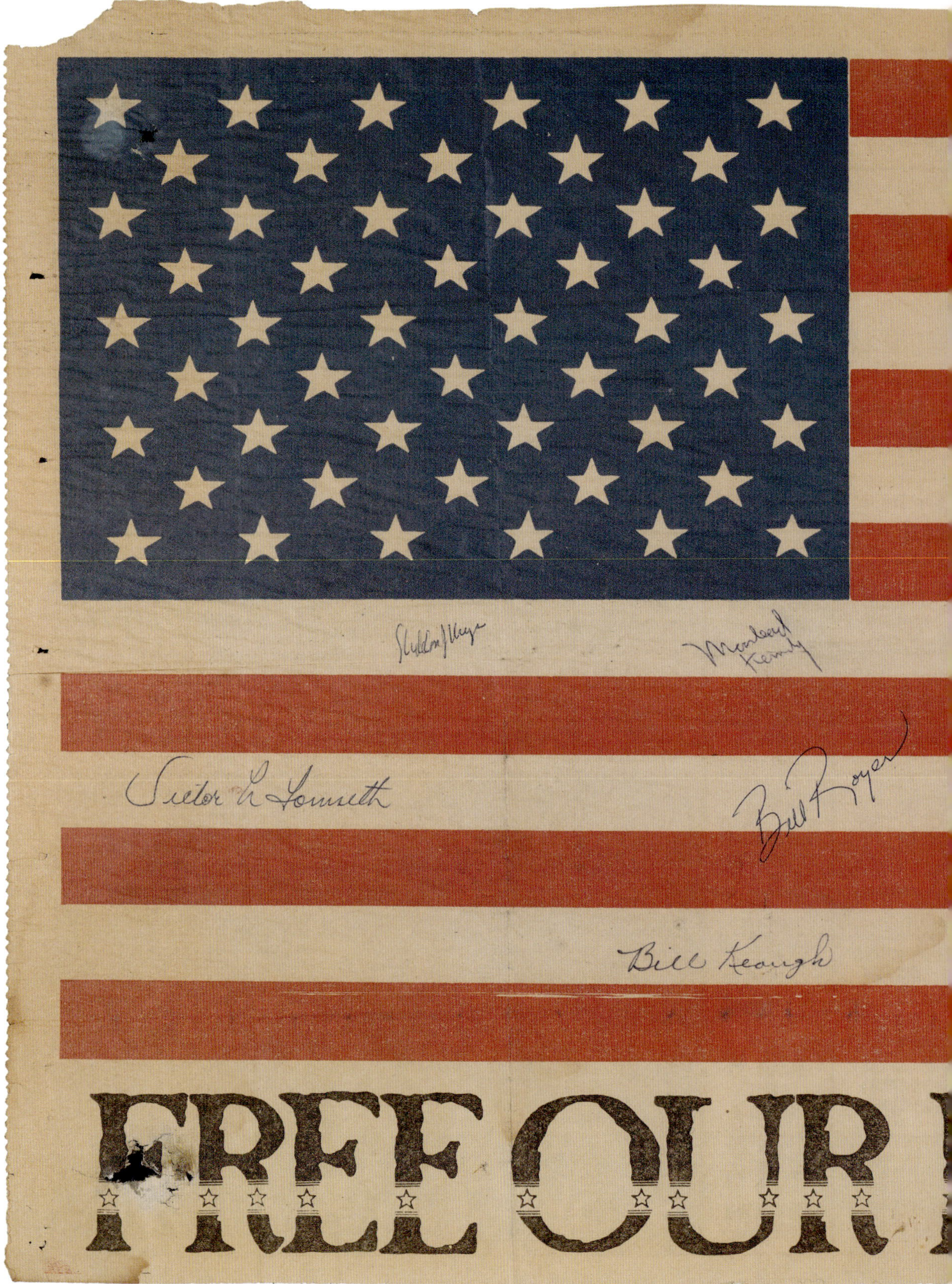
FREE OUR

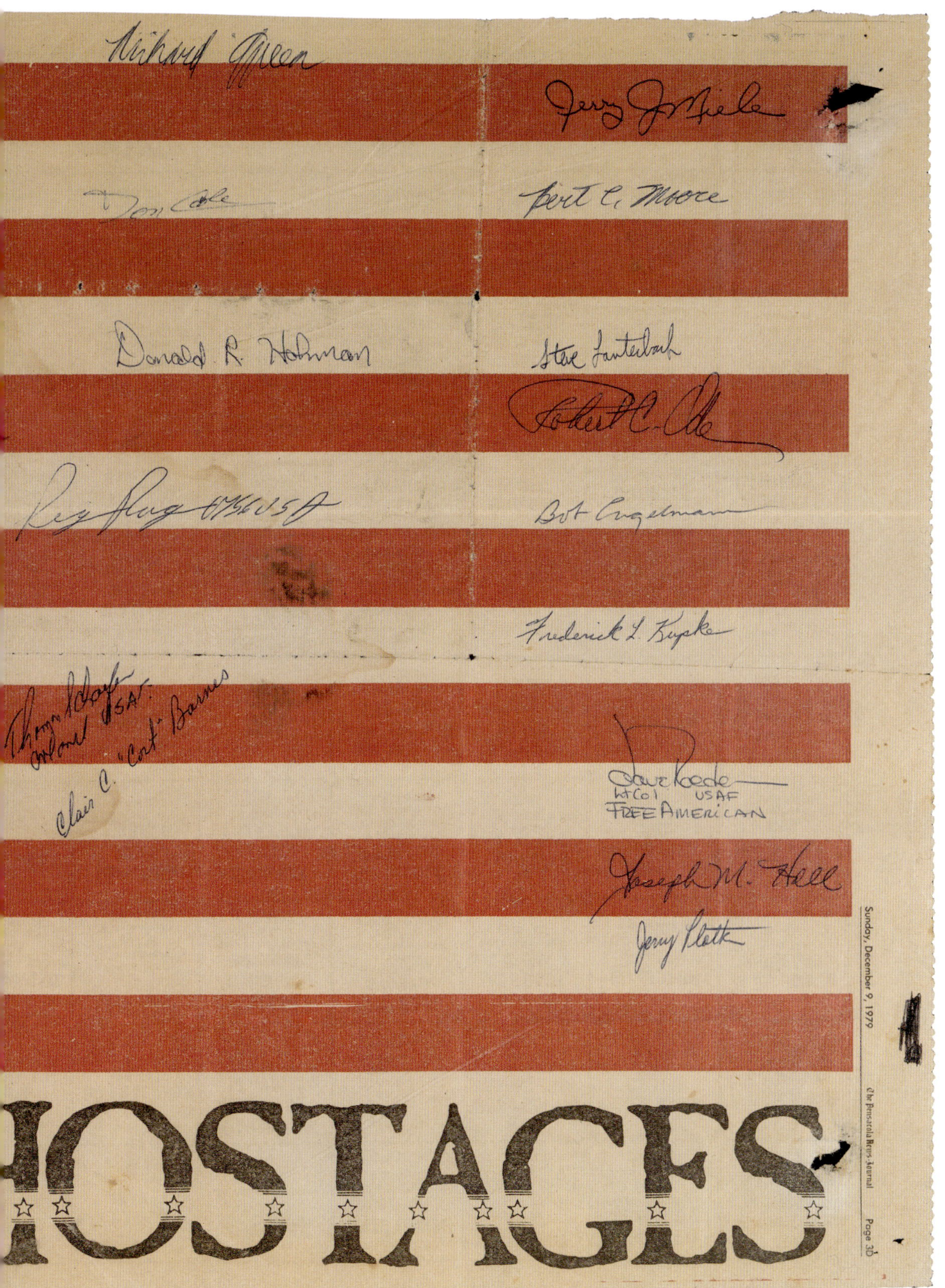
Donald R. Hohman
Frederick L. Kupke
LtCol USAF
FREE AMERICAN
Joseph M. Hall
HOSTAGES
Sunday, December 9, 1979
The Pensacola News-Journal
Page 30

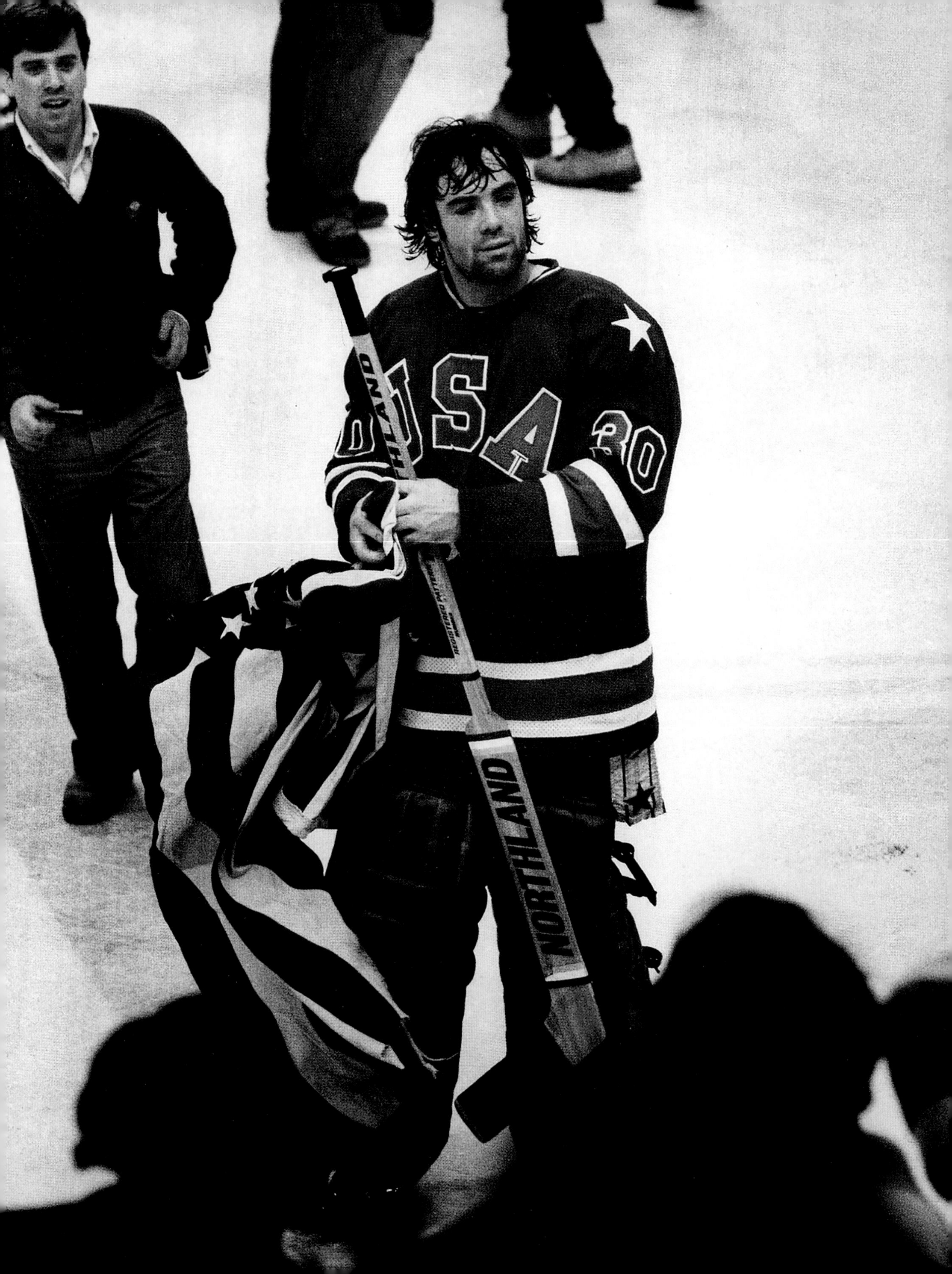
NORTHLAND
USA
30
NORTHLAND

MIRACLE ON ICE FLAG

Miracle on Ice

DATE: February 22 and 24, 1980

EVENT LOCATION: Lake Placid Olympic Center Arena (now the Herb Brooks Arena, named in honor of the 1980 US Olympic hockey coach), Lake Placid, New York

CURRENT FLAG LOCATION: Private collection of Jim Craig

***Opposite:** Team USA's goalie Jim Craig with the United States flag after their gold medal win against Finland, Lake Placid, New York, February 24, 1980*

In February 1980, it seemed like the world was mired in war and conflict. The Vietnam War had officially ended just five years earlier with the unconditional surrender of the South Vietnamese government (page 156). On November 4, 1979, militant Iranian college students had overrun the US embassy in Tehran and were still holding fifty-three Americans hostage (page 167). The Cold War was simmering, with Soviets moving into Afghanistan at the request of the Afghan government in late December 1979 (a move that would cause the United States and sixty other countries to boycott the 1980 Summer Olympics in Moscow).

It was this background that set the stage for the "Ice-Cold War": The US Olympic hockey team was set to battle the Soviet Union on the ice in Lake Placid, New York, in the medal round of the 1980 Winter Olympics. The Soviet ice hockey team had dominated the Olympics for twenty years. The only gold medal the US men's ice hockey team had ever won was at the 1960 Squaw Valley Winter Games in California. The Soviets had earned gold medals in 1964, 1968, 1972, and 1976. Out of the top twelve teams, the US hockey squad was ranked number seven. The Soviets were ranked number one.

At that time, professional athletes were banned from competing in Olympic Games by the International Sports Federation. This meant that America's best hockey players in the National Hockey League (NHL) could not participate. The US team was made up of college students who, prior to the fall of 1979, had not played together. In the first round, the Americans averaged five goals per game, an outstanding achievement. They won four games and tied one. But the Soviets averaged 9.8 goals in their first-round games, handily winning all five contests.

Four teams made it to the medal round: the United States, the Soviet Union, Finland, and Sweden. The two winning teams of the first games of the finals would play for the gold.

On February 22, 1980, the US and Soviet teams took to the ice. Shockingly, about nine minutes into the final period, the US scored a goal to tie the game, 3–3. Shortly after, US team captain Mike Eruzione scored what would become the winning goal. When the clock ticked down to zero, ABC sportscaster Al Michaels made the iconic pronouncement, "Do you believe in miracles? Yes!"—giving the moment its moniker, "Miracle on Ice." At the Olympic arena and in front of TVs across the nation, America went wild.

But it wasn't over. Two days later, the United States faced Finland in the gold medal game. Amazingly, the Americans repeated the feat of beating a team that was by all accounts superior. They defeated Finland 4–2, claiming the gold.

At the stadium, a fan, Peter Cappuccilli Jr., had draped an American flag over the rink's glass at the end of the game. He called out to goalie Jim Craig to come and take it. The celebration was so chaotic that Cappuccilli ended up climbing over the wall to hand the flag to Craig. Just as Cappuccilli approached him, TV cameras caught Craig trying to spot his father in the crowd. Cappuccilli draped the flag over Craig's shoulders as he continued to search for his father in the stands. Craig's mother, Margaret, had passed away from cancer in 1977. Craig wanted to share the moment with his father, grateful for all the sacrifices his parents had made for him to reach that pinnacle.

The Miracle on Ice was a glimmer of hope for Americans after decades of troubled times. The American team's success was so unexpected and the flag's role so spontaneous that it sealed the moment in the hearts of people around the world. Craig still has the Miracle on Ice flag in his possession.

BORN IN THE U.S.A. ALBUM COVER FLAG

Born in the U.S.A.

DATE: June 4, 1984

EVENT LOCATION: Annie Leibovitz Studio

CURRENT FLAG LOCATION: Unknown

Bruce Springsteen's "Born in the U.S.A." has blared from loudspeakers at political rallies for decades. However, the song is not the all-American anthem many believe it to be. "Born in the U.S.A." concerns the plight of the many Vietnam War veterans who returned to an America that had grown tired of the cost of the war and who were (unlike the soldiers who returned from World War II and Korea) often looked down on and disparaged for their service. Many Americans considered the war to have been a wasteful and immoral endeavor, adding insult to injury for veterans.

"Born in the U.S.A." highlights this tragedy and the irony that the veterans who had fought for their country to stem the spread of communism in Southeast Asia had now been abandoned by their country at a time when they needed support in finding jobs and housing, health care, mental health care, and other resources even still, a decade after the war's end. The paradox in Springsteen's ballad exists in the juxtaposition between the chorus, which arrives as a patriotic cheer—"Born in the U.S.A.!"—and the verses, which depict the lived experience of many veterans of the Vietnam era.

***Opposite:** Bruce Springsteen's* Born in the U.S.A. *album cover, photograph by Annie Leibovitz, New York City, 1984*

Renowned photographer Annie Leibovitz shot the now-famous cover for the album that featured this ballad and carried the same title: *Born in the U.S.A.* True to his blue-collar, common-man canon, Springsteen appears in the photograph in blue jeans and a white T-shirt, shown from behind, with a red ballcap in his back pocket, set against a backdrop of the red and white stripes of the flag—all classic symbols for America.

As Springsteen later told *Rolling Stone* magazine in an interview published on May 18, 2006, "I was very conscious of being an American musician and addressing the issues of the day. There was a sense that the flag was up for grabs, that you had the right in staking out your claim to its meaning and to the kind of country you wanted your kids to grow up in."

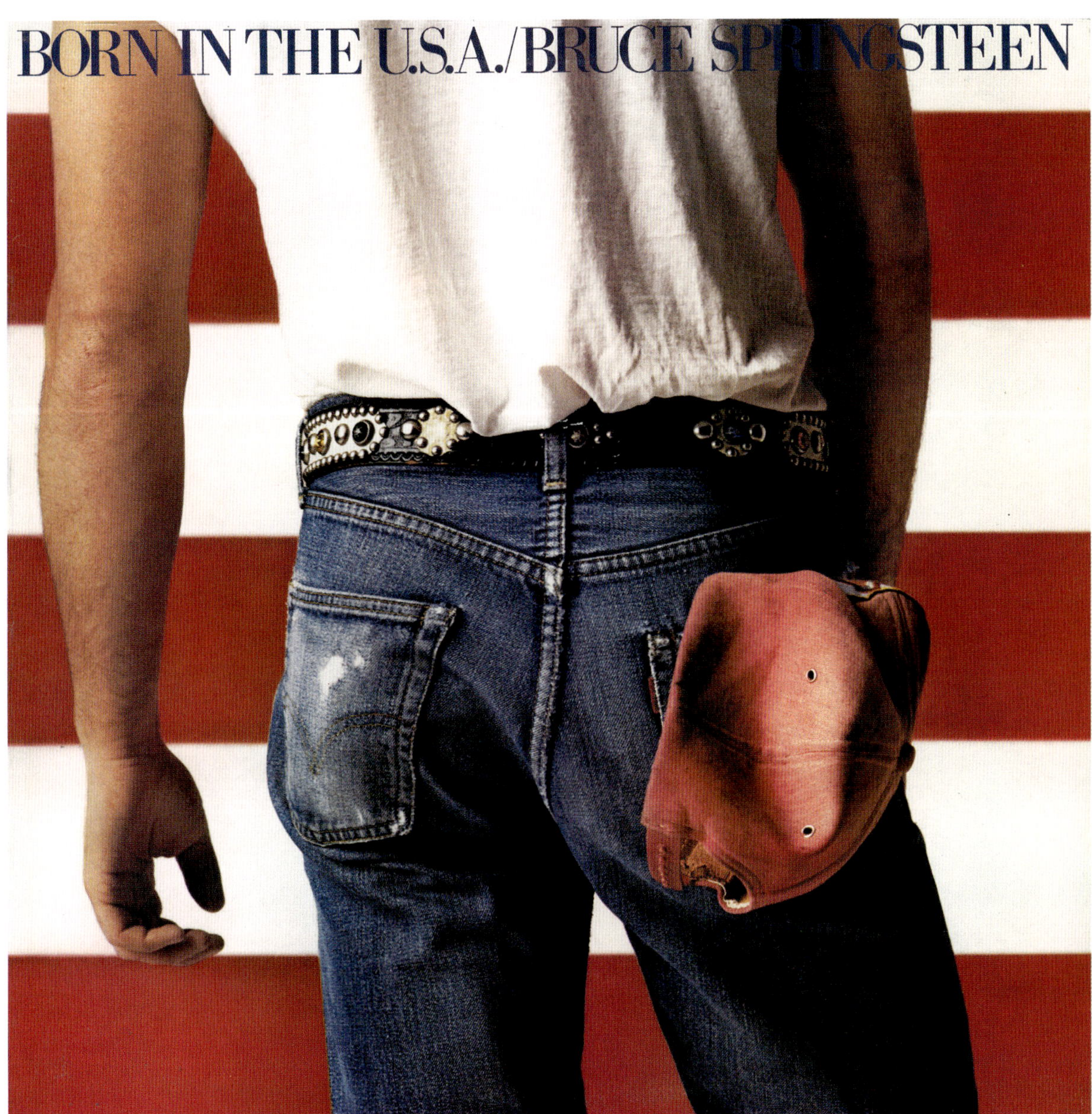
BORN IN THE U.S.A./BRUCE SPRINGSTEEN

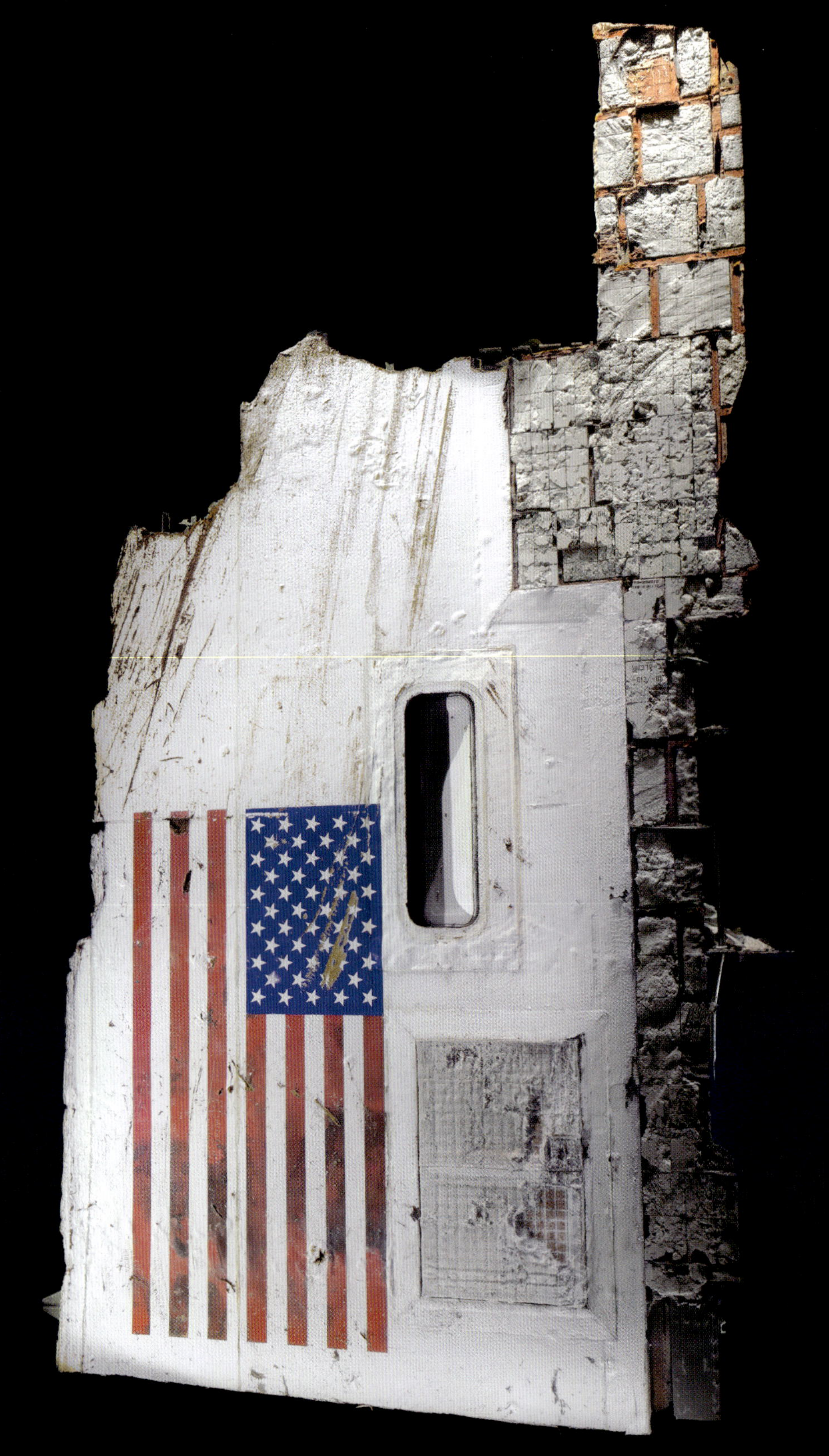

CHALLENGER **FUSELAGE FLAG**

A Reminder of Loss and Courage

DATE: January 28, 1986

EVENT LOCATION: Kennedy Space Center, Florida

CURRENT FLAG LOCATION: *Forever Remembered* Exhibit, Kennedy Space Center Visitor Complex, Cape Canaveral, Florida

Opposite: *Space Shuttle* Challenger *recovered fuselage section with American flag,* Forever Remembered *Exhibit, Atlantis Pavilion, Kennedy Space Center Visitor Complex, Florida, 2017*

Anyone alive at the time and old enough to understand what had happened remembers where they were when they heard that the Space Shuttle *Challenger* had exploded during launch on January 28, 1986. Notably, on the twenty-fifth mission of NASA's Space Shuttle program, *Challenger* carried the first civilian space explorer, high school teacher Christa McAuliffe, who had planned to teach lessons from space. That all ended when a joint on one of the solid rocket boosters was breached by the burning solid fuel. The escaping flames impinged on the craft's external tank, which held liquid hydrogen and liquid oxygen. The tank failed from the heat and exploded, destroying the *Challenger* orbiter. All seven souls aboard were lost in the accident.

Over a period of seven months, divers and salvage teams scoured the floor of the Atlantic Ocean off Cape Canaveral, searching for debris. One of the larger sections recovered was a portion of the left side of the shuttle body that contained a graphic of the American flag. The recovered debris of the orbiter, boosters, and external tank was entombed in two abandoned Minuteman missile silos at Launch Complexes 31 and 32 on the Cape Canaveral Air Force Station (now the Cape Canaveral Space Force Station).

Seventeen years later, on February 1, 2003, Space Shuttle *Columbia* burned up while reentering Earth's atmosphere. As had been the case for *Challenger*, the cause of *Columbia*'s destruction occurred during launch. A briefcase-size piece of insulating foam on the spacecraft's external tank broke free and collided with the left wing at 500 miles per hour (805 kph). The foam penetrated the edge of the wing, creating a hole. Upon reentry, friction caused by the orbiter's interface with Earth's atmosphere melted the wing's interior. The spacecraft was no longer able to maintain flight orientation, and it broke apart from the aerodynamic forces. All seven astronauts were lost. Again, months of recovery effort, this time in Texas and Louisiana, were needed to retrieve the orbiter debris.

With the end of the Space Shuttle program and decommissioning of the active orbiters in 2011, plans were made to display the retired Space Shuttle *Atlantis* at the Kennedy Space Center Visitor Complex. A tribute to the crews of *Challenger* (STS-51L) and *Columbia* (STS-107) was designed for presentation in the *Atlantis* display pavilion. Along with individual display cases housing personal effects from the *Challenger* and *Columbia* crewmembers' careers, a recovered piece from each of the orbiters was also added to the exhibit. For *Columbia*, the recovered flight deck window frames were chosen. Pine needles from the forest it landed in are still visible in the crevices of the frame. The recovered section of fuselage with the American flag was selected for *Challenger*. There were three American flag emblems on each shuttle. Two were located on either side of the orbiter's fuselage a little more than halfway to the tail. Originally, a flag was placed on the top of the left wing. This location was moved to the right wing in the latter years of the program. This remnant of the spacecraft displays scorch marks on the flag, streak scars in the thermal blankets, and fractured thermal tiles. The dynamic stresses of the disasters are visible in these poignant reminders of loss.

In 2016, NASA test director Mike Ciannilli created the Apollo, Challenger, Columbia Lessons Learned Program (ACCLLP) to ensure that the errors and oversights that contributed to the loss of spacecraft and crews in those spaceflight programs would not be forgotten. The program also seeks to highlight the ideas, actions, plans, and responses that have made NASA one of the most successful organizations in the US government. Through the ACCLLP, NASA employees are introduced to the history of NASA's tragedies and triumphs and the lessons learned from them.

AFRICAN AMERICAN FLAG, BY DAVID HAMMONS

Outrageously Magical Things

DATE: 1990

EVENT LOCATION: *Black USA* exhibition, Museum Overholland, Amsterdam

CURRENT FLAG LOCATIONS: Museum of Modern Art, New York City, National Museum of African American History and Culture, Washington, DC, and The Broad, Los Angeles, California

Many flags have endeavored to send a message by playing off the design of the traditional American flag, including the Thin Blue Line flag (hailing the work of police and safety officers) and the Pride flag (celebrating the LGBTQIA+ community, see page 163). David Hammons's *African American Flag* is another example of using the American flag as a template. Hammons substituted the blue and white with the green and black of the Pan-African flag, which was created by Marcus Garvey in 1920 for the Universal Negro Improvement Association and African Communities League (UNIA-ACL). The UNIA-ACL was a Black nationalist organization founded in 1914 with the aim of advancing the standing of people of African descent around the world. The colors from the Pan-African flag give Hammons's flag new meaning. The color black,

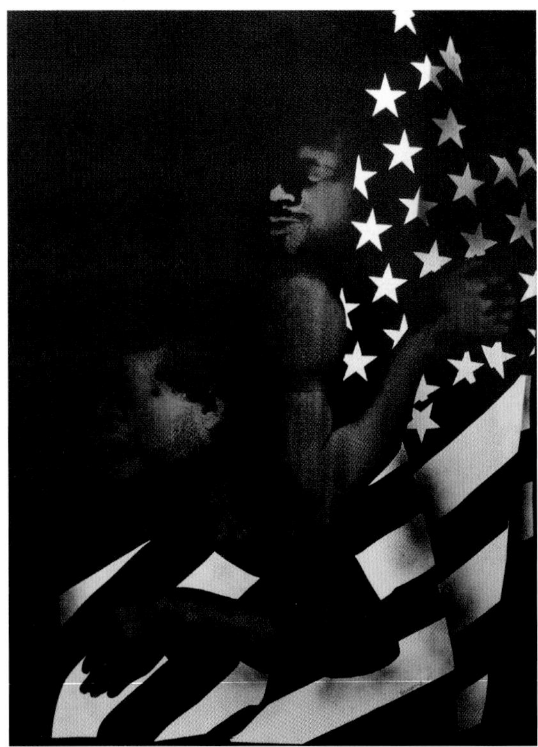

***Above:** David Hammons's* Black First, America Second, *grease, pigment, and silkscreen on paper, 1970*

***Opposite:** David Hammons's* African American Flag, *1990*

substituted for white in the stripes and stars, symbolizes the Black people. The green of the canton, replacing the traditional blue, represents the verdant nature of Africa. The red stripes symbolize the blood spilled in the fight for Black liberation. Beyond this, *African American Flag* gives Black Americans a symbol that says and shows they are both Black and American—not one or the other.

Hammons is highly regarded in the art world for his groundbreaking work and the variety of mediums he works with, which encompass performance art, printmaking, drawing, painting, sculpture, collage, photography, and videography. He has received many accolades, including Guggenheim and MacArthur fellowships. His work focuses on the Black experience while avoiding trite stereotypes and themes. Hammons's 1970 piece *Black First, America Second* is a double self-portrait, showing two versions of himself covered by an American flag. Hammons stated that the artwork and its title are straightforward in their meaning—that Hammons views his race as a priority to his country.

Hammons's *African American Flag* has become a common sight at protests in support of Black rights. It is carried at Black Lives Matter marches. It is flown to protest violence against Black Americans (page 192). It is used as a symbol of Black pride. Versions of the flag are held in some of the nation's most prestigious museums, including The Broad, the Museum of Modern Art, and the Smithsonian National Museum of African American History and Culture. Referring to the artwork *African American Flag* in *Smithsonian* magazine, Tuliza Fleming, the curator of American art at the museum, stated, "Artists have celebrated, interpreted, and provided new interpretations of the American flag for hundreds of years. I think the celebration of freedom embodied in the symbol of the American flag includes the right to critically evaluate it through an artistic lens."

Appropriating an iconic symbol like the flag of the United States and making it into a new cultural statement is bold and risky. Yet as Hammons himself observed, "Outrageously magical things happen when you mess around with a symbol."

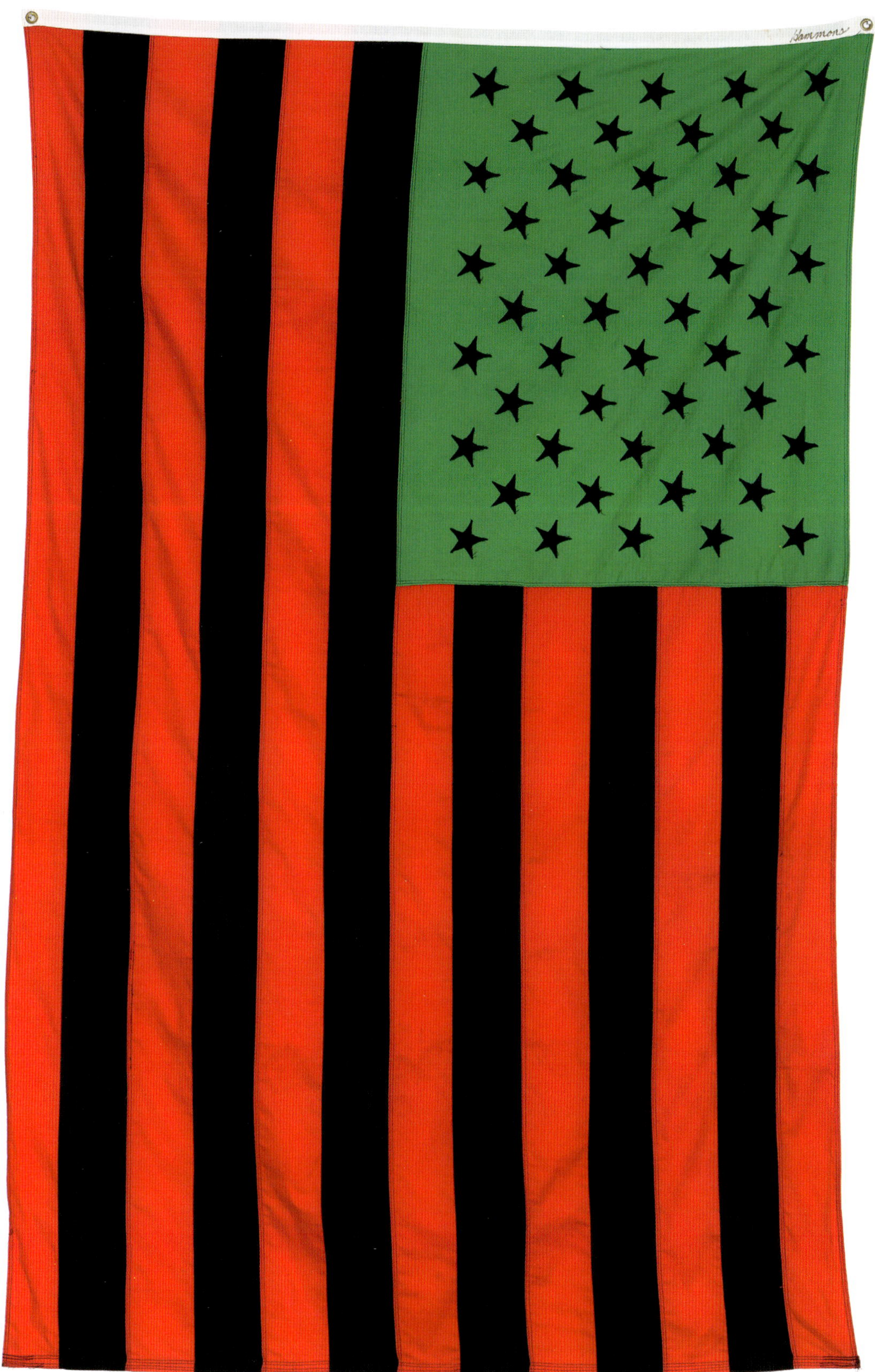
Hammons

2001 *to* 2025

America in the Twenty-First Century

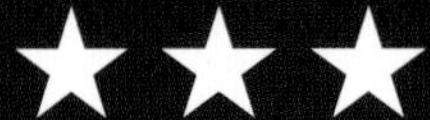

THE UNITED STATES BEGAN THE TWENTY-FIRST century by suffering the worst attack on American soil since Pearl Harbor. The events of September 11, 2001, shook the country to its core. A growing divide between conservative and liberal approaches to governing continued to widen until there was an attempt to upset the results from the 2020 presidential election and the Capitol was taken over by rioters. The American flag was present to witness both tragic and disturbing events. Yet the flag was also on display to acknowledge the resilience of Americans after natural disasters, like the Joplin, Missouri, tornado, and dramatic achievements, like the US women's gymnastics team winning an Olympic gold medal in Paris.

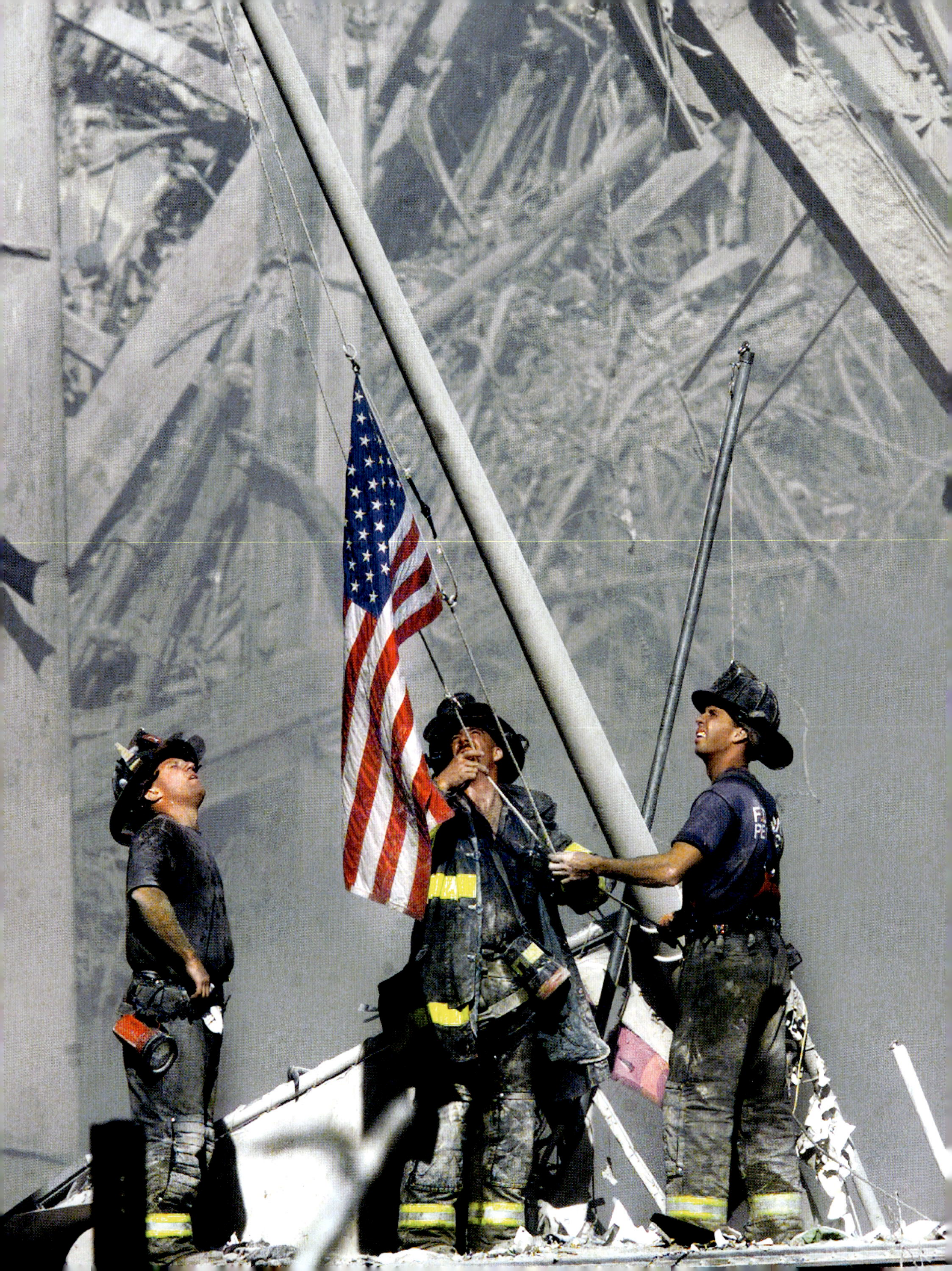

9/11 FLAG

Raising the Flag at Ground Zero

DATE: September 11, 2001

EVENT LOCATION: World Trade Center, New York City

CURRENT FLAG LOCATION: 9/11 Memorial & Museum, New York City

Opposite: *Three firefighters—(from left) George Johnson, Dan McWilliams, and Billy Eisengrein—raise the American flag with a background of destruction from the 9/11 attack, New York City, September 11, 2001.*

Thomas E. Franklin, photojournalist for *The Record* newspaper of Woodland Park, New Jersey, shouldn't have been at work on September 11, 2001. He happened to stop by the newsroom just as news broke that a plane had struck one of the World Trade Center towers. Like so many journalists that morning, unable to enter New York City, he made his way to the New Jersey side of the Hudson River. Eventually, a colleague helped him hitch a boat ride across the river. Once dropped off in Manhattan, Franklin began photographing the destruction and recovery efforts. By 5:00 p.m., he was running out of digital storage space in his camera's memory card. In an August 31, 2021, interview, Franklin related the experience of taking his famous photograph, *Raising the Flag at Ground Zero.*

> *I saw these three firemen fumbling with the flag, getting ready to raise it. It didn't immediately register to me what they were about*

> *to do, but I knew it seemed significant. So I moved into position where I could observe what they were doing . . . then very quickly, in a short burst, they hoisted the flag up a pole and I shot a burst of photographs.*

Franklin didn't realize the magnitude of the photo he made at the time. The image "didn't really stand out in any way," he said.

Franklin's photo of firefighters George Johnson, Dan McWilliams, and Billy Eisengrein raising the American flag against the backdrop of the destruction caused by the 9/11 attacks was the first glimmer of hope on that dark day. McWilliams had taken the flag from a nearby yacht, fittingly named the *Star of America*. The firefighters found a flagpole sticking out of the rubble and attached the flag.

Reminiscent of the Star-Spangled Banner surviving the battle at Fort McHenry (page 25) and the raising of the flag on Mount Suribachi on Iwo Jima (page 109), *Raising the Flag at Ground Zero* was a reminder and a symbol of America's resilience and strength. The image's poignancy only grew over time as the scope of loss, especially the New York City Fire Department's 343 casualties that day, became clear.

Raising the Flag at Ground Zero was photographed on September 11, 2001—the first of many heartbreaking days that were to unfold over the next months. Coupled with the strike on the Pentagon and the brave actions of the passengers and crew aboard Flight 93, who stopped a third attack at the cost of their own lives, it was the worst assault on American soil since Pearl Harbor (page 94). Along with the symbolism of the American flag, the firefighters who raised Old Glory on 9/11 became symbols for all the brave first responders who headed straight into the disaster zone—many realizing they may not make it out.

JOPLIN TORNADO FLAG

An Icon of Resilience

DATE: May 22 and 29, 2011
EVENT LOCATION: Joplin, Missouri
CURRENT FLAG LOCATION: Unknown

Eighty-five-year-old Hugh Hills had just pulled dinner out of the oven when he saw the storm warning on TV. He wrapped himself in a quilt and hid inside a closet while the tornado tore the second story off his home. Hills escaped unharmed. Not everyone else in Joplin, Missouri, was that lucky.

The tornado that hit Joplin on May 22, 2011, was the costliest tornado event in US history. Earlier in the day, weather forecasters at the National Weather Service had been monitoring a low-pressure system in the upper Great Plains. The predictions for severe weather quickly expanded south through the lower Midwest. The first tornado watch for the area was issued at 1:30 p.m. At 5:34 p.m., a funnel cloud formed about 4 miles (6.4 km) southwest of downtown Joplin. It was later determined that the twister began at an EF0 rating, the lowest level on the Enhanced Fujita Scale, which is used to measure the destructive force of tornados. The strength of the vortex grew quickly, and twelve minutes later, it was at EF5—the

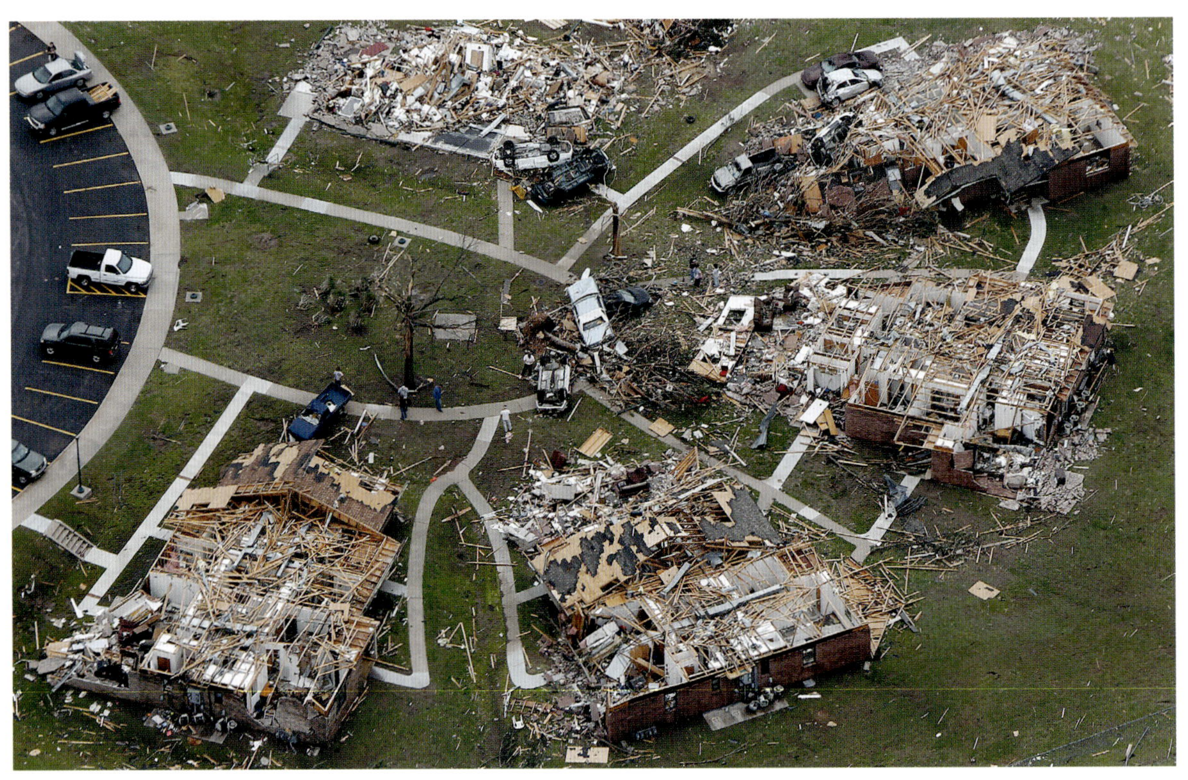

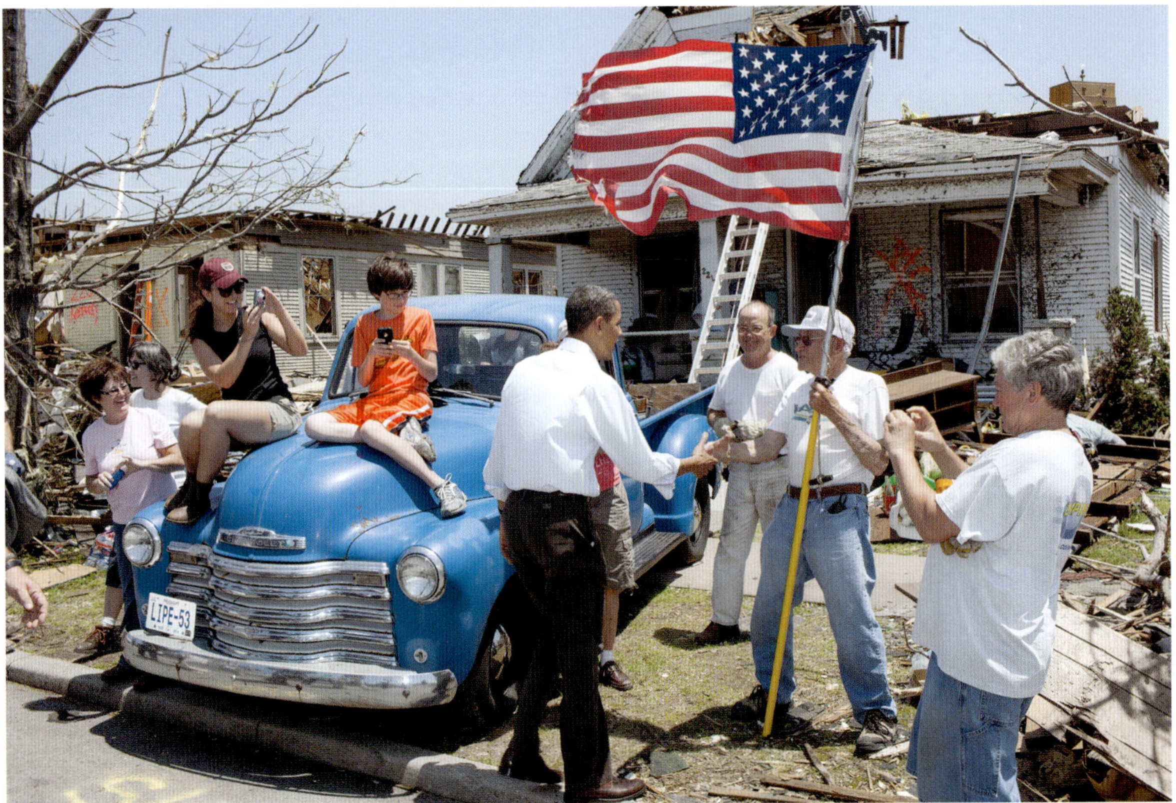
LIPE-53

Opposite, top: *Aerial view of damage from the May 22, 2011, Joplin tornado*

Opposite, bottom: *President Barack Obama greets Hugh Hills, eighty-five, in front of his home a week after the Joplin tornado, Joplin, Missouri, May 29, 2011.*

highest EF rating. It swept through the industrial park located southeast of downtown Joplin. By 6:00 p.m., the twister had moved out of the major Joplin residential areas and was losing power. The storm continued southeast and dissipated. It had torn a gash through the heart of Joplin in less than twenty minutes. Nearby communities received major damage as well.

Joplin's civil defense warning sirens had sounded at 5:17 p.m., giving residents at least seventeen minutes to take shelter. Though most residents were able to take cover, the tornado was so intense and powerful that 158 people lost their lives. Another 1,100 were injured. Some houses were completely swept away. Cars and large trucks were tossed hundreds of yards. At its widest track, the tornado was over 1 mile (1.6 km) wide, and it stayed on the ground for over 20 miles (32 km). More than 4,000 structures were destroyed and another 4,000 damaged. Maximum winds were estimated at more than 200 miles per hour (320 kph). In total, the tornado caused over $2.8 billion in losses to Joplin and surrounding communities. (In 2012 and 2013, Joplin received more than $158 million in recovery funding from the federal government. Another $200 million came from donations.)

A week after the tornado, on May 29, 2011, President Barack Obama came to Joplin to witness firsthand the destruction and comfort the survivors. He spoke with Hills, who was carrying a makeshift flagpole with an American flag, in front of his ruined home. White House photographer Pete Souza captured the moment—and with it, the ever-present resilience that rises up in the American people in the face of hardship, forever symbolized by the red, white, and blue of the nation's flag.

GEORGE FLOYD PROTEST FLAG

Boiling Point

DATE: May 25, 2020
EVENT LOCATION: Minneapolis, Minnesota
CURRENT FLAG LOCATION: Unknown

"I can't breathe!" These were George Floyd's last words as Minneapolis policeman Derek Chauvin knelt on his neck for nine minutes and twenty-nine seconds. Three other officers (J. Alexander Kueng, Thomas Lane, and Tou Thao) watched Chauvin suffocate Floyd without intervening, even while bystanders were screaming at them to stop. On May 25, 2020, Floyd, a middle-aged Black man, lost consciousness and died on a Minneapolis city street at the hands of the people paid to protect him. Protests broke out all over the United States and the world. At the rallies, some protesters carried upside-down flags—the symbol for distress. Still others burned American flags. Banners were spattered with fake blood or emblazoned with angry words: *No justice, no peace. Black Lives Matter. White silence is violence. Enough! I can't breathe.*

The American flag is normally ubiquitous at demonstrations and rallies protesting the government or its actions. In the case of the George Floyd protests, when you look at photographs of the many large protests from around the country, almost no American flags can be seen. Those that were carried were altered or defaced in some way. One can only

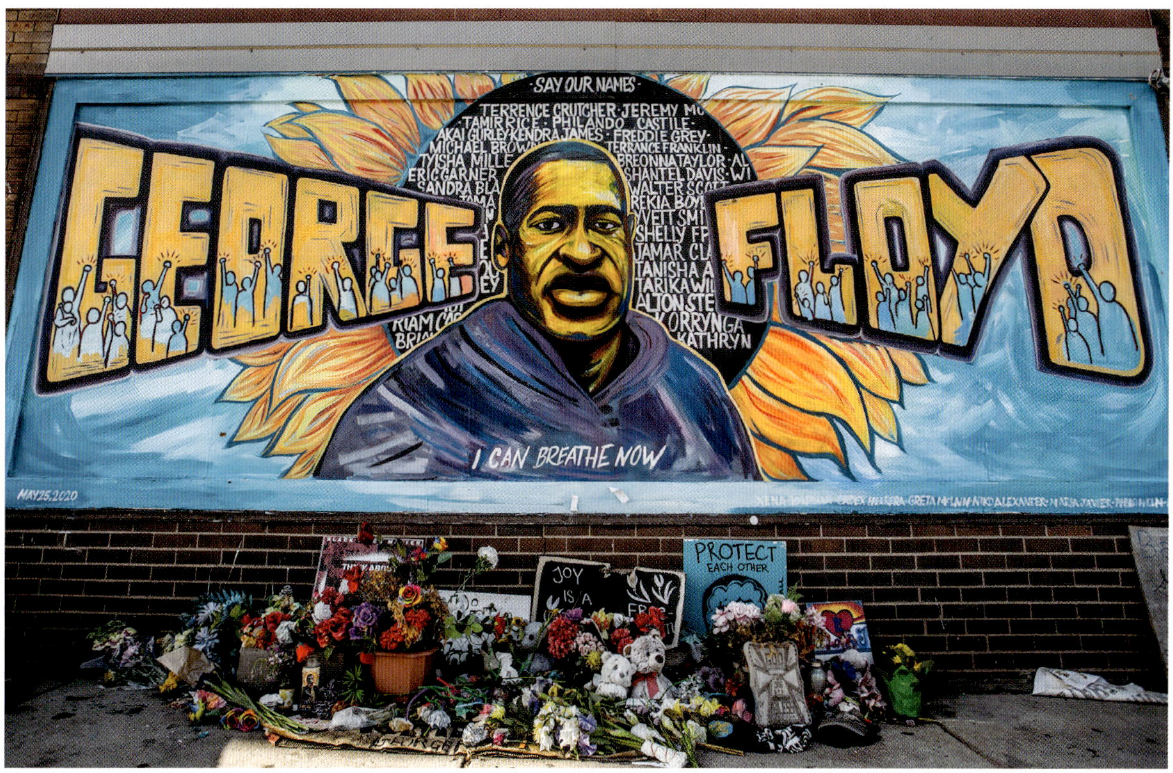

Above: *A mural of George Floyd, near the site of his murder, on the first anniversary of his death, George Floyd Square, Minneapolis, Minnesota, May 25, 2021*

Following: *A demonstrator carries a US flag upside down, a sign of distress, during a protest of the killing of George Floyd, Minneapolis, Minnesota, May 28, 2020.*

assume that the demonstrators felt that the flag no longer represented their vision of America.

One image in particular stands out: a man running with an upside-down American flag in front of a burning Minneapolis liquor store. The image is disturbing and inspiring at the same time. The flag is backlit by the light from the fire, almost appearing to be on fire itself. The man is no more than a silhouette behind the banner. It is a haunting visual metaphor for the idea that the nation and all it stands for—justice, liberty, and equality—was on fire. The photograph encapsulates the extreme frustration and anger the death of Floyd prompted.

George Floyd's murder was the latest in a series of deaths of Black Americans while in police custody. From 2017 to 2019, more than eighty Black citizens around the United States died while in police detention. Just six weeks earlier, on March 13, 2020, Breonna Taylor, a first responder herself, who was unarmed, had been shot and killed by Louisville police officers while they executed a no-knock search warrant at her apartment.

Floyd's death caused a paradigm shift in the public's view of these incidents. What had seemed like isolated events now clearly appeared

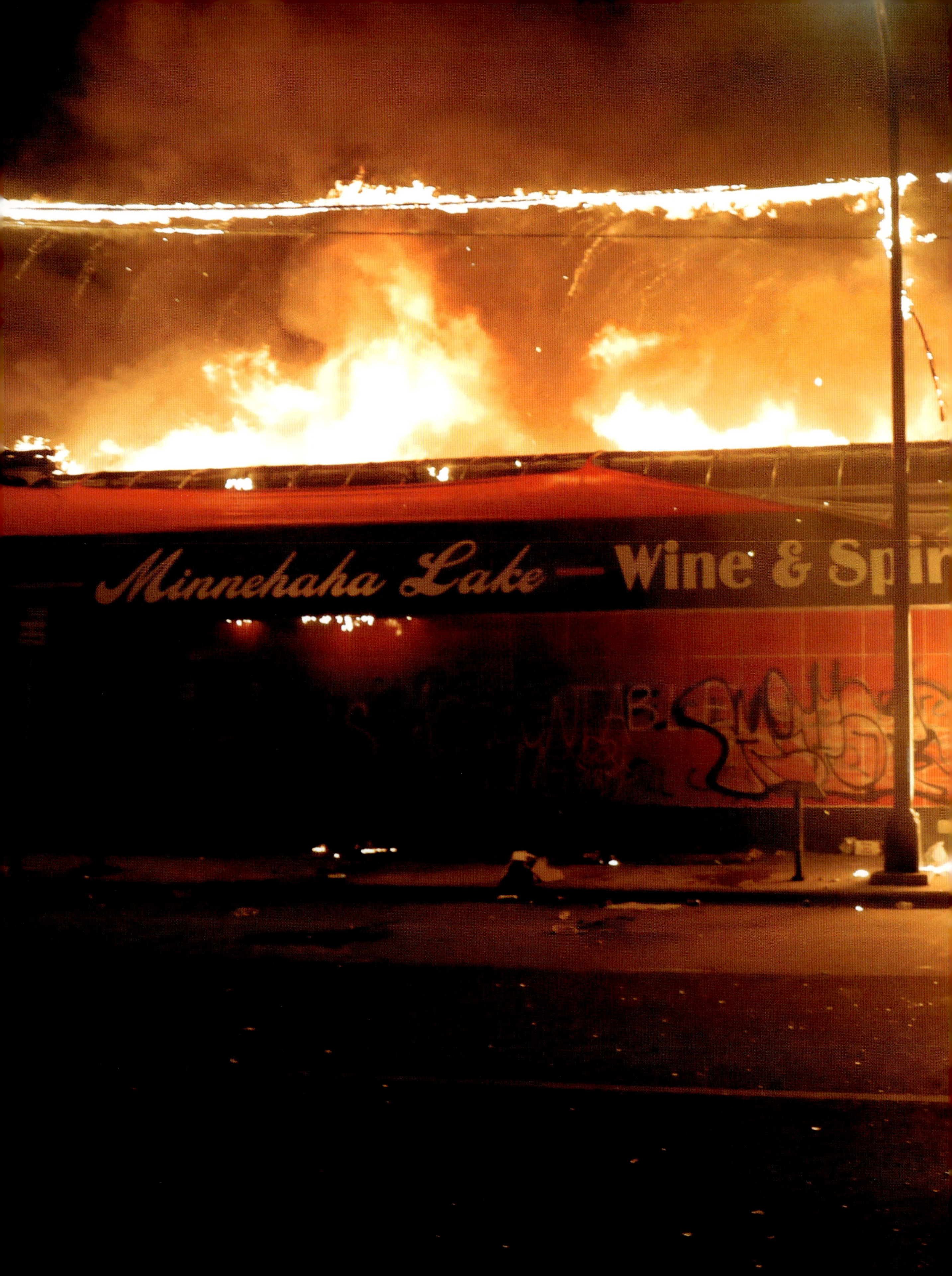

Minnehaha Lake
Wine & Spir

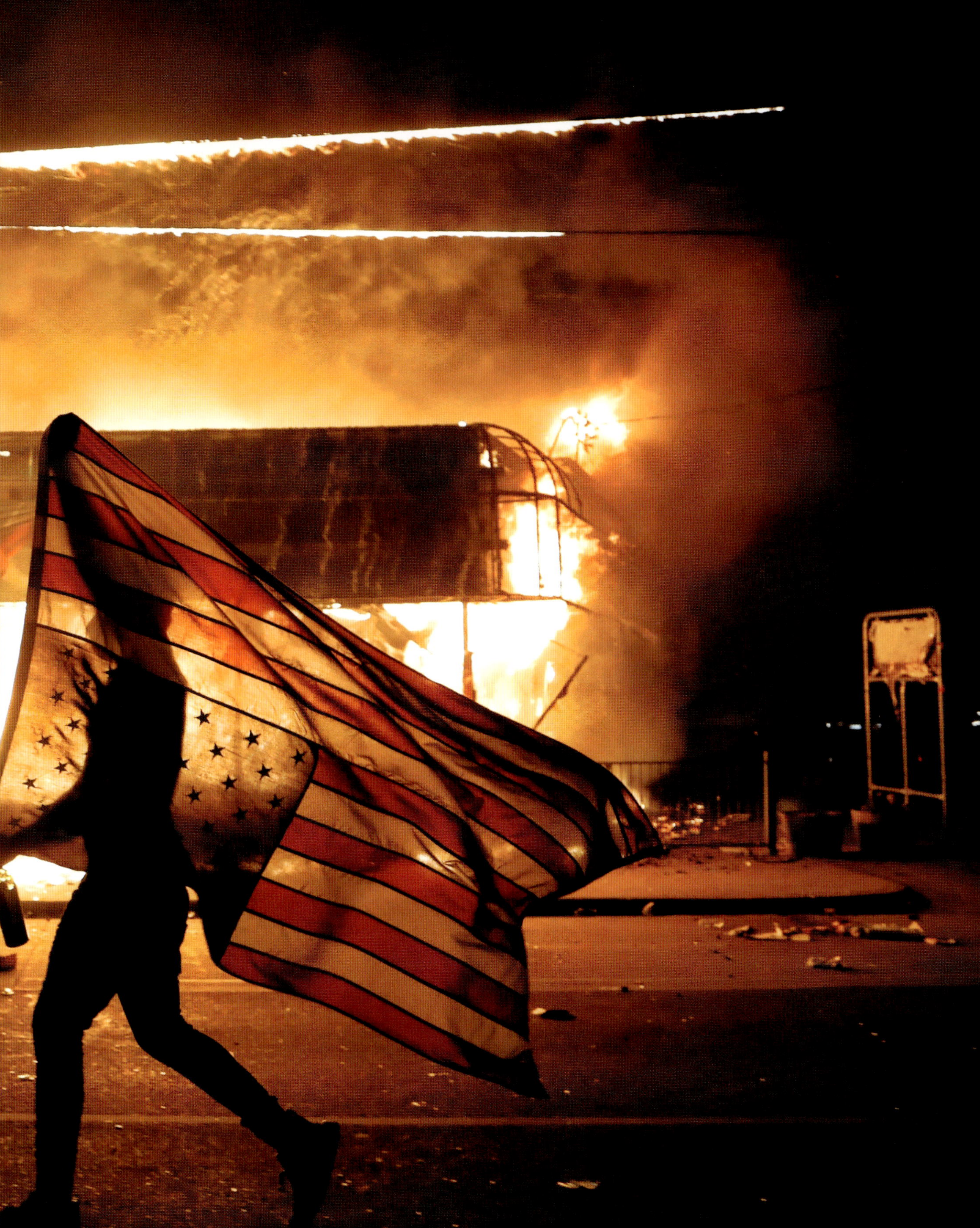

to be a systemic crisis of abuse by police officers—specifically against people of color. The community's reaction echoed the aftermath of the beating of Rodney King by police in Los Angeles, California, on March 3, 1991, and their later acquittal. This time, many of the demonstrations around the country and the world were organized by Black Lives Matter, a movement initially formed in response to the acquittal of George Zimmerman, who shot and killed Trayvon Martin in Sanford, Florida, on February 26, 2012.

In the months before Martin's death, Zimmerman had made multiple reports of suspicious persons in the development where he was the neighborhood watch coordinator. All the questionable persons Zimmerman reported to the police were Black. On the night in question, Martin was returning from a convenience store to the house where he was staying. Zimmerman stated that he noticed Martin walking through the neighborhood in the rain and became concerned because of recent burglaries in the area.

Zimmerman, twenty-eight, confronted the young Black man. They fought (though it is unclear who started the altercation), and Zimmerman shot and killed the unarmed seventeen-year-old. He claimed it was self-defense and was eventually found not guilty of second-degree murder.

The rage surrounding the killing of Trayvon Martin and acquittal of Zimmerman was rekindled with the killing of George Floyd. Many of the protests in response to the Floyd incident became violent. Businesses were burned and some looting of stores occurred, but mainly the protesters took their wrath out on the police, damaging and burning law enforcement vehicles and stations. Officers responded with tear gas and rubber bullets. Several protesters were shot. At least one died. A few officers were shot as well.

Since 2020, some progress has been made in reforming police tactics and procedures. Police departments across the nation have enacted changes in their pursuit and detainment policies and have banned certain tactics (like choke holds). Various cities (Denver, for example) have created mental health response teams that can accompany or replace police response to individuals experiencing a mental health crisis. Yet even with these changes, deaths of Black Americans in police custody continue at the same rate as before the tragic killing of George Floyd.

The four officers involved in Floyd's death—Chauvin, Kueng, Lane, and Thao—were convicted of both state and federal charges.

JANUARY 6TH FLAG

The Insurrection

DATE: January 6, 2021
EVENT LOCATION: Washington, DC
CURRENT FLAG LOCATION: Unknown

The riot at the US Capitol on January 6, 2021, had been going on for more than three hours before President Donald J. Trump tweeted a video telling his supporters who had stormed the building to go home. His staff, family, and fellow Republicans had been begging him for hours to get on live TV and tell the rioters to leave. Yet in the same video, he again falsely claimed the 2020 presidential election had been stolen from him.

Some of the most disturbing images of the insurrection show demonstrators attacking and hitting officers from the US Capitol Police and the DC Metropolitan Police with flagpoles carrying American flags, reminiscent of the photograph *The Soiling of Old Glory* (page 161). Though it is often the case that rioters wave the American flag with an obvious lack of understanding of the banner's historic roots (for example, the story of the Gadsden flag, page 11), it is still heartbreaking to see the flag, for which so much blood and life has been sacrificed in the name of democracy, used as a weapon against democracy itself.

It was one of the darkest days in American democracy and US history. Not since 1814, when the British burned the US Capitol and the

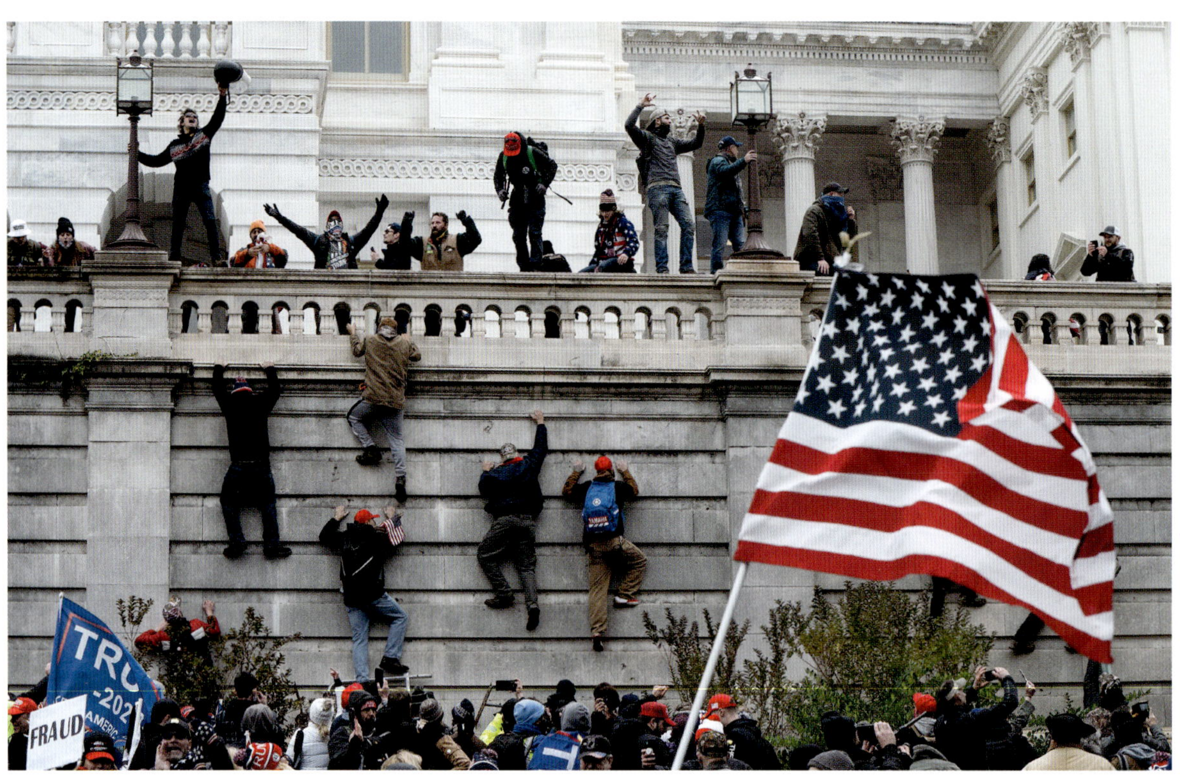
FRAUD

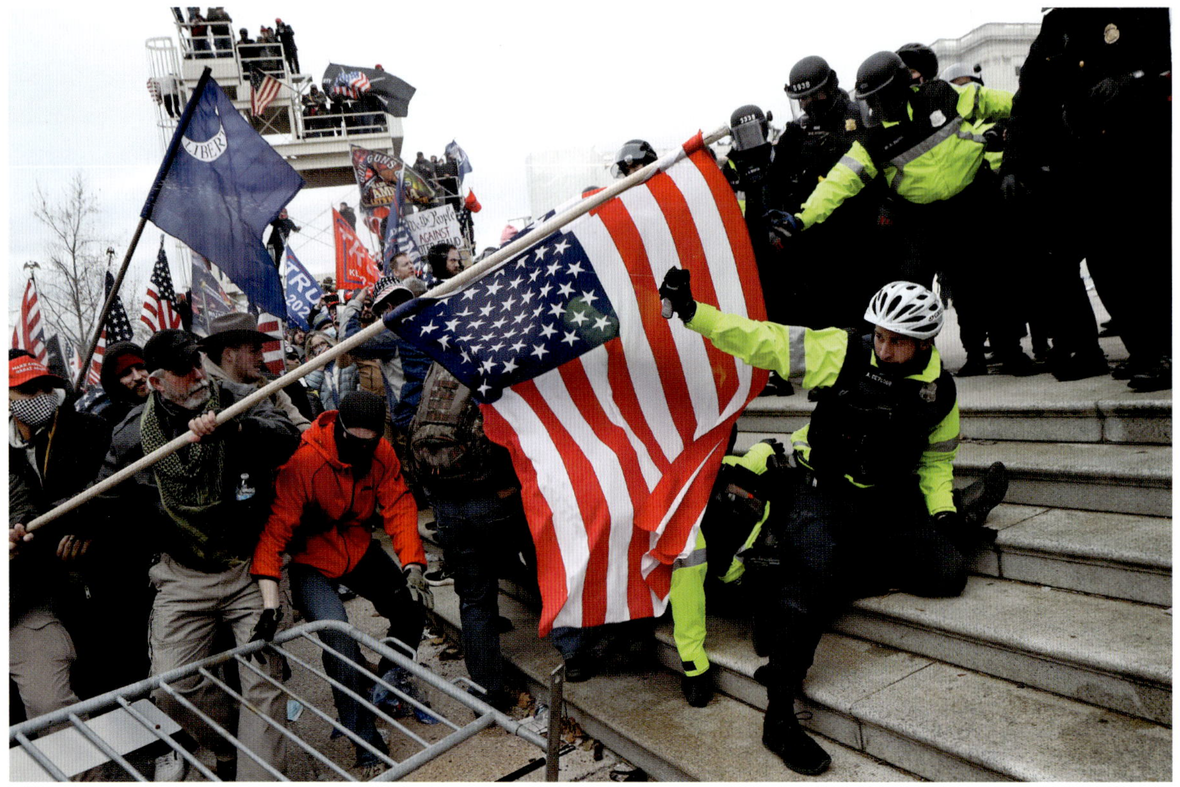

Opposite, top: Rioters scaling the U.S. Capitol on January 6, 2021

Opposite, bottom: Capitol Police being attacked with the flag

Presidential Mansion (as the White House was referred to at the time) during the War of 1812 (page 25), had any group taken over the seat of power in the United States' capital.

The 2020 presidential election was one of the most heated contests in recent history. Long before any ballots were cast, President Donald Trump was claiming that if he didn't win reelection, it would be a sign that it was rigged for his opponent, former vice president Joe Biden. When Biden was declared the winner, Trump refused to concede, and he and his supporters spread unsubstantiated stories about tampering with voting machines, dead people voting, and even interference by deceased Venezuelan President Hugo Chavez. To this day, no evidence of widespread organized fraud in the 2020 election has ever been produced.

Yet Trump's supporters in Congress and elsewhere persisted. They concocted a scheme to win the Electoral College by declaring some states' electors illegitimate and sending their own slate of delegates, who would negate votes for Biden and instead vote for Trump. Part of this plan hinged on Vice President Mike Pence declaring the duly designated electors' votes void on January 6, 2021, during the official congressional count of the Electoral College ballots. Pence refused, stating that he did not have the constitutional authority to do so.

Tapes of the president's rally at the Ellipse (a park just south of the White House) show him telling his supporters, "We fight like hell. And if you don't fight like hell, you're not going to have a country anymore." Later in the speech, he said, "I know that everyone here will soon be marching over to the Capitol building to peacefully and patriotically make your voices heard." As the electoral vote count began in Congress, the insurrectionists marched toward the Capitol, pushing past barricades and police officers. They assaulted and stormed the Capitol. They broke windows and doors. The rioters defaced the interior of the Capitol with graffiti and excrement. They broke furniture and damaged artworks.

The insurrectionists caused more than $2.5 million in damage to the Capitol building and grounds in less than six hours—with some estimates reaching $30 million. More than 1,000 assaults occurred on officers, and 140 officers were injured. One officer and four rioters died during or shortly after the skirmish. Nearly 1,600 rioters were indicted on charges ranging from entering or remaining in a restricted federal building or grounds to seditious conspiracy. Of those, more than 1,000 pled guilty. More than 130 rioters were charged with assaulting law enforcement officers or feloniously obstructing, impeding, or interfering with a law enforcement officer during a civil disorder. For defendants who went to trial, more than 99 percent were found guilty.

In 2022, when Trump announced he was running for president again, the idea that he might win the office seemed far-fetched, given his loss in 2020 and the events that took place that day at the Capitol. But the Democrats had their own issues in a sitting president, Joe Biden, who at times seemed feeble—to the point that he withdrew from the race in July 2024, a mere 107 days before the election. He was replaced on the ballot by Vice President Kamala Harris. But Trump did win this time, and he promised retribution for his enemies and mercy for his supporters—including the January 6 rioters. He made good on that promise, pardoning all the convicted rioters except for fourteen members of the Proud Boys, for whom he let the verdicts stand but commuted the sentences to time served. James Comey, former FBI director, referred to the pardons as "an obscenity."

Though the insurrection and subsequent pardons widened the fractures we see today, politically, socially, and culturally, we can take heart in the commitment of our people to our nation. Even in the face of the January 6, 2021, insurrection, our republic held fast. High above all the flags carried by the rioters that day, the American flag flew over the East Entrance to the Capitol, a sign that the nation, and democracy, stands intact.

2024 USA WOMEN'S GYMNASTICS TEAM FLAG

Pure Joy

DATE: July 30, 2024
EVENT LOCATION: Paris, France
CURRENT FLAG LOCATION: Unknown

National flags are omnipresent at the Olympics. Teams carry their country's banner during the opening of the Games. At medal ceremonies, a nation's flag is raised for each of the gold, silver, and bronze medals its athletes win. In the Parade of Flags, the participating nations' ensigns are carried single file behind the Greek flag in the closing ceremony. The Olympics are a joyous celebration of the world's premier athletes and national pride.

One of the most memorable Olympic moments for the United States was at the Paris Summer Games in 2024, when the women's gymnastics team—made up of Simone Biles, Jade Carey, Jordan Chiles, Sunisa Lee, and Hezly Rivera—won the gold in the artistic all-around event. After the win, the medalists were photographed jumping for joy and proudly holding the American flag. After years of dedication and discipline, these athletes had triumphed together to become the best women's gymnastics team in the world.

The win was a particular achievement for Biles. At the Tokyo Summer Games in 2021, she withdrew from the competition after recognizing that she wasn't able to continue due to her mental health. She told reporters,

Opposite, top: *The USA Gymnastics Women's Team celebrates their artistic all-around gold medal at the Paris Summer 2024 Olympic Games, July 30, 2024.*

Opposite, bottom: *Simone Biles celebrating the team's gold medal in Paris.*

"I just felt like it would be a little bit better to take a back seat, work on my mindfulness. And I knew that the girls would do an absolutely great job. And I didn't want to risk the team a medal for . . . my screwups, because they've worked way too hard for that." Without Biles, the USA women's gymnastics team won the silver medal in the artistic team all-around event that year.

Biles is considered one of the greatest Olympians and gymnasts of all time. She now has eleven Olympic and thirty World Championship medals. But her career came at a price. In 2018, she revealed that she was one of the survivors of sexual abuse committed by Larry Nassar, who, during his tenure as the team doctor for USA Gymnastics and Michigan State University, is believed to have sexually assaulted more than 500 girls and women. Biles's resilience after this trauma, and the bravery she showed in speaking about it and, later, prioritizing her mental health over the pressure to win, only add to her legacy.

Some moments in Olympic history remain burned into our collective memory, like the Miracle on Ice (page 173). The USA women's gymnastics team's gold medal win in Paris is one of those pinnacles of achievement that reminds us why athletic competition is important. We see individuals work together to accomplish goals that seem impossible and push themselves to perform at levels higher than they ever imagined they could. These moments become metaphors for the country, proving that we all can overcome what seem to be insurmountable hurdles.

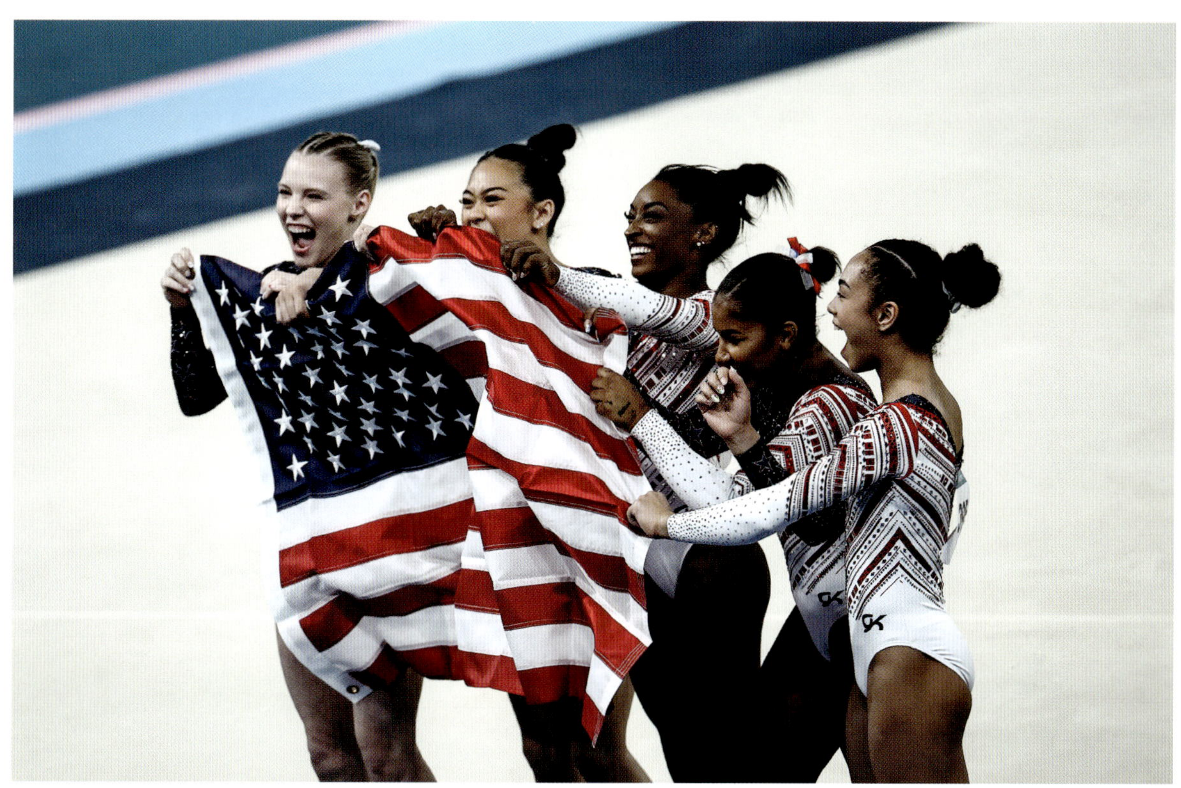

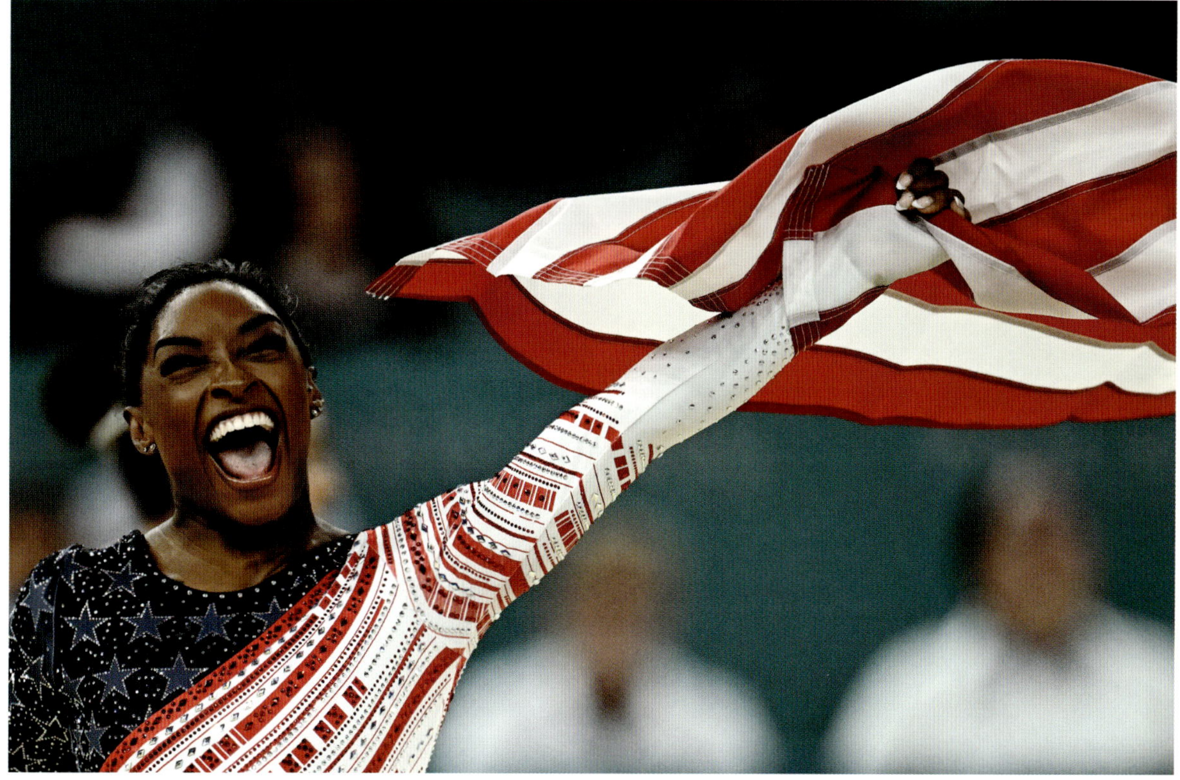

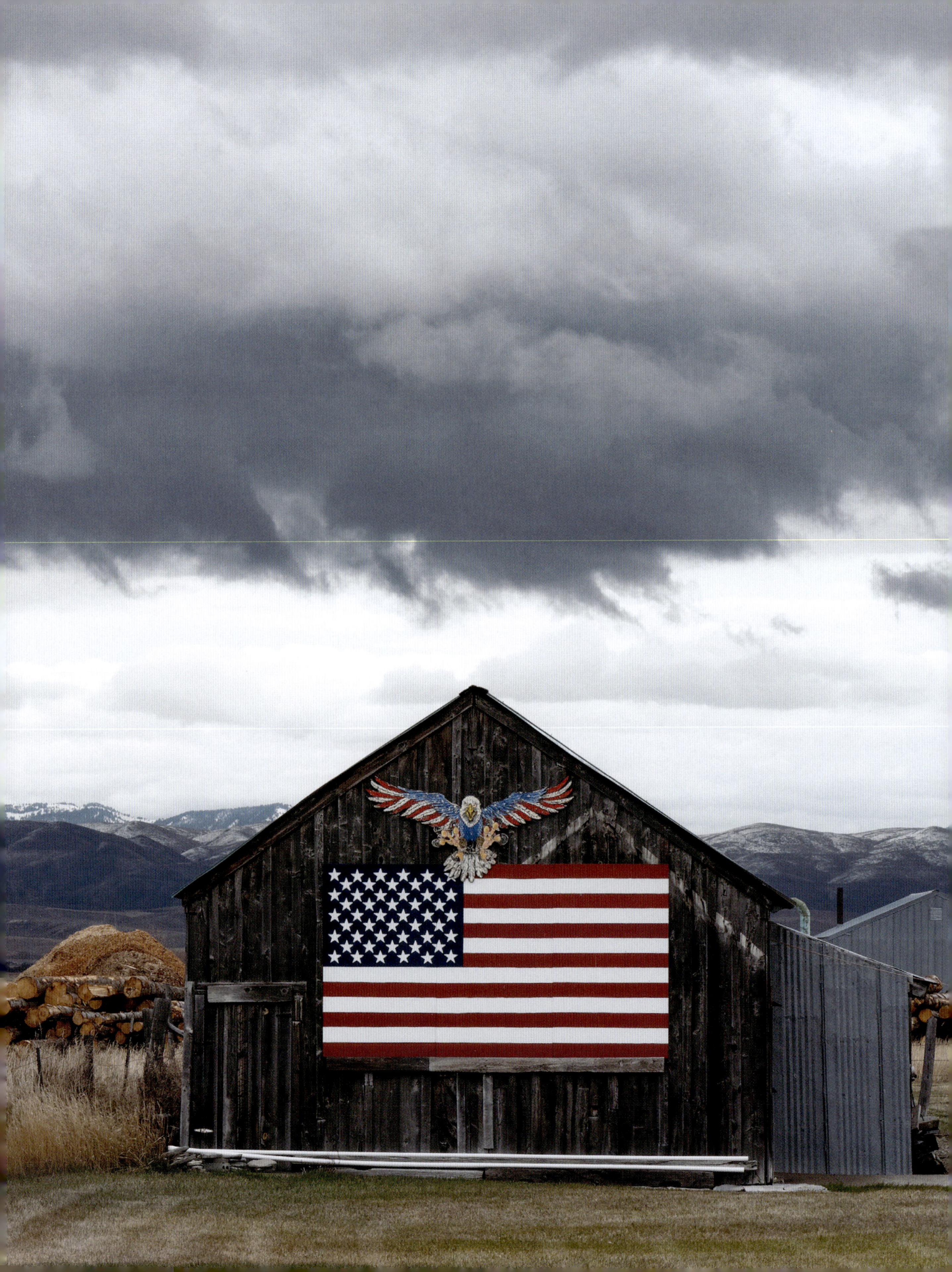

AUTHOR'S NOTE

IN 2026, WE CELEBRATE the 250th anniversary of the United States—two and a half centuries filled with moments of success, as well as failures and setbacks. The American flag has stood witness to so many of these events, symbolizing the country's resilience, strength, idealism, ingenuity, and bravery.

The stories behind *Old Glory*'s flags chronicle the history of this great American pursuit of democracy—an ongoing endeavor. As our flag evolved through the addition of states and its role as a political symbol, so did our interpretation and amendments of the Constitution, along with the wisdom we've gained from it.

Over the course of its 250-year history, America has experienced cycles of poverty and prosperity, conflict and concord, and tragedy and triumph. As Spanish philosopher George Santayana once said, "Those who cannot remember the past are condemned to repeat it." My hope is that the stories and flags of *Old Glory* illuminate the country's history in a new way, helping us usher in the next 250 years.

Opposite: *Near Paris, Idaho, 2022*

HONORING THE FLAG

UNITED STATES CODE, TITLE 4, CHAPTER 1: THE FLAG

1. Flag; stripes and stars on

The flag of the United States shall be thirteen horizontal stripes, alternate red and white; and the union of the flag shall be forty-eight stars, white in a blue field.

2. Same; additional stars

On the admission of a new State into the Union one star shall be added to the union of the flag; and such addition shall take effect on the fourth day of July then next succeeding such admission.

3. Use of flag for advertising purposes; mutilation of flag

Any person who, within the District of Columbia, in any manner, for exhibition or display, shall place or cause to be placed any word, figure, mark, picture, design, drawing, or any advertisement of any nature upon any flag, standard, colors, or ensign of the United States of America; or shall expose or cause to be exposed to public view any such flag, standard, colors, or ensign upon which shall have been printed, painted, or otherwise placed, or to which shall be attached, appended, affixed, or annexed any word, figure, mark, picture, design, or drawing, or any advertisement of any nature; or who, within the District of Columbia, shall manufacture, sell, expose for sale, or to public view, or give away or have in possession for sale, or to be given away or for use for any purpose, any article or substance being an article of merchandise, or a receptacle for merchandise or article or thing for carrying or transporting merchandise, upon which shall have been printed, painted, attached, or otherwise placed a representation of any such flag, standard, colors, or ensign, to advertise, call attention to, decorate, mark, or distinguish the article or substance on which so placed shall be deemed guilty of a misdemeanor and shall be punished by a fine not exceeding $100 or by imprisonment for not more than thirty days, or both, in the discretion of the court. The words "flag, standard, colors, or ensign," as used herein, shall include

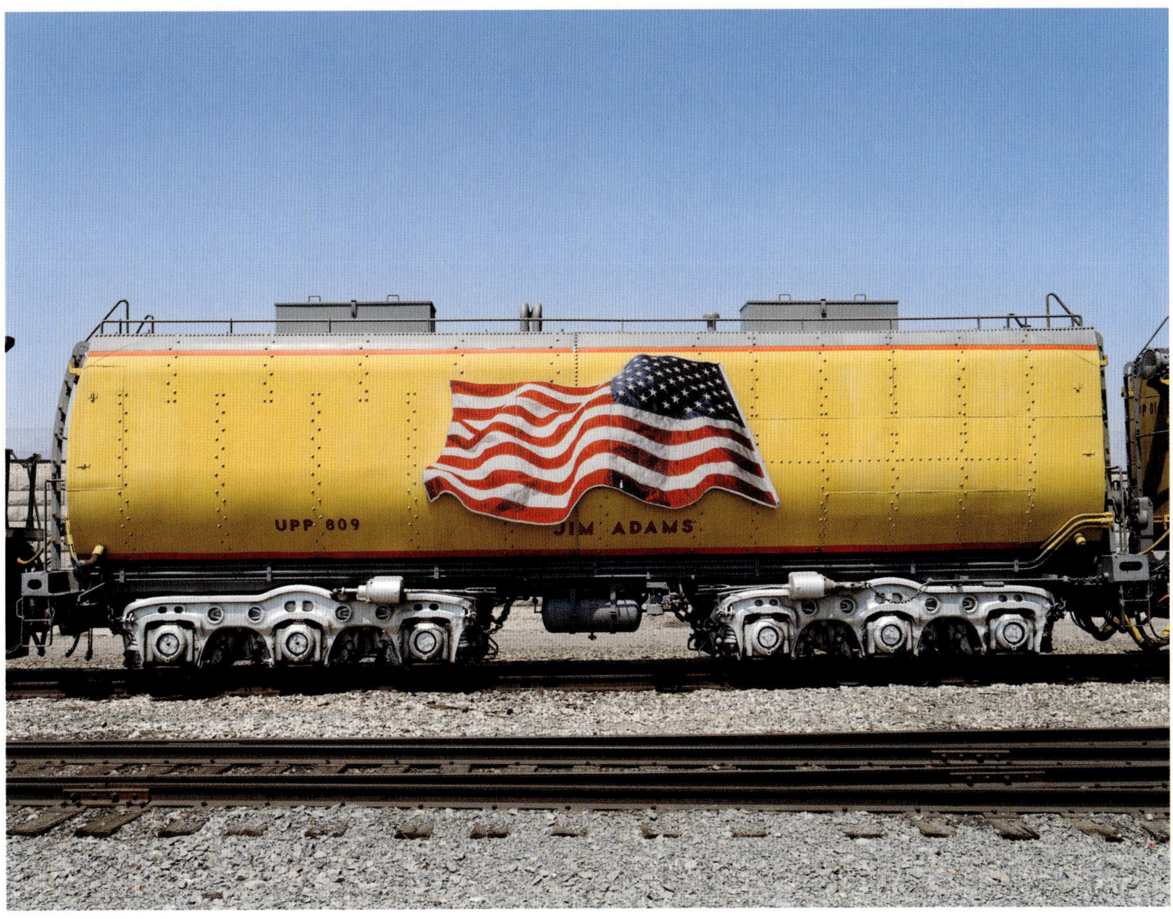

Ogden, Utah, 2024

any flag, standard, colors, ensign, or any picture or representation of either, or of any part or parts of either, made of any substance or represented on any substance, of any size evidently purporting to be either of said flag, standard, colors, or ensign of the United States of America or a picture or a representation of either, upon which shall be shown the colors, the stars and the stripes, in any number of either thereof, or of any part or parts of either, by which the average person seeing the same without deliberation may believe the same to represent the flag, colors, standard, or ensign of the United States of America.

4. Pledge of allegiance to the flag; manner of delivery

The Pledge of Allegiance to the Flag: "I pledge allegiance to the Flag of the United States of America, and to the Republic for which it stands, one Nation under God, indivisible, with liberty and justice for all," should be rendered by standing at attention facing the flag with the right hand over the heart. When not in uniform men should remove any non-religious headdress with their right hand and hold it at the left shoulder, the hand being over the heart. Persons in uniform should remain silent, face the flag, and render the military salute. Members of

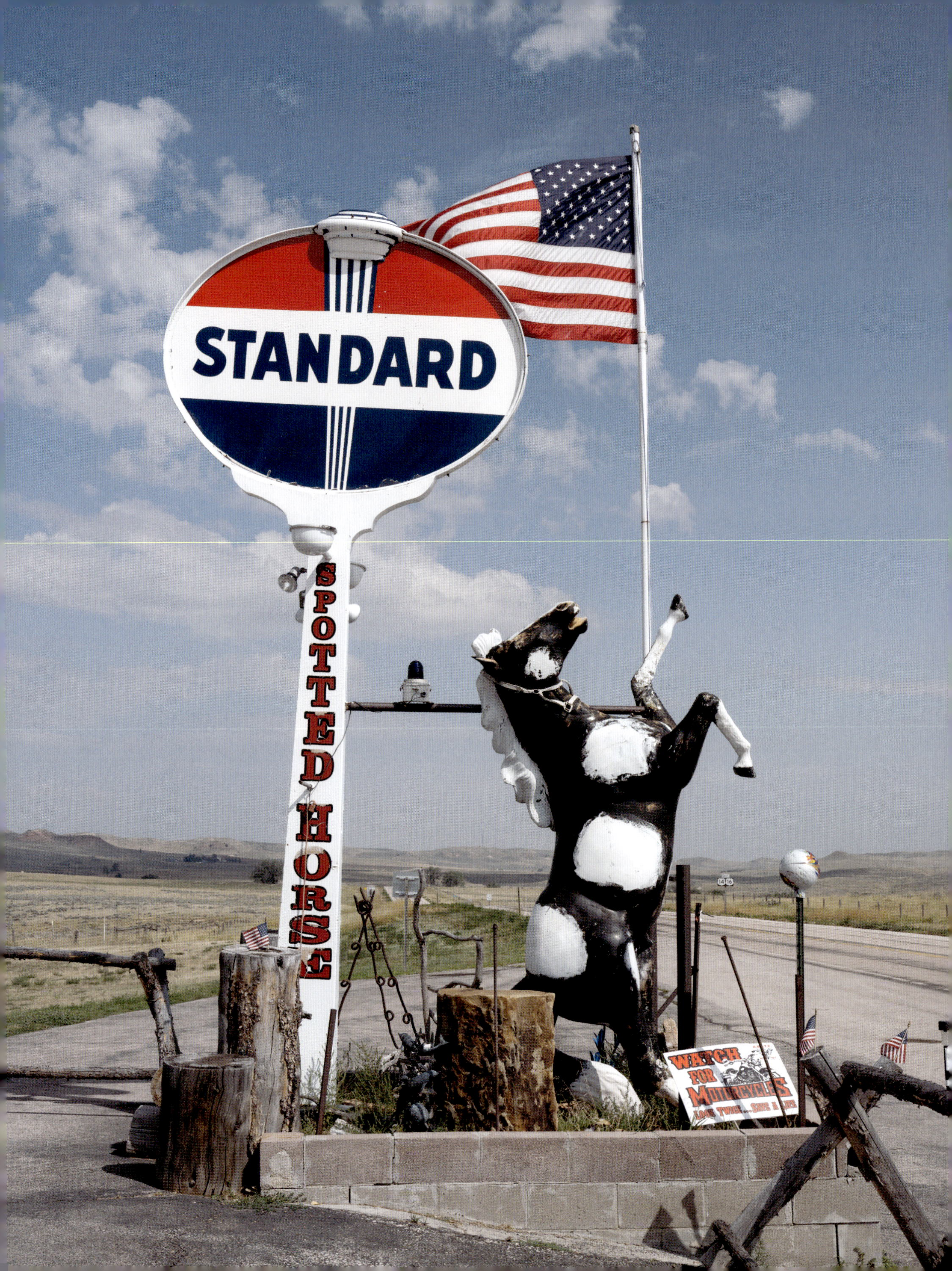
STANDARD
SPOTTED HORSE
WATCH
FOR
MOTORCYCLES

the Armed Forces not in uniform and veterans may render the military salute in the manner provided for persons in uniform.

5. Display and use of flag by civilians; codification of rules and customs; definition

The following codification of existing rules and customs pertaining to the display and use of the flag of the United States of America is established for the use of such civilians or civilian groups or organizations as may not be required to conform with regulations promulgated by one or more executive departments of the Government of the United States. The flag of the United States for the purpose of this chapter shall be defined according to title 4, United States Code, Chapter 1, Section 1 and Section 2 and Executive Order 10834 issued pursuant thereto.

6. Time and occasions for display

(a) It is the universal custom to display the flag only from sunrise to sunset on buildings and on stationary flagstaffs in the open. However, when a patriotic effect is desired, the flag may be displayed twenty-four hours a day if properly illuminated during the hours of darkness.

(b) The flag should be hoisted briskly and lowered ceremoniously.

(c) The flag should not be displayed on days when the weather is inclement, except when an all-weather flag is displayed.

(d) The flag should be displayed on all days, especially on

- New Year's Day, January 1
- Inauguration Day, January 20
- Martin Luther King Jr.'s birthday, third Monday in January
- Lincoln's Birthday, February 12
- Washington's Birthday, third Monday in February
- National Vietnam War Veterans Day, March 29
- Easter Sunday (variable)
- Mother's Day, second Sunday in May
- Armed Forces Day, third Saturday in May
- Memorial Day (half-staff until noon), the last Monday in May
- Flag Day, June 14
- Father's Day, third Sunday in June
- Independence Day, July 4
- National Korean War Veterans Armistice Day, July 27
- Labor Day, first Monday in September
- Constitution Day, September 17
- Columbus Day, second Monday in October
- Navy Day, October 27
- Veterans Day, November 11
- Thanksgiving Day, fourth Thursday in November
- Christmas Day, December 25
- and such other days as may be proclaimed by the President of the United States
- the birthdays of States (date of admission)
- and on State holidays.

(e) The flag should be displayed daily on or near the main administration building of every public institution.

(f) The flag should be displayed in or near every polling place on election days.

Opposite: *Recluse, Wyoming, 2023*

(g) The flag should be displayed during school days in or near every schoolhouse.

7. Position and manner of display

The flag, when carried in a procession with another flag or flags, should be either on the marching right; that is, the flag's own right, or, if there is a line of other flags, in front of the center of that line.

(a) The flag should not be displayed on a float in a parade except from a staff, or as provided in subsection (i) of this section.

(b) The flag should not be draped over the hood, top, sides, or back of a vehicle or of a railroad train or a boat. When the flag is displayed on a motorcar, the staff shall be fixed firmly to the chassis or clamped to the right fender.

(c) No other flag or pennant should be placed above or, if on the same level, to the right of the flag of the United States of America, except during church services conducted by naval chaplains at sea, when the church pennant may be flown above the flag during church services for the personnel of the Navy. No person shall display the flag of the United Nations or

ARTICLES OF THE US MILITARY CODE OF CONDUCT

★★★

The Code of Conduct provides guidance for the behavior and actions of members of the Armed Forces of the United States. This guidance applies not only on the battlefield but also in the event that a service member is captured and becomes a prisoner of war. The code is delineated in six articles.

ARTICLE I:

I am an American, fighting in the forces that guard my country and our way of life. I am prepared to give my life in their defense.

ARTICLE II:

I will never surrender of my own free will. If in command, I will never surrender the members of my command while they still have the means to resist.

ARTICLE III:

If I am captured I will continue to resist by all means available. I will make every effort to escape and aid others to escape. I will accept neither parole nor special favors from the enemy.

ARTICLE IV:

If I become a prisoner of war, I will keep faith with my fellow prisoners. I will give no information or take part in any action which might be harmful to my comrades. If I am senior, I will take command. If not, I will obey the lawful orders of those appointed over me and will back them up in every way.

ARTICLE V:

When questioned, should I become a prisoner of war, I am required to give name, rank, service number, and date of birth. I will evade answering further questions to the utmost of my ability. I will make no oral or written statements disloyal to my country and its allies or harmful to their cause.

ARTICLE VI:

I will never forget that I am an American, fighting for freedom, responsible for my actions, and dedicated to the principles which made my country free. I will trust in my God and in the United States of America.

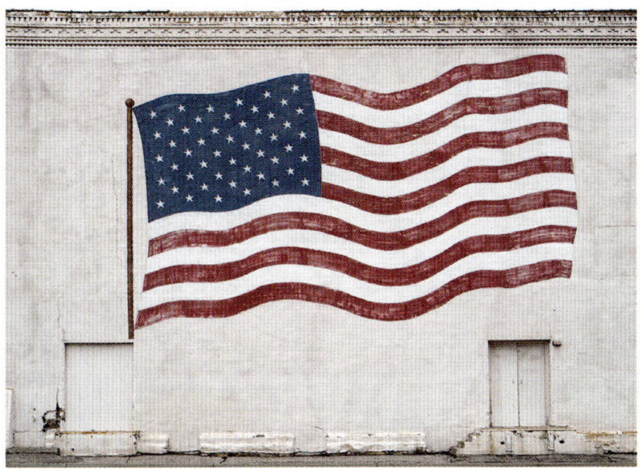

Rapid City, South Dakota, 2023

any other national or international flag equal, above, or in a position of superior prominence or honor to, or in place of, the flag of the United States at any place within the United States or any Territory or possession thereof: Provided, That nothing in this section shall make unlawful the continuance of the practice heretofore followed of displaying the flag of the United Nations in a position of superior prominence or honor, and other national flags in positions of equal prominence or honor, with that of the flag of the United States at the headquarters of the United Nations.

(d) The flag of the United States of America, when it is displayed with another flag against a wall from crossed staffs, should be on the right, the flag's own right, and its staff should be in front of the staff of the other flag.

(e) The flag of the United States of America should be at the center and at the highest point of the group when a number of flags of States or localities or pennants of societies are grouped and displayed from staffs.

(f) When flags of States, cities, or localities, or pennants of societies are flown on the same halyard with the flag of the United States, the latter should always be at the peak. When the flags are flown from adjacent staffs, the flag of the United States should be hoisted first and lowered last. No such flag or pennant may be placed above the flag of the United States or to the United States flag's right.

(g) When flags of two or more nations are displayed, they are to be flown from separate staffs of the same height. The flags should be of approximately equal size. International usage forbids the display of the flag of one nation above that of another nation in time of peace.

(h) When the flag of the United States is displayed from a staff projecting horizontally or at an angle from the window sill, balcony, or front of a building, the union of the flag should be placed at the peak of the staff unless the flag is at half-staff. When the flag is suspended over a sidewalk from a rope extending from a house to a pole at the edge of the sidewalk, the flag should be hoisted out, union first, from the building.

(i) When displayed either horizontally or vertically against a wall, the union should be uppermost and to the flag's own right, that is, to the observer's left. When displayed in a window, the flag should be displayed in the same way, with the union or blue field to the left of the observer in the street.

(j) When the flag is displayed over the middle of the street, it should be suspended vertically with the union to the north in an east and west street or to the east in a north and south street.

(k) When used on a speaker's platform, the flag, if displayed flat, should be displayed above and behind the speaker. When displayed from a staff in a church or public auditorium, the flag of the United States of America should hold the position of superior prominence, in advance of the audience, and in the position of honor at the clergyman's or speaker's right as he faces the audience. Any other flag so displayed should be placed on the left of the clergyman or speaker or to the right of the audience.

(l) The flag should form a distinctive feature of the ceremony of unveiling a statue or monument, but it should never be used as the covering for the statue or monument.

(m) The flag, when flown at half-staff, should be first hoisted to the peak for an instant and then lowered to the half-staff position. The flag should be again raised to the peak before it is lowered for the day. On Memorial Day the flag should be displayed at half-staff until noon only, then raised to the top of the staff. By order of the President, the flag shall be flown at half-staff upon the death of principal figures of the United States Government and the Governor of a State, territory, or possession, as a mark of respect to their memory. In the event of the death of other officials or foreign dignitaries, the flag is to be displayed at half-staff according to Presidential instructions or orders, or in accordance with recognized customs or practices not inconsistent with law. In the event of the death of a present or former official of the government of any State, territory, or possession of the United States, the death of a member of the Armed Forces from any State, territory, or possession who dies while serving on active duty, or the death of a first responder working in any State, territory, or possession who dies while serving in the line of duty, the Governor of that State, territory, or possession may proclaim that the National flag shall be flown at half-staff, and the same authority is provided to the Mayor of the District of Columbia with respect to present or former officials of the District of Columbia, members of the Armed Forces from the District of Columbia, and first responders working in the District of Columbia. When the Governor of a State, territory, or possession, or the Mayor of the District of Columbia, issues a proclamation under the preceding sentence that the National flag be flown at half-staff in that State, territory, or possession or in the District of Columbia because of the death of a member of the Armed Forces, the National flag flown at any Federal installation or facility in the area covered by that proclamation shall be flown at half-staff consistent with that proclamation. The flag shall be flown at half-staff 30 days from the death of the President or a former President; 10 days from the day of death of the Vice President, the Chief Justice or a retired Chief Justice of the United States, or the Speaker of the House of Representatives; from the day of death until interment of an Associate Justice of the Supreme Court, a Secretary of an executive or military department, a former Vice President, or the Governor of a State, territory, or possession; and on the day of death and the following day for a Member of Congress. The flag shall be flown at half-staff on Peace Officers Memorial Day, unless that day is also Armed Forces Day. As used in this subsection—

(1) the term "half-staff" means the position of the flag when it is one-half the distance between the top and bottom of the staff;

(2) the term "executive or military department" means any agency listed under sections 101 and 102 of title 5;

(3) the term "Member of Congress" means a Senator, a Representative, a Delegate, or the Resident Commissioner from Puerto Rico; and

(4) the term "first responder" means a "public safety officer" as defined in section 1204 of title I of the Omnibus Crime Control and Safe Streets Act of 1968 (34 U.S.C. 10284).

***Opposite:** Bighorn, Wyoming, 2023*

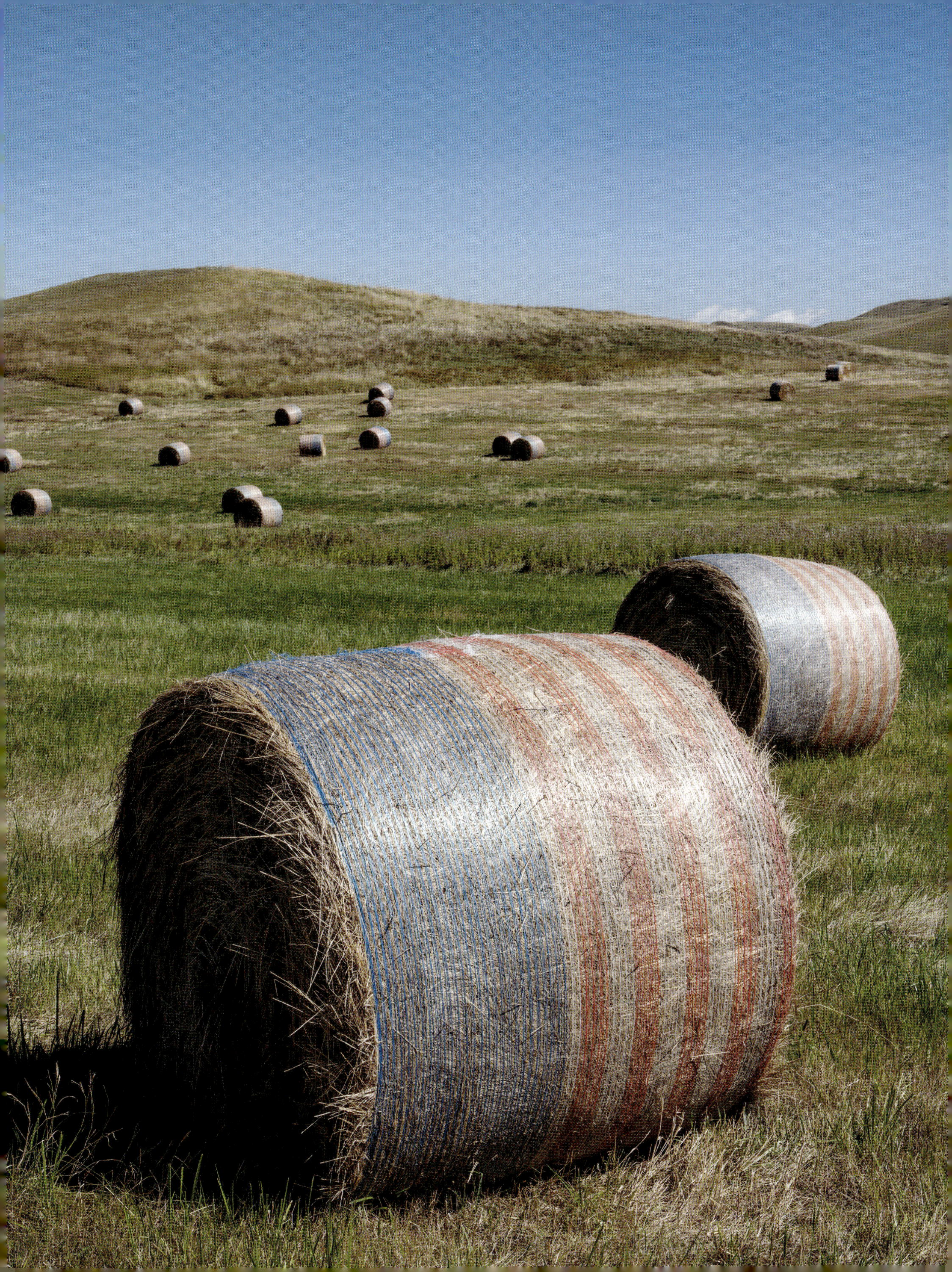

(n) When the flag is used to cover a casket, it should be so placed that the union is at the head and over the left shoulder. The flag should not be lowered into the grave or allowed to touch the ground.

(o) When the flag is suspended across a corridor or lobby in a building with only one main entrance, it should be suspended vertically with the union of the flag to the observer's left upon entering. If the building has more than one main entrance, the flag should be suspended vertically near the center of the corridor or lobby with the union to the north, when entrances are to the east and west or to the east when entrances are to the north and south. If there are entrances in more than two directions, the union should be to the east.

8. Respect for flag

No disrespect should be shown to the flag of the United States of America; the flag should not be dipped to any person or thing. Regimental colors, State flags, and organization or institutional flags are to be dipped as a mark of honor.

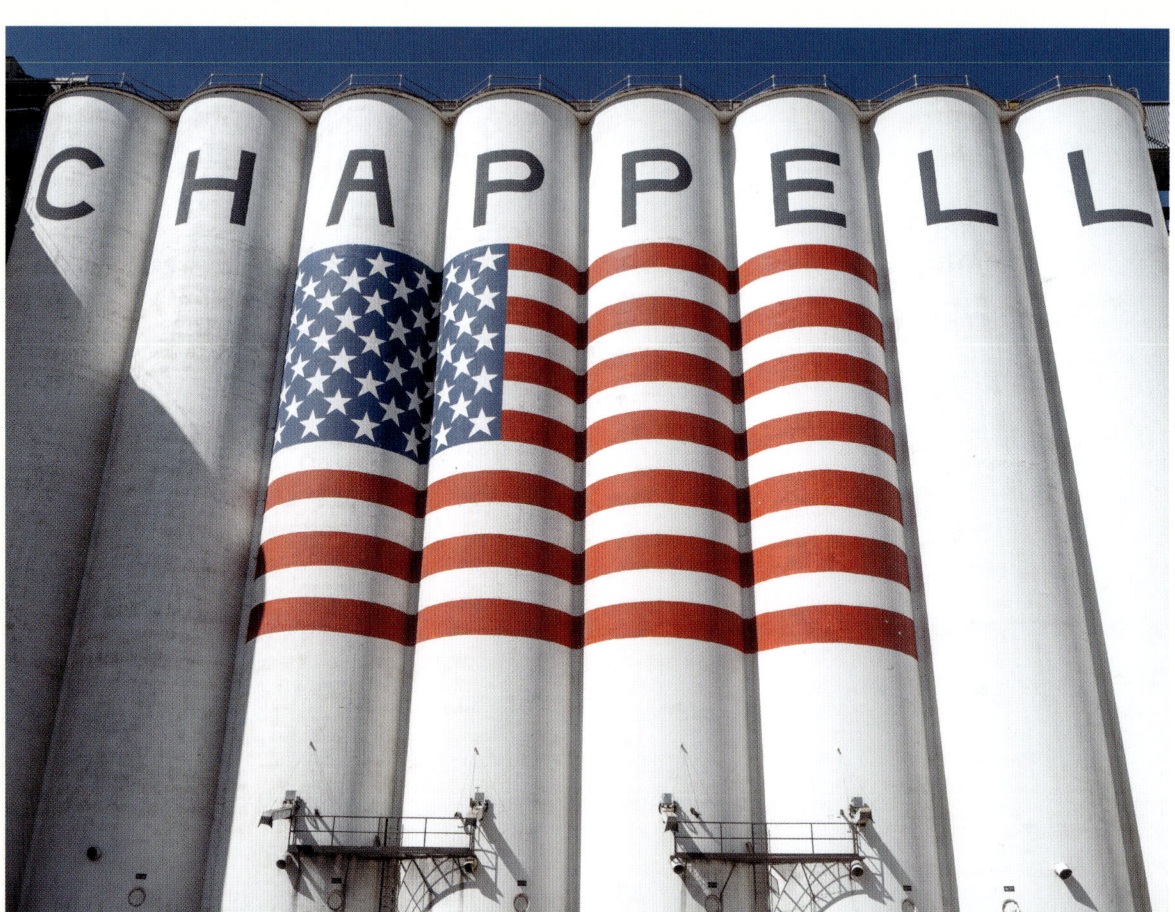

Chappell, Nebraska, 2025

(a) The flag should never be displayed with the union down, except as a signal of dire distress in instances of extreme danger to life or property.

(b) The flag should never touch anything beneath it, such as the ground, the floor, water, or merchandise.

(c) The flag should never be carried flat or horizontally, but always aloft and free, except as may be necessary in limited circumstances and done in a respectful manner as part of a military or patriotic observance.

(d) The flag should never be used as wearing apparel, bedding, or drapery. It should never be festooned, drawn back, nor up, in folds, but always allowed to fall free. Bunting of blue, white, and red, always arranged with the blue above, the white in the middle, and the red below, should be used for covering a speaker's desk, draping the front of the platform, and for decoration in general.

(e) The flag should never be fastened, displayed, used, or stored in such a manner as to permit it to be easily torn, soiled, or damaged in any way.

(f) The flag should never be used as a covering for a ceiling.

(g) The flag should never have placed upon it, nor on any part of it, nor attached to it any mark, insignia, letter, word, figure, design, picture, or drawing of any nature.

(h) The flag should never be used as a receptacle for receiving, holding, carrying, or delivering anything.

(i) The flag should never be used for advertising purposes in any manner whatsoever. It should not be embroidered on such articles as cushions or handkerchiefs and the like, printed or otherwise impressed on paper napkins or boxes or anything that is designed for temporary use and discard. Advertising signs should not be fastened to a staff or halyard from which the flag is flown.

(j) No part of the flag should ever be used as a costume or athletic uniform. However, a flag patch may be affixed to the uniform of military personnel, firemen, policemen, and members of patriotic organizations. The flag represents a living country and is itself considered a living thing. Therefore, the lapel flag pin being a replica, should be worn on the left lapel near the heart.

(k) The flag, when it is in such condition that it is no longer a fitting emblem for display, should be destroyed in a dignified way, preferably by burning.

9. Conduct during hoisting, lowering or passing of flag

During the ceremony of hoisting or lowering the flag or when the flag is passing in a parade or in review, all persons present in uniform should render the military salute. Members of the Armed Forces and veterans who are present but not in uniform may render the military salute. All other persons present should face the flag and stand at attention with their right hand over the heart, or if applicable, remove their headdress with their right hand and hold it at the left shoulder, the hand being over the heart. Citizens of other countries present should stand at attention. All such conduct toward the flag in a moving column should be rendered at the moment the flag passes.

10. Modification of rules and customs by President

Any rule or custom pertaining to the display of the flag of the United States of America, set forth herein, may be altered, modified, or repealed, or additional rules with respect thereto may be prescribed, by the Commander in Chief of the Armed Forces of the United States, whenever he deems it to be appropriate or desirable; and any such alteration or additional rule shall be set forth in a proclamation.

THE STAR-SPANGLED BANNER
(ORIGINAL VERSES, SPELLING, AND PUNCTUATION)

by Francis Scott Key

O say can you see, by the dawn's early light,
What so proudly we hail'd at the twilight's last gleaming,
Whose broad stripes and bright stars through the perilous fight
O'er the ramparts we watch'd were so gallantly streaming?
And the rocket's red glare, the bomb bursting in air,
Gave proof through the night that our flag was still there,
O say does that star-spangled banner yet wave
O'er the land of the free and the home of the brave?

On the shore dimly seen through the mists of the deep
Where the foe's haughty host in dread silence reposes,
What is that which the breeze, o'er the towering steep,
As it fitfully blows, half conceals, half discloses?
Now it catches the gleam of the morning's first beam,
In full glory reflected now shines in the stream,
'Tis the star-spangled banner—O long may it wave
O'er the land of the free and the home of the brave!

And where is that band who so vauntingly swore,
That the havoc of war and the battle's confusion
A home and a Country should leave us no more?
Their blood has wash'd out their foul footstep's pollution.
No refuge could save the hireling and slave
From the terror of flight or the gloom of the grave,
And the star-spangled banner in triumph doth wave
O'er the land of the free and the home of the brave.

O thus be it ever when freemen shall stand
Between their lov'd home and the war's desolation!
Blest with vict'ry and peace may the heav'n rescued land
Praise the power that hath made and preserv'd us a nation!
Then conquer we must, when our cause it is just,
And this be our motto—"In God is our trust,"
And the star-spangled banner in triumph shall wave
O'er the land of the free and the home of the brave.

Opposite: *U.S. Capitol Dome, Washington, DC, 2014*

Following: *Midwest, Wyoming, 2004*

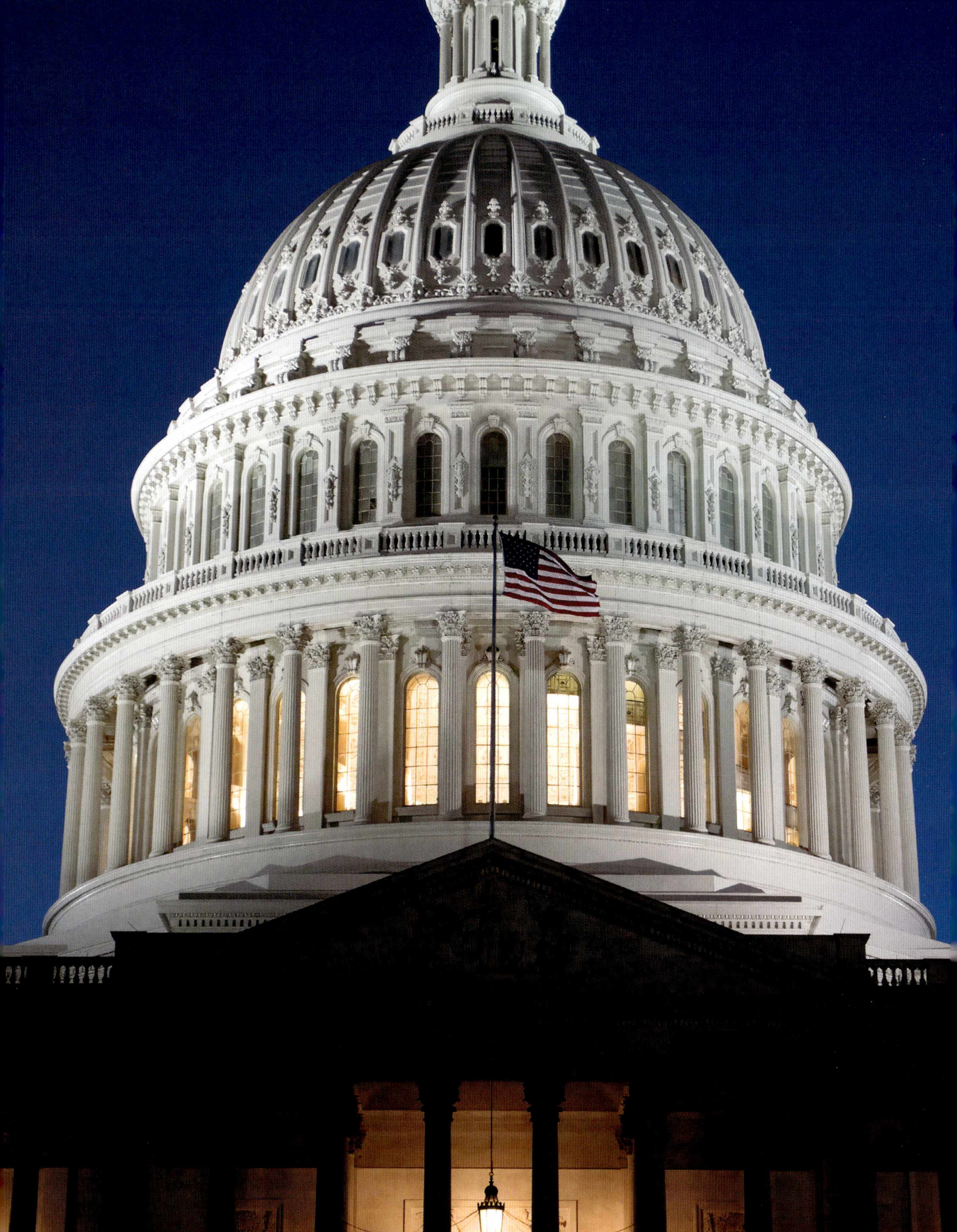

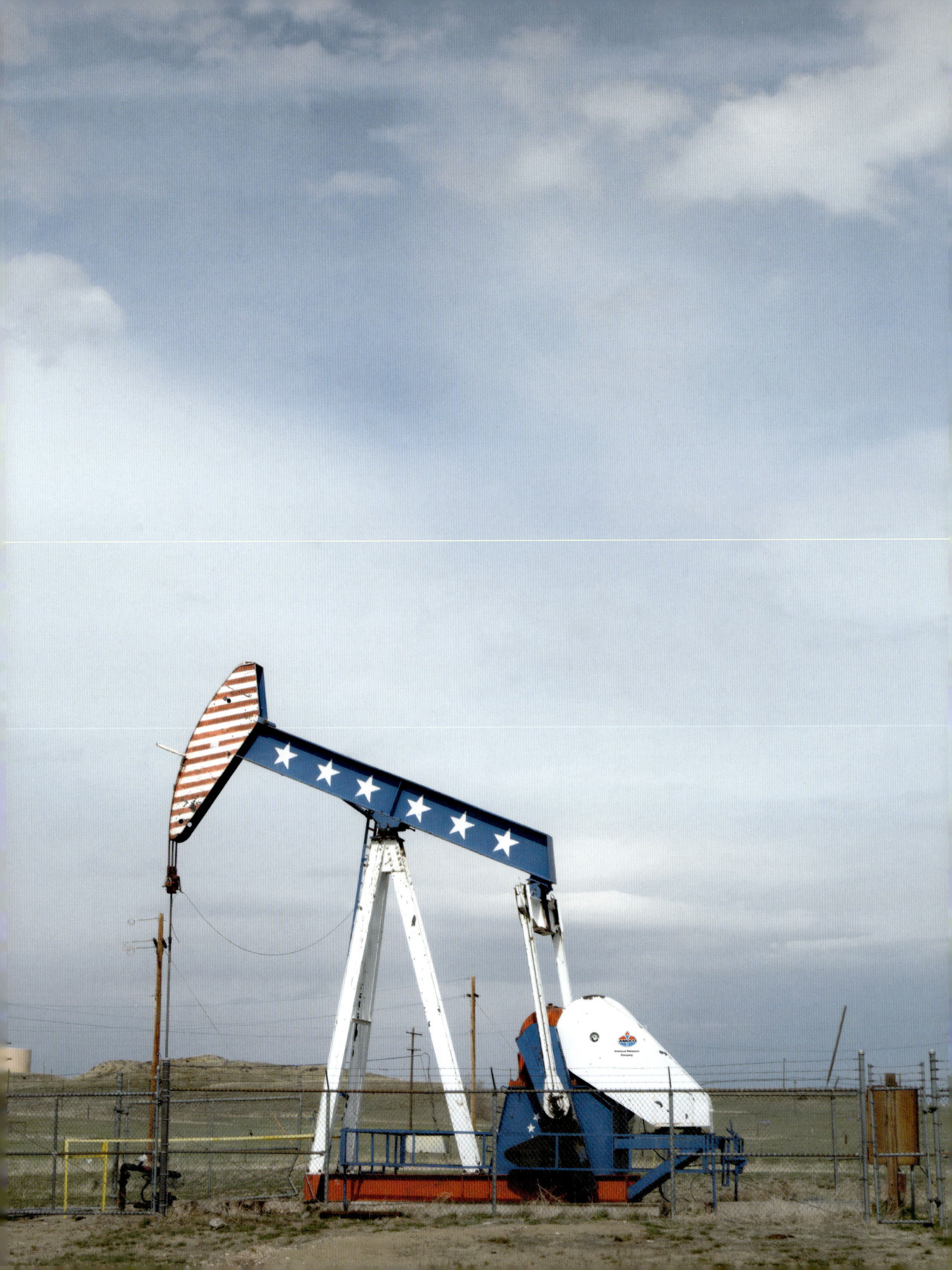
AMOCO

ACKNOWLEDGMENTS

THROUGH THE PROCESS OF making this book, I have been assisted by many individuals, all of whom have helped make this a more accurate and full telling of the American flag's relationship to the history of the United States.

I am indebted to many curators and museum personnel who gave me feedback and assistance, including: Lori Fidler at Revolutionary Spaces; Beth Ann Downey and Trish Norman at the Museum of the American Revolution; Callie Raspuzzi at the Bennington Museum; Kelly Cardwell at the Fort Stanwix National Monument; Analiese Oetting at the National Museum of American History; Marilyn Van Winkle at the Autry Museum of the American West; Mason Christensen, Karly Byrd-Nowsch, Lori Strelecki, and Ken Corcoran at the Pike County Historical Society at the Columns Museum; Kim Taylor at the Brinton Museum; Patrick Hargis, Joel Bragg, Fiona Robinson, and Patrick Thomas at the Fort Douglas Military Museum; Stephanie Mahan at the Arizona Capitol Museum; Heather Joines Mason and James B. Hill at the John F. Kennedy Presidential Library and Museum; Sabrina Christiansen at the Museum at Bethel Woods; and Ryan Pettigrew at the Richard Nixon Presidential Library and Museum.

Peter Keim and Kevin Keim graciously allowed me to use several flag images from their wonderful book *A Grand Old Flag*. Anthony Iasso generously let me include pictures from his collection at Rare Flags. David Groeninger kindly provided honest feedback on early versions of the essays. I thank Manuel DeLeon and Sandy Plasner for their generous hospitality. Thanks to Steve and Lynn Spencer for their many considerations. I greatly appreciate Doug Sperling sharing his Iranian Hostage signed flag. I was introduced to the Brinton Museum and made several images, which are included in the book, while participating in a Jentel Artist Residency in Banner, Wyoming.

Several books about the stories and individuals featured in *Old Glory* were invaluable in my research: *Defiance of the Patriots* by Benjamin L. Carp; *He Kept the Colors* by L. E. Johnson; *Artifacts of the Battle of Little Big Horn* by Will Hutchison; *Aboard the LCC 60* by Howard Vander Beek; *Don Jose: An American Soldier's Courage and Faith in Japanese Captivity* by Ezequiel L. Ortiz and James A. McClure; and *Code of Honor* by John A. Dramesi.

My wife, Amy, is my rock and support system. I thank her with all my heart.

Support from the team at Black Dog and Leventhal helped make this book more than I could have hoped. Abby Knudsen and Philip Verdirame's assistance have been invaluable. Executive Director of Marketing and Publicity Moira Kerrigan and Senior Director of Marketing and Publicity Allison McGeehon are the best! The editing team, including Kate Karol and Nancy Ringer, improved the manuscript immensely. Production Director Lillian Sun made sure everything came together. This project was a real design challenge, and Nina Simoneaux is a design wizard! My deep appreciation goes to Publisher and Editorial Director Lia Ronnen.

My editor, Shoshana Gutmajer, seems to have no end to her patience and insight. She has shepherded me through two books now, and I'm not sure I could do it without her guidance, acumen, and grace.

PHOTO CREDITS

ii–iii; v: Roland Miller; **vi–vii:** Jean Leon Gerome Ferris / Library of Congress; **viii:** NASA; **x:** Roland Miller; **x–xi:** Leif Skoogfors / Getty Images; **xi:** The Cargill Company; **xvi–xvii:** Roland Miller; **2–3:** Courtesy of Revolutionary Spaces; **6:** Museum of the American Revolution, 2003.00.0662; **8–9:** Courtesy of the Peter Keim Collection; **12:** Marko Bulgakov; **13:** Benjamin Franklin, Library of Congress; **16–17:** Edward Percy Moran / Library of Congress; **20:** University of Wisconsin–Madison; **21:** National Parks Service / Volunteer Dan Umstead; **22–23:** Bennington Museum, Bennington, Vermont; **24:** Ann Ronan Pictures / Print Collector / Getty Images; **26–27:** Courtesy of National Museum of American History, Smithsonian Institution; **28 and 31:** Courtesy of the Peter Keim Collection; **34–35:** Autry Museum; 81.G.5A; **37:** Image courtesy of the Mystic Stamp Co.; **39:** Fort Sumter and Fort Moultrie National Historical Park Museum; **40:** National Parks Service; **41:** Library of Congress; **42–43:** Frederic Edwin Church; **47:** Courtesy of the Dearborn Historical Museum; **48–49:** Roland Miller / Courtesy of the Dearborn Historical Museum; **50–51:** Courtesy of National Museum of American History, Smithsonian Institution; **53:** U.S. Steam-Power Book and Job Printing; **56–57:** Roland Miller / Courtesy of the Pike County Historical Society at the Columns Museum; **61; 62–63:** Andrew J. Russell; **66–67:** Roland Miller / Courtesy of the Brinton Museum; **68, 70:** Courtesy of National Museum of American History, Smithsonian Institution; **71:** Courtesy of Anthony Iasso; **74:** Roland Miller / Courtesy of the Fort Douglas Museum; **75:** William Dinwiddie / Library of Congress; **76, 79:** Arthur Mole and John Thomas, Library of Congress; **81:** Underwood & Underwood / Library of Congress; **85:** Detroit Publishing Co. / Library of Congress; **86:** Russell Lee / Library of Congress; **88 (top):** Arthur Rothstein / Library of Congress; **(bottom)**: Dorothea Lange / Library of Congress; **91:** Title page to "Wonder Woman" from *All-Star Comics* #8 (Oct. 1941). © & ™ DC Comics. Written by William Moulton Marston. Art by Harry G. Peter. Used with permission. Rights reserved.; **95 (left):** National Archives; **95 (right) and 96–97:** Roland Miller / Courtesy of the Arizona Capitol Museum Collection, 1990.244.001; **98:** © Anthony Plascencia—USA TODAY NETWORK via Imagn Images; **100–101:** Dorothea Lange / National Archives; **101:** Library of Congress; **102:** Dorothea Lange / Library of Congress; **103:** Courtesy of National Museum of American History, Smithsonian Institution; **104:** Gordon Parks / Library of Congress; **106:** © 2025 Figge Art Museum, successors to the Estate of Nan Wood Graham / Licensed by VAGA at Artists Rights Society (ARS), NY; **108:** Courtesy of National Museum of American History, Smithsonian Institution; **110–111:** Joe Rosenthal / Associated Press; **113:** National Archives; **114:** Courtesy of National Museum of American History, Smithsonian Institution; **120, 122:** © 2025 Jasper Johns / Licensed by VAGA at Artists Rights Society (ARS), NY; **124, 126, and 127 (top):** Abbie Rowe / National Park Service; **127 (bottom):** Joel Benjamin / Courtesy of the John F. Kennedy Presidential Library & Museum; **128–129:** Abbie Rowe / National Park Service; **132–133:** Matt Herron; **134–135:** Silver Screen Collection / Getty Images; **136:** *Easy Rider* © 1969, renewed 1997 Columbia Pictures Industries, Inc., All Rights Reserved, Courtesy of Columbia Pictures; **137:** Heritage Auction Galleries of Dallas, Texas; **140–142:** NASA; **146–147:** Courtesy of the Museum at Bethel Woods; **148:** © Ken Kolsbun; **150 (left):** Ryan Pettigrew / Richard Nixon Presidential Library and Museum; **150 (right):** Bettmann / Getty

Images; **152:** Leonard Detrick / *New York Daily News* Archive / Getty Images; **154:** Paul Connell / *The Boston Globe* / Getty Images; **155:** Bettmann / Getty Images; **157 (top):** Circa Images / GHI / Universal History Archive / Universal Images Group / Getty Images; **(bottom):** Owen Franken / Getty Images; **160–161:** Stanley Forman; **164 (left):** Flag by Gilbert Baker. Photograph courtesy of the Gilbert Baker Foundation, **(right):** Courtesy of GLBT Historical Society; **165:** Mick Hicks; **166:** Paul J. Richards / AFP / Getty Images; **169–171:** Roland Miller / Courtesy of Doug Sperling; **172:** Marvin E. Newman / *Sports Illustrated* / Getty Images; **177:** Courtesy of Sony Music Entertainment; **178:** Roland Miller / Courtesy Kennedy Space Center Visitor Center; **182:** David Hammons / Courtesy Tilton Gallery, New York; **183:** © 2025 David Hammons / Artists Rights Society (ARS), New York; **186:** © Thomas E. Franklin—USA TODAY NETWORK via Imagn Images; **190 (top):** Keith Myers / *Kansas City Star* / Tribune News Service via Getty Images; **(bottom):** Pete Souza / National Archives; **193:** © Chris Tuite / ImageSPACE / MediaPunch; **194–195:** AP Photo / Julio Cortez; **198 (top):** AP Photo / Jose Luis Magana; **(bottom):** Reuters / Leah Millis; **203 (top):** Anne-Christine Poujoulat / AFP / Getty Images; **(bottom):** Loic Venance / AFP / Getty Images; **204–221:** Roland Miller.

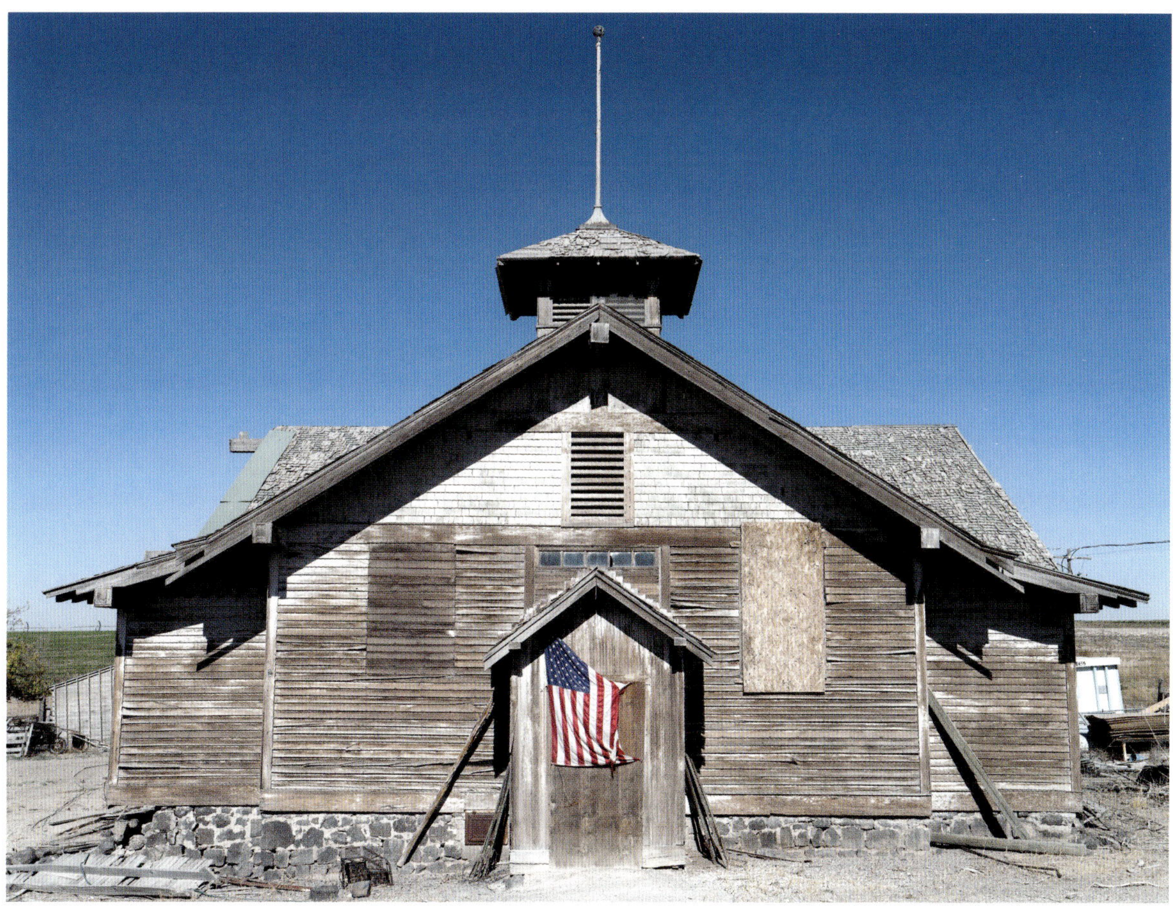

Hazelton, Idaho, 2022

ROLAND MILLER, a native of Chicago, studied photography at Utah State University, earning both his BFA and MFA degrees. He spent thirty-two years working in higher education as a professor and administrator. Miller is the author of *The Space Shuttle: A Mission-by-Mission Celebration of NASA's Extraordinary Spaceflight Program* (Artisan, 2022); *Orbital Planes* (Damiani Editore, 2022); and *Abandoned in Place* (University of New Mexico Press, 2016). In 2017, Miller guided astronaut Paolo Nespoli as he photographed the interior of the International Space Station during Expeditions 52 and 53. They coproduced a book of these images, *Interior Space* (Damiani Editore, 2020). Miller's photography has been exhibited at museums across the United States and internationally, including the Galleria del Cembalo in Rome, Italy, and the Southeast Museum of Photography at Daytona State College in Daytona Beach, Florida. Miller's photographs are held in many public and private collections, such as the Museum of Contemporary Photography in Chicago, and the NASA Art Collection in Washington, DC.